D1031249

Small Business Marketing Strategies

ALL-IN-ONE

for dummies®
A Wiley Brand

Presented by

U.S. CHAMBER OF COMMERCE

for dummies®
A Wiley Brand

Small Business Marketing Strategies, All-in-One For Dummies®

Published by: **John Wiley & Sons, Inc.,** 111 River Street, Hoboken, NJ 07030-5774, www.wiley.com

Copyright © 2016 by John Wiley & Sons, Inc., Hoboken, New Jersey

Published simultaneously in Canada

For general information on our other products and services, please contact our Customer Care Department within the U.S. at 877-762-2974, outside the U.S. at 317-572-3993, or fax 317-572-4002. For technical support, please visit www.wiley.com/techsupport.

Wiley publishes in a variety of print and electronic formats and by print-on-demand. Some material included with standard print versions of this book may not be included in e-books or in print-on-demand. If this book refers to media such as a CD or DVD that is not included in the version you purchased, you may download this material at http://booksupport.wiley.com. For more information about Wiley products, visit www.wiley.com.

Library of Congress Control Number: 2016936125

ISBN 978-1-119-23691-7 (pbk); ISBN 978-1-119-23693-1 (ebk); ISBN 978-1-119-23692-4 (ebk)

Manufactured in the United States of America

33614057651738

10 9 8 7 6 5 4 3 2 1

Contents at a Glance

Table of Contents

Introduction

Welcome to *Small Business Marketing Strategies All-In-One For Dummies!*

Because you picked up this book, it's a good bet that you're a small business owner or marketer who works with small businesses. You likely want to find out as much as you can about how small businesses are marketing themselves in today's fast-changing world of social media, websites, blogs, mobile phones, and other platforms, media, and post-modern doohickeys. You want to know how you can turn tweets, likes, shares, comments, photos, blogs, profiles, apps, and so forth into dollars. Well, if that's the case, you've come to the right place.

This book presents and explains a wide variety of information, all aimed at enlightening you on what you need to know to achieve success. Whether you need know-how and advice on the basics of current marketing practices, discovering and defining your clients, using Facebook or Twitter to promote your business, leveraging content marketing to draw in customers and potential customers, launching a campaign, optimizing your content for search engines — or kick it old school with broadcast, print, and outdoor ads, you'll find the help you need here.

The aim of this book is to provide you with the very best ideas, concepts, and tools for marketing small businesses. Using the info here, you should be able to create marketing campaigns that speak to real people in the language they use day in and day out. And you should be able to avoid many common mistakes that end up turning your customers off or wasting your time. Marketing is a tricky business. But you probably already knew that.

About This Book

This book is a generous conglomeration of material from a number of Dummies marketing and social media books, carefully selected with an eye toward getting you going with an overall marketing program.

For a tiny fraction of the amount you'd pay to get a marketing MBA, this book delivers an easily understandable road map to today's most innovative and effective marketing techniques and strategies. The information you find here is firmly grounded in the real world. This book isn't an abstract collection of theoretical, pie-in-the-sky mumbo-jumbo that sounds good but doesn't work when you put it to the test. Instead, you'll find only the best information, the best strategies, and the best techniques that are working on today's business environment, both online and off.

This book is also meant to be at least a little fun. Marketing doesn't have to be a bore — especially nowadays, when it seems to be merging with entertainment and interpersonal communication in ways that wouldn't have been dreamt of even a decade ago. At any rate, maintaining a sense of humor can be vital when facing the challenges that all small business folk face from time to time.

Within this book, you may note that some web addresses (URLs) break across two lines of text. If you're reading this book in print and want to visit one of these web pages, simply key in the web address exactly as it's noted in the text, pretending as though the line break doesn't exist. If you're reading this as an ebook, you've got it easy — just tap the web address to be taken directly to the web page.

Foolish Assumptions

This book makes a few assumptions about you. For example, you are interested in marketing (duh). You own or work for or with a small business (also duh). Maybe you've already started or at least conceived of a marketing campaign and are looking for tips to refine the techniques you're already developing. Or perhaps it's something you think may want to try, to boost your income and enlarge your customer base, and are looking to read up on it before you make your move. You'll find a lot to like in these pages.

If you have little or no experience in marketing so far, no worries. There's plenty of fundamental information here as well. The early chapters will get you up and running on the core concepts.

It's also safe to assume that you can — or believe you can — use a computer, a smartphone, and the web and other services of the all-powerful Internet. You may not be a gearhead, but you can tap, click, and search with the best of them.

Finally, this book assumes you're eager to scoop up and implement new tips and tricks and that you're willing to acquire some new perspectives on the topic.

Icons Used in This Book

Icons are handy little graphic images that are meant to point out particularly important information about starting your own business. Throughout this book, you find the following icons, conveniently located along the left margins:

TIP

This icon directs you to tips and shortcuts you can follow to save time and do things the right way the first time.

REMEMBER

Remember the important points of information that follow this icon, and your business will be all the better for it.

WARNING

Danger! Ignore the advice next to this icon at your own risk. Heeding this info can save you boatloads of trouble.

TECHNICAL STUFF

This one points out slightly advanced material that you can safely skip if you're in a hurry. But by all means, read these if you want to stretch yourself a bit.

EXAMPLE

This icon points out specific real-life examples to illustrate a point.

Beyond the Book

In addition to the material in the print or ebook you're reading right now, this product also comes with some access-anywhere goodies on the web. No matter how hard you work at marketing, you'll likely come across a few questions where you frankly don't have a clue. To view this book's Cheat Sheet, simply go to www.dummies.com and search for "Small Business Marketing Strategies Cheat Sheet" in the Search box.

Where to Go from Here

If you're new to marketing, you may want to start at the beginning of this book and work your way through to the end. What a radical concept. A clear path of information and practical advice leading to success awaits you. Simply turn the page and you're on your way. But you can start anywhere. If you've already studied or done some real-world marketing and are short of time (and who isn't?), feel free to use the table of contents and index to zero in on particular topics of interest to you right now, whether that's creating a board on Pinterest, upping your visibility in online directories, or working with direct mail.

Regardless of how you find your way around this book, the sincere hope of this endeavor is that you'll not just amp up your marketing prowess, but enjoy the journey as well. Good luck!

1
Setting Up Your Marketing Foundation

Contents at a Glance

Chapter 1

Framing the Marketing Process

You're not alone if you opened this book looking for an answer to the question, "What is marketing, anyway?" Everyone seems to know that marketing is an essential ingredient for business success, but when it comes time to say exactly what it is, certainty disappears from the scene.

People aren't sure if marketing, advertising, and sales are the same or different things. And they're even less sure about what marketing involves and how to do it well.

To settle the matter right up-front, here's a plain-language description of what marketing — and this book — is all about.

REMEMBER

Marketing is the process through which you win and keep customers.

>> Marketing is the matchmaker between what your business is selling and what your customers are buying.

>> Marketing covers all the steps involved in tailoring your products, messages, online and off-line communications, distribution, customer service, and all other business actions to meet the desires of your most important business asset: your customer.

>> Marketing is a win-win partnership between your business and its market.

REMEMBER

Marketing isn't about talking *to* your customers; it's about talking *with* them. Marketing relies on two-way communication between your business and your buyers. This chapter gives you a clearer idea of what the marketing process is.

Seeing the Big Picture

Marketing is a nonstop cycle. It begins with customer knowledge and goes around to customer service before it begins all over again. Along the way, it involves product development, pricing, packaging, distribution, advertising and promotion, and all the steps involved in making the sale and serving the customer well.

Following the marketing wheel of fortune

Every successful marketing program — whether for a billion-dollar business or a solo entrepreneur — follows the marketing cycle illustrated in Figure 1-1. The process is exactly the same whether yours is a start-up or an existing business, whether your budget is large or small, whether your market is local or global, and whether you sell through the Internet, via direct mail, or through a bricks-and-mortar location.

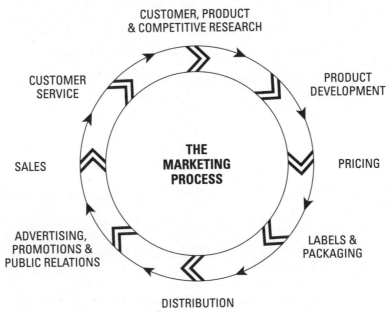

FIGURE 1-1:
The marketing wheel of fortune.

© *John Wiley & Sons, Inc.*

Just start at the top of the wheel and circle around clockwise in a never-ending process to win and keep customers and to build a strong business in the process.

As you loop around the marketing wheel, here are the marketing actions you take:

1. **Conduct research to gain knowledge about your customers, product, market area, and competitors.**

2. **Tailor your product, pricing, packaging, and distribution strategies to address your customers' needs, your market environment, and your competitive realities.**

3. **Create and project marketing messages to reach your prospective customers, inspire their interest, and move them toward buying decisions.**

4. **Go for and close the sale — but don't stop there.**

5. **After you make the sale, begin the customer service phase.**

    Work to develop relationships and ensure high levels of customer satisfaction so that you convert the initial sale into repeat business, loyalty, and word-of-mouth advertising for your business.

6. **Interact with customers to gain insight about their wants and needs and their use of and opinions about your products and services.**

    Combine customer knowledge with ongoing research about your market area and competitive environment. Then use your findings to fine-tune your product, pricing, packaging, distribution, promotional messages, sales, and service.

And so the marketing process goes around and around.

REMEMBER

Successful marketing has no shortcuts — you can't just jump to the sale. To build a successful business, you need to follow every step in the marketing cycle, and that's what the rest of this book is all about.

Understanding the relationship between marketing and sales

People make the mistake of thinking *marketing* is a high-powered or dressed-up way to say *sales*. Or they treat marketing and sales as two independent functions that they mesh together under the label *marketing and sales*.

REMEMBER

In fact, sales is an essential part of marketing, but it's not and never can be a replacement for the full marketing process. Selling is one of the ways you communicate your marketing message. It's the point at which you offer the product, you make the case, the customer makes a purchasing decision, and the business-to-customer exchange takes place.

MARKETING: THE WHOLE IS GREATER THAN THE PARTS

Advertising. Marketing. Sales. Promotions. What are the differences? The following story has circulated the marketing world for decades and offers some good answers for what's what in the field of marketing communications:

- If the circus is coming to town and you paint a sign that says, "Circus Coming to the Fairgrounds Saturday," that's *advertising*.

- If you put the sign on the back of an elephant and walk it into town, that's *promotion*.

- If the elephant walks through the mayor's flower bed, that's *publicity*.

- And if you get the mayor to laugh about it, that's *public relations*.

- If the town's citizens go to the circus and you show them the many entertainment booths, explain how much fun they'll have spending money there, and answer their questions — and they ultimately spend a lot of money at the circus — that's *sales*.

Because marketing involves far more than marketing communications, a second part to this circus analogy shows how the story might continue if it went on to demonstrate where research, product development, and other components of the marketing process fit in:

- If, before painting the sign that says, "Circus Coming to the Fairgrounds Saturday," you check community calendars to see whether conflicting events are scheduled, study who typically attends the circus, and figure out what kinds of services and activities they prefer and how much they're willing to pay for them, that's *market research*.

- If you invent elephant ear pastries for people to eat while they're waiting for elephant rides, that's *product development*.

- If you create an offer that combines a circus ticket, an elephant ear, an elephant ride, and an elephant photo, that's *packaging*.

- If you get a restaurant named Elephants to sell your elephant package, that's *distribution*.

- If you ask everyone who took an elephant ride to participate in a survey, that's *customer research*.

- If you follow up by sending each survey participant a thank-you note, along with a two-for-one coupon to next year's circus, that's *customer service*.

- And if you use the survey responses to develop new products, revise pricing, and enhance distribution, you've started the *marketing process* all over again.

WARNING

Without all the marketing steps that precede the sale — fitting the product to the market in terms of features, price, packaging, and distribution (or availability), and developing awareness and interest through advertising, publicity, and promotions — even the best sales effort stands only a fraction of a chance for success.

Jump-Starting Your Marketing Program

Small business leaders are most likely to clear their calendars and make marketing a priority at three predictable moments:

>> At the time of business start-up

>> When it's time to accelerate business growth

>> When they experience a bump on the road to success, perhaps due to a loss of business because of economic or competitive threats

You may have opened this book because your business is in the midst of one of those three situations right now. As you prepare to kick your marketing efforts into high gear, remember that marketing isn't just about selling. It's about attracting customers with great products and strong marketing communications, winning them over, and then retaining their business by exceeding their expectations. As part of the reward, you achieve repeat business, loyalty, new customer referrals, and a better shot at long-term business success.

The following sections can help you get a leg up on beginning your marketing program.

Marketing a start-up business

If your business is just starting, your marketing plan needs to address a set of decisions that existing businesses have already made. Existing companies have images to build upon, whereas your start-up business has a clean slate upon which to write exactly the right story.

TIP

Before sending messages into the marketplace, answer these questions:

>> What kind of customer do you want to serve? (See Book 1, Chapter 2.)

>> How will your product compete with existing options available to your prospective customer? (See Book 1, Chapter 2.)

>> What kind of business image will you need to project to gain your prospect's attention, interest, and trust?

EXAMPLE

A business setting out to serve corporate clients would hardly want to announce itself by placing flyers on community bulletin boards. On the other end of the spectrum, a start-up aiming to win business from cost-conscious customers would probably be better off announcing a promotion-packed open house than placing large ads full of praise from affluent business leaders.

If you're marketing a start-up business, pay special attention to these first few chapters. They can help you identify your customers, make pricing decisions, present your product, size up your competition, and set your goals and objectives.

Growing your business

Most established businesses grow their revenues by following one of the following routes:

>> Grow market share by pulling business away from competitors. (See Book 1, Chapter 3.)

>> Grow customer share either by prompting larger transactions during each visit or by generating more frequent repeat business.

>> Grow interest in new offerings that generate additional sales volume for your business. (See Book 1, Chapter 2.)

REMEMBER

Almost always, the most cost-efficient route to higher sales volume is to look inside your business first, shore up your product and service offerings, and strengthen your existing customer satisfaction and advertising spending levels *before* trying to win new prospects, which requires significantly more effort and expense.

Scaling your marketing to meet your goal

Small business owners often feel overwhelmed by the marketing task. They aren't sure how much money they should dedicate to the effort, whether they need to hire marketing professionals, how to weight efforts between traditional media and online communications, and whether they need to create new ads, brochures, and websites to get the job done.

Do those uncertainties sound familiar? If so, detour around the questions and get into forward motion by first putting your marketing task in perspective. Ask these questions:

» How much business are you trying to gain?

» How many clients do you want to add?

Whether you're launching a new business or accelerating the growth of an existing enterprise, defining what you're trying to achieve makes everything easier.

EXAMPLE

A social-service agency may set a goal to raise $100,000 in donor funds. An accounting firm may want to attract six corporate clients. A retailer may want to build an additional $50,000 in sales. A doctor may want to attract 100 patients for a particular new service. An e-publisher may want to achieve 500 downloads.

By setting your goal first (more on this important step in Book 1, Chapter 4), the process of creating your marketing plan becomes a focused, goal-oriented, and vastly easier activity.

How Small Business Marketing Is Different

All marketing programs follow the same set of steps in the marketing process (refer to Figure 1-1 earlier in this chapter), but the similarities between big business marketing and small business marketing stop there. Budgets, staffing, creative approaches, and communication techniques vary hugely between an international mega-marketer and a comparatively micro-budget marketer like, well, you.

This book is for *you.* Here's why.

Dollar differences

As a small business marketer, you already know one difference between your marketing program and those of the corporate behemoths that loom over you in all directions: The big guys have the big budgets. They talk about a couple hundred thousand dollars as a discretionary line-item issue. You talk about a couple hundred dollars as an amount worthy of careful consideration. The advice in this book is scaled to your budget, not to the million-dollar jackpots you see referenced in most other marketing books.

Staffing differences

Look at the organization chart of any major corporation. Nearly always, you find a marketing vice president. Under that position you see a bunch of other professionals, including advertising directors, sales managers, online and social-media marketing managers, research directors, customer service specialists, and so on. In contrast, strong small businesses blend marketing with the leadership function. The small business organization chart often puts responsibility for marketing in the very top box, the one with the owner's name, which likely puts *you* in the essential role of overseeing marketing as a hands-on task.

Creative differences

The top-name marketers routinely spend six figures to create ads with the sole purpose of building name recognition and market preference for their brands, often without a single word about a specific product or price.

Small businesses take a dramatically different approach. They want to develop name recognition just like the biggest advertisers, but their ads have to do double duty. You know firsthand that each and every small business marketing investment has to deliver immediate and measurable market action. Each effort has to stir enough purchasing activity to offset the marketing cost involved. The balancing act — and the focus of the chapters in Book 5 — is to create marketing communications that build a clear brand identity while also inspiring the necessary consumer action to deliver inquiries, generate leads, and prompt sales — *now*.

Strategic differences

In big businesses, bound copies of business plans are considered part of the furnishings, whereas in many small businesses, the very term *marketing plan* provokes a pang of guilt.

TIP

Truth is, creating a marketing plan is pretty straightforward and reasonably manageable. It's one of those pay-a-little-now-or-pay-a-lot-more-later propositions. If you invest a bit of time up-front to plan your annual marketing program, implementation of the plan becomes the easy part. But without a plan, you'll spend the year racing around in response to competitive actions, market conditions, and media opportunities that may or may not fit your business needs.

The small business marketing advantage

As a small business owner, you may envy the dollars, people, and organizations of your big business counterparts, but you have some advantages they envy as well.

The heads of Fortune 500 firms allocate budgets equal to the gross national products of small countries to fund the research required to get to know and understand their customers. Meanwhile, you can talk with your customers face to face, day after day, at virtually no additional cost.

Because the whole point of marketing is to build and maintain customer relationships, no business is better configured to excel at the marketing task than the small business.

What's more, today's customers don't just crave interactive communication with the businesses they buy from — they demand it. In the biggest of big businesses, shifting from one-way communication to two-way, interactive communication involves monumental shifts in how the business markets. Meanwhile, for your small business, shifting toward interactive marketing is simply a matter of making the choice to get online, get social, get talking, and get involved in two-way communications that give your business a marketing edge.

Making Marketing Your Key to Success

It's the simple truth that without customers, a business is out of business.

Marketing is the key to achieving customer interest, winning customer purchases, earning customer satisfaction and loyalty, and keeping your small business *in* business.

Put in terms like that, marketing is the single most important activity in any business — including yours. The fact that you're holding this book means you've made a commitment, and that gives you an edge over many of your competitors. Go for it!

Chapter 2

Defining Your Customers

Every marketer mulls the same questions: Who are my customers? How did they hear about me? Why do they buy from me? How can I reach more people like them?

Successful businesses use the answers to these questions to influence every product-design, pricing, distribution, and communication decision they make. This chapter focuses on the only boss that really matters in business: the person with an interest in your product or service and an open billfold. Whether your business is starting up, running at full pace, or in need of a turnaround, you can use the information in this chapter to get in tune with the customers who will make or break your bottom line.

>> If your business is going great guns, use this chapter to create a profile of your best customers so that you can attract more just like them.

>> If your business feels busy but your sales and profits are weak, this chapter can help you differentiate between the customers who are costing you time and money and the ones who are making you money — so you can direct your marketing efforts at the moneymakers.

>> If your sales have hit a frustrating plateau — or worse, if they're sliding downhill — you need to get and keep more customers, period. That means knowing everything you can about who is buying products or services like the ones you're selling and what it will take to make those people buy from you.

The best products aren't *sold* — they're *bought*. You never hear a customer say he *bought* a lemon at the used car lot. Nope, someone *sold* him that lemon — but hopefully not you or your business. If you're a good marketer, you aren't *selling* anyone anything. Instead, you're helping customers select the right products to solve their problems, address their needs, or fulfill their desires. You're helping them *buy*.

As a result, you can devote the bulk of your marketing efforts to the steps that take place long before and after money changes hands. These efforts involve targeting customers, designing the right product line, communicating your offerings in terms that address customers' wants and needs, and interacting after the sale in a way that builds loyalty and repeat business. This chapter spotlights everything you need to know about your products and the reasons your customers want to buy those products from you.

REMEMBER

Business leaders don't work for themselves; they work for their customers.

Anatomy of a Customer: Knowing Who Your Customers Are

Understanding who's who among your clientele is called *market segmentation* — the process of breaking down your customers into segments that share distinct similarities.

Here are some common market segmentation terms and what they mean:

>> **Geographics:** Segmenting customers by their physical locations to determine the regions, counties, states, countries, zip codes, and census tracts where current and therefore likely prospective customers live.

>> **Demographics:** Segmenting customers into groups based on factors such as age, sex, race, religion, education, marital status, income, and household size.

>> **Psychographics:** Segmenting customers by lifestyle characteristics, behavioral and purchasing patterns, beliefs, values, and attitudes about themselves, their families, and society.

>> **Geodemographics:** A combination of geographics, demographics, *and* psychographics. Geodemographics, also called *cluster marketing* or *lifestyle marketing,* is based on the age-old idea that birds of a feather flock together — that people who live in the same area tend to have similar backgrounds and consuming patterns. Geodemographics helps you target your marketing efforts by pinpointing neighborhoods or geographic areas where residents share the age, income, lifestyle characteristics, and buying patterns of your prospective customers.

TIP

If you want to search deeper with these segmentations, check out Google Keyword Planner (https://adwords.google.com/KeywordPlanner) and Facebook Ads (www.facebook.com/business/ads-guide).

These sections examine these market segmentation terms in plain English so you have a better idea who your customers are and can identify them.

Collecting customer information

People with the profile of your current customers are apt to become customers as well. That's why target marketing starts with customer knowledge. Small businesses fall into two groups: those with customer databases and those that serve customers whose names and addresses they never capture. A medical clinic or auto repair shop falls into the first group. A sandwich shop or convenience store likely falls into the second group, although even those who don't automatically collect customer names and information can use loyalty programs or contests to collect valuable customer data.

The more you know about current customers, the better prepared you are to target and reach more people just like them. Start by doing some research.

Do-it-yourself fact-finding

You can get a good start on conducting customer research without ever walking out the front door of your business. Start by focusing on information you can collect through customer communications and contacts:

>> **Collect addresses from shipping labels and invoices in order to group customers by location and purchase type.**

>> **Monitor the origin of incoming phone calls.** When prospects call your business, find out where they're from and how they found you.

Keep questions conversational and brief. Remember that customers are calling to *receive* information, not to become research subjects.

- Use the caller identification feature on your phone to collect the incoming phone number prefix and area code, which can enable you to track the geographic origin of customer calls.

- Your phone service provider may be able to furnish lists of incoming call area codes or dialing prefixes for your reference.

>> **Track responses to ads and direct mailers.** Include a call to action that inspires a reaction. When prospects respond, collect their addresses and other information to build not just a database but also an inquiry profile.

>> **Study web reports to find out more about visitors to your website.** Work with the firm that hosts and manages your site to discuss available reports and how to mine the information you collect. Also, enter your web address into Google Analytics (`www.google.com/analytics`) to access data about site visitors, including their geographic origin, language, and other facts.

Be aware, though, that some Internet providers hide the geographic origin of users under the label "undefined," and others bundle all traffic, which means you may see a good many site visitors from a distant location not relevant to your business.

>> **Check with merchant processor company.** It may have data about past transactions about customers that you can use.

Beyond studying telltale signs for the geographic origins of your business, put your small business advantage to use and actually talk with your customers, using these approaches:

>> **Survey your customers.** Use online survey services available through sites such as `www.surveymonkey.com`, which allow you to choose from a range of templates and collect responses from up to ten questions from 100 people for free. Or you can create and email a survey to customers on your own or use contest forms to collect information.

If your business attracts foot traffic, consider surveying customers in person. Whether you survey all customers or limit your effort to every *n*th customer (every tenth one, for example), keep the question period short, keep track of responses, and time interviews so that your findings reflect responses from customers during various days and weeks.

When surveying customers, keep these cautions in mind:

- Establish and share your company's privacy policy to assure customers that you respect and protect the information you collect.

- If you collect information online, visit the website of the Online Privacy Alliance (`http://privacyalliance.org`) and click "For Businesses" for policy guidelines.

- If you question customers in person, don't risk treating long-standing customers like strangers to your business. Instead of asking, "Is this your first visit?" try to get at the answer indirectly, asking questions such as, "Have you been here since we moved the reception area?" or, "Have you stayed with us since we started our wine reception?" Savvy restaurateurs don't have to ask at all. They know that if a customer asks for directions to the restroom, that person is likely a first-time patron. On the other hand, a waiter who overhears a customer recommending a certain menu item to a tablemate can make a safe guess that the patron is a repeat guest.

- Realize that informal studies aren't statistically valid, but they provide interesting insights that help you better understand at least an informally assembled cross section of your clientele.

WARNING

- One other caution: Many retailers request zip codes before processing credit card transactions, both to aid in fraud prevention and to obtain customer data. In 2011, the California Supreme Court ruled such requests illegal. Know the rules in your state before posing the question.

>> **Observe your customers.** Without asking a single question, you can find out a lot from observing customer behavior. What kinds of cars do your customers drive? How long do they spend during each visit to your business? Do they arrive by themselves or with others? Do those who arrive alone account for more sales or fewer sales than those who arrive accompanied by others? Where do they pause or stop in your business?

TIP

If your website has Google Analytics installed, you can use the "flow chart" feature to see how visitors flow through your website or web store.

EXAMPLE

Your observations help you define your customer profile while also leading to product decisions, as shown in these examples:

- A small theme park may find that most visitors stay for two hours and 15 minutes, which is long enough to want something to eat or drink. This can lead to the decision to open a café or restaurant.

- A retailer may realize that women who shop with other women spend more time and money, which may lead to a promotion that offers lunch for two after shopping on certain days of the week.

- A motel may decide to post a restaurant display at a hallway entry where guests frequently pause.

TIP

Tap online resources that unlock the power of your customer data, giving you knowledge about where in your local market area you can find prospective customers that match the profile of your current and best customers.

Calling in the pros

Doing it yourself doesn't mean doing it all on your own. As you're conducting customer research, here are places where an investment in professional advice pays off:

>> **Questionnaires:** Figure out what you want to discover and create a list of questions. Then consider asking a trained market researcher to review your question wording, sequence, and format. After your questions are set, you can distribute the survey on your own or with professional help. Either way, have someone with design expertise prepare a questionnaire that makes a good visual impression on your business's behalf. Include a letter or introductory paragraph explaining why you're conducting research and how you'll protect the privacy of answers.

>> **Phone or in-person surveys:** Professional researchers pose questions that don't skew the results. Asking the questions yourself easily lets your biases, preconceptions, and business pressures leak through and sway responses. Plus, customers are more apt to be candid with third parties. (If you need proof, think of all the things people are willing to say behind someone's back that they'd never say to the person's face. The same principle applies in customer research.)

>> **Online surveys:** Professional online survey tools are free unless you want to reach very large survey groups, in which case reasonably priced packages are available. If only a portion of your clientele is active online, be sure to accompany online surveys with off-line surveys in order to capture the opinions of those who don't use the Internet.

>> **Focus groups:** If you're assembling a group of favorite clients to talk casually about a new product idea, you're fine to go it alone. But to get opinions from outsiders or insight into sensitive topics such as customer service or pricing, use a professional facilitator who is experienced in managing group dynamics so that a single dominant participant doesn't steer the group outcome.

To obtain outside assistance, contact research firms, advertising agencies, marketing firms, and public-relations companies. Explain what you want to accomplish and ask whether the company can do the research for you or direct you toward the right resources.

TIP

Two good starting points are the Association of Small Business Development Centers (www.asbdc-us.org) and Score (www.score.org).

Geographics: Locating your market areas

Not all businesses are geographically constrained. Most Internet businesses aren't; most restaurants are. If geography matters to your business, though, it's an essential ingredient in arriving at your customer profile.

To target your market geographically, you need to ask, "Where am I most likely to find potential customers, and where am I most apt to inspire enough sales to offset my marketing investment?" To help you answer these questions, here's some advice:

>> **Start with the addresses of your existing customers.** Wherever you have a concentration of customers, you likely have a concentration of *potential* customers. Unless you already have sky-high market share, those are the areas where you should direct your advertising efforts.

>> **Search for trends.** Google Trends (www.google.com/trends/explore) identifies search trends within a geographic area.

>> **Follow your inquiries.** Inquiries are customers waiting to happen. They are consumers whose interest you've aroused and whose radar screens you've managed to transit. Your first objective should be to convert inquiry interest into buying action. Further, by finding out where inquiries are coming from, you may discover new geographic areas to target with future marketing efforts.

>> **Locate new customer prospects in your local market area.** Identify people who match the profile of your current customers but who don't yet buy from you. By discovering where these prospects live, you also discover areas for potential market expansion.

- Contact media outlets that serve your business sector. Ask for information regarding geographic areas with a concentration of people who fit your customer profile. Advertising representatives are often willing to share information as a way to convince you of their ability to carry your marketing message to the right prospects.

- Contact your industry association. Inquire about industry market analyses that detail geographic areas with concentrated interest in your offerings. If you can export your offering beyond your regional marketplace, you may discover national or international market opportunities that you otherwise wouldn't have considered.

- Visit your library reference desk. Study the *SRDS Lifestyle Market Analyst,* a rich source of market-by-market demographic and lifestyle information, and the *CACI Sourcebook of ZIP Code Demographics,* which details the population profiles of 150 U.S. zip codes and county areas. Through these resources, you can find and target areas that have a concentration of residents with lifestyle interests that match up with your target customer profile. Other good resources, often available at your public library, include the Merchant Nexus Database, D&B's Million Dollar Database, Info USA, and Reference USA.

Each time you discover a geographic area with easy access to your business and with a concentration of residents who fit your buyer profile, add the region to your list of prospective geographic target markets.

Demographics: Collecting customer data

After you determine *where* your customers are, the next step is to define *who* they are so that you can target your marketing decisions directly toward people who fit your customer profile.

Trying to market to everyone is a budget-breaking proposition. Instead, narrow your customer definition by using demographic facts to zero in on exactly whom you serve by following these steps:

1. **Use your own general impressions to define your customers in broad terms based on how you describe their age, education level, ethnicity, income, marital status, profession, sex, and household size.**

   Answer these questions about your customers:

   - Are they mostly male or female?

   - Are they mostly children, teens, young adults, early retirees, or senior citizens?

   - Are they students, college grads, or PhDs?

   - What do they do — are they homemakers, teachers, young professionals, or doctors?

   - Are they mostly single, couples with no children at home, heads of families, grandparents, or recent empty nesters?

   - How would you describe their ethnicity and the languages they speak?

   - Based on your observations, how would you define their income levels?

   - When are they most in need of your service? A season, a month, a day, or a time of the week?

2. **Break your market into subgroups, perhaps categorized by the kinds of products the customers usually purchase or the time of year they typically do business with you.**

EXAMPLE

A restaurant that analyzes its weekday lunchtime clientele and patrons of its dinner business may discover that the two time frames draw customers with dramatically different demographic profiles. For example, perhaps the lunchtime clientele is comprised mostly of businesspeople from the nearby area, whereas the dinner traffic is largely tourist families. This finding may lead to the development of two different and highly targeted promotions: a *5 minutes or it's free* lunch offer aimed at the nearby business community and promoted through the chamber of commerce newsletter and other low-cost, local business publications; and a *Kids under 7 eat free* offer aimed at tourists and promoted through hotel desk clerks and local visitor publications.

3. **Verify your answers by asking your customers.**

Incorporate questions during inquiry and sales contacts by following the advice in the "Do-it-yourself fact-finding" section, earlier in this chapter.

WARNING

As you collect demographic information about your customers, realize that people who fit the same factual description may vary widely in their purchasing patterns. That's why it's essential that you also understand customer lifestyles and buying behaviors, covered in the next section on psychographics.

Psychographics: Customer buying behaviors

Knowing where and who your customers are allows you to select the right communication vehicles to carry your marketing messages. As you decide what to say and how to present your message, you also want to find out as much as you can about the attitudes, beliefs, purchasing patterns, and behaviors of your customers. This information helps you create marketing messages that interest your prospects and motivate them to buy from you.

Defining who isn't a prospect for your product

Sometimes, the easiest way to start your customer profiling is to think about who *isn't* likely to buy from your business. For example:

EXAMPLE

>> A manufacturer of swing sets knows that most customers aren't young professional couples living in urban lofts. It needs to talk to families whose homes have backyards.

>> A landscape and nursery business knows that it won't find many customers in downtown high-rise apartments.

>> A manufacturer of architectural siding may decide that its buyer isn't the end user — or homeowner — at all. Rather, the customer is the architect who specifies the product in the initial building design.

TIP

Don't be afraid to target the audience for your marketing messages. You can still sell to anyone who enters your business or website, but your marketing investment should target only those who best fit your customer description.

Identifying the purchase tendencies customers have in common

Based on your personal impressions and also on information you discover through conversations and surveys (see advice earlier in the "Calling in the pros" section), make a list of common traits shared by your best customers by answering the following questions:

>> Do they buy on impulse or after careful consideration?

>> Are they cost-conscious or more concerned about the quality and prestige of the purchase?

>> Are they loyal shoppers who buy from you on a frequent basis or are they one-time buyers?

>> Do they buy from your business exclusively or do they also patronize your competitors?

>> Do they reach you through a certain channel — for example, your satellite office or your website — or do they contact you via referrals from other businesses or professionals?

EXAMPLE

A retailer in a vacation area might organize customers into the following subgroups:

>> **Geographic origin:** Local residents, in-state visitors, out-of-state visitors, and international visitors.

>> **Activity interest:** Golfers, skiers, campers, and business travelers/convention guests.

REMEMBER

By creating customer subgroups, you'll see patterns emerge. Certain customer groups account for higher sales volume, more frequent purchases, purchases of certain types of products, purchases during certain seasons or hours, purchases through your website rather than in person, and so on. When you know the tendencies of various segments, you know what to offer to each target group.

Determining Which Customers Buy What

Marketing is a matter of resource allocation. No budget — not even those of mega-brands like General Motors or Apple— is big enough to do it all. At some point, every marketer has to decide to aim its dollars toward the markets and products that have the best chance of delivering results and providing a good return on the marketing investment. These sections look at what you need to know about who buys what.

Viewing your sales by market segment

The best marketers aim promotions precisely at target audiences they believe have the interest and ability to purchase the featured product. Take these steps as you match segments of your market with the categories of your product line they're most likely to want to purchase:

1. **Break down your sales by product categories to gain a clear picture of the types of products you sell, the sales volume each category produces, and the type of customer each attracts.**

2. **Use your findings to determine which product categories offer the best potential growth opportunities and also to clarify which segments of your clientele are most likely to respond to marketing messages.**

3. **Weight your marketing expenditures and develop your marketing messages and media plans to achieve your targeted sales goals through promotions that appeal to clearly defined customer segments.**

EXAMPLE

A furniture manufacturer may divide its products into office, dining, and children's lines — each meeting the demands of a different market segment and even employing a different distribution and retailing strategy. The manufacturer would follow three separate marketing-communications strategies, placing primary emphasis (and budget allocation) on promoting the line most apt to deliver top sales volume over the upcoming period.

EXAMPLE

An accounting firm may sort its clientele both by type of service purchased and by client profile. It may target individual clients for tax-return business during the year's first quarter, target high-net-worth clients for estate- and tax-planning right after the April 15 tax-filing deadline, and target business clients for strategic planning services in early fall, when those customers are thinking about their business plans for the upcoming year.

After you're clear about which segments of your customer base are most apt to purchase which products, you'll have the information you need to develop and communicate compelling promotions and offers. You may also discover clues to new-customer development. For example, studying sales patterns may lead to the finding that certain products or services provide a good point of customer entry to your business, arming you with valuable knowledge you can use in new-customer promotions.

Table 2-1 shows how a motel might categorize its market so that it can discover the travel tendencies of customers in each geographic market area and respond with appropriate promotional offers.

TABLE 2-1 ## Market Segmentation Analysis: Mountain Valley Motel

	Hometown	Rest of Home State	Neighboring States	Other National/ International
Total Sales				
$712,000	$56,960	$462,800	$128,160	$64,080
	8%	65%	18%	9%
Sales by Length of Stay				
1-night stay	$48,416	$83,304	$19,224	$3,204
2-night stay	$2,848	$231,400	$70,488	$32,448
3–5 night stay	none	$101,816	$32,040	$28,428
6+ night stay	$5,696	$46,280	$6,408	none
Sales by Season				
Summer	$5,696	$277,680	$96,120	$54,468
Fall	$11,962	$55,536	$12,816	$6,408
Winter	$4,557	$37,024	$6,408	none
Holiday	$22,783	$23,140	none	none
Spring	$11,962	$69,420	$12,816	$3,204

With detailed market knowledge, you can make market-sensitive decisions that lead to promotions tailored specifically to consumer patterns and demands. The following examples show how the motel featured in Table 2-1 can use its findings to make marketing decisions:

» **Local market guests** primarily stay for a single night and mostly during the holiday season, making them good targets for local year-end promotions. Additionally, 10 percent of local guests stay for six nights or longer, likely while undergoing household renovations or lifestyle changes. This long-stay business tends to occur during nonsummer periods when motel occupancy is low, so the motel may want to consider special offers to attract more of this low-season business.

» **Half of statewide guests** spend two nights per stay, although nearly a third spend three to six nights, which proves that the motel is capable of drawing statewide guests for longer stays. This information may lead to an add-a-day promotion.

» **National and international guests** account for approximately one-quarter of the motel's business. Because these guests are a far-flung group, the cost of trying to reach them in their home market areas via advertising would be prohibitive. Instead, the motel managers might research how these guests found out about the motel. If they booked following advice from travel agents, tour group operators, or websites, the managers could cultivate those sources for more bookings. Or, if the guests made their decisions while driving through town, the motel may benefit from well-placed billboard ads and greater participation in travel apps and review sites that influence traveler behavior.

Conduct a similar analysis for your own business:

» How do your products break down into product lines? (See the later section, "Getting to Know Your Product: Seeing It through Your Customer's Eyes" for more information about this important topic.)

» What kind of customer is the most prevalent buyer for each line?

Then put your knowledge to work. If one of your product lines attracts customers who are highly discerning and prestige–oriented, think twice about a strategy that relies on coupons, for example.

Matching customers with distribution channels

Distribution is the means by which you get your product to the customer. A good distribution system blends knowledge about your customer (see the first half of this chapter) with knowledge of how that person ended up with your product (that's what distribution is about). It's often a surprisingly roundabout route.

EXAMPLE

To demonstrate, take a look at how visitors might arrive at a local museum. Suppose that 50,000 visitors walk through the turnstiles every year. Suppose that 10,000 of those visitors are school groups, 5,000 are tour groups, 5,000 prepurchased tickets through local motels and hotels, 5,000 prepurchased tickets through the websites of the museum and the regional visitor bureau, 5,000 have tickets distributed by partner businesses as part of special promotional programs, and 20,000 are either museum members or independent visitors.

Based on these numbers, the museum is distributing its tickets through the following channels:

>> Educators (possibly influenced by curriculum directors)

>> Tour companies (possibly influenced by state or local travel bureaus)

>> Lodging establishment front desks (probably influenced by hotel and motel marketing departments)

>> The Internet (possibly influenced by state or local travel bureaus)

>> Partner businesses (influenced by museum networking)

>> The museum entrance gate (influenced by museum marketing efforts)

By allocating guest counts and revenues to each of the channels, the museum would arrive at the distribution analysis shown in Table 2-2. By studying the findings, the museum can determine which channels are most profitable and which are most likely to respond positively to increased marketing efforts.

TABLE 2-2   **Channel Distribution Analysis**

Distribution Channel	Ticket Revenue	Number of Guests/ Percent of Total	Sales Revenue/ Percent of Total
Educators	$5.00	10,000/20%	$50,000/16%
Tour companies	$6.00	5,000/10%	$30,000/10%
Motels/hotels	$6.50	5,000/10%	$32,500/11%
Internet			
Museum website	$8.00	3,000/6%	$24,000/8%
Visitor bureau website	$6.50	2,000/4%	$13,000/4%

Distribution Channel	Ticket Revenue	Number of Guests/ Percent of Total	Sales Revenue/ Percent of Total
Museum entry gate			
Museum members	$3.00	5,000/10%	$15,000/5%
Independent visitors	$8.00	15,000/30%	$120,000/39%
Partnering businesses	$4.00	5,000/10%	$20,000/7%

You can create your own channel analysis, providing your business with information about how customers reach your business and the levels of sales activity that each channel generates. Put your findings to work by taking these steps:

1. **Track sales changes by distribution channel.**

   If one distribution channel starts declining radically, give that channel more marketing attention or enhance another channel to replace the revenue loss.

2. **Compare percentage of sales to percentage of revenue from each channel.**

   Channels that deliver lower-than-average income per unit should involve a lower-than-average marketing investment or deliver some alternative benefit to your business. For example, in the case of the museum in Table 2-2, the tickets distributed through partnering businesses deliver lower-than-average revenue and likely require a substantial marketing investment. Yet they have an alternative benefit — they introduce new people to the museum and therefore cultivate membership sales, donations, and word-of-mouth support.

3. **Communicate with the decision makers in each distribution channel.**

   When you know your channels, you know whom to contact with special promotional offers. For example, if school groups arrive at a museum because the museum is on an approved list at the state's education office, that office is the decision point, and it's where the museum would want to direct marketing efforts. If school groups arrive because art or history teachers make the choice, the museum would want to get information to those art or history teachers.

As part of your channel analysis, consider whether your business can reach and serve prospective customers through new distribution channels, whether that means introducing online sales, off-premise purchase locations, new promotional partnerships, or other means of reaching those who fit your target customer profile but who don't currently buy from your business.

Catering to screen-connected customers

In addition to everything you find out about your customers — who they are, where they live, how they buy, and what they want — realize that one common denominator applies to all: They're all influenced by the Internet.

Even if your customers are among the rare few who aren't online, you can bet that their purchase decisions are affected by input from those who are.

Research shows that 89 percent of consumers find online channels trustworthy sources for product and service reviews, and an even greater percentage use online media before purchasing products, even in their local market area. Go to Book 2, Chapter 2 for information on preparing your business to connect with your customers online. It's where they are, so it's where your business needs to meet and interact with them.

Getting to Know Your Product: Seeing It through Your Customer's Eyes

The first step toward stronger sales is to know everything you possibly can about the products you sell and the reasons your customers buy.

Look beyond your primary offerings to consider the full range of solutions your business provides. Likely you'll discover your offerings are more diverse than you first realize, a finding that can lead to stronger, more targeted marketing efforts.

EXAMPLE

Consider the products of a lakeside resort. The owners would list the number of cabins, seats in the restaurant, and rowboats for rent. Then they'd include the shopping opportunities in the resort's bait shop. Their list may also include summer youth camps, winter cross-country ski packages, all-inclusive corporate retreats, and such intangibles as family memories, based on their finding that many reservations are motivated by an emotional response to the lakeside setting as an annual vacation site.

Similarly, a law office might describe its products by listing the number of wills, estate plans, incorporations, bankruptcies, divorces, adoptions, and lawsuits it handles annually. And if it's well managed, the lawyers will know which of those product lines are profitable and which services are performed at a loss in return for the likelihood of ongoing, profitable relationships.

What about your business?

>> What do you sell? How much? How many? What times of year or week or day do your products sell best? How often is a customer likely to buy or use your product?

>> What does your product or service do for your customers? How do they use it? How does it make them feel? What problem does it solve?

>> How is your offering different from and better than your competitors'?

>> How is it better than it was even a year ago?

>> What does it cost?

>> What do customers do if they're displeased or if something goes wrong?

By answering these questions, you gain an understanding of your products and the ability to steer their future sales.

When service is your product

If your business is among the great number of companies that sell services rather than three-dimensional or packaged goods, from here on when you see the word *product,* think *service.* In your case, service *is* your product.

Today, nearly 80 percent of all Americans work in service companies. Services — preparing tax returns, writing wills, creating websites, styling hair, or designing house plans, to name a few — aren't things that you can hold in your hands. In fact, the difference between services and tangible products is that customers can see and touch the tangible product *before* making the purchase, whereas when they buy a service, they commit to the purchase before seeing the outcome of their decisions, relying heavily on their perception of the reputation of your business.

Your product is what Google says it is

Chances are great that before people contact you or your business directly they check you out online. Close to a hundred million names are searched on Google every day. Before buying products, visiting businesses, or meeting others, people look online to see which businesses dominate the first screens of their search results. You should too.

Customers also look online to see whether their search results turn up credible and trust-building information about your business, including links to positive and descriptive sites and, increasingly, Google +1 recommendations from people they know and regard highly.

TIPS FOR EGO-SURFERS: FIND OUT HOW YOU LOOK ONLINE

Ego-surfing, also known as *Googling yourself* or *vanity searching,* starts with typing your name into a search engine and often ends with you wondering how Google matched your name to the list of results you see.

"The first step is to search for yourself early and often," says Janine Warner, founder of DigitalFamily.com and author of *Websites DIY For Dummies.* "Then set up an alert at `www.google.com/alerts` so Google will email you every time it discovers your name online."

When you go ego-surfing, Janine shares these insider tips:

- **Don't stop with Google.** Also check and optimize your search results in Bing, DuckDuckGo, and the many other search engines out there.

- **Look beyond the first results you see.** Use the search engine's filters to adjust results. Choose the News and Blog links to see whether you've been mentioned recently, or use the Images and Video links to find photos and footage linked to your name online.

- **Search online phone and address directories.** Also, plug your business street address into Google Maps to pinpoint the location and see a photo from street level. If you can prove the information is incorrect, outdated, or worse, Google and other sites will update the information.

- **Search social media sites.** Many allow you to change privacy settings to control how much information is available to people you haven't accepted as "friends." Visit `http://namechk.com` to check name availability on dozens of social media sites.

- **Check business directories.** ZoomInfo (`www.zoominfo.com`) lists more than 50 million people, searchable by name, company, title, industry keywords, and location. Create a profile to manage what appears when people search your name.

- **Realize that your own searches may deliver a distorted view of your search ranking.** Google factors in your location and search history when it delivers search results, so your past searches may influence your results. Similarly, if you live in Los Angeles and your friend lives in New York, the two of you will get different results for your name search, just as you'd both get different results if you search words like *accountant, restaurant,* and *parks.*

- **Go incognito to get the best search results.** The Google Chrome web browser includes a way to surf without revealing your location, IP address, browser history, and other identifiable information. As a result, you get clean Google search results that aren't affected by the search engine's ability to track your search history. You can download Google Chrome for free, and like most web browsers, it's quick and easy to install. To surf incognito, click on the wrench icon in the top-right corner of the browser window, and from the drop-down menu choose "New incognito window."

"In case you think incognito searches are just for those who don't want others to know their nefarious online activities, think again," Janine says. "I've taught journalists and business executives all over the world to use free web proxy sites to surf anonymously, especially in places where your online activity can get you killed or kidnapped. The free web proxy service Hide My Ass (www.hidemyass.com) always gets a laugh when I mention it in a speech, but protecting your online identity and reputation is no joke."

This sidebar is based on information by Janine Warner. For more about her books, speaking engagements, and videos, visit www.JanineWarner.com *and* www.DigitalFamily.com.

TIP

See for yourself: Conduct searches for your business name, product name, product category, personal name, and keywords customers may use when seeking information about you and your business. Does your business appear prominently — with links to positive information — in search results for keywords customers are likely to be using? If so, pat yourself on the back and keep up the good work on your online identity. For search tips, check out the sidebar, "Tips for ego-surfers: Find out how you look online."

Illogical, Irrational, and Real Reasons People Buy What You Sell

Online searches and customer opinion research results reveal what people believe about your product, your product category, what your offering means to them personally, and why they make what otherwise may seem like illogical buying decisions. Think about it:

>> Why pay $5 for a loaf at the out-of-the-way Italian bakery if they can buy bread for under a dollar at the grocery store?

>> Why pay nearly double for a Lexus than for a Toyota if some models of both are built with many of the same components?

>> Why seek cost estimates from three service providers and then choose the most expensive bid if all three propose nearly the same solution?

Why? Because people rarely buy what you think you're selling.

REMEMBER

People don't buy your *product.* They buy the promises, the hopes, or the satisfaction that they believe your product will deliver.

They buy the $5 loaf of salt-crusted rosemary bread because they believe it's worth it, perhaps because it tastes superior or maybe because it satisfies their sense of worldliness and self-indulgence. They opt for the high-end car for the feeling of safety, quality, prestige, and luxury it delivers. They pay top price for services perhaps because they like having their name on a prestigious client roster — or maybe because they simply like or trust the high-cost service provider more than the lower-cost ones.

People may choose to buy from your business over another simply because you make them feel better when they walk through your door.

REMEMBER

Don't fool yourself into thinking that you can win customers simply by matching your competitor's features or price. People decide to buy for all kinds of irrational reasons. They buy because they see some intangible and often impossible-to-define value that makes them believe the product is a fair trade for the asking price. Often, that value has to do with the simple truth that they like the people they're dealing with. Never underestimate the power of a personal relationship.

Buying Decisions: Rarely about Price, Always about Value

Customers decide to buy based on their perception of the value they're receiving for the price they're paying. Whatever you charge for your product, that price must reflect what your customer thinks your offering is worth. If nothing distinguishes your product, it falls into the category of a commodity, for which customers are unwilling to pay extra.

If a customer thinks your price is too high, expect one of the following:

>> The customer won't buy.

>> The customer *will* buy but won't feel satisfied about the value, meaning you win the transaction but sacrifice the customer's goodwill and possibly the chance for repeat business.

>> The customer will tell others that your products are overpriced.

Before you panic over a customer calling you high-priced, keep in mind that the dissatisfied customer's negative word-of-mouth is only bad news if others respect the person's opinions regarding price and value. It's often better to lose the business of a cherry-picking bargain hunter than to sacrifice your profit margins trying to price to that person's demanding standards. If your prices are on the high end, though, be certain that the quality, prestige, and service — the *value* — that you offer is commensurate with your pricing. Also realize that it's possible to *underprice* your offering. If a prospect thinks your product is worth more than its price tag, expect one of the following:

>> You may sacrifice the sale if the prospect interprets the low price as a reflection of a second-rate offering.

>> You may make the sale, but at a lower price (and lower profit margin) than the customer is willing to pay, leaving lost revenue and possibly customer questions following the transaction.

>> The customer may leave with the impression that you're a discounter — a perception that may steer future opinions and purchase decisions.

WARNING

Unless you aim to own the bargain-basement position in your market (a dangerous strategy because some other business can always go lower), you're better off providing excellent value and setting your prices accordingly.

Calculating the value formula

During the split second it takes for customers to rate your product's value, they weigh a range of attributes:

>> What does it cost?

>> What is the quality?

>> What features are included?

>> Is it convenient?

>> Is it reliable?

>> Can they trust your expertise?

>> How is the product supported?

>> What guarantee, promise, or ongoing relationship can they count on?

These considerations start a mental juggling act, during which customers determine your offering's value. If they decide that what you deliver is average, they'll expect a low price to tip the deal in your favor. On the other hand, if they rank

Defining Your Customers

aspects of your offering well above those of competing options, they'll likely be willing to pay a premium for the perceived value.

REMEMBER

Customers match high prices with high demands. Remember the sign you used to see in print shops and auto repair garages? "Good, fast, and cheap — choose any two"? How times have changed. Today's customers expect the companies they buy from to offer price, quality, *and* speed. But here's the good news: They expect you to be *competitive* in all three areas but *exemplary* in only one. Here are some well-known examples:

>> Costco = Price

>> Nordstrom = Service

>> 7-Eleven = Convenience

>> FedEx = Reliability

>> Apple = Quality

Riding the price/value teeter-totter

Price emphasizes the dollars spent. Price is what you get out of the deal. Value is what you deliver to customers. Value is what they care most about and what your communications should emphasize.

Pricing truths

When sales are down or customers seem dissatisfied, small businesses turn too quickly to their pricing in their search for a quick-fix solution. Before reducing prices to increase sales or satisfaction levels, think first about how you can increase the value you deliver. Consider the following points:

>> Your customer must perceive your product's value — or the worth of the solution your product delivers — to be greater than the asking price.

>> The less value customers equate with your product, the more emphasis they put on low price.

>> The lower the price, the lower the perceived value.

>> Customers like price reductions way better than price increases, so be sure when you reduce prices that you can live with the change, because upping prices later may not sit well.

>> Products that are desperately needed, rarely available, or one-of-a-kind are almost never price-sensitive.

Penny-pinching versus shooting the moon

Tell a person he needs angioplasty surgery, and he'll pay whatever the surgeon charges — no questions asked. But tell him he's out of dishwasher detergent, and he'll comparison shop. Why? Because one product is more essential, harder to substitute, harder to evaluate, and needed far less often than the other. One is a matter of life and death, the other mundane. See Table 2-3 to determine where your product fits on the price–sensitivity scale.

TABLE 2-3   ## Price Sensitivity Factors

Price Matters Less if Products Are	Price Matters More if Products Are
Hard to come by	Readily available
Purchased rarely	Purchased frequently
Essential	Nonessential
Hard to substitute	Easy to substitute
Hard to evaluate and compare	Easy to evaluate and compare
Wanted or needed immediately	Easy to put off purchasing until later
Emotionally sensitive	Emotion-free
Capable of providing desirable and highly beneficial outcomes	Hard to link to a clear return-on-investment
One-of-a-kind	A dime a dozen

Evaluating your pricing

Give your prices an annual checkup. Here are factors to consider and questions to ask:

>> **Your price level:** Compared to competitors' offerings, how does your offering rank in terms of value and price? How easily can the customer find a substitute — or choose not to buy at all? (See Book 1, Chapter 3.)

>> **Your pricing structure:** Do you include or charge extra for enhanced features or benefits? What promotions, discounts, rebates, or incentives do you offer? Do you offer quantity discounts? Does your pricing motivate desired customer behavior, for example by offering a discount on volume purchases, contract renewals, or other incentives that are factored into your pricing to reduce hesitation and inspire future purchases?

>> **Pricing timetable:** How often do you change your pricing? How often do your competitors change their pricing? Do you anticipate competitive actions or market shifts that will affect your pricing? Do you expect your costs to affect your prices in the near future? Do you need to consider any looming market changes or buyer taste changes?

Raising prices

Customers either resist or barely register price hikes. Their reaction largely depends on how you announce the change. One of the worst approaches is to simply raise prices with a take–it–or–leave–it announcement. Far better is to include new pricing as part of a menu of pricing options, following these tips:

TIP

>> **Accompany price hikes with lower-priced alternatives.** Examples include bulk-purchase prices, slow-hour or slow-season rates, and bundled product packages that provide a discount in return for the larger transaction.

>> **Announce a new range of products instead of simply high- and low-priced options.** Research shows that, though customers often opt for the lower of two price levels, when three price levels are provided, they choose the mid-range or upper level rather than the least expensive.

>> **Give customers choices by unbundling all-inclusive products.** By presenting product components and service agreements as self-standing offerings customers can self-tailor a lower-priced offering.

>> **Give advance notice of price increases.** In service businesses, don't make customers discover increases on their invoices. Allow them time to accommodate new pricing in their budgets. In retail businesses, give customers the opportunity to stock up before price hikes take effect.

>> **Believe in your pricing.** Especially when you raise prices, be certain that your pricing is a fair reflection of your product's cost and value. Then instill that belief throughout your business.

Presenting prices

The way you present prices can inspire your prospects — or confuse or underwhelm them. Use Table 2-4 and the following advice to show your prices in the most favorable light:

>> **Don't let your price presentation get too complex.** Table 2-4 presents examples for presenting prices in a straightforward, visually attractive manner that communicates clearly without misleading consumers.

>> **Do make the price compelling.** In a world of outlet malls, online bargains, and warehouse stores, "10 percent off" isn't considered a deal.

>> **Do support pricing announcements with positive benefits your product promises to deliver.** Price alone is never reason enough to buy.

TABLE 2-4 **Pricing Presentation Do's and Don'ts**

Do	Don't	Why
Announcing a new St. Louis number to remember — $89 per night	We've just cut our nightly rates — $89 midweek; some restrictions apply	The first approach makes the deal sound noteworthy, whereas the second approach provides no positive rationale and implies that "small print applies."
Sofa and loveseat $1,995	Sofa and loveseat $1,995.00	When prices are more than $100, drop the decimal point and zeroes to lighten the effect.
½ off second pair	25% off two or more	Complicated discounts are uninspiring, and "½ off" sounds like double the discount of 25% off when you buy two.
Regularly $995; now $695 while supplies last	30% off	A third off sounds more compelling than 30% off, but showing a $300 reduction is stronger yet. "While supplies last" adds incentive and urgency.
$17.95; we pick up all shipping and handling	$14.95 plus shipping/handling	The word "plus" alerts the consumer that the price is only the beginning. Calculate and include shipping and handling to remove buyer concern and possible objection.
State and local taxes apply	State and local taxes extra	"Extra" goes into the same category as "plus" when it comes to pricing.

The Care and Feeding of a Product Line

You have two ways to increase sales:

1. **Sell more to existing customers.**

2. **Attract new customers.**

Figure 2-1 presents questions to ask as you seek to build business from new and existing customers through new and existing products.

FIGURE 2-1: Questions to ask as you assess your sales growth options.

How can we sell more **Existing Products** to **Existing Customers**	How can we initiate sales of **Existing Products** to **New Customers**
What **New Products** would build business with **Existing Customers**	What **New Products** can we offer to attract **New Customers**

© John Wiley & Sons, Inc.

REMEMBER

Products get old. They follow a life cycle (refer to Figure 2-2) that begins with product development and proceeds until the product reaches old age, at which time its growth rate halts and sales decline.

FIGURE 2-2: Sales follow a predictable curve throughout the product life cycle.

Product Reaches Maturity

Increased Promotion — Growth Rate Slows

Competitors Enter — Similar Products Introduced

Repeat Purchase and New Sales — Price Wars

New Product Sales — Sales Decline

Development — Product Withdrawal or Reinvention

Introduction — Growth — Maturity — Saturation — Decline

© John Wiley & Sons, Inc.

Enhancing the appeal of existing products

At least annually, small businesses need to assess whether their products still appeal to customers. When customers lose interest, a company needs to adjust features, services, pricing, or packaging — or make other changes to sustain or reignite buyer interest. Here are some of your options:

EXAMPLE

WARNING

>> **Same product, new use:** Start by looking for ways you can re-present the product to win new purchases by established and new customers.

A historic example of re-presenting a product comes from Arm & Hammer baking soda. When consumers stopped baking, sales of baking soda tumbled. Arm & Hammer responded by reintroducing baking soda — this time not as a recipe ingredient but rather as a refrigerator deodorizer. Today, that repurposing has led Arm & Hammer into a role as a leading supplier of cleaning and household solutions.

>> **Same product, new promotional offer:** Examine ways to update how you offer your product to customers, including new distribution, customer-responsive pricing, or new packages combining top-selling products with others your customers may not have tried.

Be sure your new offer provides advantages that address customer wants and needs. Before you offer a new "deal," be sure that you can say yes to the following question: Does this provide customers with a better, higher-value way to buy the product? For advice to follow, see the sidebar, "Innovation isn't for the self-absorbed," later in the chapter.

>> **Same product, new customer:** Expand the market for existing products through low-risk, introductory trial offers or samples or through free seminars, guest lectures, or events that attract the kinds of people you target as customers and develop their interest in your offerings.

Raising a healthy product

Sales follow a predictable pattern as a product moves through the life cycle illustrated in Figure 2-2. The following descriptions explain the marketing steps and sales expectations that accompany each phase of the product's life:

WARNING

>> **Introductory phase:** At the beginning of a product's life cycle, you want to build awareness, interest, and market acceptance while working to change existing market purchase patterns. Use introductory offers to gain trial and drive sales to speed up your cost/investment recovery.

Although prompting early sales through low pricing is tempting be careful, how you introduce a product determines how its image is established. If customers link the product with a low price, that first impression will stick and limit your ability to increase prices later. Better to set the price where it belongs relative to your product value and to gain sales through heavy start-up advertising and, if necessary, carefully crafted promotional offers.

>> **Growth phase:** The product enters this phase after it's adopted by the first 10 to 20 percent of the market, called the *innovators* or *early adopters.* The

masses follow this pace-setting group, and when the masses start buying, growth takes off and competitors enter. Consider promotions and special offers to protect and build market share.

>> **Maturity:** When the product reaches maturity, its sales are at their peak level, and sales growth starts to decline.

>> **Saturation phase:** At this phase, the market is flooded with options. Sales come largely from replacement purchases. Use pricing offers and incentives to recruit new customers and win them from competitors.

>> **Declining phase:** When the product reaches the point of deep sales decline, a business has only a few choices. One is to abandon the product in favor of new offerings, perhaps introducing phase-out pricing to hasten the cycle closure. Another is to let the product exist on its own with minor marketing support and, as a result, lowered sales expectations. Yet a third option is to reinvent the product's usage, application, or distribution to gain appeal with a new market; it's best to take this revitalizing step when a product reaches its maturity rather than after its appeal is in decline.

Developing new products

Whether it's to seize a new market opportunity or to offset shrinking sales with replacement products, one of the most exciting aspects of business is introducing new products. It's also one of the most treacherous because it involves betting your business resources on a new idea.

As you pursue product development, ask these questions:

>> What current product can you significantly update or enhance to address changing customer wants and needs?

>> What altogether new idea will satisfy currently unaddressed wants and needs of your customers and prospective customers?

>> What market trend can you address with a new product?

WARNING

Companies develop many new products to address fads that may or may not become lasting trends. Before capitalizing on a fad, consider these factors:

>> Only a fraction of hot fads launch marketplace trends. Most come and go quickly, so have a plan to get in and get out of the market quickly if interest ebbs.

>> Be sure you aren't entering the market too late. Take a second to review Figure 2-2, the product life cycle. If other companies have already introduced

offerings to address the fad, and if those products have already reached the saturation phase, then your new offering will have to come with pricing and other incentives to win business from the lineup of competitors already in the field.

Here are questions to ask during the research stage of product development:

>> Is it unique? Is another business already producing it, and, if so, will your product be materially different — and better?

>> Does it deliver customer value? If this is an upgrade of an existing product, how is it different in a way that matters to customers?

>> Will it appeal to a growing market? What is its customer profile?

>> Is it feasible? What will it cost to produce or deliver, and how much can you charge for it?

>> Does it fit with your company image? Is it consistent with what people already believe about you, or does it require a leap of faith?

>> Is it legal and safe? Does it conform to all laws? Does it infringe on any patents? Does it have safety concerns?

>> Can you make and market it? Do you have the people and cash resources to back it? Can you get it to market? Do sales projections support the cost of development, introduction, and production?

WARNING

As you study new product ideas, beware of the following:

>> Features that don't inspire your customer

>> Features that don't deliver clear customer benefit

>> Product enhancements that don't add significant product value

>> "New" products that are really old products in some newfangled disguise that means nothing to customers

>> Products that don't fit within your expertise and reputation

>> Products that address fads or trends that are already starting to wane

One last caution: If you're introducing a product that's the very first of its kind, budget sufficiently to achieve customer knowledge and a fast following. Otherwise you may lose the advantage to a competitor who arrives second but with a better offering and marketing effort. As proof, consider how AltaVista was eclipsed by Google or how MySpace was overtaken by Facebook.

Managing your product offerings

Product line management is less about what you're selling than about what the market is buying. Keep your focus on your customers — on what they value — not just today, but tomorrow.

Make a list of products you sell and the revenue that each offering generates. Concentrate only on the end products you deliver. For example, a law office provides clerical services, but because those services are part of other products and aren't the reason people do business with the attorneys in the first place, they shouldn't show up on the firm's product list.

To get you started, Table 2-5 shows products for a bookstore.

TABLE 2-5   **Independent Bookstore Product Line Analysis**

Product	Product Revenue	Percentage of Revenue
Books	$250,000	43.4%
Magazines	$95,000	16.5%
Coffee and pastries	$95,000	16.5%
Greeting cards and gift items	$55,000	9.5%
Audiobooks	$45,000	7.8%
Audiobook rentals	$18,500	3.2%
Pens and writing supplies	$18,000	3.1%

Follow these steps to prioritize and manage your product line:

>> **Sell more of what customers are buying.** Study your list for surprises. You may find some products that are performing better than you realized. This knowledge will alert you to customer interests that you can ride to higher revenues. For example, nearly one-third of all revenues at the bookstore featured in Table 2-5 come from beverage/pastry and magazine sales (combined). This finding may support a decision to move the magazine display nearer to the cafe, giving each area a greater sense of space and bringing consumers of both offerings into nearer proximity (and therefore buying convenience).

>> **Promote products that you've hidden from your customers.** You may have a product line that's lagging simply because your customers aren't aware of it. When the bookstore in Table 2-5 realized that only 3 percent of revenues

were from sales of pens and writing supplies, the owners boosted the line by giving it a more prominent store location. The result? Sales increased. Had the line continued to lag, though, the owners were ready to replace it with one capable of drawing a greater response.

>> **Move fast-selling items out of prime retail positions.** Give the spotlight to harder-to-sell offerings or give the slower-selling items visibility by placing them near top sellers. In the case of the bookstore in Table 2-5, moving a display of greeting cards closer to the popular pastry counter led to increased sales.

>> **Back your winners.** Use your product analysis to track which lines are increasing or decreasing in sales and respond accordingly. If the bookstore in Table 2-5 is fighting a decline in book sales whereas sales of reading accessories and gifts are growing, the owners may decide to address the trend by adding lamps, bookends, and even reading glasses.

>> **Bet only on product lines that have adequate growth potential.** Before committing to new product strategies, project your return on investment. For example, Table 2-5 shows that a little more than 3 percent of sales result from audiobook rentals. Doubling this business would increase annual revenues by only $18,500. Realizing this, the owners asked: What's the likelihood of increasing this business — and at what cost? On the other hand, increasing cafe sales by 20 percent would realize $19,000 of additional revenue, which the owners determined was a safer marketing bet and a stronger strategic move.

Chapter 3

Sizing Up the Market

No matter how unique your offering, no matter how much you think you play on a "field of one," and even if you're the only hitching post in a one-horse town, you have competition.

When Alexander Graham Bell called to Mr. Watson through his newfangled invention in 1876, he had competition already. He held in his hand the one and only such device in the whole world, yet from its moment of inception, the telephone had to fight for market share. It had to compete with all the existing and more familiar means of message delivery, and it was certain to spawn a crop of copycat products to vie for message delivery in the future.

Competition may not be obvious or direct, but it's always present. The sooner you face it and plan for it, the better. Use the information in this chapter to gauge and grow your share of business.

Playing the Competitive Field

Competition is the contest among businesses to attract customers and sales. The opposite of competition is a *monopoly*, where a single company has complete control of an industry or service offering.

Competition occurs whenever winning attention is necessary for selection and survival. In nature, the peacock's tail, the rose's scent, and the apple's sweetness are the marketing tools. In business, the battle is fought and won with product innovations and marketing programs designed to attract customers to one business over another.

Thanks to the forces of competition, the free enterprise system is undergoing constant improvement. Here are a few examples of what competition does:

>> It prompts product upgrades and innovations.

>> It leads to higher quality and lower prices.

>> It enhances selection.

>> It inspires business efficiencies.

These sections take a closer look at the ins and outs of competition and what you need to know about remaining competitive.

Speaking the language of competition

Your sales figures provide your first indication of how you're doing in your competitive arena. If they're strong and growing, your business is on the right track. If they're sliding downhill, you have your work cut out for you. This section defines the terms to know in order to evaluate and improve your position in the competitive field.

Market share

Market share is your slice of the market pie — or your portion of all the sales of products like yours that are taking place in your market area. For example, suppose that you manage a movie theater in a market with a dozen other movie theaters within a reasonable driving distance. Your market share is the percentage that your theater captures of all the movie tickets sold by all 13 movie theaters. See the "Calculating Your Market Share" section later in this chapter for tips on how to determine and grow your market share.

Share of customer

Share of customer is the percentage that you capture of all the purchases that each individual customer *could* make at your business. Continuing with the movie theater example, in addition to tickets, the theater sells popcorn, soda, candy, movie posters, gift certificates, and so on. Every customer who purchases a movie ticket — nothing else — represents an opportunity to seize a greater share of customer, also known as *share of billfold.*

Share of opportunity

Share of opportunity measures all those people who could but don't buy products like the ones you sell.

EXAMPLE

Years ago, Coca-Cola released research documenting that nearly 6 billion people in the world were consuming, on average, 64 ounces of fluid a day. Of that total intake, only 2 ounces of the liquid consumed was Coca-Cola. Coca-Cola officials used this information as the basis of an effort to increase what the company termed its *share of stomach.*

EXAMPLE

An insurance brokerage sells life insurance, which provides a solution for peace of mind. Its competition comes from competing insurers and all the other ways people address their desire for financial security, including everything from investing in stocks to stashing money under the mattress to buying lottery tickets. The insurance brokerage may want to think in terms of how to increase its *nest egg share.*

Find a "stomach share" analogy for your business. What satisfaction does your product address? What solution does your business provide? It's not likely that you'll be able to arrive at a firm calculation of the total size of the opportunity your business addresses, but simply by thinking in terms of why people buy your offering and how they participate with your business, you may land on new promotional ideas that lead to a greater share of business.

Knowing what you're up against

Your business faces three kinds of competition:

REMEMBER

>> **Direct competitors that eat into your market share:** They offer the same kinds of products or services that you do and appeal to customers in the same markets that you do business.

Your market share increases when you lure business from direct competitors to your business.

>> **Indirect competitors that erode your share of customer:** For instance, if you sell paint but your customer buys a paintbrush somewhere else, that paintbrush seller is an indirect competitor because it's capturing your customer's secondary sale. Similarly, if you own a marketing company and your client also uses a sales coach to build business, the sales coach is your indirect competitor.

TIP

To increase your share of customer, find a way to serve as a one-stop solution by offering your primary product and also the secondary, complementary, or add-on products that customers currently obtain elsewhere.

>> **Phantom competitors that block your share of opportunity:** One of the biggest obstacles to a purchase — and therefore the biggest *phantom competition* — is your customer's inclination to buy nothing or to find some alternative or do-it-yourself solution instead of buying what you're selling. Taking the paint store example a step further, if you offer a choice between enamel and latex paint but your customers opt for vinyl siding (which never needs paint), a siding outlet is a phantom competitor capable of blocking your business. For that matter, if customers decide that their houses can go another year without a paint job, the option to do nothing is your phantom competitor.

TIP

To increase your share of opportunity, discover your phantom competitors and then make your product an easier, more satisfying, and more valuable alternative.

Understanding how to compete

All else being equal, most customers opt for the product with the lowest price. If you want to charge more, make sure that everything else *isn't* equal between you and your lower-priced competitor. Most competitors fall into one of the following two categories:

>> **Price competitors** emphasize price as their competitive advantage. To succeed as a price competitor, a business must be prepared to offset lower profit margins with higher sales volume. It also must be prepared to lose its only competitive edge if another business offers a lower price.

>> **Nonprice competitors** gain business through a distinction other than low price. They win business based on superior quality, prestige, service, location, reputation, uniqueness of offering, or customer convenience. They must offer an overall value that customers perceive to be worth a higher price tag. They also need to be able to clearly communicate their quality distinction — for instance: *Zero defects, Phone calls returned in four hours,* or *Delivery in 30 minutes or it's free.*

Winning Your Share of the Market

You win market share by taking business from your direct competitors, thereby reducing their slice of the market pie while increasing your own. Here's what you must do:

1. **Get to know your direct competition.**

If prospects don't buy from your business, where do they go instead?

2. **Find out why your customers buy from competing businesses over yours.**

3. **Determine how to win business from direct competitors by enhancing or communicating the value of your offerings in a way that makes them more attractive than the competing alternatives.**

The following sections go into more detail on how to accomplish these steps.

Defining your direct competition

The first step toward gaining market share is to acknowledge that you have competition and to get real about which businesses are winning the sales that you're working to capture. On an annual or regular basis, ask yourself the questions outlined in this section.

With which businesses does your business directly compete?

When people consider buying your product or service, which other businesses do they think of at the same time?

Be realistic as you name your direct competitors. Just because a retailer sells jewelry in New York City, it doesn't necessarily compete with Tiffany's. Your direct competitors are businesses that provide your customers a similar offering and a reasonable alternative to your product or service.

REMEMBER

If you have a service business, your direct competitors are those companies that you regularly go up against as you try to win contracts or jobs. If you're a retailer, your direct competitors are the businesses whose shopping bags your customers carry as they walk by your store or the business names you overhear while customers deliberate whether to buy your product or some alternative. Investigate by conducting customer research (see Book 1, Chapter 2).

How does your business stack up against its direct competitors?

Invest some time discovering the strengths and weaknesses of your competitors. Shop their stores, call their offices, visit their websites, or take any other steps to approach them in the manner your customers approach your business. Compare how their offerings, their presentations, their brand images, and the experience of dealing with their businesses compares with the offerings of your business.

Evaluate each competitor:

>> What are this competitor's strengths?

>> What are this competitor's weaknesses?

>> What could your business do differently to draw this competitor's customers over to your business?

Among your direct competitors, how does your business rank?

Are you the top-tier player in your competitive arena or are you on the low end of the spectrum trying to become a more dominant player? Here are approaches for pegging your place in your competitive field:

>> Compare how your business ranks with competitors based on number of employees, sales volume, or any other indicator you can ballpark.

>> Compare your market share with the share of each competitor. (See the section "Calculating Your Market Share" later in this chapter.)

TIP

>> Evaluate your *top of mind* ranking — sometimes called your *mind share.* When prospects are asked to name three to five businesses in your field, does your name consistently make the list? You can easily find new competitor lists using the free search tool from www.semrush.com by searching your service name. For example: Miami Auto Repair.

If so, you can be pretty sure that your business has top-tier mind share in its competitive arena. Keep listening and you'll discover the names of the businesses your customer thinks are your direct competitors. And if you don't hear your business name, listen anyway, because when you know which businesses *are* in the top-of-mind category, you can begin to analyze what they do differently to achieve the prominence you seek.

Moving up the competitive ladder

Most businesses misdirect their time and energy by tackling the wrong competitors. They take on the biggest names in their market area instead of the biggest threats to their business. As you develop your competitive plan of attack, follow these steps:

1. **Start by winning market share from the businesses you're actually losing customers to** *today.*

   Do this even if it involves facing the harsh reality that your customers consider your business among a less prestigious group than you wish they did. After you name your current competitors, study their offerings, their marketing, and the customer service they provide as you honestly evaluate how your business compares.

2. **Make a list of the companies you** *wish* **you were running with.**

   Evaluate why you're not in that group. Is it because of your business's image or location? Does the nature of your clientele mark you as a lower-level player? Or do your products and pricing prevent you from competing with the biggest names in your business arena?

3. **Consider whether changing competitive levels is advantageous.**

   Assess whether your business is more apt to be successful at its current competitive level (think of the big-fish-in-a-small-pond concept) or at the next competitive level (where perhaps you can compete for more lucrative business but where competition may be stiffer and where customers may be fewer or more demanding).

If you decide that your business would be better off competing with more visible and prestigious businesses in your arena, commit to making the changes necessary to get the market to see you through new eyes.

Calculating Your Market Share

Having a sense of your market share provides a good indication of your competitive rank and a way to monitor your growth within your target market. These sections help you figure out your business's market share.

Sizing up your target market

To calculate your share of the market, first define the size of the market in which you compete.

The *total* market includes the entire nation or world — a market area that matters enormously to major global marketers like Nike or Levi's. But to a small business like yours, what matters is your *target* market — the one within the sphere of your business's influence. You can assess your target market's size by using the following criteria:

>> **Geographic targeting:** Where are your customers, and how many are there? For example, a retailer may determine that its geographic target market consists primarily of people who live or vacation within a two-hour drive of the retailer's place of business. An accountant may determine that her geographic target market is concentrated within the city limits. A consultant may target businesses within a five-state region.

>> **Customer targeting:** How many people or businesses actually fit your customer profile? (See Book 1, Chapter 2 for profiling information.) An office furniture manufacturer may target all the nation's office-furnishing retail establishments, along with architects and interior designers who specify office furnishings. An online florist may focus exclusively on wedding planners and brides-to-be within a single state or region.

>> **Product-oriented targeting:** Sometimes, the most effective way to measure your target market's size is through an analysis of how many sales of products like yours occur in the market. For instance, a microbrewery may measure its share of a market as a percentage of all premium beer sold in its geographic target area. (The microbrewery wouldn't measure its sales against *all* beer sales; it would focus on premium beer sales, because that's the microbrewery's sphere of business influence.) Likewise, an attorney who specializes in land-use planning would assess the number of land-use cases in the target market area before trying to calculate market share.

Doing the math

After you have a good sense of your total target market's size, you can use several approaches to calculate your share:

>> **Unit sales:** Some businesses can easily figure out the total number of products like theirs sold each year. A motel manager in a region that collects a hotel occupancy tax, for instance, could divide the tax the motel pays by the total area-wide tax collection to arrive at the motel's share of the market.

>> **Number of potential customers:** If you know that 30,000 adults are in your target market area, and if you can make an educated guess that one in ten of them — or 10 percent — is a consumer of services like yours, you can assume that your business has a total potential market of 3,000 adults. If you serve 300 of those adults, you have a 10 percent share of your target market.

TIP

To aid in your guesswork, visit the reference area of your library and flip through the Standard Rate and Data Service (SRDS) *Local Market Audience Analyst* to find out about consumers in your market area.

For instance, imagine a fabric and sewing supply store that serves a geographic area that includes 7,000 homes within a 15-minute drive of the store. The owners could find out from the *Local Market Audience Analyst* that 18.5 percent of the households in the area participate in home sewing. If the store's owners multiply the 7,000-household market area by 18.5 percent, they'll discover that they have 1,295 potential customers in their geographic market area. If the owners currently serve 250 of these potential customers, they have a market share of just less than 20 percent — meaning plenty of opportunity for growth.

>> **Total sales volume:** Another way to estimate market share is to calculate how much people spend at businesses like yours in your market area each year and then divide that figure by your sales revenue. For example, if annually in your market area people spend a total of $1 million on products like those you sell, and if your business does $100,000 annually in sales, then you have a 10 percent market share.

TIP

Regional business journals and newspapers compile lists that rank sales by businesses in specific industries or service sectors. Businesses submit their revenues (often slightly inflated, so read them with a realistic eye) as a basis for appearing in these lists. Study the lists for your industry to find clues to regional sales revenues in your field.

EXAMPLE

MARKET SHARE: SAMPLE CALCULATION

Suppose that Green Gardens, a residential landscaping business, serves a market area that includes 20,000 houses, of which approximately 10 percent use landscape services. Thus, the potential residential landscape service market is 2,000 homes. If Green Gardens serves 200 homes, it has a 10 percent market share.

Another way to look at market share is by dollar volume. Green Gardens could estimate the revenues of each of its competitors and then add those figures to the Green Gardens revenue figure to produce a rough estimate of total target market residential landscape service sales. If target market sales total $4 million, and if Green Gardens has annual sales of $600,000, Green Gardens has a 15 percent market share.

If Green Gardens combines its knowledge of market share based on unit sales (number of houses served) *and* market share based on dollar volume, its owners would see that they have a 10 percent share of all houses served, yet they have a 15 percent share of total dollar volume. This finding could lead them to conclude that they serve larger-sized accounts than some of their competitors. And based on that, they should have a small celebration!

Increasing Your Market Share

If you're in business and you're ringing up sales, you can rest assured that your business enjoys at least some level of market awareness and market share. But you can be equally certain that not everyone knows about or buys from your business. No brand in the world has 100 percent brand awareness, let alone 100 percent market share, so be reasonable with your market share goals and growth expectations.

Also, as you seek to increase market share, steer clear of these land mines:

>> **Avoid "buying" market share through price reductions.** Don't sacrifice your bottom line as you prepare to welcome new customers through the door. Before you go the price-slashing route, glance through the pricing advice in Book 1, Chapter 2.

>> **Be ready before issuing an invitation to new customers.** Don't procrastinate, but do give yourself time to be sure you're ready to make a great first impression. Run through the following checklist before launching a new business development effort:

- **Current customer satisfaction levels:** Are your current customers happy with your product? Are they happy with your business in general? Do they return to your business again and again, or do you have a high turnover rate? Do customers speak well on your behalf? Are your customer satisfaction levels sky-high?

- **Customer service adjustments:** Before working to draw in new customers, make changes that will enhance your customer experience and service levels, increasing the odds that you'll develop lasting and loyal customer relationships. Start by studying current customer reviews, ratings, and input, looking for legitimate service or product complaints you can address before reaching out to new customers. Then, beyond righting wrongs, get proactive. Do you need to fine-tune your product offering — how you price it, how you package and present it, or even how you guarantee it? Do you need to improve how you interact with customers? This may include everything from enhancing your business environment to revising your on-hold telephone message to improving the speed and user-friendliness of your website.

- **Business readiness:** Do you have the inventory (or, if you own a service business, the staff, talent, and capacity) to deliver what you're offering? Is your staff well-informed and ready to help prospects become buyers when they respond to your marketing messages?

WHEN MARKET SHARE MEANS MARKET SATURATION

The common rule is that a 25 percent market share is considered a dominant market position. As you calculate your market share, watch closely as it reaches a dominant position. When it gets there, take time to celebrate, for sure, but also be aware that as your share edges farther upward, it will near a level called market saturation.

Market saturation occurs when a business captures the sales of about 40 percent of the potential customers within its target market, at which point one of several things tends to happen:

- **Competitors start to eat into market share.** After a business begins to saturate its marketplace, competitors realize the opportunity and enter to seize a share of the sales.

- **The dominant business gets complacent.** Quality control often gets lax and customers begin to stray.

- **Customers' interest or need wanes.** By the time a business gains dominant market share, often customers have bought the products they need and, other than replacements, their purchases grow few and far between.

- **The business seeks new opportunities.** With market saturation comes the need for change. Businesses that dominate their market areas seek growth by opening new markets or introducing new products. Most of all, they restore their emphasis on customer service and satisfaction — the very thing that made the business a success in the first place.

Don't turn from a growing market too soon, but don't cling exclusively to a saturated market too long. Use market share knowledge as your steering wheel.

Chapter 4

Setting Your Goals

D oes the following description sound a little or a lot like you?

You don't know where to start with your marketing efforts. You don't know how much you should spend. You don't know whether you need to hire someone to take on the marketing task. You aren't sure what you should be saying or to whom. In fact, you aren't even certain what you're trying to accomplish with your marketing efforts.

If that description sounds familiar, this chapter is for you, because getting clear about your marketing goals simplifies everything.

After you actually state what you want to achieve, marketing becomes a pretty reasonable task. For example, an accounting firm may determine that it wants to add three new corporate clients over the coming year. A retail establishment may want to gain $200,000 in new sales. A commercial cleaning business may want to take on five more business contracts.

When small business owners are clear about where they want to go, they nearly always get there. In huge companies, the process of getting all the departments focused on the same goal is like herding cats. But small businesses have fewer people to orchestrate, and the owner's will can more clearly affect the actions of the full business team. As a small business marketer, if you start with a goal, a plan, and a reasonable budget for achieving your desired outcome, chances are you'll get where you want to go.

Where Are You Going, Anyway?

Mission. Vision. Goals. Objectives. What's what?

Some consultants do nothing but lead corporations and organizations through the *visioning* process, helping them clarify why they exist, what they hope to achieve, and how they intend to get where they want to be.

Small companies rarely have the funds to dedicate to this kind of a strategic process. For that matter, they rarely have time to stop and think about what they're trying to accomplish beyond the survival objective of bringing in enough revenue to cover the expenses. That's why your business will have an edge — and a greater chance for success — if you devote some time upfront to setting your sights and aiming yourself and your business in the right direction.

Understanding the "vision" thing

Well-run businesses set annual goals that are supported by the foundation of a business vision and mission. The terms *vision* and *mission* are often used interchangeably, but there is a fine-line difference.

REMEMBER

Your *vision* is a statement of what your company strives to be. It defines your desired future. It's the big picture of where you're going. Your company's *mission*, on the other hand, is the path you plan to follow to achieve success.

A hallmark example of clearly defined vision and mission statements comes from the Oregon Trail, the 19th-century trek from Missouri to Oregon. If ever an organization needed a vision to overshadow the mission's rigor and to guide all goals and objectives, it was this 2,200-mile journey across America.

> **Oregon Trail vision:** To find a better life.

> **Oregon Trail mission:** To travel by wagon to Oregon.

Even if your own challenges pale in comparison to those of America's pioneers (and with any luck, they do!), your organization will still benefit from clarity about what you're working to achieve. You may come up with vision and mission statements, or you may combine the two in a single statement of purpose, following the examples of success stories in the upcoming section.

Either way, by defining what your business seeks to achieve you'll create a barometer by which to measure every planning and marketing decision your business makes.

Knowing your statement of purpose

Your business will be stronger if you put into writing the ultimate reason that you come to work every day. Consider these questions as you work on your company's reason for being:

>> Why did you get into this business in the first place?

>> What need did you see that you felt you could fulfill better than anyone else?

>> What makes your business different from others?

>> What commitment do you make to those you deal with — from employees to suppliers to customers?

>> What's the ultimate reason for your work?

WARNING

Turning a profit is a desired result of your success, but don't let the bottom line become your purpose. Instead, articulate what positive change you want to create through your business. Doing so defines the heart and soul of your company and the driving force behind all the decisions that you make. From there, success — and profits — should flow.

Looking for success stories

Most successful companies display their statements of purpose throughout their workplaces and in their written communications. Check annual reports and websites to find the statements of purpose from the business world's well-known success stories.

EXAMPLE

Here are some examples:

>> **Google:** To organize the world's information and make it universally accessible and useful.

>> **Microsoft:** To help people and businesses throughout the world to realize their full potential.

>> **Boys & Girls Clubs of America:** To enable all young people, especially those who need us most, to reach their full potential as productive, caring, responsible citizens.

>> **Coca-Cola Company:** To refresh the world. To inspire moments of optimism and happiness. To create value and make a difference.

Setting Your Goals

Now it's your turn: Use the formula in Figure 4-1 to create a sentence that serves as the beacon for your business. As you develop your statement, think in terms of your vision (what positive change you want to achieve) and your mission (how you'll make your vision real).

Formula for a Purpose Statement

BEGIN WITH

A verb that describes the change you want to make

THEN ADD

A clause summarizing the need your business addresses

AND YOU HAVE

The Purpose Statement for your company

FIGURE 4-1:
Developing a
statement of
purpose.

© John Wiley & Sons, Inc.

Defining Goals and Objectives Simply

More than just business buzzwords, *goal*, *objective*, *strategy*, and *tactic* fit together to take your small business from ideas to action.

>> **Goal:** The overall sales or professional target that your marketing program seeks to achieve. Your goal is an expression of a realistic and clearly defined target, usually accompanied by a time frame.

>> **Objective:** The measurable result that will be necessary to achieve the goal. A plan usually has several objectives that define the major means by which you'll meet the goal.

>> **Strategy:** The plan for achieving each measurable objective.

>> **Tactic:** An action you'll take to enact your strategy.

Figure 4-2 shows how these elements come together.

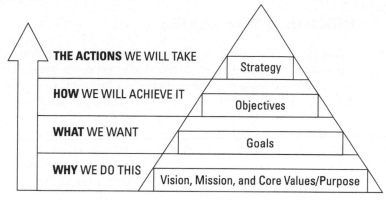

FIGURE 4-2:
The planning
pyramid.

Setting goals and objectives

The line between goals and objectives is razor thin, and many marketers spend undue time trying to differentiate between the two. The truth is that you can run a perfectly successful company without drowning in goal-versus-objective details. Yet sure enough, the minute you decide to skip the whole drill, some banker, venture capitalist, or major partner will ask you to define how you've set your goals and objectives, and you'll be left tongue-tied in the meeting. If that happens, the following descriptions can bail you out:

>> **Your goal** is what you want to achieve during the upcoming marketing period to move toward the vision you've set for your company.

>> **Your objectives** define how your business will achieve its goal over the upcoming year.

EXAMPLE

A local newspaper may set an annual goal to increase readership by 5 percent in order to more fully achieve its vision to serve as the region's most trusted information vehicle. The goal defines *what* the newspaper wants to achieve, but not *how* it will achieve it. Here are some objectives a newspaper might set to increase readership by 5 percent:

A Verb	A Noun	A Precise Description of the Desired Change
To introduce	a new section	aimed at young, affluent, urban professionals
To gain	5 percent	market share from Competitor X
To improve	delivery time	by one hour daily

Setting Your Goals

Planning strategies

Strategies are the plans for achieving business objectives. They're practical, achievable, and action-oriented. Strategies generally detail changes that a business intends to make to the four marketing functions called the *marketing mix* (or the *four p's*): pricing, product, promotion, and place (also known as distribution).

REMEMBER

Cast your goals and objectives in cement when you create your marketing plan each year, but keep your strategies flexible so you can adjust them in response to competitive forces, economic realities, or new opportunities. Just remember that the only strategy worth pursuing is one that directly supports your goals and objectives.

Putting goals, objectives, and strategies into action

After you're clear about your marketing goal, every action becomes a building block toward achieving that ultimate desired end.

WARNING

Small businesses sometimes confuse goals and strategies. Opening a new office, beginning to sell a new product, or increasing prices in June are strategies, not goals. Knowing your strategies without being clear about the goal you're trying to reach is like wandering in the woods wearing a blindfold.

EXAMPLE

In Figure 4-3, you can see how all parts of the business program fit together in the plan for a microbrewery.

Following the fail-safe planning sequence

Successful marketers follow the same lock-step marketing scenario:

1. **Conduct market research.**

   Doing so ensures that you know everything you can about your customer, your product, your competition, and your business environment. Follow the steps outlined in Book 1, Chapters 2 and 3.

2. **Establish marketing goals and objectives.**

   The previous sections of this chapter are full of instructions on this step.

3. **Set the marketing strategies and determine the marketing mix that you'll employ to achieve your objectives.**

   The preceding section guides you through this step.

4. **Choose your marketing tools and tactics.**

   That's what the rest of this book is about.

Purpose: To make a difference by creating great beer to drink in the warm, lively atmosphere of our brewpub, contributing to the success of events and celebrations, and supporting important causes in the community that surrounds us.

Annual Goal:
Increase gross revenues by 10%.

Objectives:
Increase brewpub business by 20%.
Increase case sales by 8%.
Increase revenue from ancillary products and services by 20%.

Strategies:

Place or Distribution Strategy

- Broaden retail distribution to increase taps in regional bars and restaurants.
- Broaden wholesale distribution to increase grocery and convenience store sales.
- Establish a retail outlet in the brewpub for sale of logo items.

Pricing Strategy

- Increase prices by 3–5% to adjust for cost increases and to align better with premium labels.
- Establish bulk pricing for multi-keg or multiple-case orders.

Product Strategy

- Create a mobile pub unit that can be loaned to event hosts.
- Establish a line of logo items to be sold online and in a new brewpub outlet.
- Create beer-brewing classes to drive business during slow seasons and daytime hours.

Promotion Strategy

- Use broadcast and social media advertising to build brand awareness.
- Use social media to promote beer-brewing classes and mobile pub events.
- Link all communications to a website landing page featuring logo items and mobile pub events.
- Sponsor community events and participate in community fundraisers that align with our mission and the mission of our key retail partners.

FIGURE 4-3: A brewpub's marketing purpose, goal, objective, and strategies.

Setting Your Goals

Never, ever start with Step 4. In other words, never decide on your tactic — whether to run an ad or hire a new distributor or take on a new partner — until you know your strategies. Because when you know your strategies, you know your objectives, which means that you know your goals, which means that you know where you want your business to go. After that, all that's left is to establish interim milestones and measure results along the way, fine-tuning your tools and tactics as necessary until you reach your goal.

Tactics *follow* strategies — not vice versa.

Budgeting to Reach Your Goals

Small business marketing budgets include two variables: time and money. You can reach customers with paid advertising and marketing communications or you can reach them through personal contacts, which requires time but little if any cash outlay.

Networking and sales calls have long served as an alternative to costly advertising outreach. But in today's marketplace, those who can devote time to marketing have powerful additional tools in their arsenal: social media and digital communications.

Turn to Book 4 for three chapters that cover connecting with customers online through social media. If your customers are online, and if you're willing to commit the time to meet and interact with them through your website, social media channels, and other sites, then your need for marketing dollars can be offset by your investment of time. This section helps you weigh the balance.

Talking realistically about small business marketing budgets

The most important commitment you can make to your marketing program is to establish and stick to a budget. Whether you're budgeting time, money, or both, cover these four points:

>> Establish a marketing budget.

>> Spend the allocated time or funds on a planned marketing program.

>> View the allocation as an important business investment.

>> Manage the program well.

If you cut back on marketing, you put your business on a dangerous downhill slide. Sure, you recoup some money — or time — when you make the budget cut, but following that one-time savings, look at what happens. With the reduction comes fewer communication efforts. With fewer communications, sales decline. Declining sales reduce your overall revenues, which means you have even fewer resources to allocate for future marketing.

Think long and hard before trimming your marketing budget because it's the one expense item designated specifically to attract and keep customers.

Knowing how much you should spend

How much money you spend on marketing depends on the type of business you have and the marketing tools you employ. Everyone wants a magic formula, but there isn't one, especially today when so much marketing happens online rather than through paid advertising. Remember the following:

>> Mature businesses in established markets with low growth goals can get away with low marketing investments of as little as 2 to 5 percent of sales. Companies that target high growth must invest far more.

>> Businesses whose sales come primarily from subcontracting can spend almost no cash on marketing, whereas businesses that need to win the attention of a broad cross section of retail customers must budget enough to gain visibility through paid media ads, online communications, and promotions.

>> Businesses with customers who are active online and in social media networks can establish communication and ongoing interaction with little or no cash investment, though don't fool yourself into believing that social media and online marketing is free. At the least, you need to allocate time, which may translate to money if you hire staff or outside resources to establish and manage a truly effective online presence.

Only a decade ago, marketing success — especially for business-to-consumer marketers — relied heavily on how much money a business could invest in efforts to push its message into the marketplace. Today, success results not from merely pushing marketing messages but from forming two-way interactions with customers, both personally and through the Internet.

Dollars no longer make or break marketing effectiveness. Today's marketers need to budget both money and time to communicate with *and* listen to customers — interacting, responding, and developing two-way relationships as a result.

Setting Your Goals

TIP

As you determine how much to allocate for marketing, consider

>> **The nature of your business and your market:** Businesses that market to other businesses tend to allocate a lower percentage of sales to marketing than businesses that market to a wide range or number of consumers. It's the proverbial rifle versus shotgun difference. The business-to-business marketer can set its sights and reach its customers directly, whereas the business-to-consumer marketer must reach a broader audience, usually involving costly investments of time and money.

>> **The maturity of your business:** Start-up businesses need to invest more heavily than established businesses, in part to cover extraordinary one-time costs that existing businesses have behind them and in part to accelerate communications to gain first-time prospect awareness.

>> **The size of your market area:** Businesses that serve customers who are primarily located within a short drive or walk from the business location can target marketing communications into a concise market area. As a result, they can probably allocate a lower investment than businesses that have to build awareness and interest in statewide, national, or even international markets.

>> **Your competition:** Businesses that are the only game in town have to enhance their marketing efforts if several competitors suddenly open nearby. And businesses that are the underdog and want to take on the leaders must invest accordingly.

>> **Your objective and task:** The most important consideration in setting your budget is to understand your growth goals. The more aggressive they are, the more time and money you need to budget for marketing. For example, if you're planning to launch a new product or open a new location, you need to increase your marketing efforts to gain awareness, interest, and action and to fund the training, marketing support, and additional advertising required to make your plan possible.

TIP

You'll find many forms to help you allocate funding for your marketing program if you search online for "marketing budget templates." The template best-suited for your marketing budget depends on the nature of your program — whether you're marketing business-to-business, business-to-consumer, primarily through events and networking, primarily using online and social media communications, or primarily through paid advertising. Here's a sampling of websites that offer free templates for you to choose from:

>> **SCORE Annual Marketing Budget Template:** www.score.org/resources/annual-marketing-budget-template

» **Google Spreadsheet Marketing Budget Template for Start-ups:** http://
davidcummings.org/2011/11/25/google-spreadsheet-marketing-
budget-template-for-startups/

» **Microsoft Marketing Budget Planner Template:** www.microsofttemplates.
org/microsoft-excel-templates/marketing-budget-planner-template.
html

» **Sharp Mind Marketing Budget Template:** http://sharpmindmarketing.
com/wp-content/uploads/2011/07/Marketing-Budget-OnlineSMM.pdf

EXAMPLE

YOUR MONEY OR YOUR TIME? HOW COMPANIES DECIDE

Some businesses decide *not* to invest significant dollars in advertising. Instead, they direct their resources at sales presentations, networking efforts, community and industry trade shows and events, and online communications, through which they can establish contact and interact with customers and prospective customers.

That doesn't mean they aren't investing in marketing. They're investing time (and supporting dollars) rather than relying exclusively on costly and traditional advertising vehicles. Here are examples of businesses that rely more heavily on an investment of time than money:

- An attorney who wants to attract regional corporate clients may serve as a board member and volunteer counsel for a community nonprofit organization, knowing that this will generate working relationships with fellow board members who fit the target client profile.

- A regional ski resort that wants to attract more families from the local market area may decide to offer free ski lessons and rentals to all fifth graders as a way to establish relationships directly rather than via paid marketing communications.

- A hair salon that wants to build business may shift its emphasis from paid ads to pay-per-click search ads and social networking, aiming to reach customers at the moment they're considering salon services. The salon can direct online interest to a landing page that features a special offer and reservation invitation, converting customers to leads with no cash investment beyond initial site setup. See Part III for information on how to connect with customers online.

2

Getting Started with Your Campaign

Contents at a Glance

Chapter 1

Tech Tools to Have

This chapter reviews useful tools and resources to make your marketing plan easier to execute. Before you start, you may also want to check out Book 4, Chapter 1, which focuses on measurement tools for traffic, costs, and campaign performance.

As you select tools and schedule tasks from suggestions in this chapter, remember to enter them on your Social Media Marketing Plan and Social Media Activity Calendar (Book 2, Chapter 3).

Try to select at least one tool from each category:

>> Resource, news, and blog sites that cover online marketing and social media

>> Content-distribution tools

>> Tools for notifying search engines and directories of updates

>> URL-clipping tools

>> Shopping widgets for social media, if appropriate

>> Buzz-tracking tools to monitor mentions of your business

TIP

You can always jump right into the social media scene and figure out these things later, but your efforts will be more productive if you build the right framework first.

Keeping Track of the Social Media Scene

Unless you take advantage of online resources, you'll never be able to stay current with the changes in social media. Here's a quick look at how much the landscape changed in the course of just a few years:

>> Use of social media continued its explosive growth. According to the Pew Center for the Internet and American Life, 72 percent of all Internet users also use social media. And one-fifth of Internet users access three or more social media channels.

>> Facebook purchased WhatsApp, an instant messaging application, for $19 billion.

>> The month-long FIFA World Cup tournament (for soccer) generated more than 3 billion interactions on Facebook and 672 million tweets in summer 2014.

>> Social media fueled the remarkable fundraising phenomenon of the Ice Bucket Challenge for the ALS Society, raising more than $100 million for research into Lou Gehrig's disease.

>> New social media platforms continued to pop up, proving that the power of innovation is still strong. Watch for action on Apple Music and Spotify (music listing), Sobrr (short-lived social messaging), and Sulia (content sharing by experts), among others.

>> Multiple social media services went belly up. Casualties of the social media wars included Google's social network Orkut and Eons, a social media site targeted at baby boomers.

To keep current on the changing tides, subscribe to feeds about social marketing from social marketing blogs or news services; check at least one source weekly. Also, review traffic trends on social media services weekly; they're amazingly volatile. Table 1-1 lists some helpful resource sites.

TABLE 1-1 Social Media Resources

Name	URL	Description
BIG Marketing for Small Business	`www.bigmarketingsmallbusiness.com`	Social media, online, and offline marketing tips
HubSpot	`http://blog.hubspot.com`	Inbound marketing blog about attracting the right prospects to your site and converting them into customers
Marketing Land	`http://marketingland.com`	Internet marketing news
MarketingProfs	`www.marketingprofs.com/marketing/library/100/social-media`	Social media marketing tips, including business-to-business (B2B)
MarketingSherpa	`www.marketingsherpa.com/library.html`	Social networking research
Mashable	`http://mashable.com/social-media`	Premier social media guide
TopRank Online Marketing Blog	`www.toprankblog.com`	Blog about online and social marketing
SiteProNews	`www.sitepronews.com`	Social media and search engine news
Social Media Examiner	`www.socialmediaexaminer.com`	Online social media magazine advising businesses on use of social media to achieve marketing goals
Social Media Marketing Group on LinkedIn	`www.linkedin.com/groups?gid=66325`	Professional, nonpromotional discussion group
Social Media Today	`www.socialmediatoday.com`	Online community for marketing and PR professionals dealing with social media
TechHive	`www.techhive.com`	Technology news site
TechCrunch	`http://techcrunch.com`	Technology industry blog
Techmeme	`http://techmeme.com`	Top technology news site
Twitter Marketing Kickstart Tool Kit	`https://biz.twitter.com/download-our-marketing-kickstart-tool-kit`	Tool to improve Twitter performance by modifying your presence, profiles, and tweets

Saving Time with Content-Distribution Tools

Social media marketing obviously can quickly consume all your waking hours — and then some. Just the thought of needing to post information quickly to Facebook, Twitter, Google+, LinkedIn, social bookmarks, blogs, Pinterest, or social news services might make any social marketer cringe.

Time to work smarter, not harder, with content-distribution tools to post your content to many places at once for tasks like the following:

>> **Routine maintenance:** Use a content-distribution tool whenever you make updates according to your Social Media Activity Calendar. What a timesaver.

>> **Quick event postings:** Share information from a conference, trade show, meeting, or training session from your phone by sending short text updates to Twitter and LinkedIn. Or take a picture with your smartphone and send it to Instagram, Twitter, and Facebook. To send something longer, use a distribution tool to post to your blog and Facebook.

>> **Daily updates:** Group all social media services that you may want to update with rapidly changing information, such as a daily sale or the location of your traveling cupcake cart by the hour.

REMEMBER

If you have more than three social media outlets or frequently update your content, choosing at least one distribution tool is a must-have way to save time.

Some businesses prefer to craft custom postings for Facebook, Twitter, and other services based on the specific audience and content needs of each channel, while others find this too time-consuming. Do what seems right for your business: Automate *cross-postings* (set up a service so that postings on one social media service automatically appear on others to save time), customize by channel, or mix and match.

In addition to Hootsuite, OnlyWire, and other tools described in the next few sections, you can use really simple syndication (RSS) to feed content to users and to your various social media profiles. Keep in mind, however, that RSS works best with highly technical audiences.

Considering alternative content distribution services

You can select from several content-distribution services to *syndicate* (copy) your content from one social media service to another. All the services work roughly the same way, but each has its own peculiarities. Choose the one that's the best fit for you.

TIP

Some free plugins are available for WordPress (www.wordpress.com) for this purpose. Another good resource is https://ifttt.com/recipes/collections/40-recipes-to-streamline-your-social-media.

REMEMBER

Reconfigure your settings on content-distribution tools whenever you decide to add or drop a social media service or create a new, special-purpose group for marketing purposes.

Buffer

An easy-to-use app, Buffer (https://bufferapp.com) allows you to preschedule content distribution to multiple social media platforms. It uses its own built-in link shortener to gather and compare data about the performance of posts on various channels.

Hootsuite

Self-described as "the leading social media dashboard," Hootsuite (http://hootsuite.com) has expanded from its origins as a way to manage only the Twitter experience. From scheduling to stats, Hootsuite now integrates more than 35 social media channels, allowing multiservice postings from one location to Twitter, Facebook, LinkedIn, Foursquare, Google +, Instagram, YouTube, and your blog, among others.

OnlyWire

OnlyWire (http://onlywire.com) updates up to 50 social networks simultaneously. It also passes updates between WordPress sites, RSS feeds, and social media channels.

OnlyWire also offers several handy mini-apps at http://onlywire.com/tools to facilitate sharing items quickly:

>> A developer API to custom-program content exchanges among your social media channels

>> A Chrome toolbar add-in that lets you quickly share web pages you like with your Facebook and Twitter accounts

>> A WordPress plug-in that automatically submits your WordPress posts to the social media services you've selected

>> An app to deliver material from RSS feeds to your selected social media channels

Postling

Like Hootsuite, Postling (`https://postling.com`) lets you cross-post to all major social networking services and blogging platforms: Facebook, Twitter, Linke-dIn, WordPress, Tumblr, Flickr, CitySearch, and more. You can post immediately or schedule posts to go out at a later time. When people respond to your posts, Postling organizes those responses in one place and allows you to answer them from the Postling site. Postling emails a daily recap of the most recent activity on your social network sites, Yelp and Citysearch reviews, and relevant metrics, such as click through rates. You can also add other users for specific social media channels to help you respond to posts.

TweetDeck

Owned by Twitter, this tweet management tool at `https://about.twitter.com/products/tweetdeck` lets you schedule tweets, track engagement, and organize multiple accounts in one convenient location.

UberSocial

If you're on your smartphone all the time, UberSocial (`http://www.ubersocial.com`) may be perfect for you. This Twitter smartphone app, available for Android, BlackBerry, and iPhone, allows users to post and read tweets. Features vary slightly between the three devices, but all integrate LivePreview, which enables users to view embedded links next to tweets without closing the app and opening a new browser, making it an efficient way to use Twitter on your smartphone. Other features include cross-posting to Facebook, managing multiple accounts, and sending tweets of more than 140 characters.

Putting RSS to work

If you don't use one of the preceding tools, which automatically take care of RSS aggregation, then you need to consider the following section. If you do use of the preceding tools, then you can skip this section. RSS technology, which has been around for a decade, is still a viable way to distribute (syndicate) information for publication in multiple locations. The familiar orange-and-white icon shown in Figure 1-1 gained prominence years ago as a way to notify others automatically about often-updated content such as headlines, blogs, news, or music: an RSS feed.

FIGURE 1-1:
The RSS icon.

The published content — called a *feed* — is provided for free in a standardized format that can be viewed in many different programs. RSS feeds are read on the receiving end in an RSS reader, a feed reader, or an aggregator. Readers come in three species:

>> **Standalone:** Such as FeedDemon

>> **Add-ons:** Compatible with specific applications, such as an RSS plug-in for a WordPress blog

>> **Web-based:** Like Mozilla Firefox's Live Bookmarks, which adds RSS feeds to a user's Favorites folder

Feeds may be delivered to an individual subscriber's desktop, email program, or browser Favorites folder, or they can be reproduced on another website, blog page, or social media page.

TECHNICAL STUFF

You can offer an RSS feed from your site, blog, or social media pages — or display your own or others' RSS feeds on your pages. This feature requires some technical skills. If you're not technically inclined, ask your programmer to handle the implementation.

Subscribing is easy: Users simply click the RSS icon and follow directions. After that, the RSS reader regularly checks the list of subscribed feeds and downloads any updates. Users can receive automatic alerts or view their updates on demand. The provided material is usually a linkable abstract or headline, along with the publisher's name and date of publication. The link opens the full article or media clip.

Subscribers not only receive timely updates from their favorite sites, but they also can use RSS to collect feeds from many sites in one convenient place. Rather than check multiple websites every day, for instance, political junkies can have RSS feeds about Congress delivered automatically from *The Huffington Post, The Nation, The Washington Post,* and *The New York Times.*

TIP

Unless you're targeting a market that's highly proficient technically, be cautious about using RSS as your only option for sharing content except in technology fields. The general public sees RSS as too technical or complicated, and many feed readers have been shut down recently.

Be sure to enter your choices for content distribution on your Social Media Marketing Plan and create a schedule for distributing updates (daily? weekly? monthly?) on your Social Media Activity Calendar.

If you're interested in RSS, you'll find the resources in Table 1-2 helpful.

TABLE 1-2   ## RSS Resources for Technical Audiences

Name	URL	Function
Atom	www.xml.com/lpt/a/1619	Atom feed details
Feedage.com	www.feedage.com	Directory of RSS feeds
FeedBurner	http://feedburner.google.com	Create, manage, and monitor RSS feeds
FeedDemon	www.feeddemon.com	Free-standing RSS reader for Windows
FeedForAll	www.feedforall.com	RSS feed creation tool
Netvibes	www.netvibes.com	Combination personal aggregator and social network
NewsFire	www.newsfirerss.com	RSS reader for Macs

RSS offers a distinct advantage for sharing site content with readers: one-time-and-forget-about-it installation. After RSS is installed on your site or blog, you don't have to do anything except update your master site. You don't even have to type an entry like you do with the other content-distribution tools. Everyone who subscribes gets your feed automatically, and you know that they're prequalified prospects because they've opted in.

From a user's point of view, RSS means that after requesting a feed, the user doesn't have to go anywhere or do anything to receive updates because updates arrive at her fingertips.

TECHNICAL STUFF

Unfortunately, RSS coordinates with social media distribution services only if you (or your programmer) enable your other social media pages to accept and display your RSS feed. Alternatively, your programmer may be able to use a tool like the OnlyWire API (www.onlywire.com/socialapi) to configure your RSS feed to accept updates for distribution to social media.

TIP

A newer format for syndication, an Atom feed operates similarly to RSS but uses different technical parameters. Although many blogs use Atom feeds, the older RSS format remains more popular overall. Some sites offer or accept only one or the other, so your choice of source and destination services partly drives your selection of syndication format. For more information about Atom and RSS, see www.atomenabled.org or http://nullprogram.com/blog/2013/09/23.

Notifying Search Engines about Updates

Some people think that search engines, especially Google, know everything about everybody's websites all the time. Not so. Even the Google grandmaster needs a tip now and again. Even though all search engines routinely *crawl* or *spider* (visit and scan) websites to keep their own results current and relevant, your cycle for updates won't necessarily match their cycles for crawling.

TIP

Make sure that submit your website and sitemap to Google Webmaster Tools at www.google.com/webmasters/tools.

REMEMBER

Keeping search engines updated is valuable: Your site is not only more likely to appear in relevant search results, but its ranking will also improve from frequent updates.

The solution — *pinging* — is a simple way to get the attention of search engines and directories whenever you update your blog or website. Pinging has several other uses online: confirmation that a site or server is operating, as a diagnostic tool for connectivity problems, or confirming that a particular IP address exists.

Pinging can be done on demand by using a third-party service, or you can configure your blog, RSS feed, and some other sites to do it automatically. Generally, you simply enter the name of your blog or post, enter your URL, select your destination(s), and click the Submit button. The service then broadcasts a message that your site contains a new post or other content.

TIP

Select only one pinging service at a time. Search engines don't take kindly to double pinging.

WordPress, TypePad, Blogger, and most other blog services offer built-in, automatic pinging every time you post. On some smaller blog hosts, you may have to set up pinging (or submit to search engines) in a control panel. Table 1-3 summarizes some of the most popular pinging options.

TABLE 1-3   **Pinging Resources**

Name	URL	Description
Feed Shark	`http://feedshark.brainbliss.com`	Free ping service for blogs, RSS feeds, and podcasts
GooglePing	`http://googleping.com`	Ping search engines without registering
King Ping	`www.kping.com`	Paid, automated pinging for blogs, tweets, and online publishers
Pingdom	`www.pingdom.com`	Paid service that monitors whether your site is up and running
PingFarm	`www.pingfarm.com`	Free ping service that notifies search engines when you update your site or blog
Pinging and SEO	`www.seostrategies.pro/seo/369/pinging-for-seo-explained`	Article explaining pinging and SEO benefits
Pingler	`http://pingler.com`	Free and paid services for pinging multiple sites on a regular schedule; useful for developers and hosts
Ping-O-Matic!	`http://pingomatic.com`	Ping service for blogs to search engines

REMEMBER

Be sure to enter your choices for a pinging service on your Social Media Marketing Plan. If pinging isn't automatic, enter a task item for pinging below each update on your Social Media Activity Calendar.

Snipping Ugly URLs

The last thing you need when microblogging (on sites like Twitter) is a URL that takes up half your 140-character limit. Long, descriptive URLs that are useful for search engines are also messy in email, text messages, text versions of e-newsletters, and blogs, not to mention making it difficult to retweet within the limit. The solution is to snip, clip, nip, trim, shave, or otherwise shorten ungainly URLs with a truncating service. Take your choice of those in Table 1-4 or search for others.

The downside is that the true owner of shortened URLs may be a mystery, so it doesn't do much for your branding. Figure 1-2 shows a typical URL-truncating service and the result.

TABLE 1-4   **URL Snipping Services**

Service Name	URL	Notes
2 Create a Website	`http://blog.2createawebsite.com/?s=URL+shortners`	Comparison review article
Bitly	`https://bitly.com`	Free and paid versions, with history, stats, and preferences
Ow.ly	`http://ow.ly/url/shorten-url`	Hootsuite's URL shortener, free
Snipurl	`http://snipurl.com`	Stores, manages, and tracks traffic on short URLs, free
TinyURL	`http://tinyurl.com`	One of the oldest and best-known truncators, free
Twitter	`http://t.co`	Link-shortening service; used only on Twitter, which automatically shortens links in tweets to a t.co link; can still use third-party link shorteners

FIGURE 1-2: Enter a long URL at Bitly and receive a short URL in return.

Source: bitly.com

REMEMBER

As always, enter the name of your URL-snipping service on your Social Media Marketing Plan. To make it easier to track URLs and their snipped versions, select just one service.

Using E-Commerce Tools for Social Sites

If money makes the world go 'round, e-commerce takes the cybersocial world for a dizzying spin. There have been many different options for promoting or linking to your online store from blogs and social networks, but several applications now let you sell directly (or indirectly) from social media pages. These sections explain what is essential to know for selling stuff online.

Always check the terms of service on social media sites to be sure you aren't violating their rules. Some services may prohibit selling directly from their site.

Selling through links

The easiest way to sell from social networks and blogs is simply to post a banner or a text link to your own website or to other sites (Etsy, for example) that sell your products. Additionally, you can post images on a site like Facebook with links to your website or other sites.

The Healing Waterfall does this in a sophisticated manner, as shown in Figure 1-3. Clicking an item on its Facebook storefront (www.facebook.com/TheHealingWaterfall/) takes shoppers to the Healing Waterfall's shopping website at www.guidedimagerydownloads.com to fill their carts and check out.

Displaying products on social media services

If you're looking for a more seamless experience, consider e-commerce tools that display items from your existing online store on your blog or social media pages, and then either link automatically back to your web store to complete the transaction or permit users to purchase directly from the social media page.

E-commerce widgets are minidisplays of products; these changeable badges (which appear onscreen as a large button with multiple links) link to an existing web store. If you already have an online store, check your shopping cart or *check stand provider* (the section of your online store that totals orders and takes payments) to see whether it offers a widget for social media, like the one shown in Figure 1-4.

Link to website store

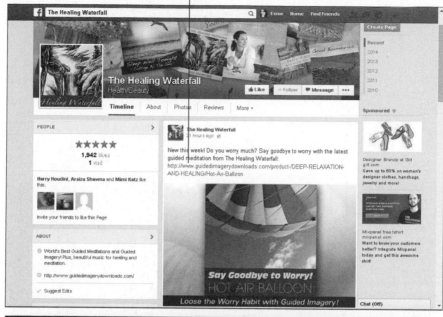

FIGURE 1-3: Product offerings can begin on Facebook (top) and link to a separate shopping website (bottom).

Badge

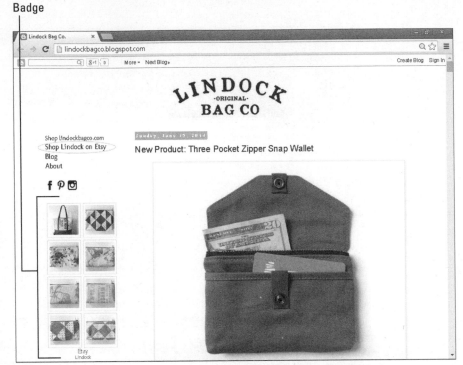

Reproduced with permission of Julie Brzezinski

FIGURE 1-4:
The Etsy mini-badge on the left side of this blog drives traffic to the Etsy shop for the Lindock Bag Company.

TIP

Many vendors of online stores offer widgets or apps with shopping or promotional functionality for use on specific social media services. For instance, SouthernTots.com uses the Soldsie app to conduct sales on Instagram (http://instagram.com/southerntots) and Facebook (www.facebook.com/southerntots) by using the comment function on those sites.

Combining a virtual storefront with a payment service

By comparison, a *virtual storefront* on a social media service either imports products from an online store already in place on your website or allows products to be uploaded directly from a freestanding, online store like Etsy. At the check stand stage, these storefronts link to your regular web store or to a third-party site to process the transactions. Although virtual storefront strategies may be a useful way to cast a wider net for customers, they may complicate your recordkeeping when used in addition to a web store.

TIP

E-commerce tools described in this chapter, which let you promote and sell only your own products, are quite different from social shopping services, which aggregate products from multiple sources, often suggested by consumers themselves and linking viewers back to your website.

REMEMBER

Third-party e-commerce tools that link to PayPal or other payment services generally don't integrate with inventory and accounting packages in the way that a full-featured shopping cart on your website might. If your business inventory system doesn't link to the shopping cart on your website, you may need to adjust those records manually.

If you use a virtual storefront in addition to an existing store on your own website but don't track inventory automatically, you can track the source of your sales another way. For tracking purposes, create separate SKUs for products that will be listed on different online store locations or set a different price — for example, discounting items specifically for your Twitter audience. However, this approach doesn't work with automated inventory controls.

Reviewing sample products for selling on social media

The following sections discuss some of the many specific tools and products available for selling products through social media. Consider these items examples in the range of products available. You should research and evaluate products to meet your own needs.

Ecwid

Ecwid (www.ecwid.com) is a complete e-commerce solution for websites, blogs, Facebook, Tumblr, and more. Facebook shoppers complete the entire process, including checkout, on Facebook. Additional social media integration to share purchases and recommend products is also available for Facebook, Twitter, Pinterest, Google+, and Tumblr.

Because the contents of your web store are mirrored on several sites, you can easily update your product catalog simultaneously at all sites and manage all the online locations from one dashboard. Prices range from free for up to ten products to $99 per month for unlimited products. All packages include a free Facebook store.

EARTHEGY GAINS ENERGY FROM FACEBOOK SALES

Chrisy Bossie founded Earthegy, a retailer of crystals and healing jewelry, in August 2010 with a shop on Etsy and products spread out on her dining room table. She soon added a blog, a Facebook page, and Facebook advertising to her marketing mix.

"Facebook advertising brought me a ton of qualified customers," explains Bossie, who tightly targets her Facebook ads to women, ages 35 to 60, who are interested in crystal healing and energy jewelry.

"Customers grew my business to the point [that] I outgrew other selling venues and needed my own e-commerce site." In 2012 she launched her site at www.earthegy.com (see the nearby figure) and quickly gained subscribers to a new weekly newsletter. At the same time, she continues her blog to capture Google rankings and drive traffic to her online store.

She added shopping to her Facebook presence, using an app provided by 3dcart (www.3dcart.com), which powers her online web store as well. As seen in the following figure, Shop Earthegy appears as a tab in the top navigation (below the header graphic). It also appears to the left of the timeline on her main page. Although Bossie has more than 1,000 products on her main website, the app previews only about 40 of them on Facebook. Because the app pulls products from one specified category in her store, Bossie cleverly created a New at Earthegy category in the top-left navigation column on her main site. Because products in the New category change constantly, this approach keeps the Facebook display fresh.

Bossie recently says that 35 percent of her sales appear to have come directly from Facebook, but she thinks those numbers are understated. "Customers who now go directly to my website often first found me on Facebook, but the Facebook referral doesn't show up now because they know how to find me directly."

Although she finds Google Analytics useful for keeping an eye on her website, Bossie prefers a real-time view. "I can see what people are searching for; if it's a product I don't carry, I'll start hunting for it." She even watches orders as they near the end of the checkout process. "A lot of the time, I'll be pulling those products from inventory and packing them while a customer is still checking out. It makes for faster shipping times, and a huge reason my customers become repeat customers is because I ship as fast as I possibly can."

While she plays around with Pinterest a bit, and cross-posts from Facebook to Twitter, Bossie keeps her marketing efforts focused. "Because of Facebook's effectiveness, I spend all of my time and effort there to generate sales and interest in my products."

She earned that effectiveness the hard way. Bossie offers some of her lessons learned for maximizing the potential of Facebook:

- Photos, photos, photos! Links and videos don't get nearly the reach as good photos do.

- Make sure your website information is easy to find. Fill out your About page on Facebook. There's no sense promoting your products on Facebook if people can't find where to purchase them. (For every product photo that Bossie posts, she includes a direct link to the store detail page in the caption.)

- Because people prefer information to ads, include stories and interesting tidbits about your products.

- Don't be afraid to use the Delete and the Block and Ban options if people post negative comments.

- Don't demand action from those who Like your Facebook page via your timeline. They are gracing you with an audience. If you start asking them to do things, they'll leave.

(continued)

(continued)

Passionate about her business, Bossie continues to run Earthegy as a one-woman band, working from dawn to dusk, like most entrepreneurs. Even when she's away from home, she constantly monitors her Facebook page on a smartphone. And, yes, she still has crystals spread out on her dining room table.

Earthegy's web presence:

- `www.earthegy.com`

- `www.facebook.com/earthegy`

- `www.facebook.com/earthegy/app_30729455954` (store)

- `www.blog.earthegy.com`

- `https://plus.google.com/114937442286552466800/posts?hl=en`

- `https://twitter.com/earthegy`

Reproduced with permission of Earthegy

Shopify

Shopify (www.shopify.com) is a full-featured store builder that lets Facebook users browse your catalog and purchase products directly from Facebook. A free Facebook store is included with monthly web-based plans, which range from a $14 starter package to $179 for unlimited storage. If you don't already have or want a web-based store, you can select a Facebook-only plan (www.shopify.com/facebook) with unlimited products starting at $9 per month. Per-transaction credit card fees are charged in addition. All plans have a 14-day free trial.

TIP

When selecting a storefront solution for your website, investigate which ones offer either the ability to use the same solution on social media platforms or provide widgets for social media compatibility. Many companies have added this feature in response to demand.

Storefront Social

Made specifically for Facebook, Storefront Social (www.storefrontsocial.com) allows you to sell directly from Facebook using PayPal, Google Checkout, or Authorize.net for credit cards. You can forward shoppers to your web-based store to conclude the purchase or to see additional products. Offering a free seven-day trial and flat monthly fees from $9.95 for 100 products to $29.95 for 1,000 products, Storefront Social is an affordable selling solution for small- to medium-size stores.

StoreYa

StoreYa (www.storeya.com) is a cost-effective solution for selling on Facebook, blogs, websites, and/or in a mobile environment, with links to your primary store to complete a sale (see Figure 1-5). StoreYa allows you to import your products from other e-commerce programs. It includes multiple social media marketing tools to increase sales, as well as store statistics. Pricing varies by the number of products (SKUs) in your catalog, starting with a free version for 20 products and rising to enterprise level, with several affordable levels in between. It offers a free 14-day trial period.

Other resources for selling on social media

Table 1-5 lists other e-commerce widgets, storefronts, and resources you may want to check out.

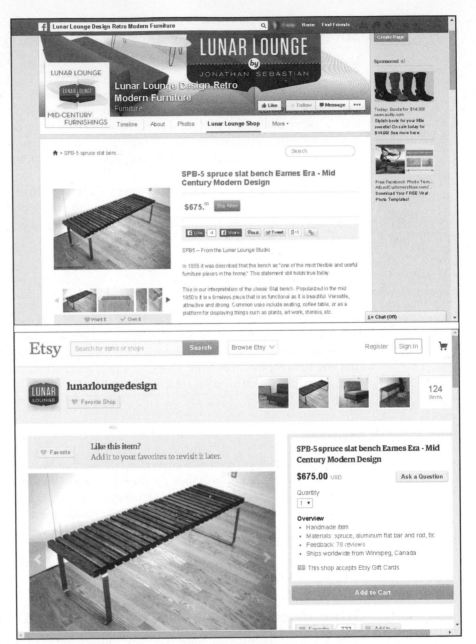

FIGURE 1-5:
Lunar Lounge uses the e-commerce solution from StoreYa on its Facebook page (top); clicking the Buy Now button opens Lunar Lounge's Etsy shop (bottom).

TIP

Watch for news from Twitter about buying online directly from a tweet. Twitter recently began testing a Buy button with some test partners to make it fun and simple to shop from mobile devices.

TABLE 1-5

Social E-Commerce Widgets, Storefronts, and Resources

Name	URL	Notes
Amazon	`https://widgets.amazon.com`	E-commerce widgets for the Amazon store that can be placed on multiple social network, blog, or web pages
Big Cartel	`http://bigcartel.com`	Hosted e-commerce website geared toward artists, clothing designers, and bands; capability to set up freestanding e-commerce sites and add to a Facebook site
Bigcommerce	`http://www.bigcommerce.com`	E-commerce platform that allows you to design a web store and add a widget to Facebook
eBay	`http://developer.ebay.com/businessbenefits/money`	E-commerce widget for your eBay store
E-junkie	`www.e-junkie.com`	Cart or Buy Now buttons for social media or blog; fee based on size and volume; handles charges for downloaded items (for example, music or whitepapers)
Etsy	`www.etsy.com`	Directions for using e-commerce widget for your Etsy store
Highwire	`www.highwire.com`	Multichannel storefront for use on your own website and/or eBay, Facebook, Google, or mobile site
Mercantec	`www.mercantec.com/google`	Snippet generator that adds shopping cart to sites, blogs, or social networks; has analytics
PayPal	`https://developer.paypal.com/docs/classic/products`	E-commerce Adaptive Payment API that lets programmers build small applications on social networks
Soldsie	`http://new.soldsie.com`	An app for Facebook and Instagram that allows you to sell on those sites through uploaded photos and user comments
Storefront Social	`http://storefrontsocial.com`	Allows you to create a Facebook shop in minutes
Wishpond	`http://corp.wishpond.com/social-promotions`	Apps to run promotions, such as coupons, contests, or group sales, on Twitter and Facebook

Keeping Your Ear to the Social Ground

The onslaught of data from social media sites can be overwhelming. To garner some value from all the noise, you can take advantage of certain tools to monitor what's being said about your company.

TIP

When should you start to worry? Some experts suggest that a negative comment appearing within the first 20 results on a Google search on your name, brand, or product could be a sign of trouble. Don't worry about a one-off negative comment on a minor site.

Social media monitoring is about who's saying what. It's about your brand, your products, and your reputation. It's not the same as social media measurement, which deals with traffic statistics, conversion rates, and return on investment (ROI). These sections take a closer look at what's important when monitoring what others are saying about your business.

TECHNICAL STUFF

Bring user feedback directly to you. Place a free feedback widget on your site from `http://shoutbox.widget.me` or `http://getbarometer.com`. This feature takes some programming knowledge; if you're not up to the task, ask your programmer. You can find some monitoring tools for specific types of services in the sections that follow.

Deciding what to monitor and why

If you didn't have anything else to do, you could monitor everything. That situation isn't realistic, so you need to set some constraints. Start with your goal and ask yourself what you want to accomplish. For example, you may want to

>> Track what's being said about your company and products, both positive and negative.

>> Conduct competitor or market research.

>> Stay up-to-date on what's happening in your industry.

>> Watch trends in terms of mentions, topics of interest, or volume of comments.

>> Gain a competitive advantage.

>> Monitor the success of a specific press release, media campaign, or product promotion.

>> Monitor infringement of trademark or other intellectual property.

>> Obtain customer feedback so you can improve your products and services.

After you decide your goal, it should be obvious what search terms or keywords to monitor. Your list may include

>> Your company name

>> Your domain name

>> Names of executives and staff who speak with the public

>> Product names and URLs

>> Competitors' names

>> Keywords

>> Topic tags

Deciding which tools to use

The number of monitoring tools is almost as great as the amount of data they sift through. Research your options and choose at least one tool that monitors across multiple types of social media. Depending on the social media services you're using, you might want to select one from each appropriate service category, as well.

The frequency with which you check results from these tools will depend on the overall visibility of your company, the schedule for your submissions to different services, and the overall intensity of your social media presence. For some companies, it might be a daily task. For others, once weekly or even once per month will be enough.

TIP

If you're not sure where to start, begin with weekly Google Alerts to monitor the web and daily `Mention.com` alerts to monitor social media. Add one tool each for blogs and Twitter, if you use them actively or think people may be talking about your business on their own. Adjust as needed.

Using free or inexpensive social monitoring tools

If you don't have a lot of money in your budget, you can pick one or more of the tools in the following sections to monitor across multiple types of social media.

REMEMBER

Mark your choices on your Social Media Marketing Plan. If the tool doesn't offer automated reporting, you'll need to enter the submission task, as well as the review task, on your Social Media Activity Calendar.

Addictomatic: Inhale the Web

Addictomatic (http://addictomatic.com/about) lets you "instantly create a custom page with the current buzz on any topic." It searches hundreds of live sites, including news, blog posts, videos, and images, and it offers a bookmarkable, personalized dashboard for keeping track of your updates.

Brand24

An affordable brand-monitoring tool, Brand 24 (http://brand24.net) starts at $19 per month with a 14-day free trial. It includes both sentiment and data analysis to provide a good sense of the buzz around your product, brand, business, or search term. It covers multiple social media outlets, including Facebook, Twitter, and Blip TV, with alerts daily or more often. Additional features available with more expensive plans allow you to review customer behavior, actions, and posts.

Google Alerts

One of the easiest and most popular of free monitoring services, Google Alerts (www.google.com/alerts) are notifications of new results on up to 1,000 search terms. Alerts can be delivered via email or RSS feed.

You can receive results for news articles, websites, blogs, video, and Google books and forums.

You set the frequency with which Google checks for results and other features from your My Alerts dashboard page. Think of Alerts as an online version of a clipping service. Yahoo! (http://alerts.yahoo.com) offers something similar.

Google Trends

Google Trends (www.google.com/trends) is a useful market research tool. It not only provides data on the hottest current searches, but also compares the number of searches on the terms you enter to the total number of searches on Google overall during the same time frame. Click the word Trends in the top left of the navigation bar and select the Explore option in the drop-down list. Click Add Term to insert the search phrase that interests you.

From the top horizontal navigation you can choose to refine your research by selecting options from the dropdowns under Worldwide (location), 2004–Present (time frame), All categories (topic area), or Web Search (content type.) Select the Subscriptions option in the drop-down list to receive email notification of trending searches and stories.

HowSociable

Type any brand name at www.howsociable.com, as shown in Figure 1-6, to see how visible it is in social media. The free version checks "one brand with 12 different metrics and limited features." The paid upgrade checks 24 more channels. Click any element for additional detail, as shown on the report for the Department of Homeland Security in Figure 1-6.

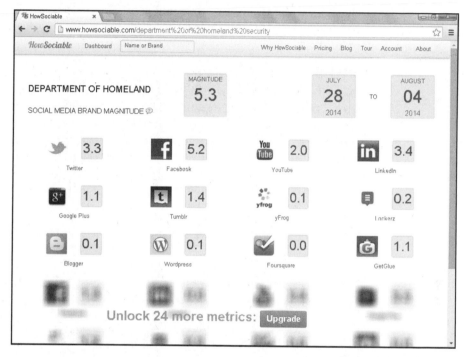

FIGURE 1-6: HowSociable displays social media visibility for the Department of Homeland Security.

IceRocket

Meltwater's IceRocket (www.icerocket.com) is a free monitoring tool that covers millions of blogs, as well as Twitter and Facebook, in 20 languages. By the way, this is one of the places left where you can post the URL for your blog to make sure it gets found in search engines.

IFTTT (If This Then That)

If This Then That (www.ifttt.com) is an automation tool that lets you write a script (called a *Recipe*) to receive notifications and accomplish other tasks online. You can easily use IFTTT to manage your online reputation. It's easiest to browse existing, public Recipes to find one that monitors your desired social media platforms; then tweak the Recipe to include the search terms you want to monitor.

Mention

Mention (`https://en.mention.com`) monitors multiple social networks, news sites, forums, blogs, or any web page in 42 languages. It offers several helpful features: first, the ability to export data, filtered by time and source, which allows you to compare your results to competitors' results; and second, real-time alerts plus a daily or weekly digest by email. Its free basic plan allows one user, one alert, and up to 250 mentions per month, but doesn't include analytics. Paid versions — which have higher limits on the number of alerts, mentions, and users — start at $29 per month, but all include a free 14-day trial.

social mention

The site social mention (`http://socialmention.com`) tracks and measures what's being said about a specific topic in real time across more than 100 social media services. It provides a social ranking score based on its own definition of *popularity* — which includes self-defined criteria of strength, sentiment, passion, and reach — for every search. Figure 1-7 shows the results for the term Ice Bucket Challenge (which had received more than 1 billion views on YouTube by September 2014.) For more information on measuring sentiment, see Book 2, Chapter 3.

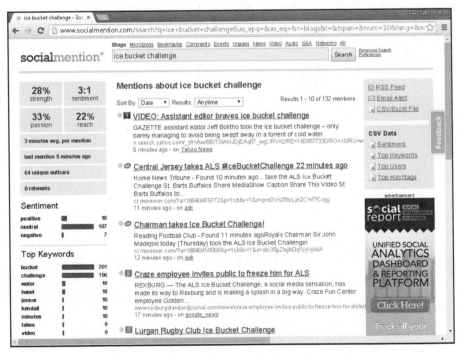

FIGURE 1-7: social mention provides a social-ranking score based on its definition of popularity.

Source: www.socialmention.com

You can select to monitor only specific services and choose among service categories of bookmarks, blogs, microblogs, comments, news, networks, video, audio, images, Q&A, or all. Although you can input only one term at a time, the results may go back 30 months or more.

TIP

If you select the CSV/Excel File option on the search results page, you can download all pages of the resulting display with details. Doing so makes it easy to create graphs showing changes in various criteria over time. For instance, you might be able to pinpoint how an active social media campaign changes the Sentiment results for your company.

In addition, social mention aggregates trends (www.socialmention.com/trends) in near-real-time about social media discourse — which is also handy for doing market research.

TECHNICAL STUFF

The site also offers real-time widgets (http://socialmention.com/tools) to place on your site or in your browser bar. The browser is a simple plug-in, but your programmer will need to copy and paste the widget code onto your site.

Sprout Social

A high-end package of social media tools, Sprout Social (www.sproutsocial.com) includes a comprehensive monitoring feature that combines all alerts, messages, and actions into a single stream that can be analyzed to discover trends. You can watch for social media comments about your business, brand, products, competitors, or industry topics in near real-time. Prices start at $59 per user per month but include a 30-day free trial.

Talkwalker Alerts

A comparable alternative to Google Alerts, Talkwalker (www.talkwalker.com/alerts) monitors the web for mentions of your brand, competitors, name, events, or other keywords. It provides email updates to your email inbox or RSS reader on a daily or weekly basis. Free for up to 100 alerts, Talkwalker Alerts does not cover social media. However, the paid Pro versions of Talkwalker (www.talkwalker.com/en/social-media-intelligence) include multiple social media sources, higher limits on the number of alerts, and other features. Prices start at approximately $650 per month, with a 14-day free trial.

Topsy

Topsy (www.topsy.com) is a free, real-time search engine for social media, including links, tweets, influencers, photos, and/or images. Ranking results based on daily conversations about terms entered, Topsy also offers social trends and social analytics.

Trackur

Trackur (www.trackur.com) tracks all forms of social media, including Facebook, Google+, Reddit, blogs, news, networks, RSS feeds, tweets, images, and video (some sources are available only with paid plans). In addition to displaying conversational content, Trackur presents trends and analyzes any website that mentions a term being monitored. You can get a free account that includes one saved search and 100 results. Monthly plans start with 50 search terms at $97 per month. All paid plans come with a free 10-day trial.

WhosTalkin.com

WhosTalkin.com (www.whostalkin.com) is another free, real-time search tool. It surveys 60 social media services for current conversations in the categories of blogs, news, networks, videos, images, forums, and tags. It lacks the reporting capabilities of social mention, but it does include actual comments. WhosTalkin.com provides results for only one term at a time but offers a browser search plug-in API.

Measuring the Buzz by Type of Service

The number of monitoring tools competing for market share is astonishing. The following tables are not intended to be comprehensive lists, but simply to provide some idea of what's out there.

Table 1-6 lists tools for monitoring blogs and forums; Table 1-7 tools for news, RSS, and geolocation sites; Table 1-8 tools for Twitter; and Table 1-9, some high-end tools at the enterprise level. You can always search for free tools in each category to get more options.

TABLE 1-6   **Blog- and Forum-Monitoring Tools**

Name	URL	Description
Attentio	http://attentio.com	Multilingual social media monitoring; fee.
Bloglines	www.bloglines.com	Delivers blog search content in an RSS feed.
BlogSearchEngine	www.blogsearchengine.org	Search for blogs by topic area or search term.
Meltwater IceRocket	www.icerocket.com	Trend and buzz monitor for blogs, Twitter, and Facebook.
sovrn	www.sovrn.com	Free tool to help publishers monetize their websites and social media, reach their target audiences, and build relationships. Includes reports on user behavior, demographics, and actions.

TABLE 1-7   ## Social News and RSS Tools

Name	URL	Description
Google News	`http://news.google.com`	Keyword search of Google News
Yahoo! News	`http://news.yahoo.com`	Keyword search of Yahoo! News

REMEMBER

To ensure that your blog appears in a timely fashion in blog-monitoring tools, submit your blog to each one and set up pinging (which you can read about in the section "Notifying Search Engines about Updates," earlier in this chapter).

TABLE 1-8   ## Twitter Monitoring Tools

Name	URL	Description
Hashtagify.me	`http://hashtagify.me`	Manage your own hashtags and receive alerts when hashtags are used.
SocialOomph	`www.socialoomph.com`	Formerly TweetLater.com, one-stop shop to monitor and manage Twitter; paid version includes blogs, Facebook, LinkedIn, RSS feeds, and more.
Twitter's TweetDeck	`https://about.twitter.com/products/tweetdeck`	Twitter tool to create searches and track hashtags, events, or topics.
Twitter Search	`https://twitter.com/search-home`	Twitter's own search filter with advanced queries.

TABLE 1-9   ## Fee-Based, Enterprise-Level Monitoring Tools

Name	URL	What It Does
BrandsEye	`www.brandseye.com`	Paid service tracks online conversations with monitoring and insight tools.
eCairn Conversation	`www.ecairn.com`	Integrates and analyzes multiple social media sources for marketing and PR pros.
Lithium	`www.lithium.com/products-solutions/social-media-analytics`	Monitors community engagement as part of an integrated social media management package.
NielsenOnline	`www.nielsen.com/us/en/solutions/measurement/online.html`	Deep web analysis of consumer-generated content in online communities, message boards, groups, blogs, opinion sites, and social networks.

(continued)

TABLE 1-9 *(continued)*

Name	URL	What It Does
Salesforce.com	`www.salesforcemarketingcloud.com/products/social-media-listening`	Detailed monitoring of social media buzz about industry, competitors, and/or brand. Analyze customer desires, evaluate content engagement, and assess campaign reaction.
Spiral16	`www.spiral16.com/technology`	Advanced software tool for brand monitoring and sentiment; includes sophisticated reporting.
Sysomos' Heartbeat	`www.sysomos.com/products/overview/heartbeat`	Real-time monitoring and measurement tool for buzz and sentiment.

Figure 1-8 shows the results of a typical Twitter search.

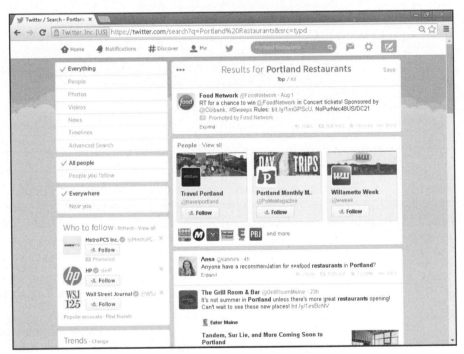

FIGURE 1-8:
Results page from Twitter search for Portland restaurants.

Source: Twitter

Chapter 2

Making the Business Case for Social Media

I n the best of all worlds, *social media* — a suite of online services that facilitates two-way communication and content sharing — can become a productive component of your overall marketing strategy. These services can enhance your company's online visibility, strengthen relationships with your clients, and expand word-of-mouth advertising, which is the best type.

Given its rapid rise in popularity and its hundreds of millions of worldwide users, social media marketing sounds quite tempting. These tools require minimal upfront cash and, theoretically, you'll find customers flooding through your cyber-doors, ready to buy. It sounds like a no-brainer — but it isn't, especially as social media channels mature into a pay-to-play environment with paid advertising.

Has someone finally invented a perfect marketing method that puts you directly in touch with your customers and prospects, costs nothing, and generates profits faster than a perpetual motion machine produces energy? The hype says yes; the real answer, unfortunately, is no. Although marketing nirvana may not yet be at hand, the expanding importance of social media in the online environment may mean that your business needs to participate anyway.

This chapter provides an overview of the pros and cons of social media to help you decide whether to join the social whirl, and it gives a framework for approaching a strategic choice of which media to use.

Making Your Social Debut

Like any form of marketing, social media takes some thought. It can become an enormous siphon of your time, and short-term profits are rare. Social media marketing is a long-term commitment.

So, should you or shouldn't you invest time and effort in this marketing avenue? If you answer in the affirmative, you immediately confront another decision: What form should that investment take? The number of options is overwhelming; you can never use every technique and certainly can't do them all at once.

Figure 2-1, which compares the percentages of small businesses using various social media to attract new customers, shows that most businesses use LinkedIn and/or Facebook. Although some U.S. small businesses have taken a wait-and-see attitude, more and more are trying social media. According to an August 2013

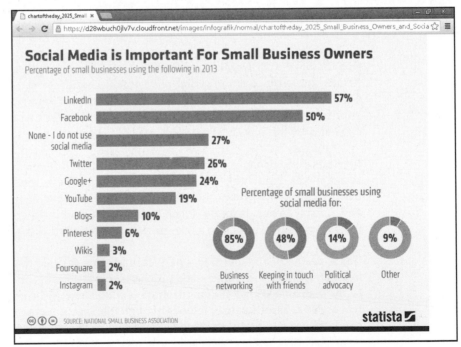

FIGURE 2-1: Most companies using social media focus on LinkedIn or Facebook.

Reproduced by permission of Statista, Inc.

survey from the National Small Business Association (`www.nsba.biz/wp-content/uploads/2013/09/Technology-Survey-2013.pdf`), 73 percent of small businesses used some form of social media, up from 47 percent in 2010. Those businesses on the sidelines give the best reason in the world for not participating — their customers aren't there.

Defining Social Media Marketing

The bewildering array of social media (which seem to breed new services faster than rabbits can reproduce) makes it hard to discern what they have in common: shared information, often on a peer-to-peer basis. Although many social media messages look like traditional broadcasts from one business to many consumers, their interactive component offers an enticing illusion of one-to-one communication that invites individual readers to respond.

The phrase *social media marketing* generally refers to using these online services for *relationship selling* — selling based on developing rapport with customers. Social media services make innovative use of new online technologies to accomplish the familiar communication and marketing goals of this form of selling.

TIP

The tried-and-true strategies of marketing (such as solving customers' problems and answering the question, "What's in it for me?") are still valid. Social media marketing is a new technique, not a new world.

This book covers a variety of social media services (sometimes called social media *channels*) and uses the phrase *social media site* to refer to a specific, named online service or product.

You can categorize social media services, but they have fuzzy boundaries that can overlap. Some social media sites fall into multiple categories. For instance, some social networks and online communities allow participants to share photos and include a blog.

Here are the different types of social media services:

>> **Social content-sharing services:** These services facilitate posting and commenting on text, videos, photos, and podcasts (audio).

● **Blogs:** Websites designed to let you easily update or change content and allow readers to post their own opinions or reactions.

Examples of blog tools are WordPress, Typepad, Blogger, and Tumblr. Blogs may be hosted on third-party sites (apps) or integrated into your own website using software. Figure 2-2 shows an example of a blog at www . muybuenocookbook . com, which was built using a WordPress template.

- **Videos:** Examples are YouTube, Vimeo, Vine.co, or Ustream. Figure 2-3 shows a how-to video from YouTube.

- **Images:** Flickr, Photobucket, Instagram, Snapchat, SlideShare, Pinterest, or Picasa.

- **Audio:** Podbean or BlogTalkRadio.

FIGURE 2-2:
The WordPress blog for Muy Bueno uses strong graphics to gain attention.

Reproduced by permission of Yvette Marquez-Sharpnack, MuyBuenoCookbook.com

>> **Social networking services:** Originally developed to facilitate the exchange of personal information (messages, photos, video, and audio) to groups of friends and family, these full-featured services offer multiple functions. From a business point of view, many social networking services support subgroups that offer the potential for more targeted marketing. Common types of social networking services include

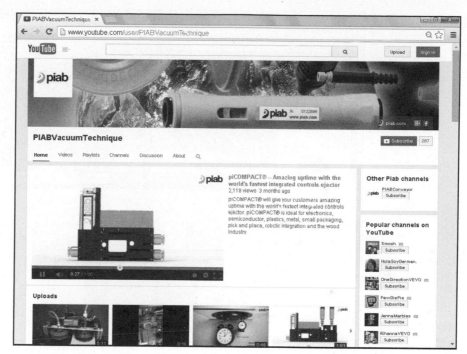

FIGURE 2-3:
A YouTube channel can be an integral part of a social media strategy.

- **Full networks:** Such as Facebook, Google+, or MeetMe.com. Figure 2-4 shows how the Lodge at Mountain Springs Lake Resort uses its Facebook page to attract leads.

- **Short message networks:** Such as Twitter or Plurk, which are often used for sharing announcements, events, sales notices, and promotions. Figure 2-5 shows how Blue Bottle Coffee uses its Twitter account at `https://twitter.com/bluebottleroast` to enable a dialog with its customers.

- **Professional networks:** Such as LinkedIn and small profession-specific networks.

- **Specialty networks:** They target specific groups, rather than the general public within a vertical industry, demographic, or activity segment, as opposed to by profession or job title.

>> **Social bookmarking services:** Similar to private bookmarks for your favorite sites on your computer, social bookmarks are publicly viewable lists of sites that others have recommended. Some are

  - **Recommendation services:** Such as StumbleUpon and Delicious.

  - **Social shopping services:** Such as Kaboodle and ThisNext.

Reproduced by permission of Mountain Springs Lake Corp.

FIGURE 2-4:
The Lodge at
Mountain Springs
Lake Resort uses
its Facebook
presence to
attract leads for
weddings.

- **Other bookmarking services organized by topic or application:** Such as sites where readers recommend books to others using bookmarking techniques.

>> **Social news services:** On these peer-based lists of recommended articles from news sites, blogs, or web pages, users often vote on the value of the postings. Social news services include

- Digg

- Reddit

- Other news sites

>> **Social geolocation and meeting services:** These services bring people together in real space rather than in cyberspace:

- Foursquare

- Meetup

- Other GPS (Global Positioning System) applications, many of which operate on mobile phones

- Other sites for organizing meet-ups and *tweet-ups* (gatherings organized by using Twitter)

FIGURE 2-5: Twitter can be used to make announcements (top) or facilitate dialogue with customers (bottom), as shown on the Twitter page for Blue Bottle Coffee.

>> **Community-building services:** Many comment- and content-sharing sites have been around for a long time, such as forums, message boards, and Yahoo! and Google groups.

Making the Business Case for Social Media

Other examples are

- **Community-building sites:** They have multiple sharing features, such as Ning.

- **Wikis**: Such as Wikipedia, for group-sourced content.

- **Review sites:** Such as TripAdvisor, Yelp, and Epinions, to solicit consumer views.

As you surf the web, you can find dozens, if not hundreds, of social tools, *apps* (freestanding online applications), and *widgets* (small applications placed on other sites, services, or desktops). These features monitor, distribute, search, analyze, and rank content. Many are specific to a particular social network, especially Twitter. Others are designed to aggregate information across the social media landscape, including such monitoring tools as Google Alerts, Mention.net, or Social Mention, or such distribution tools as RSS (Really Simple Syndication), which allows frequently updated data to be posted automatically to locations requested by subscribers

The chapters in Book 4 cover many of these tools in detail.

Understanding the Benefits of Social Media

Social media marketing carries many benefits. One of the most important is that you don't have to front any cash for most social media services. Of course, there's a downside: Most services require a significant investment of time to initiate and maintain a social media marketing campaign.

As you read the following sections, think about whether each benefit applies to your needs. How important is it to your business? How much time are you willing to allocate to it? What kind of a payoff would you expect? Column 2 in Figure 2-6 shows how other small businesses rate the relative effectiveness of social media in meeting their goals.

Casting a wide net to catch your target market

The audience for social media is huge. In June 2014, Facebook claimed almost 1.32 billion monthly active users, of which 1.08 billion were mobile users. Slightly more than 81 percent of Facebook's traffic comes from outside the United States and Canada.

Digital Marketing Tactics Used by US SMBs, March 2013
% of respondents

	Currently in use	Most effective
Website	86.6%	33.9%
Social media	77.3%	24.9%
Email for marketing/promotion	65.8%	19.6%
Email for customer service	61.3%	14.0%
Videos and photos	54.6%	13.2%
SEO	53.8%	16.2%
Blogs and white papers	52.7%	13.4%
Email for prospecting	48.2%	9.5%
Online store or other ecommerce solution	26.3%	10.9%
Online events (webinars and shows)	26.3%	10.1%
Paid search words	23.2%	8.4%
Paid banner ads on search engines and/or other websites	22.7%	9.8%
Mobile/SMS communication	19.6%	3.4%
Mobile apps	18.2%	6.2%

Source: Vocus and Inc. Magazine, "The State of Digital Marketing for SMBs," June 12, 2013

159135   www.**eMarketer**.com

FIGURE 2-6: The effectiveness of social media marketing compared to other marketing tactics.

Reproduced by permission of eMarketer

When compared to Google, this social media behemoth is in tight competition for the U.S. audience. In July 2014, Facebook tallied 167.35 million unique U.S. visitors, while Google surpassed it with 177.03 million. Keep in mind, of course, that visitors are conducting different activities on the two sites.

Twitter claims more than 271 million monthly active users and totes up about 500 million *tweets* (short messages) daily. A relatively small number of power users are responsible for the majority of tweets posted daily. In fact, about 44 percent of users create Twitter accounts without ever posting. More people read tweets than are accounted for, however, because tweets can be read on other websites.

Even narrowly focused networking sites claim hundreds of thousands of visitors. Surely, some of the people using these sites must be your customers or prospects. In fact, one popular use of social media is to cast a wide net to capture more potential visitors to your website. Figure 2-7 shows a classic conversion funnel, which demonstrates the value of bringing new traffic to the top of the funnel to produce more *conversions* (actions taken) at the bottom.

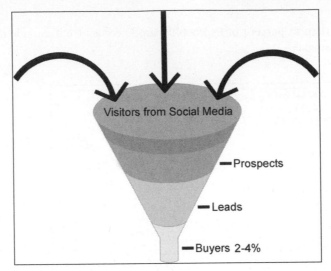

© John Wiley & Sons, Inc.

FIGURE 2-7:
The classic conversion funnel shows that only 2 to 4 percent of funnel entries yield desired results.

The conversion funnel works like this: If more people arrive at the top of the funnel, theoretically more will progress through the steps of prospect and qualified lead to become a customer. Only 2 to 4 percent, on average, make it through a funnel regardless of what action the funnel conversion depicts.

TIP

Book 2, Chapter 3 discusses how you can assess traffic on social media sites using Quantcast, Alexa, or other tools, and match their visitors to the profiles of your customers. Generally, these tools offer some information free, although several are freemium sites with additional data available only with a paid plan.

Branding

Basic marketing focuses on the need for branding, name recognition, visibility, presence, or top-of-mind awareness. Call it what you will — you want people to remember your company name when they're in need of your product or service. Social media services, of almost every type, are excellent ways to build your brand.

REMEMBER

Social media works for branding as long as you get your name in front of the right people. Plan to segment the audience on the large social media services. You can look for more targeted groups within them or search for specialty services that may reach fewer people overall but more of the ones who are right for your business.

Building relationships

You will hear repeatedly that social media marketing takes time to produce sales results. If you're focused on short-term benefits, you'd better shake that thought loose and get your head into the long-term game. To build effective relationships in social media, you're expected to

>> Establish your expertise.

>> Participate regularly as a "good citizen" of whichever social media world you inhabit; follow site rules and abide by whatever conventions have been established.

>> Avoid overt self-promotion.

>> Avoid using hard-sell pressure techniques.

>> Provide value with links, resources, and unbiased information.

Watch for steady growth in the number of your followers on a particular service or the number of people who recommend your site to others; increased downloads of *white papers* (articles that provide detailed information on a topic); or repeat visits to your site. All these signs indicate you're building relationships that may later lead, if not to a direct sale, then to a word-of-web recommendation to someone who does buy.

In the world of social media, the term *engagement* refers to the length of time and quality of interaction between your company and your followers.

REMEMBER

Social media is a long-term commitment. Other than little experiments or pilot projects, don't bother starting a social media commitment if you don't plan to keep it going. Any short-term benefits you see aren't worth the effort you have to make.

Improving business processes

Already, many clever businesses have found ways to use social media to improve business processes. Though individual applications depend on the nature of your business, consider leveraging social media to

>> Promptly detect and correct customer problems or complaints.

>> Obtain customer feedback and input on new product designs or changes.

>> Provide tech support to many people at one time; if one person has a question, chances are good that others do, too.

» Improve service delivery, such as cafes that accept to-go orders on Twitter or Facebook, or food carts that notify customers where and when their carts will arrive.

» Locate qualified new vendors, service providers, and employees by using professional networks such as LinkedIn.

» Collect critical market intelligence on your industry and competitors by watching content on appropriate social media.

» Use geolocation, tweets, and mobile search services to drive neighborhood traffic to brick-and-mortar stores during slow times and to acquire new customers.

REMEMBER

Marketing is only part of your company, but all of your company is marketing. Social media is a ripe environment for this hypothesis, where every part of a company, from human resources to tech support, and from engineering to sales, can be involved.

Improving search engine rankings

Just as you optimize your website, you should optimize your social media outlets for search engine ranking. Now that search engines are cataloging Twitter and Facebook and other appearances on social media, you can gain additional front-page real estate for your company on Google and Yahoo!/Bing (which now share the same search algorithms and usually produce similar results).

Search engines recognize some, but not all, appearances on social media as inbound links, which also improve the page rank of your site.

TIP

Use a core set of search terms and keywords across as many sites as possible. Book 2, Chapter 4 deals with search engine optimization, including tactics to avoid because they could get you in trouble for spamming.

Optimization pays off in other ways: in results on real-time searches, which are now available on primary search engines; on external search engines that focus on blogs or other social media services; and on internal, site-specific search engines.

Selling when opportunity arises

Conventional thinking says that social media is designed for long-term engagement, for marketing and branding rather than for sales. However, a few obvious selling opportunities exist, particularly for business-to-consumer (B2C) companies, that won't offend followers:

>> **Sell music and event tickets.** SoundCloud and ReverbNation, which cater to music and entertainment, are appropriate social media sites for these products.

>> **Include a link to your online store on social shopping services.** Recommend products — particularly apparel, jewelry, beauty, and decor — as Stylehive does.

>> **Offer promotional codes or special deals to followers.** Offering codes or deals on particular networks encourages your followers to visit your site to make a purchase. You can also announce sales or events.

>> **Place links to online or third-party stores like Etsy.com (see Book 2, Chapter 1) on your profile pages on various services.** You can rarely sell directly from a social media service, but some permit you to place widgets that visually showcase your products and link to your online store, PayPal, or the equivalent to conclude a transaction.

>> **Include a sign-up option for your e-newsletter.** It offers a bridge to sales.

The chart in Figure 2-8 shows a HubSpot survey of the percentage of companies that succeeded in acquiring a customer by way of a lead generated from a specific social media service. Survey respondents included both B2B (business-to-business) and B2C (business-to-consumer) companies.

TIP

Include sales offers within a stream of information and news to avoid turning your social media site into a series of never-ending advertisements.

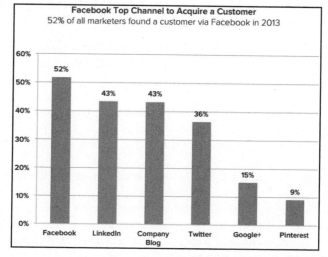

FIGURE 2-8: Companies have been successfully finding customers through social media for a few years now.

Reproduced by permission of HubSpot, Inc.

Saving money on advertising

Although time is money, the magic word is *free.* If you're a start-up company, free social media is likely the only advertising you can afford. If you decide to approach social media for this purpose, construct your master campaign just as carefully as you would a paid one:

>> Create a plan that outlines target markets, ad offers, publishing venues, and schedules for different ad campaigns.

>> If necessary, conduct comparative testing of messages, graphics, and offers.

>> Monitor results and focus on the outlets that work best at driving qualified visits that lead to conversions.

>> Supplement your free advertising with search engine optimization, press releases, and other forms of free promotion.

REMEMBER

Advertising is only one part of marketing!

As you see traffic and conversions building from your social media marketing campaigns, you may want to reduce existing paid advertising campaigns. Just don't stop your paid advertising until you're confident that you have an equally profitable stream of customers from social media. Of course, if your ad campaign isn't working, there's no point continuing it.

Understanding the Cons of Social Media

For all its upsides, social media has its downsides. As social media has gained in popularity, it has also become increasingly difficult to gain visibility among its hundreds of millions of users.

In fact, sometimes you have to craft a campaign just to build an audience on a particular social media site. It's quite similar to conducting optimization and inbound link campaigns so that your site is found in natural search results.

TIP

Don't participate in social media for its own sake or just because everyone else is.

By far, the biggest downside in social media is the amount of time you need to invest to see results. You need to make an ongoing commitment to review and respond to comments and to provide an ongoing stream of new material. An initial commitment to set up a profile is just the tip of the iceberg.

WARNING

Keep in mind that you need to watch out for the addictiveness of social media. Individually and collectively, social media is the biggest-ever time sink. If you doubt that, ask yourself whether you became addicted to news alerts during the 2012 presidential campaign, or couldn't take your eyes off live coverage of the ESA's comet landing. Or maybe you play Candy Crush or other video games with a passion, continuously run instant messaging, check email every ten seconds . . . you get the idea. Without self-discipline and a strong time schedule, you can easily become so socially overbooked that other tasks go undone.

As you consider each of the social media options in this book, also consider the level of human resources needed. Do you have the time and talents yourself? If not, do other people within your organization have the time and talent? Which other efforts will you need to give up while making room for social media? Will you have to hire new employees or contract out services, leading to hard costs for this supposedly "free" media?

Integrating Social Media into Your Overall Marketing Effort

Social media is only part of your online marketing. Online marketing is only part of your overall marketing. Don't mistake the part for the whole.

Consider each foray into social marketing as a strategic choice to supplement your other online marketing activities, which may include

>> **Creating and managing a marketing-effective website:** Use content updates, search engine optimization (SEO), inbound link campaigns, and event calendar postings to your advantage.

>> **Displaying your product or service's value:** Create online press releases and email newsletters. Share testimonials and reviews with your users and offer affiliate or loyalty programs, online events, or promotions.

>> **Advertising:** Take advantage of pay-per-click ads, banners, and sponsorships.

REMEMBER

Social media is neither necessary nor sufficient to meet all your online marketing needs.

Use social media strategically to

>> Meet an otherwise unmet marketing need.

>> Increase access to your target market.

>> Open the door to a new niche market.

>> Move prospects through the conversion funnel.

>> Improve the experience for existing customers.

For example, the website for Fluid IT Services (www.fluiditservices.com) links to Facebook, Twitter, and LinkedIn profiles sites, as well as its blog (www.fluiditservices.com/blog), to attract its audience.

To get the maximum benefit from social media, you must have a *hubsite,* the site to which web traffic will be directed, as shown in Figure 2-9. With more than 1 billion websites online, you need social media as a source of traffic. Your hubsite can be a full website or a blog, as long as the site has its own domain name. It doesn't matter where the site is hosted — only that you own its name, which appears as www.yourcompany.com or http://blog.yourcompany.com. Though you can link to http://yourcompany.wordpress.com, you can't effectively optimize or advertise a WordPress address like this. Besides, it doesn't look professional to use a domain name from a third party.

Consider doing some sketching for your own campaign: Create a block diagram that shows the relationship between components, the flow of content between outlets, and perhaps even the criteria for success and how you'll measure those criteria.

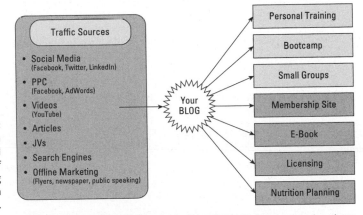

FIGURE 2-9: All social media channels and other forms of online marketing interconnect with your hub website.

Reproduced with permission of Watermelon Mountain Web Marketing, watermelonweb.com

Developing a Strategic Social Media Marketing Plan

You may have written an overall marketing plan when you last updated your business plan and an online marketing plan when you first created your website. If not, it's never too late. For business planning resources, see the Starting a Business page at `www.sba.gov/category/navigation-structure/starting-managing-business/starting-business`.

You can further refine a marketing plan for social media marketing purposes. As with any other marketing plan, you start with strategy. A Social Media Marketing Goals statement (Figure 2-10 shows an example) would incorporate sections on strategic goals, objectives, target markets, methods, costs, and return on investment (ROI).

Here are some points to keep in mind when putting together your strategic marketing overview:

>> The most important function of the form isn't for you to follow it slavishly, but rather to force you to consider the various facets of social media marketing before you invest too much effort or money.

>> The form also helps you communicate decisions to your board of advisors or your boss, in case you need to make the business case for getting involved in social media.

>> The form provides a coherent framework for explaining to everyone involved in your social media effort — employees, volunteers, or contractors — the task you're trying to accomplish and why.

Book 1, Chapter 3 includes a Social Media Marketing Plan, which helps you develop a detailed tactical approach — including timelines — for specific social media services, sites, and tools.

The following sections talk about the information you should include on this form.

Establishing goals

The Goals section prioritizes the overall reasons you're implementing a social media campaign. You can prioritize your goals from the seven benefits of social media, described in the earlier section "Understanding the Benefits of Social Media," or you can add your own goals. Most businesses have multiple goals, which you can specify on the form.

Social Media Marketing Goals

Related to Hub Site (URL): _____

Prepared by: _____ **Date:** _____

Business Profile

Is the social media plan for a new or established company?

○ New company ○ Existing company, years in business:

Does the company have an existing brick-and-mortar operation?

○ Yes ○ No

Does the company have an existing website or web presence?

○ Yes ○ No

Does the company have an existing blog or social media presence?

○ Yes ○ No
If yes, list all current URLs for social media.

Will your site serve:

○ Business ○ Consumers

What type of business is the website for?

○ Manufacturer ○ Service provider ○ Retailer
○ Distributor ○ Professional

What does the company sell?

○ Goods ○ Services

Describe your goods or services:

What geographical range does the social media campaign address?

○ Local (specify) ○ Regional (specify)
○ National (specify if not US) ○ International (specify)

Social Media Campaign Goals

Rank the applicable goals of your social media campaign from 1-7 with 1 your top goal

_____ Increasing traffic/visits to hub site

_____ Branding

_____ Building relationships

_____ Improving business process (e.g. customer service, tech support)

_____ Improving visibility in natural search

_____ Increasing sales revenue

_____ Saving money on paid advertising

Financial Profile

Social Media Campaign Budget for First Year

Outside development, contractors, includes writing, design, technical $ _____

Special content production (e.g. video, podcasts, photography): $ _____

Marketing/paid ads on social media $ _____

Inhouse labor (burdened rate) $ _____

Other costs, e.g. tools, equipment $ _____

TOTAL: $ _____

Break-even point: $ _____   Within: _____ ◯ mo ◯ yr

Return on investment: _____ %   Within: _____ ◯ mo ◯ yr

Objectives

Repeat for appropriate objectives for each goal within timeframe specified (for instance, 1 year).

Traffic objective (# visitors per month): _____   Within: _____

Conversion objective: _____ %   Within: _____

Sales objectives (# sales per month): $ _____   Within: _____

Average $ per sale: $ _____   Within: _____

$ revenue per month: $ _____   Within: _____

Other objectives specific to your site, e.g. for branding, relationships, search ranking

_____   Within: _____

_____   Within: _____

_____   Within: _____

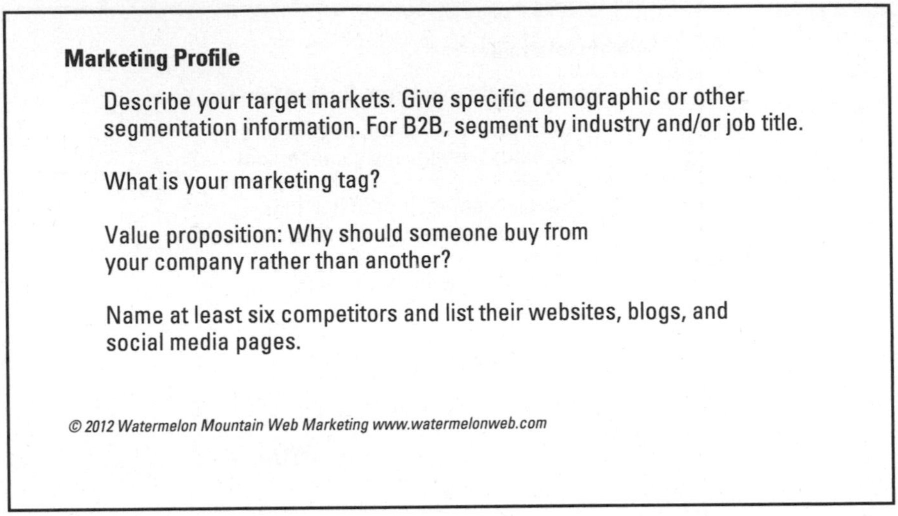

Marketing Profile

Describe your target markets. Give specific demographic or other segmentation information. For B2B, segment by industry and/or job title.

What is your marketing tag?

Value proposition: Why should someone buy from your company rather than another?

Name at least six competitors and list their websites, blogs, and social media pages.

FIGURE 2-10: Establish your social marketing goals, objectives, and target market definition on this form.

Reproduced with permission of Watermelon Mountain Web Marketing, watermelonweb.com

Consult Table 2-1 to see how various social media services rank in terms of helping you reach some of your goals.

TABLE 2-1 Matching Social Media Services to Goals

Service	Customer Communication	Brand Exposure	Traffic to Your Site	SEO
Facebook	Good	Okay	Good	Good
Google+	Good	Good	Okay	Okay
Instagram	Poor	Good	Good	Poor
LinkedIn	Okay	Good	Good	Okay
Pinterest	Good	Good	Okay	Good
SlideShare	Okay	Good	Poor	Poor
Twitter	Good	Good	Good	Good
YouTube	Okay	Okay	Good	Okay

Adapted from data sources at `www.cmo.com/articles/2014/3/13/_2014_social_intro.html`

Setting quantifiable objectives

For each goal, set at least one quantifiable, measurable objective. "More customers" isn't a quantifiable objective. A quantifiable objective is "Increase number of visits to website by 10 percent," "add 30 new customers within three months," or "obtain 100 new followers for Twitter account within one month of launch." Enter this information on the form.

Identifying your target markets

Specify one or more target markets on the form, not by what they consume, but rather by who they are. "Everyone who eats dinner out" isn't a submarket you can identify online. However, you can find "high-income couples within 20 miles of your destination who visit wine and classical music sites."

You may want to reach more than one target market by way of social media or other methods. Specify each of them. Then, as you read about different methods in this book, write down next to each one which social media services or sites appear best suited to reach that market. Prioritize the order in which you plan to reach them.

Book 2, Chapter 3 suggests online market research techniques to help you define your markets, match them to social media services, and find them online.

TIP

Think niche! Carefully define your audiences for various forms of social media, and target your messages appropriately for each audience.

Estimating costs

Estimating costs from the bottom up is tricky, and this approach rarely includes a cap. Consequently, costs often wildly exceed your budget. Instead, establish first how much money you're willing to invest in the overall effort, including in-house labor, outside contractors, and miscellaneous hard costs such as purchasing software or equipment. Enter those amounts in the Cost section.

Then prioritize your social marketing efforts based on what you can afford, allocating or reallocating funds within your budget as needed. This approach not only keeps your total social marketing costs under control but also lets you assess the results against expenses.

TIP

To make cost-tracking easier, ask your bookkeeper or CPA to set up an activity or a job within your accounting system for social media marketing. Then you can easily track and report all related costs and labor.

Valuing social media ROI

Return on investment (ROI) is your single most important measure of success for social media marketing. In simple terms, *ROI* is the ratio of revenue divided by costs for your business or, in this case, for your social media marketing effort.

You also need to set a realistic term in which you will recover your investment. Are you willing to wait ten weeks? Ten months? Ten years? Some forms of social media are unlikely to produce a fast fix for drooping sales, so consider what you're trying to accomplish.

Figure 2-11 presents a brief glimpse of how HubSpot clients assessed their average cost of *lead generation* (identifying prospective customers) in 2013, comparing social marketing to other forms of marketing. It's just a guide. Keep in mind that the only ROI or cost of acquisition that truly matters is your own.

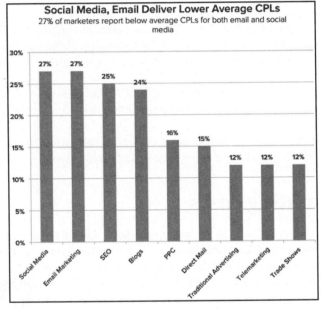

FIGURE 2-11:
Social media and email show a lower cost per lead (CPL) generated compared to other forms of marketing.

Reproduced by permission of HubSpot, Inc.

Costs usually turn out to be simpler to track than revenues that are traceable explicitly to social media. Book 2 Chapter 4 discusses techniques for figuring ROI and other financial metrics in detail.

REMEMBER

Whatever you plan for online marketing, it will cost twice as much and take twice as long as anticipated.

A social media service is likely to produce results only when your customers or prospects are already using it or are willing to try. Pushing people toward a service they don't want is quite difficult. If in doubt, first expand other online and offline efforts to drive traffic toward your hubsite.

AGLOW WITH BRAND VALUE FROM SOCIAL MEDIA

Alpenglow Sports has been selling mountain gear on the north shore of Lake Tahoe, California, for more than 35 years, long before the existence of the Internet and web marketing. Now it uses social media to share its passion for mountain sports — skiing, trail running, hiking, backpacking, and rock climbing — and to convey its strong commitment to the community and to the environment.

According to owner and CEO Brendan Madigan, the company promotes itself regionally, with some social media posts targeted specifically to various locations in California. Alpenglow's market, he explains, is roughly 40 percent locals and 60 percent visitors, including many second-home owners who drive to Tahoe from elsewhere in the state.

Unlike many companies, Alpenglow has not used its eight-year-old website (`http://alpenglowsports.com`, seen in the following figure) for e-commerce, though that may change in the future. The site currently consists of a blog, a registration portal for its annual Alpenglow Mountain Festival, and a gallery of strong images that convey its brand message.

Source: Alpenglow Sports

(continued)

(continued)

Madigan explains that in keeping with the company's spirit of adventure, Alpenglow began doing social media in 2009 without a master plan. "I've always felt that social media should portray the passion that we all have for the mountain sports we do. Accordingly, I just started a Facebook page [see the following figure] and began to learn as I went along." One summer, some of the shop employees ascended and then skied down Mt. Denali in Alaska, posting updates on Facebook of their adventure. When they returned, they discovered many people had been following their progress. "That was undoubtedly a light-bulb moment for me regarding the marketing power of a free resource!" Madigan exclaims.

With that triumph in hand, Alpenglow added Twitter and then Instagram. "When you are portraying a mountain lifestyle, there is rarely something as effective as simple images. One image can say a lot about your brand and what you love to do."

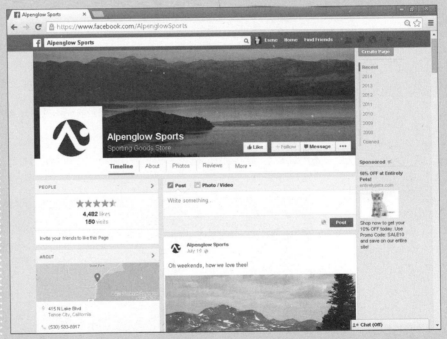

Source: Alpenglow Sports

Alpenglow doesn't look for social media to provide a direct ROI through product sales. "I've always felt that if you are pitching sales your brand will lose, especially in the small brick and mortar arena." Madigan feels that if he conveys the fun and thrill of mountain sports, the ROI will come organically. It doesn't hurt that the company's employee-athletes are an amazing inspiration, as well as a great source of information and experience.

To keep things "authentic," Madigan manages the social media outlets himself, working with a creative partner only to develop content for larger events or offline advertising. "I try to abide by a 90/10 split for fun posts versus some type of product/sale post. I feel that anything more than that will turn off customers. Plus, while we have financial realities, promoting cheesy sales pitches just isn't as fun as posting a photo of the backcountry powder skiing you did that morning that had an epic sunrise!"

The effort is time-consuming, but to Madigan it's all part of an expression of life in the mountains. He tries to post to Facebook daily at either 9 a.m. or 4 p.m. Twitter and Instagram are more likely to be on the fly, when he catches a great photo of wildflowers, a sunrise, or glittering snow. On occasion, he will use Hootsuite for a more scheduled rollout of messages. Overall, social media is a six- to ten-hour-per-week commitment.

To monitor the results of all this activity, Alpenglow uses Talkwalker and Google Alerts. Madigan finds it essential to "keep an ear to the ground," so he can address both praise and criticism quickly, and respond promptly to any questions that arise. He uses Google Analytics to track web traffic primarily during mountain festivals.

Notwithstanding Facebook Insights, "I don't think there is a realistic way to actually measure a direct ROI for social marketing," Madigan says. "Because we aren't currently fixated on driving traffic to an e-commerce site, we have some degree of flexibility."

In addition to social media, Alpenglow includes e-newsletters, search engine optimization, press releases, and traditional print and radio ads in its marketing mix. For paid online advertising, Madigan uses Facebook advertising only to boost successful posts. (See Book 4, Chapter 2.) "With the 8-percent Facebook algorithm, it is quite hard to reach our followers. Usually we only do this during our Mountain Festivals or other important events that warrant enhanced exposure. We generally target our audiences to sport-specific followers or geographic regions," he explains.

Madigan reemphasizes the importance of passion to other business owners. "You have only 8 seconds to make an impression — and as a business owner or marketer, it is your responsibility to capture [your customers' attention]. Be fun, educational, and daring in your social posts. I always ask myself 'Does this post portray what gets me out of bed in the morning?' Pretty simple when it comes down to it."

Here are addresses for Alpenglow Sports' web presence:

- `http://alpenglowsports.com`
- `www.facebook.com/AlpenglowSports`

(continued)

(continued)

- http://instagram.com/alpenglowsports
- http://twitter.com/alpenglowsports
- www.yelp.com/biz/alpenglow-sports-tahoe-city
- http://alpenglowsports.wordpress.com
- http://plus.google.com/100026260159126807522/posts

Chapter 3

Plotting a Social Media Marketing Strategy

ook 2, Chapter 2 talks about making the business case for social media marketing, looking at the question of whether you should or shouldn't get involved. That chapter is about strategy, goals, and objectives — this one is about tactics. It helps you decide which social media services best fit your marketing objectives and your target market. Let your customers and prospects drive your selection of social media alternatives. To see the best return on your investment in social media, you need to try to use the same social media as they do. This principle is exactly the same one you apply to all your other marketing and advertising efforts. Social media is a new tactic, not a new world.

REMEMBER

Fish where your fish are. If your potential customers aren't on a particular social media outlet, don't start a campaign on that outlet.

This chapter shows how to use online market research to assess the match between your target markets and various social media outlets. After you do that, you're ready to start filling out your own Social Media Marketing Plan, covered in Book 2, Chapter 4.

Locating Your Target Market Online

Nothing is more important in marketing than identifying and understanding your target audience (or audiences). After you can describe your customers' and prospects' demographic characteristics, where they live, and what social media they use, you're in a position to focus your social marketing efforts on those people most likely to buy your products or services. (Be sure to include the description of your target market on your Social Media Marketing Goals statement, discussed in Book 2, Chapter 2.)

Because social media techniques focus on inexpensive ways to reach niche markets with specific messages, they're tailor-made for a guerrilla marketing approach. As with all guerrilla marketing activities, target one market at a time.

Don't dilute your marketing budget or labor by trying to reach too many audiences at a time. People still need to see your message or brand name at least seven times to remember it. Trying to boost yourself to the forefront of everyone's mind all at once is expensive.

REMEMBER

Focus your resources on one niche at a time. After you succeed, invest your profits in the next niche. It may seem counterintuitive, but it works.

Don't let setting priorities among niches paralyze you. Your choice of niches usually doesn't matter. If you aren't sure, go for what seems to be the biggest market first, or the easiest one to reach.

Segmenting Your B2C Market

If you have a business-to-consumer (B2C) company, you can adapt the standard tools of *market segmentation*, which is a technique to define various niche audiences by where they live and how they spend their time and money. The most common types of segmentation are as follows:

>> Demographics

>> Geographics

>> Life stages

>> Psychographics or lifestyle

>> Affinity or interest groups

These categories affect not only your social media tactics but also your graphics, message, content, offers, and every other aspect of your marketing.

Your messages need to be specific enough to satisfy the needs and wants of the distinct subgroups you're trying to reach.

Suppose that you want to sell a line of organic, herbal hair care products using social media. If you described your target market as "everyone who uses shampoo" on your Social Media Marketing Goals statement (see Book 2, Chapter 2), segment that market into different subgroups before you select appropriate social marketing techniques.

When you're creating subgroups, keep these concepts in mind:

>> **Simple demographics affect your market definition.** The use of fragrances, descriptive terms, and even packaging may vary by gender. How many shampoo commercials for men talk about silky hair? For that matter, what's the ratio of shampoo commercials addressed to women versus men?

>> **Consider geography.** Geography may not seem obvious, but people who live in dry climates may be more receptive to a message about moisturizers than people who live in humid climates. Or, perhaps your production capacity constrains your initial product launch to a local or regional area.

>> **Think about life stages.** For instance, people who dye their hair look for different hair care products than those who don't, but the reason they color their hair affects your selling message. (Teenagers and young adults may dye their hair unusual colors in an effort to belong to a group of their peers; older men may hide the gray with Grecian Formula; women with kids may be interested in fashion, or color their hair as a pick-me-up.)

>> **Even lifestyles (psychographics) affect decisions.** People with limited resources who are unlikely to try new products may respond to messages about value and satisfaction guarantees; people with more resources or a higher status may be affected by messages related to social grouping and self-esteem.

>> **Affinity or interest groups are an obvious segmentation parameter.** People who participate in environmental organizations or who recycle goods may be more likely to be swayed by a "green shampoo" appeal or shop in specific online venues.

Different niche markets are drawn to different social media activities in general and to specific social media service providers in particular. In the following several sections, we look in detail at different online tools you can use to explore the parameters that seem the most appropriate for segmenting your audience and selecting specific social media sites.

For more information on market segmentation and research, see the latest edition of *Small Business Marketing Kit For Dummies* by Barbara Findlay Schenck (John Wiley & Sons, Inc.).

The most successful marketing campaigns are driven by your target markets, not by techniques.

Demographics

Demographic segmentation, the most common type of market differentiation, covers such standard categories as gender, age, ethnicity, marital status, family size, household income, occupation, social class, and education.

Sites such as Quantcast (www.quantcast.com) and Alexa (www.alexa.com) provide basic demographic information compared to the overall Internet population, as shown in Figure 3-1. Quantcast also displays the distribution by subcategory within the site. Alexa's free version now provides only limited information, although it does offer a seven-day free trial. As you can see, the sites don't always share the same subcategory breakdowns or completely agree on the data. However, either one is close enough for your social marketing purposes.

Use these tools to check out the demographic profile of users on various social media services, as well as your own users and those of your competitors. For instance, by comparing the demographics on Quantcast, you can see that LinkedIn appeals to an audience that is older, more male-dominated, and better educated than visitors to Facebook.

Look for a general match between your target audience and that of the social media service you're considering.

Always check for current demographic information before launching your social media campaign. For details by channel, try www.pewinterest.org/2013/12/30/demographics-of-key-social-networking-platforms.

Geographics

Marketing by country, region, state, city, zip code, or even neighborhood is the key for location-based social media outlets, such as Foursquare, or any other form of online marketing that involves local search.

Source: Quantcast.com and Alexa

FIGURE 3-1:
Quantcast (top)
and Alexa
(bottom) provide
demographic
profiles
comparing users
of a site (in this
case, LinkedIn)
with the general
Internet
population.

Geographic segmentation also makes sense if your business draws its primary target audience from within a certain distance from your brick-and-mortar storefront. For example, geographic segmentation makes sense for grocery stores, barber shops, gas stations, restaurants, movie theaters, and many other service providers, whether or not your social media service itself is location-based.

Many social media services offer a location search function to assess the number of users within your geographical target area:

>> **Twitter users near a specified location** (http://twitter.com/search-advanced): Enter a zip code or place name in the Near This Place text box to find users within 15 miles of your designated location. On the search results page that appears, select both People and Near You in the left column. You may be able to alter the 15-mile default distance in the search box at the top of the results page.

>> **LinkedIn users within a certain radius** (www.linkedin.com/search): In the Location drop-down list in the left column, select Located In or Near in the Location drop-down list. Additional options appear, including a Country drop-down list, a Postal Code text box, and a Within drop-down list, with choices of radius from 10 to 100 miles. After clicking Search, the number of results appears at the upper left of the center column, above the list of names. You can filter further by the degree of connection, if you want.

>> **Facebook users near a certain location** (www.facebook.com/ads/audience_insights/): Click the Find Friends link at the top of the page. In the option box that appears in the right column, type the location where you want to search in the Current City area (for example, Albuquerque). Select other filters you want to search by in the other option areas.

Unfortunately, Facebook doesn't give you a total number of the potential people you may want to reach. See Book 4, Chapter 2 for more on Facebook.

TIP

If you can't determine the number of potential users for a social media channel within your specific geographic location, use the Help function on the social media channel, check the blog, or contact the company.

Several companies combine geographical information with demographics and behavioral characteristics to segment the market more finely. For example, the Nielsen Claritas PRIZM system, available from Tetrad (www.tetrad.com/demographics/usa/nielsen/ – tab-prizm), offers demo-geographic data organized into 66 distinct sub-segments, some of which are described in Table 3-1. (You can download the entire list at www.tetrad.com/pub/prices/PRIZMNE_Clusters.pdf.) These segments, shown in Figure 3-2, can be viewed at the zip-code level using the tool at www.claritas.com/MyBestSegments/Default.jsp?ID=20.

TABLE 3-1 Top-Level Demo-Geographic Social Groups from Nielsen PRIZM

Name	Description
Urban Uptown	Wealthiest urban (highest-density) consumers (five subsegments)
Midtown Mix	Midscale, ethnically diverse, urban population (three sub-segments)
Urban Cores	Modest income, affordable housing, urban living (four sub-segments)
Elite Suburbs	Affluent, suburban elite (four sub-segments)
The Affluentials	Comfortable suburban lifestyle (six sub-segments)
Middleburbs	Middle-class suburbs (five sub-segments)
Inner Suburbs	Downscale inner suburbs of metropolitan areas (four sub-segments)
Second City Society	Wealthy families in smaller cities on fringes of metro areas (three sub-segments)
City Centers	Middle-class, satellite cities with mixed demographics (five sub-segments)
Micro-City Blues	Downscale residents in second cities (five sub-segments)
Landed Gentry	Wealthy Americans in small towns (five sub-segments)
Country Comfort	Upper-middle-class homeowners in bedroom communities (five sub-segments)
Middle America	Middle-class homeowners in small towns and exurbs (six sub-segments)
Rustic Living	Most isolated towns and rural areas (six sub-segments)

Life stages

Rather than look at a target market solely in terms of demographics, *life stage analysis* considers what people are doing with their lives, recognizing that it may affect media behavior and spending patterns.

Usage may also differ by life stages, as shown in Table 3-2. Note that the set of life stages described in the table may not accurately reflect the wider range of today's lifestyles.

You're looking for a fit between the profile of your target audience and that of the social media service.

REMEMBER

With more flexible timing for going through life passages, demographic analysis isn't enough for many types of products and services. Women may have children later in life; many older, nontraditional students go back to college; some retirees reenter the workforce to supplement Social Security earnings. What your prospective customers do each day may influence what they buy and which media outlets they use more than their age or location.

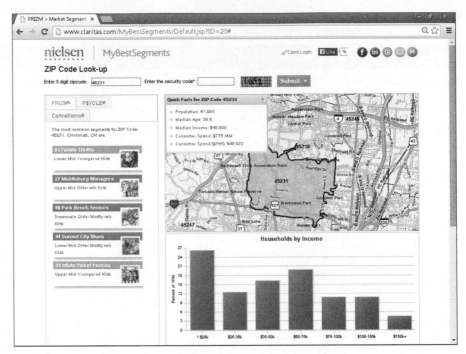

FIGURE 3-2:
Nielsen's Claritas tool allows you view market segmentation at the zip-code level.

TABLE 3-2   # Life Stage Segmentation

Life Stage	Products They Buy
Single, no children	Fashion items, vacations, recreation
Married, no children	Vacations, cars, clothing, entertainment
New nesters, children under 6	Baby food and toys; furniture and new homes
Full nest, youngest over 6	Children's items, activities, and education
Full nest, children over 16	College, possibly travel and furniture
Empty nest, children gone	Travel, cruises, vacations
Retired couples	Moves to warmer climates, housing downsizing
Solitary working retiree	Travel, vacations, medical expenses
Retired solitary survivor	Medical expenses

Source: Adapted from `http://academic.brooklyn.cuny.edu/economic/friedman/mmmarket segmentation.htm#C1`*.*

For instance, the Pew Research Center's Internet and American Life Project found in January 2014 that 28 percent of cellphone users access a social networking site on a typical day, with the most likely users being higher educated, higher income, young, black, or Hispanic (www.pewinternet.org/fact-sheets/social-networking-fact-sheet).

Psychographics or lifestyle

Psychographic segmentation divides a market by social class, lifestyle, or the shared activities, interests, and opinions of prospective customers. It helps identify groups within a social networking service or other, smaller, social networks that attract users who meet your desired profile.

Behavioral segmentation, which is closely related, divides potential buyers based on their uses, responses, or attitudes toward a product or service. To obtain this information about your customers, consider including a quick poll as part of your e-newsletter, website, or blog. Although the results from those who reply may not be exactly representative of your total customer base — or that of prospective customers — a survey gives you some starter data.

REMEMBER

Don't confuse the psychographic profile of a group with personality traits specific to an individual.

Psychographic segmentation helps you identify not only where to promote your company but also how to craft your message. For instance, understanding your specific target group, its mindset, and its lifestyle might help you appeal to customers such as the Innovators shown in Figure 3-3, who might be interested in your high-end line of fashion, home decor, or vacation destinations. Or you might target Experiencers for an amazing new cosmetics line, a wild new restaurant, or an energy drink.

TIP

To develop a better understanding of psychographic profiling, take the quick VALS (Values and Life Styles) survey yourself at www.strategicbusinessinsights.com/vals/presurvey.shtml.

Affinity groups

Segmenting by *affinity group* (a group of people who share similar interests or participate in similar activities) fills in the blank at the end of the "People who like this interest or activity also like . . . " statement. Because psychographic segmentation uses Activity as a subsection, that approach is somewhat similar.

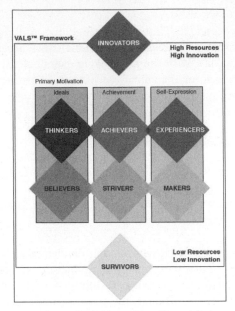

FIGURE 3-3:
Psychographic segmentation is shown on the VALS (Values and Life Styles) chart.

Reproduced with permission of Strategic Business Insights (SBI)

For example, in Figure 3-4, Quantcast estimates other interests of visitors to Goodreads (www.goodreads.com) based on their browsing behavior under the Audience Interests option. (This data is available only for *Quantified sites* — for example, sites for which the site owners have verified the data.) An alpha symbol [α] in the upper-right of a Quantcast results page indicates a verified site, and a yellow caution symbol indicates an unverified one. On Alexa, scroll down to the Related Links section for a list of the top ten sites related to the target site in various ways, or click Categories with Related Sites to view sites that fit within the same classifications as the target site.

For information on clickstream analysis (where visitors come from and where they go), see Book 4, Chapter 2.

By using Quantcast and Alexa in this way, you can obtain public information about visits to specific social media services or to your competitors' or other related businesses' websites. You can also use these services to profile your own business, although your website might be too small to provide more than rough estimates. If your business is too small, estimate the interest profile for your target market by running Quantcast for a verified, large corporation that offers a similar product or service.

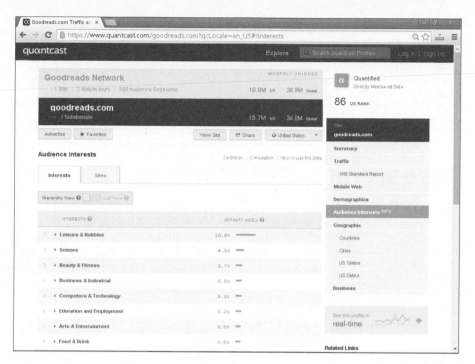

FIGURE 3-4:
Quantcast estimates topics that interest users of Goodreads.

Source: Quantcast.com

TIP

Sign up for free, direct measurement of your apps and websites at `www.quantcast.com/user/signup`. Alexa charges for similar services, but it does allow you to claim your site for free at `www.alexa.com/siteowners/claim`. Otherwise, consider polling your customers to find out more about their specific interests.

You can also use Google Trends (`www.google.com/trends/explore#cmpt=q`) to search by the interest categories shown in Table 3-3. Click All Categories at the top of the page to open a drop-down list. Google Trends uses real-time search data to estimate customer interest in various topics over time. You can select specific keywords, time periods, or locations for additional detail.

TABLE 3-3   **Main Categories Available on Google Trends**

Arts & Entertainment	Autos & Vehicles	Beauty & Fitness
Books & Literature	Business & Industrial	Computers & Electronics
Finance	Food & Drink	Games
Health	Hobbies & Leisure	Home & Garden
Internet & Telecom	Jobs & Education	Law & Government

(continued)

Plotting a Social Media
Marketing Strategy

TABLE 3-3 *(continued)*

News	Online Communities	People & Society
Pets & Animals	Real Estate	Reference
Science	Shopping	Sports
Travel		

Researching B2B Markets

Market research and social media choices for business-to-business (B2B) markets are somewhat different from business-to-consumer (B2C) markets because the sales cycle is different. Usually, B2B companies have a longer sales cycle, high-ticket purchases, and multiple people who play a role in closing a sale; consequently, B2B marketing requires a different social media presence.

In terms of social media, more B2B marketing efforts focus on branding, top-of-mind visibility, customer support, customer loyalty, and problem-solving compared to more sales-focused messages from B2C companies.

TIP

One key step in B2B marketing is to identify people who make the buying decision. Professional social networks such as LinkedIn, Networking for Professionals, or others on `www.sitepoint.com/social-networking-sites-for-business` may help you research people on your B2B customer or prospect lists.

According to research by the Content Marketing Institute, more than 90 percent of all B2B marketers use some form of social media. As shown in Figure 3-5, B2B firms may emphasize different forms of social media than B2C businesses. In many cases, the choice of social media varies by company size, industry type, experience with social media, and the availability of budgetary and human resources.

For more information on using social media for B2B marketing, visit one of these links:

>> `https://smallbusiness.yahoo.com/advisor/83-exceptional-social-media-marketing-statistics-2014-160016146.html`

>> `www.socialmediaexaminer.com/SocialMediaMarketingIndustry Report2014.pdf`

>> `www.mediabistro.com/alltwitter/b2c-b2b-social-marketing_b57346`

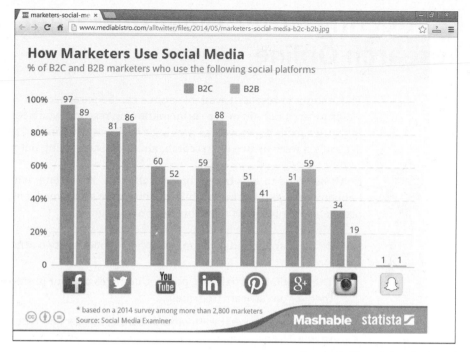

FIGURE 3-5:
B2C (left columns) and B2B (right columns) businesses often utilize different social media channels.

HubSpot (www.hubspot.com/marketing-statistics) also offers a range of B2B market research tools and webinars.

As always, the key is ensuring that your customers are using the type of social media you're considering. Use the search feature and group options on major social networking sites to test your list of existing customers. Chances are good that if a large number of your existing customers are using that service, it will be a good source for future customers as well.

In addition to participating in general market research, you might want to try SimilarSites (www.similarsites.com), which not only assists with research on social media alternatives that reach your target market, but also helps you find companies that compete with yours.

TIP

Check competing sites for inbound links from other sites, as well as their outbound links, to see how they reach their customers.

Conducting Other Types of Market Research Online

The amount of research available online can be paralyzing. A well-crafted search yields most, if not all, of the social marketing research you need. You aren't writing an academic paper; you're running a business with limited time and resources. Set aside a week or two for research, and then start laying out your approach.

TIP

Don't be afraid to experiment on a small scale. In the end, what matters is what happens with your business while you integrate social media into your marketing plan, not what happens to businesses on average.

Despite these statements, you might want to touch on two other research points:

>> **The most influential sites, posters, or pages on your preferred social media:** You can learn from them.

>> **Understanding what motivates people to use certain types of social media:** Make the content you provide meet their expectations and desires.

Identifying influencers

Whether you have a B2B or B2C company, you gain valuable insight by reviewing the comments of influencers (companies or individuals that drive the conversation within your industry sector). For example, to see the most popular posters on Twitter, use Twitaholic at `http://twitaholic.com` to view by number of updates or number of followers, as shown in Figure 3-6.

You may be surprised to find that the most frequent posters aren't necessarily the ones with the most followers, and vice versa.

For additional tools to identify influencers on various social media channels, check out the lists at Binkd (`www.binkd.com/social-media/5-tools-to-identify-your-social-media-influencers`) or Ragan (`www.ragan.com/social media/articles/9_tools_to_find_industry_influencers_47951.aspx`).

These sites can help you identify people you might want to follow for research purposes.

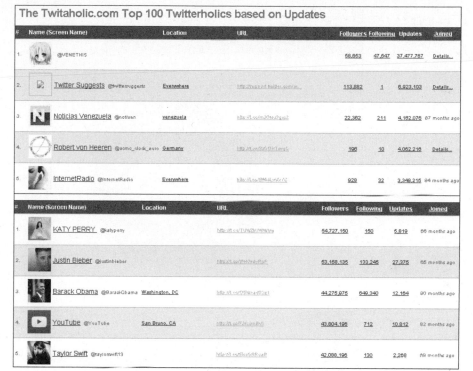

The Twitaholic.com Top 100 Twitterholics based on Updates

#	Name (Screen Name)	Location	URL	Followers	Following	Updates	Joined
1.	@VENETHIS			58,653	47,547	37,477,767	Details...
2.	Twitter Suggests @twittersuggests	Everywhere	http://support.twitter.com/n...	113,882	1	6,923,103	Details...
3.	Noticias Venezuela @notiven	venezuela	http://t.co/mJ0Nv2gie2	22,362	211	4,162,076	87 months ago
4.	Robert von Heeren @acme_clock_euro	Germany	http://t.co/Sz5DHTeceL	195	10	4,062,216	Details...
5.	InternetRadio @InternetRadio	Everywhere	http://t.co/RM4JLnKr7C	928	32	3,348,215	84 months ago

#	Name (Screen Name)	Location	URL	Followers	Following	Updates	Joined
1.	KATY PERRY @katyperry		http://t.co/TUPqZk09Q4mp	54,727,150	150	5,819	66 months ago
2.	Justin Bieber @justinbieber		http://t.co/DHXsdvRoP	53,158,135	133,245	27,375	65 months ago
3.	Barack Obama @BarackObama	Washington, DC	http://t.co/O5Wred2iz1	44,275,975	649,340	12,164	90 months ago
4.	YouTube @YouTube	San Bruno, CA	http://t.co/F3rLenBVI	43,804,196	712	10,812	82 months ago
5.	Taylor Swift @taylorswift13		http://t.co/Eks6xBRzaR	42,088,196	130	2,268	69 months ago

Reproduced with permission of Twitaholic

FIGURE 3-6: Twitaholic ranks the most influential tweeters by number of updates (top) or number of followers (bottom).

Understanding why people use social media services

The expectation that people gravitate toward different types of social media to meet different needs seems reasonable. The challenge, of course, is to match what people seek with particular social sites. The advertising network Chitika surveyed its own clients, sorting downstream referrals from social networks to websites by vertical industry type, as shown in Figure 3-7 for Facebook and Twitter. Ask yourself whether these patterns match your expectations and whether they match what you see on these sites.

A review of successful social media models may spark creative ideas for your own campaign.

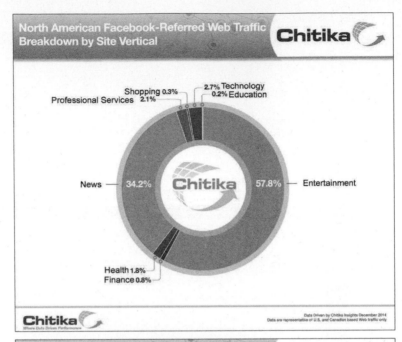

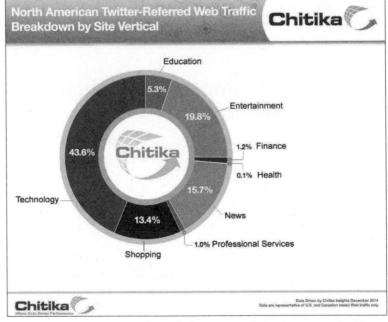

FIGURE 3-7:
Chitika analyzed
referrals from
Facebook (top)
and Twitter
(bottom) to
various types
of websites.

Reproduced with permission of Chitika, Inc.

Setting Up Your Social Media Marketing Plan

You can dive into social media marketing headfirst and see what happens. Or you can take the time to research, plan, execute, and evaluate your approach. The Social Media Marketing Plan, shown in Figure 3-8, is for people taking the latter approach.

REMEMBER

Plan your work; work your plan.

Depending on its complexity and availability of support, think in terms of a time-line of 3 to 12 months to allow time to complete the following steps. Estimate spending half your time in the planning phase, one-quarter in execution, and one-quarter in evaluation and modification. To set up your own custom social media marketing plan, follow these steps:

1. **Do market research and online observation.**

2. **Draft marketing goals, objectives, and your marketing plan using the form in Figure 3-8.**

3. **Get your marketing ducks in a row with in-house preparation.**
   - Hiring, outsourcing, or selecting in-house staff
   - Training
   - Team-building
   - Writing a social media policy document

4. **Complete preparatory development tasks.**
   - Designing advertising creatives
   - Content overview (an outline of which marketing messages you want to send out when)
   - Measurement plan and metric implementation
   - Social media tool selection and dashboard development
   - Social media activity calendar setup (discussed more later in this chapter)
   - Programming and content modifications to existing website(s), as needed

5. **Create accounts and a pilot social media program.**

6. **Evaluate the pilot program, debug it, and modify it, as needed.**

7. **Launch and promote your social media campaign one service at a time.**

8. **Measure and modify social media in a process of constant feedback and reiteration.**

Don't be afraid to build a pilot program — or several — into your plan to see what works.

Social Media Marketing Plan

Company Name _____ Date _____

Hub Site (URL of website or blog with domain name traffic will be driven to)

_____

Standard Social Media Identification Name/Handle _____

Social Media Project Director   _____

Social Media Team Members & Tasks   _____   _____

                                        _____   _____

Programming/Technical Team   _____   _____

Social Media Policy URL   _____

Check all applications used. Items noted by ☒ are strongly recommended.

SOCIAL MEDIA PLANNING

❑ **Dashboard** (Select one: Enter URL & login info)
- ○ Netvibes
- ○ Hootsuite
- ○ Other – Name:
- ○ Custom

❑ **Calendar** (Select one: Enter URL & login info)
- ○ Google Calendar
- ○ Yahoo! Calendar
- ○ Microsoft Office Calendar
- ○ Other – Name:

❑ **Social Sharing Service** (Select one: Enter URL & login info)
- ○ AddThis
- ○ ShareThis
- ○ AddtoAny
- ○ Other – Name:

❑ **Social Media Resources** (Insert one resource site or blog to follow)
- ○

SOCIAL MEDIA TOOL KIT

❑ **Monitoring** (Select at least one: Enter name, URL, & login info for all used)
- ○ Brand Reputation/Sentiment Tool with fee (e.g., BrandsEye)
- ○ Topic Monitoring Tool (e.g., Google Trends, Addict-o-matic)
- ○ HowSociable
- ○ IceRocket
- ○ Mention.com
- ○ Trackur
- ○ WhosTalkin
- ○ Blog Monitoring Tool
- ○ Twitter Monitoring Tool
- ○ Talkwalker Alerts
- ○ Google Alerts
- ○ Other – Name:

☐ **Distribution Tools** (Select at least one: Enter name, URL & login info for all used)
- ○ RSS/Atom Feeds
- ○ Buffer
- ○ Hootsuite
- ○ OnlyWire
- ○ TweetDeck
- ○ Other – Name:

☐ **Update Notification Tools** (Select at least one: Enter Name, URL & login Info for all used)
- ○ Pingdom
- ○ Feed Shark
- ○ GooglePing
- ○ King Ping
- ○ Other – Name:

☐ **URL Clipping Tool** (Select one: Enter URL & login info)
- ○ Bitly
- ○ Snipurl
- ○ TinyURL
- ○ Other – Name:

☐ **E-commerce Tool or Widget** (Select one: Enter URL & login info)
- ○ Ecwid
- ○ Storefront Social
- ○ Shopify
- ○ Etsy Widget
- ○ Amazon Widget
- ○ PayPal Widget
- ○ Other – Name:
- ○ Custom Widget

☐ **Search Engine Tools** (If needed, enter URL & login info; include submission dates)
- ○ Search Engine Ranking Tool (Select One)
- ○ Google Search Engine Submission
- ○ Bing/Yahoo! Search Engine Submission
- ○ Automated XML Feed
- ○ Specialty Search Submission Sites
- ○ Other – Name:

STANDARD SET PRIMARY KEYWORDS/TAGS

- ☐
- ☐
- ☐
- ☐
- ☐
- ☐
- ☐
- ☐

STANDARD PAGE DESCRIPTION TAG
(Enter 150-character description: Include at least four of the keywords above)

SOCIAL MEDIA SERVICES

❑ **Social Bookmarking Sites** (Select at least one: Enter name, URL, & login info for all used)
- ○ Delicious
- ○ StumbleUpon
- ○ Y! Bookmarks
- ○ Google Bookmarks
- ○ Other

❑ **Social News Sites** (Select at least one: Enter name, URL, & login info for all used)
- ○ Digg
- ○ Reddit
- ○ Newsvine
- ○ Slashdot
- ○ Other

❑ **Social Shopping & Specialty Bookmark Sites** (Enter name, URL, & login info for all used)
- ○ Kaboodle
- ○ This Next
- ○ StyleHive
- ○ Other

❑ **Blogging Site** (Enter name, URL, & login info for all used)
- ○ Primary blog
- ○ Blog directory submission site
- ○ Blog monitoring site
- ○ Blog measuring tool sites
- ○ Other

❑ **Primary Social Networking Services** (Select at least one: Enter name, URL, & login info for all used)

Facebook
- ○ Groups
- ○ Events
- ○ Metrics
- ○ Follow Us On/Like Us

Twitter
- ○ Hashtags/Lists
- ○ Tools
- ○ Metrics
- ○ Follow Us On

LinkedIn
- ○ Groups
- ○ Events/Answers
- ○ Metrics
- ○ Follow Us On

Google+
- ○ Circles
- ○ +1 (Ratings)
- ○ Metrics
- ○ Follow Us On

Pinterest
- O   Metrics
- O   Follow Us On

- O   Specialty Networks
- O   Other Professional Networks (e.g., Ryze)
- O   Other Vertical Industry Networks (e.g., DeviantArt)
- O   Other Demographic Networks (e.g., Grandparents.com)

☐ **Social Media Sharing Sites** (Enter name, URL, & login info for all used)
- O   YouTube
- O   UStream
- O   Vimeo
- O   Vine
- O   Instagram
- O   Snapchat
- O   Pinterest
- O   SlideShare
- O   Podcasts
- O   Other

☐ **Social Community Sites** (Enter name, URL, & login info for all used)
- O   Ning
- O   Forums
- O   Message Boards
- O   Other

☐ **Other Social Media Services** (Enter name, URL, & login info for all used)
- O   Geolocation (e.g., Foursquare, Google Latitude, Facebook Location)
- O   Collective Shopping (e.g., Groupon, Living Social)
- O   Social Gaming
- O   Social Mobile
- O   Other

SOCIAL MEDIA METRICS

Key Performance Indicators (Enter eight; e.g., Traffic, CPM, CPC, Conversion Rate, ROI)

☐	☐
☐	☐
☐	☐
☐	☐

☐ **Analytical/Statistical Tool** (Select at least one: Enter name, URL, & login info for all used)
- O   Google Analytics
- O   Yahoo! Analytics
- O   AWstats
- O   StatCounter
- O   SiteTrail.com
- O   Other

SOCIAL MEDIA ADVERTISING

- O   Facebook
- O   LinkedIn
- O   Twitter
- O   Other

☐ **Advertising Metrics** (for reports on impressions, clicks, CTR, CPC, CPM, etc.)

(Enter the following information for each social media advertising service, e.g. Facebook Ads, used.)
- O   Name/Account Log-in URL/User Name/Password
- O   Name/Account Log-in URL/User Name/Password

FIGURE 3-8:
Build a social media marketing plan for your company.

Plotting a Social Media Marketing Strategy

IT'S NO CONTEST: SOCIAL MEDIA WINS!

Originally founded in 1979, Whitehall Lane Winery in Napa Valley, California, was purchased by the Leonardini family in 1993. The winery now owns seven vineyards and has increased case production from 5,000 cases to almost 50,000. Whitehall Lane's first informational website, created in the late 1990s, was supplanted in 1999 with a site linked to Winetasting.com to allow online wine sales, one of the first wineries in the Napa Valley to do so.

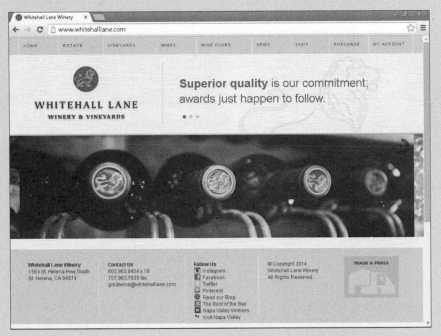

Reproduced by permission of Whitehall Lane Winery

Despite the company's growth, the Tasting Room (direct sales) at Whitehall Lane took a tough hit during the recession starting in 2007. But by 2014, it had surpassed its pre-recession sales records. How? Katie Leonardini, co-owner and vice president of direct sales (which includes overseeing the Tasting Room, e-commerce, Wine Club, and direct marketing), attributes some of the increase in the last two years to the winery's loyalty base. "Our fans don't just follow us on social media — they buy our wines, they visit our winery when they come to Napa Valley, and they join our wine club. Furthermore, they remain members of our wine club and don't cancel after 2 to 3 shipments as many members used to do in the past."

Leonardini turned to social media in 2008. "I was using it on a personal basis and knew that it would be a great way to engage those in their 20s and 30s to talk about Napa Valley and the wine industry. We had strong brand loyalty in the 50+ age group, but wanted to introduce our brand to younger segments." Her instincts obviously proved right.

She didn't have a master plan, but she knew she wanted to grow their list of friends and followers, especially those who lived outside Napa Valley so they would feel connected. "Our philosophy has always been to grow organically and not purchase followers," she explains. "We work hard to ensure that users who Like or Follow us do so because they are genuine fans of our brand and are interested in our content. We also like to reward those fans for following us faithfully.

Leonardini quickly found social media contests to be an effective way to grow the audience and build brand loyalty. The contests have strategic and tactical goals. "We use contests as tools to target specific areas on our social media, or to highlight events happening with the winery. For instance, in an effort to grow our Pinterest following and highlight different items for sale in the winery, we held a Pin and Win contest in March 2014," as shown in the nearby figure. She tries to run roughly one contest every other month. "Engagement on social channels depends on what type of contest we're running, but Facebook is generally highest based on our fan demographic there."

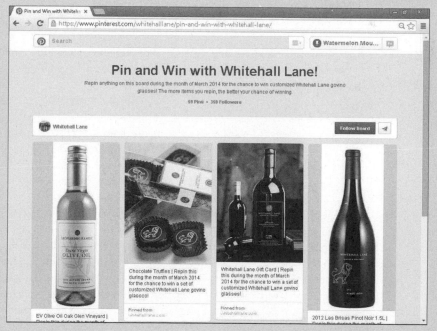

Reproduced by permission of Whitehall Lane Winery

(continued)

(continued)

Whitehall Lane also works hard to create consistencies between social media contests and what is going on in the winery, whether the goal of a contest is to build dinner attendance, increase sales from repeat customers, or increase wine club membership.

"Our contests are meant to engage our customers. We love to engage these followers, have some fun, and reward those that have been loyal to us. Finally, meeting these fans/followers in person really reinforces our philosophy." From Leonardini's point of view, social media efforts strengthen the quality of the guests, as well as the number of people, who visit the winery. "For example, if we gave away complimentary tastings on social media, our number of visitors would be larger in our tasting room, but those guests would be visiting for the free tasting, and not to explore the quality wines that we have to offer. The visitors that we gain due to our social media efforts are interested in learning more about our family business, the history of the winery, and what the advantages are in becoming a wine club member."

The company generally does not limit contests to specific market niches or segments. Because one of their goals is increased engagement, they take a more inclusive approach to getting people involved. Rather than targeting the audience narrowly by demographics, Leonardini tries to make contests that are more specific, like photo contests that every demographic can get involved in.

Wineries like Whitehall face constraints that many other businesses don't. Legally, Whitehall Lane must ensure that people submitting to its contests are above the legal drinking age. For the same reason, the company doesn't use wine as a prize for any contests. Whitehall Lane also enforces specific rules when collecting content from users (for example, in photo/video contests), so users who submit photos consent to allow use of these photos in marketing efforts.

For more than two years, Whitehall Lane has worked with Abbi Agency in Nevada. The agency manages the company's social media directly, but they work together to create the content. Abbi will generally put together the overall campaign ideas and contests and manage day-to-day operations, but the marketing team keeps the agency in the loop about specific happenings at the winery or things to be posted.

Success takes time! "The Abbi Agency follows a general schedule when posting to help keep content organized, consistent, and on-strategy," Leonardini says. "Each week, they schedule out content ahead of time, and then we check the content to ensure that it fits with our brand messaging before it goes live. All in all, between content creation and monitoring our social outlets, Abbi Agency spends 4 to 6 hours per week on our social media outlets, with more time spent during contests. Between launching and monitoring contests, they probably take a total of 8 to 12 hours, depending on how intensive they are. I correspond with my colleagues at Abbi Agency at least once a day. This ensures that we are all on the same page in terms of direction."

Whitehall Lane runs their contests and tracks analytics through Offerpop (`www.offerpop.com`), a well-known platform for social media contests and campaigns. With Offerpop, Leonardini can easily set up Facebook tabs for different types of social media contests with different goals, such as email collection, photo collection, increased engagement, customer referral, fan growth, and many more.

To determine a contest's success, Leonardini uses Offerpop analytics to see how much of the audience was engaged. Offerpop gives analytics to measure fan growth, shared contest links, entries and entry channel, page views, and many others." If we are working to establish a hashtag through a contest, we will use tools like Iconosquare and Topsy to measure the hashtag's growth during the contest's duration."

She actively cross-promotes their social contests throughout all of Whitehall Lane's social channels to reach their entire fan base. Depending on the contest, Leonardini will also blog about it and send out the information to the e-newsletter database. Whitehall Lane does include social icons on its website (see the figure above), but those drive users to Whitehall Lane's general social pages, where she posts frequently about contests to increase their visibility.

Leonardini has some very useful advice to share. "One huge lesson we have learned about social media contests is that it's important to put yourself in the user's shoes when considering whether a contest will be successful. Just because a contest is a creative, fun idea, it doesn't mean that it will be something that users will want to — or remember to — participate in. We've seen lower engagements with certain contests and have realized that these are too limiting . . . for users to participate in."

"Another great lesson we've learned is to be open to cross-promoting and working with others in our industry on social media. One of our most successful campaigns has been #MerlotMe, which was created by a dozen wineries in Napa Valley in 2013. With so many wineries working together to promote appreciation for Merlot in the month of October, it has allowed us to capitalize on the use of the hashtag and find ways to make the conversation unique for our brand."

Whitehall Lane Winery's web presence:

- `www.whitehalllane.com`
- `http://instagram.com/whitehalllane`
- `www.facebook.com/whitehalllanewinery`

(continued)

(continued)

- https://twitter.com/whitehalllane

- www.pinterest.com/whitehalllane

- http://blog.whitehalllane.com/

- http://bestofthebaytv.com/view/887

- www.visitnapavalley.com/wineries-whitehall_lane_winery_348.htm

- www.napavintners.com/winery/whitehall-lane

Chapter 4

Managing Your Cybersocial Campaign

After you create a Social Media Marketing Plan (see Book 2, Chapter 3), one major task you face is managing the effort. If you're the only one doing the work, the simplest — and likely hardest — task is making time for it. Though social media need not carry a lot of upfront development costs, it carries a significant cost in labor.

This chapter discusses how to set up a schedule to keep your social media activity from draining all your available time. If you have employees, both you and your company may benefit if you delegate some of the social media tasking to them. You can also supplement your in-house staff with limited assistance from outside professionals.

REMEMBER

For small businesses, it's your money or your life. If you can't afford to hire help to work on social media, you carve it out of the time you've allocated to other marketing activities — unless, of course, you want to add another two hours to your workday.

Finally, this chapter carries a word of caution. Make sure that everyone posting to a social media outlet knows your policy about what is and isn't acceptable, as well as how to protect the company's reputation and confidential material. As you launch your marketing boat onto the churning waters of social media, you should ensure that everyone is wearing a legal life preserver.

Managing Your Social Media Schedule

As you know from your business experience, if something isn't important enough to schedule, it never gets done. Social media, like the rest of your marketing efforts, can easily be swallowed up by day-to-day demands. You must set aside time for it and assign tasks to specific people.

TIP

Allocate a minimum of two hours per week if you're going to participate in social media, rather than set up pages and abandon them. Otherwise, you simply don't see a return from your initial investment in setup. If you don't have much time, stick with the marketing you're already doing.

Controlling the time commitment

Social media can become addictive. If you truly like what you're doing, the time problem might reverse. Rather than spend too little time, you spend too much. You might find it difficult to avoid the temptation of continually reading what others have to say about your business or spending all your time tweeting, streaming, and posting.

Just as you stick to your initial dollar budget, keep to your initial time budget, at least for the first month until you see what works. After you determine which techniques have the greatest promise, you can rearrange your own efforts as well as your team's.

REMEMBER

Social media marketing is only part of your online marketing effort, and online marketing is only part of your overall marketing.

Selecting activity days

One way to control the time you spend on social media is to select specific days and times for it. Many business people set aside regularly recurring blocks of time, such as on a quiet Friday afternoon, for marketing-related tasks, whether they're conducting competitor research, writing press releases or newsletters for the following week, obtaining inbound links, or handling their social media marketing tasks.

Other people prefer to allocate their time early in the morning, at lunchtime, or just before leaving work each evening. The time slot you choose usually doesn't matter, unless you're offering a time-dependent service, such as accepting to-go orders for breakfast burritos via Twitter.

TIP

Whatever the case, allot time for every task on your Social Media Activity Calendar, followed by the initials of the person responsible for executing the task.

Allowing for ramp-up time

Even if you're the only person involved, allow time for figuring out important information before your official social media launch date. Everyone needs time to observe, master new tools, practice posting and responding, experiment, and decide what works before you can roll out your plan.

TIP

Bring your new social media venues online one at a time. This strategy not only helps you evaluate which social media venue works, but also reduces stress on you and your staff.

Developing your social date book

There are as many ways to schedule social media activities as there are companies. Whatever you decide, don't leave your schedule to chance.

Larger companies may use sophisticated project management software. Some offer a free trial such as Basecamp (https://basecamp.com) and Smartsheet (www.smartsheet.com), while others are available as freemium proprietary solutions, such as MOOVIA (https://site.moovia.com), or as open source programs such as GanttProject (www.ganttproject.biz) or ProjectLibre (www.projectlibre.org). For more options, see http://alternativeto.net/software/smartsheet or www.techshout.com/alternatives/2013/17/smartsheet-alternatives. Alternatively, you can schedule tasks using spreadsheet software.

However, the simplest solution may be the best: Calendar software, much of which is free, may be all you need. Paid options may merge schedules for more people and allow customized report formats. Several options are listed in Table 4-1. Look for a solution that lets you

>> Choose a display by day, week, or month or longer.

>> List events or tasks in chronological format.

>> Select different time frames easily.

>> Easily schedule repeat activities without requiring duplicate data entry.

TABLE 4-1   Calendaring Software

Name	URL	Free or Paid
Calendar & Time Management Software for Windows Reviews	`http://download.cnet.com/windows/` `calendar-and-time-management-software`	Free, shareware, and paid
Connect Daily	`www.mhsoftware.com/connectdaily.htm`	Paid, free trial
EventsLink Network Website Calendar	`www.eventslink.net`	Paid, free trial
Google Calendar	`www.google.com/calendar`	Free
Mozilla Lightning Calendar	`www.mozilla.org/en-us/projects/` `calendar`	Free, open source
Trumba	`www.trumba.com/connect/default.aspx`	Paid, free trial
Yahoo! Calendar	`http://calendar.yahoo.com`	Free

TIP

If several people are involved in a substantial social media effort, select calendar software that lets you synchronize individual calendars, such as Google, Yahoo!, Mozilla Lightning, and others. Figure 4-1 shows a sample of a simple social marketing calendar using Yahoo! The calendar shows the initials of the person responsible. Clicking an event or a task reveals item details, including the time allotted to the task, the sharing level, and whether a reminder is sent and to whom. Figure 4-2 offers an example of an event detail listing in a Google calendar.

Note: Google and Yahoo! require you to set up an account before you can use their calendars.

REMEMBER

Set your calendar to private but give access to everyone who needs to be aware of your social media schedule. Depending on the design of your social media program, some outside subcontractors may need access to your calendar to schedule their own production deadlines.

Creating a social media dashboard

Your social media marketing efforts may ultimately involve many tasks: Post to multiple venues; use tools to distribute content to multiple locations; monitor visibility for your company on social media outlets; and measure results by using several analytical tools. Rather than jump back and forth among all these resources, you can save time by using a graphical dashboard or control panel.

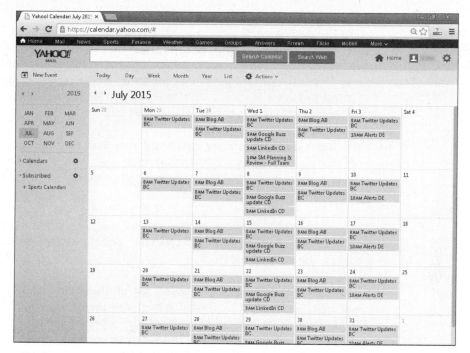

FIGURE 4-1:
Using Yahoo!
Calendar, you can
easily schedule
your social media
activities.

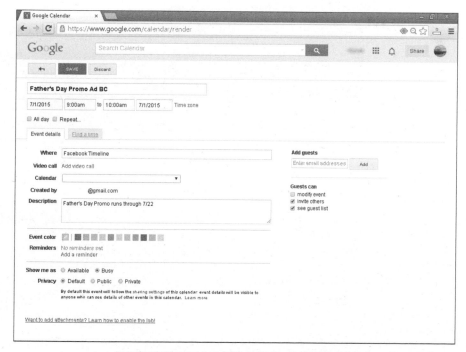

FIGURE 4-2:
On the Google
Calendar, you can
provide specifics
for a marketing
task by modifying
an event detail
window.

Managing Your
Cybersocial Campaign

Like the dashboard of a car, a social media dashboard puts the various required functions at your fingertips in (you hope) an easy-to-understand and easy-to-use visual layout. When you use this approach, the customized dashboard provides easy access in one location to all your social media accounts, tools, and metrics. Figures 4-3 and 4-4 show several tabs of a customized Netvibes dashboard — one for social media postings and another for tools.

The items on your primary dashboard may link to other, application-specific dashboards, especially for analytical tools and high-end enterprise solutions; those application dashboards are designed primarily to compare the results of multiple social media campaigns.

Table 4-2 provides a list of dashboard resources, some of which are generic (such as My Yahoo!) and others, such as Netvibes and Hootsuite (see Figure 4-5), which are specific to social media.

Before you try to build a dashboard, list all the social media sources, services, and reports you want to display, along with their associated URLs, usernames, and passwords. It will help if you indicate whether services are interconnected (for example, note whether you're using a syndication service to update multiple social media at the same time) and how often statistical reports should be updated for each service (hourly, daily, weekly, or monthly).

FIGURE 4-3:
This mock-up of a social media dashboard from Netvibes gathers the user's various social media services on the Social Media Choices tab.

Source: www.netvibes.com

FIGURE 4-4:
The Tools & Stats tab of this mock-up Netvibes dashboard displays tools for distributing, monitoring, searching, and analyzing data.

TABLE 4-2   ## Social Media Dashboard Resources

Name	URL	Description
Hootsuite	`www.hootsuite.com`	Free, customizable dashboard for social media; paid option available
MarketingProfs	`www.marketingprofs.com/ articles/2010/3454/how-to-create-your- marketing-dashboard-in-five-easy-steps`	Instructions for customizing a dashboard (you can close the pop-up window asking you to sign up)
My Yahoo!	`http://my.yahoo.com`	Free, customizable Yahoo! home page
Netvibes	`http://netvibes.com`	Free, customizable dashboard for social media
Search Engine Land	`http://searchengineland.com/ b2b-social-media-dashboard-a- powerful-tool-to-uncover-key-customer- insights-17839`	Tips on how to use a social media dashboard for B2B
uberVU	`www.ubervu.com`	Paid social media dashboard client

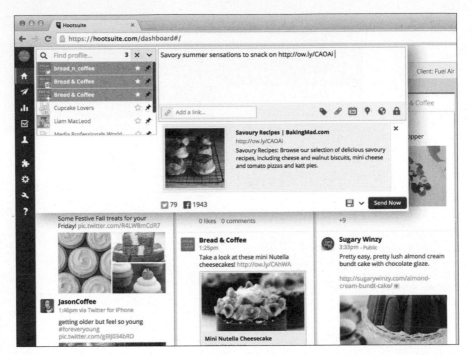

FIGURE 4-5:
The social media dashboard from Hootsuite allows you to monitor and update multiple social network services.

The more complex your social media campaign, the more functionality your dashboard needs.

TIP

Dashboards sound simple to use, but they can be a bit of a challenge to set up. In some cases, your programmer needs to create or customize *widgets* (mini applications). Plan to create and test several versions of the dashboard until everyone is satisfied with the results.

Consider implementing password access for approved users to various functions within the dashboard. Some users might be constrained to viewing reports, whereas others might be allowed to change the dashboard configuration.

Assembling Your Social Media Marketing Dream Team

Just for the moment, assume that you have employees who can — and are willing to — share the burden of social media. If you live a rich fantasy life, assume that you might even hire someone to take the lead.

In a larger company, the nexus for control of social media varies: In some cases, it's the marketing department; in others, corporate communications, public relations, sales, or customer support takes the lead.

Some companies disperse responsibilities throughout the company and have tens to dozens of people blogging and tweeting.

If your plan requires multiple employees to leverage LinkedIn profiles for B2B reasons, as well as post on multiple blogs in their individual areas of expertise and tweet current events in their departments, your need for coordination will increase.

Be cautious about asking employees to coordinate links and comments with their personal social media accounts. This task should be voluntary. Alternatively, on company time and on an account that "belongs" to your company (using a business email address), ask employees to develop a hybrid personal-and-business account where their personalities can shine. Now, individual privacy and First Amendment rights are respected on their separate personal accounts, and you have no liability for the content they post there.

TIP

No matter who does the bulk of the work — your staff members, contractors, or a combination of the two — always monitor your program randomly but regularly. In addition to getting routine reports on the results, log in to your accounts for a few minutes at various times of the day and week to see what's going on.

Seeking a skilled social media director

A good social media director should have an extroverted personality, at least in writing. This person should truly enjoy interacting with others and take intrinsic pleasure in conversation and communication. You might want to look, based on your chosen tactics, for someone who can

>> Write quickly and well, with the right tone for your market.

>> Listen well, with an ear for your target audiences and their concerns.

>> Post without using defamatory language or making libelous statements about competitors.

>> Communicate knowledgeably about your company and your products or services.

>> Recognize opportunities and develop creative responses or campaigns.

>> Work tactfully with others, alerting them when problems or complaints surface.

>> Articulate the goals of social media well enough to take a leadership role in encouraging others to explore its potential.

>> Analyze situations to draw conclusions from data.

>> Adapt to new social media and mobile technologies when they arise.

>> Learn quickly (because this field is extremely fluid).

This combination of skills, experience, and personality may be hard to find. Add to it the need to reach different submarkets for different reasons. Now you have several reasons to build a team with a leader, rather than rely on a single individual to handle all your social media needs.

TIP

You usually can't just add social media to someone's task list; be prepared to reassign some tasks to other people.

Depending on the size and nature of your social media effort, your dream team may also need someone with production skills for podcasting or videocasting, or at least for producing and directing the development of those components. Though this person may not need extensive graphical, photographic, presentation, or data-crunching skills, having some skills in each of those areas is helpful.

Hiring 20-somethings (or younger) because they're familiar with social media may sound like a good idea, but people in this age group aren't as likely to be familiar with business protocol or sensitive to business relationships, as someone older and more experienced might be. You might need to allow extra time for training, review, and revision.

Looking inside

Before implementing a social media plan, speak with your employees to invite their input, assess their level of interest in this effort, evaluate existing skill sets, and ascertain social media experience. Consider all these factors before you move forward; by rearranging task assignments or priorities, you may be able to select in-house personnel to handle this new project.

TIP

Leave time for communication, education, and training both at the beginning and on an ongoing basis.

Hiring experts

Think about using professionals for the tech-heavy tasks, such as podcasts, videocasts, or design, unless you're going for the just-us-folks tone. Professionals can get you started by establishing a model for your staff to follow, or you may want to hire them for long-term tasks such as writing or editing your blogs for consistency.

Many advertising agencies, PR firms, search engine optimizers, marketing companies, and copywriters now take on social media contracts. If you've already worked with someone you like, you can start there. If not, select social media professionals the same way you would select any other professional service provider:

>> Ask your local business colleagues for referrals.

>> Check sources such as LinkedIn and Plaxo. If appropriate, post your search criteria on your site, blog, social media outlets, and topic-related sites.

>> Request several price quotes. If your job is large enough, write and distribute a formal Request for Proposal (RFP).

>> Review previous work completed by the contractors.

>> Check references.

Creating a Social Media Marketing Policy

Even if you're the only person involved in social media marketing at the beginning, write up a few general guidelines for yourself that you can expand later. Figure 4-6 shows a sample social media policy; you can download other examples from www.itbusinessedge.com/search/?q=social+media+policy&filter= ITDownload. From the drop-down list for the first field at this link, select Policies. From the drop-down list in the second field, select Social Networking. Click Go and then download any of the sample policies from the list that appears.

Most policies address the social media issue both in terms of what employees are allowed to do on behalf of the company and what they aren't allowed to do. For example:

>> Employees may not be allowed to use personal social accounts on company time.

>> Some trained employees may be allowed to post customer support replies on behalf of the company, whereas others are responsible for new product information.

ITBUSINESSEDGE
YOUR TECHNOLOGY INTELLIGENCE AGENT

NarrowCast Group, LLC ••• 10400 Linn Station Road, Suite 100 ••• Louisville, KY 40223

Sample Social Networking Policy

The following is the company's social media and social networking policy. The absence of, or lack of explicit reference to a specific site does not limit the extent of the application of this policy. Where no policy or guideline exists, employees should use their professional judgment and take the most prudent action possible. Consult with your manager or supervisor if you are uncertain.

1. Personal blogs should have clear disclaimers that the views expressed by the author in the blog is the author's alone and do not represent the views of the company. Be clear and write in first person. Make your writing clear that you are speaking for yourself and not on behalf of the company.
2. Information published on your blog(s) should comply with the company's confidentiality and disclosure of proprietary data policies. This also applies to comments posted on other blogs, forums, and social networking sites.
3. Be respectful to the company, other employees, customers, partners, and competitors.
4. Social media activities should not interfere with work commitments. Refer to IT resource usage policies.
5. Your online presence reflects the company. Be aware that your actions captured via images, posts, or comments can reflect that of our company.
6. Do not reference or site company clients, partners, or customers without their

Reproduced with permission of QuinStreet, Inc.

FIGURE 4-6:
A basic social media policy may be enough to get you started.

For additional information and examples, see the resources listed in Table 4-3.

TIP

To increase compliance, keep your policy short and easy to read. Try to focus on what people *can do* rather than on what they can't do.

TABLE 4-3 ## Social Media Policy Resource Sites

Name	URL	Description
American Express	`www.americanexpress.com/us/small-business/openforum/articles/employee-social-media-policy`	Article titled "Employees Gone Wild: 8 Reasons You Need A Social Media Policy TODAY"
ITBusinessEdge	`www.itbusinessedge.com/search/?q=social+media+policy&filter=ITDownload`	Social media guidelines, templates, and examples; select Policies in the Type drop-down list, and Social Networking in the Topic drop-down list
LikeableMedia Blog	`www.likeable.com/blog/2013/04/5-things-brands-should-consider-for-their-social-media-policy`	Article titled "5 Must-Haves For Your Brand's Social Media Policy"

Name	URL	Description
LinkedIn	www.linkedin.com/today/post/article/20140320152546-13721119-how-to-create-a-social-media-strategy-that-actually-gets-read	Article titled "How to create a social media strategy that actually gets read"
Mashable	http://mashable.com/2012/10/06/social-media-policy-update	Article titled "Tips for Updating Your Company's Social Media Policy"
Netsphere Strategies	www.netspherestrategies.com/blog/10-items-to-include-in-your-companys-social-media-policy	Free checklist
PolicyTool for Social Media	http://socialmedia.policytool.net	Free social media policy generator
Rocket Lawyer	www.rocketlawyer.com/document/social-media-policy.rl	Free social media policy generator
Social Media Examiner	www.socialmediaexaminer.com/write-a-social-media-policy	Article titled "How to Write a Social Media Policy to Empower Employees"
Social Media Governance	http://socialmediagovernance.com/policies.php	Free database of policies for review
TechRepublic	www.techrepublic.com/article/how-to-craft-a-social-media-policy	Article titled "How to craft a social media policy"
Toolkit Cafe	http://toolkitcafe.com/social_media_policies.php	Policies toolkit ($119)

A typical policy addresses risk management, intellectual property protection, individual privacy protection, and the respect of your audience, company, and fellow employees. Given the rapidly changing world of social media, you'll have to keep your policy flexible and update it often. Try to incorporate the following suggested concepts, adapted from Mashable (http://mashable.com/2012/10/06/social-media-policy-update):

>> Hold individuals responsible for what they write.

>> Be transparent. Disclose who you are, including your company name and title.

>> Recognize that clients, prospects, competitors, and potential future employees are part of your audience.

>> Be respectful of everyone.

>> Understand the tenor of each social media community and follow its precepts.

>> Respect copyright, trademarks, and privacy rights.

>> Protect your company's confidential trade-secret and proprietary information in addition to client data, especially trade-secret information under nondisclosure agreements.

>> Do *not* allow personal social media activity to interfere with work.

TIP

The complexity of your social media policy depends on the extent of your social media marketing effort and the number of people and departments involved. Generally, the larger the company, the longer the policy.

Staying on the Right Side of the Law

Just about everything in social media pushes the limits of existing intellectual property law. So much information is now repeated online that ownership lines are becoming blurred, much to some people's dismay and damage.

When in doubt, don't copy. Instead, use citations, quote marks, and links to the original source. Always go back to the original to ensure that the information is accurate.

TIP

Watch blogs such as Mashable and TechCrunch for information about legal wrangling. New case law, regulations, and conflicts bubble up continually.

Obtaining permission to avoid infringement

You can't (legally) use extended content from someone else's website, blog, or social media page on your own site, even if you can save it or download it. Nope, not even if you include a credit line saying where it came from. Not even if you use only a portion of the content and link to the rest. Not text, not graphics, not compiled data, not photos. Nothing. Nada. Nil. Zilch.

Though small text extracts with attribution are permitted under the fair use doctrine, the copyright concept is intended for individuals and educational institutions, not for profit-making companies. If you don't obtain permission, you and your company can be sued for copyright infringement. In the best-case scenario, you can be asked to cease and desist. In the worst case, your site can be shut down, and you might face other damages.

The way around this situation is simple: Send a permission request, such as the one in the nearby sidebar, "Sample copyright permission."

Be especially careful with photographs, which are usually copyrighted. Here are a few places to find free or low-cost images legally:

>> Select from the wealth of material offered under a Creative Commons license (http://creativecommons.org). Search for items that can be used for commercial purposes or are in the public domain.

>> Search for copyright-free images from the federal government.

>> The Commons on Flickr (www.flickr.com/commons) has thousands of free photographs.

>> Search http://images.google.com. Click the Settings link in the bottom-right corner of the window, and then select Advanced Search from the pop-up menu that appears. In the Advanced Search screen that appears, scroll down to the Usage Rights drop-down list and select Free to Use or Share, Even Commercially. Note that these images may still require attribution or have other limits on use; you should still contact the copyright holder for permission.

>> Look for stock images from sources such as iStockphoto (www.istockphoto.com), Shutterstock (www.shutterstock.com), or Freerange Stock (http://freerangestock.com).

TIP

Trademarks and logos also usually require permission to use, though the logos (icons) that social media companies provide for Share This or Follow Us On functionality are fine to use without permission. If you find an image in the Press or Media section of a company's website, you can assume that you have permission to reproduce it without further permission. Generally, a disclaimer that "all other logos and trademarks are the property of their respective owners" will suffice.

REMEMBER

If it's illegal offline, it's illegal online.

Respecting privacy

Providing a disclaimer about keeping user information private is even more critical now that people sign up willy-nilly online. Individual privacy, already under threat, has become quite slippery with the Facebook Connect sign-in available on all sorts of third-party sites. Facebook Connect may make sign-ins simpler for a user, but it gives Facebook access to user behavior on the web while giving third parties access to users' Facebook profiles for demographic analysis.

SAMPLE COPYRIGHT PERMISSION

Use this sample letter when you want permission from a source for your website.

Dear _____:

Watermelon Mountain Web Marketing wants permission to use your *(information, article, screen shot, art, data, photograph)* on our *(website/blog/social media page)* at *[this URL: WatermelonWeb.com]* and in other media not yet specified. We have attached a copy of the information we want to use. If it meets with your approval, please sign the following release and indicate the credit line you want. You can return the signed form as an email message, a PDF file, a digitally signed document, a fax, or a first-class mail message. Thank you for your prompt response.

The undersigned authorizes Watermelon Mountain Web Marketing to use the attached material without limit for no charge.

Signature:

Printed name:

Title:

Company name:

Company address:

Telephone/fax/email:

Company domain name:

Credit line:

Photographs of identifiable individuals, not taken in a public space, historically have required a waiver to use for commercial purposes. When individuals post their images on Facebook, LinkedIn, MySpace, or elsewhere, they may not intend to give permission for that image to appear elsewhere.

Respect a person's space; do not post publicly viewable images of people's faces on any of your social media pages unless you have permission. For a simple photo waiver, see www.nyip.edu/photo-articles/archive/basic-model-release.

Revealing product endorsement relationships

Taking aim at companies that were arranging paid recommendations from bloggers, the Federal Trade Commission (FTC) updated its regulations for digital advertising, including blogs, in 2013. The rule (found at `www.ftc.gov/sites/default/files/attachments/press-releases/ftc-staff-revises-online-advertising-disclosure-guidelines/130312dotcomdisclosures.pdf`) requires bloggers to disclose whether they've received any type of payment or free products in exchange for a positive review. For more information, see `http://bloggylaw.com/ftc-guidelines-blogger-disclosures`.

The rule doesn't appear to apply to individuals who post a review on public review sites (such as Epinions.com, TripAdvisor, or Yelp), but it applies if you review other companies' products on your blog or send products to other bloggers to request a review.

You can find out more about this requirement from the disclosure resources listed in Table 4-4. Some bloggers, offended by the rules, have found humorous or sarcastic ways to comply; others, such as Katy Widrick, whose blog appears in Figure 4-7 (`http://katywidrick.com/about/disclosure-policy`), are simply matter-of-fact about it.

TABLE 4-4 **Legal Resource Sites**

Name	URL	Description
American Bar Association	`www.americanbar.org/groups/intellectual_property_law/resources.html`	Intellectual property resource lists
BloggyEsq	`http://bloggylaw.com/ftc-guidelines-blogger-disclosures`	Article titled "FTC Guidelines: Are You Making The Right Blogger Disclosures?"
DisclosurePolicy.org	`http://disclosurepolicy.org`	Generate free disclosure policies
Electronic Frontier Foundation	`www.eff.org`	Nonprofit focused on free speech, privacy, and consumer rights
Federal Trade Commission	`www.ftc.gov/sites/default/files/attachments/press-releases/ftc-staff-revises-online-advertising-disclosure-guidelines/130312dotcomdisclosures.pdf`	Federal guidelines for digital media disclosure

(continued)

TABLE 4-4 *(continued)*

Name	URL	Description
FindLaw	`http://smallbusiness.findlaw.com/intellectual-property.html`	Intellectual property resources
International Technology Law Association	`www.itechlaw.org`	Online legal issues
PublicLegal from the Internet Legal Research Group	`www.ilrg.com`	Index of legal sites, free forms, and documents
Nolo	`www.nolo.com/legal-encyclopedia/ecommerce-website-development`	Online legal issues
Social Media Examiner	`www.socialmediaexaminer.com/ftc-2013-disclosures`	Article titled "What Marketers Need to Know About the New FTC Disclosures"
Social Media Explorer	`www.socialmediaexplorer.com/social-media-marketing/disclosures-for-bloggers-and-brands`	Blog and brand disclosure summary
SocialMedia.org	`http://socialmedia.org/disclosure`	Social Media Disclosure Toolkit
U.S. Copyright Office	`www.copyright.gov`	Copyright information and submission
United States Patent and Trademark Office	`www.uspto.gov`	Patent and trademark information, databases, and submission
Word of Mouth Marketing Association	`www.womma.org/ethics`	WOMMA Code of Ethics resources

TIP

Regardless of what you think of the policy, reveal any payments or free promotional products you've received. You can, of course, be as clever, funny, cynical, or straightforward as you want. Feeling lazy? Auto-generate a policy at `www.disclosurepolicy.org`.

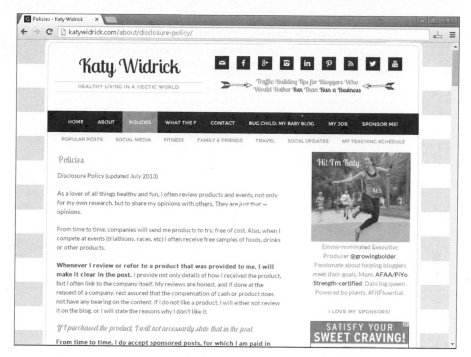

Reproduced with permission of KPWidrick

FIGURE 4-7:
This blogger
sets out a clear
acknowledgment
policy on product
endorsement.

Protecting Your Brand Reputation

It's important to start protecting your brand now by registering your company name for social media accounts. To avoid *brandjacking* (others using your company or product brand name on social media for their own purposes or to write misleading or negative things about your company), try to choose the most popular, available handle that will work across multiple sites. Use your company or product name and keep it short.

TIP

Even if you don't plan to do anything else in social media for a year or more, register your name now on Facebook, Twitter, LinkedIn, and Google+ and on any other sites you might want in the future, such as Pinterest or YouTube. You can register your name on every site while you read this book or reserve them all at once.

A number of companies now offer tools that claim to assess the quality of what people are saying about your company, products, or staff. In addition to counting how many times your name appears, they try to assess the *sentiment* of postings — whether statements are negative or positive. Some also offer an assessment of the degree of *engagement* — how enthusiastic or hostile a statement might be.

Some people then take this information, along with frequency of posting, and use their own proprietary formulas to assign a quantitative value to your online reputation, as shown in the example from Trackur (www.trackur.com) in Figure 4-8.

FIGURE 4-8:
Trackur offers an inexpensive reputation-management tool that scales up for large companies.

Be cautious about assigning too much weight to these brand reputation tools, some of which are described in Table 4-5. They may produce widely varying results, and most rely on software that can't understand complex sentences or shortened phrases with words omitted. If you think your dense sibling doesn't understand irony, don't try sarcasm with a computer.

Notwithstanding the warnings, experiment with one of the free or freemium sentiment-measuring tools in Table 4-5 to see what, if anything, people are saying. (*Freemium* tools offer a free version with limited features; more extensive feature sets carry a charge.) Those results, such as they are, will become one of many baselines for your social media effort. Unless you already have a significant web presence, you may not find much.

Of course, many of these tools are designed for use by multinational corporations worried about their reputations after negative events, such as a General Motors auto recall or the British Petroleum oil spill in the Gulf of Mexico.

For you, the sentiment results might be good for a laugh or make excellent party chatter at your next *tweet-up* (your real-world meeting arranged through tweets).

TABLE 4-5 **Brand Sentiment Resources**

Name	URL	Description
Attentio	`http://attentio.com`	Social media dashboard to track sentiment and more; paid
BrandsEye	`www.brandseye.com`	Online reputation tool; paid
Digital Sherpa	`www.digitalsherpa.com/blog/protect-online-business-reputation`	Article titled "How to Protect Your Online Business Reputation"
Mediabistro	`www.mediabistro.com/12-tips-on-fixing-your-brands-bad-reputation-a12012.html`	Article titled "12 Tips on Fixing Your Brand's Bad Reputation"
Naymz	`www.naymz.com`	Personal reputation on social media
Oracle Social Cloud	`www.oracle.com/us/solutions/social/overview/index.html`	Social relationship management tool
Reputation.com	`www.reputation.com/for-business`	Reputation monitoring tool; starts at $49/month
SDL SM2	`www.sdl.com/products/SM2`	Social media sentiment tool; paid
Sentiment 140	`www.sentiment140.com`	Twitter sentiment tool; free app
Social Fresh	`http://socialfresh.com/monitoring-your-brand-online-reputation/`	List of social monitoring tools
Trackur	`www.trackur.com/free-brand-monitoring-tools`	Reputation protection tool; freemium model

Chapter 5

Leveraging Search Engine Optimization (SEO) for Social Media

N o matter how popular social media may be, search engine optimization (SEO) must still be a part of your toolkit for a successful, broad-spectrum web presence. The goal of SEO is to get various components of your web presence to appear near the top of search results — preferably in the top ten — on general search engines or in search results for specific social media services.

You accomplish this by selecting appropriate search terms or keywords and then optimizing content, navigation, and structure to create a web page or profile that's search-friendly for your selected terms. At the same time, you maximize cross-links from social media to increase the number of inbound links to your primary website.

Fortunately, you can optimize social media, from blogs to Facebook, very much the same way that you optimize a website. Some people call this social media optimization (SMO), referring to the application of SEO techniques to social media. SMO has become even more critical with search engines such as Google moving toward personalization and semantic analysis, which skews users' results on the basis of location and past searches.

If you do a good job optimizing multiple components of your web presence — your website, blog, Facebook page, Twitter profile, and more — they may all appear near the top of Search Engine Result Pages (SERPs) on selected terms, increasing your company's share of that premium screen real estate. As mentioned in Book 2, Chapter 2, improving search engine ranking is one strategic justification for implementing a social media campaign in the first place.

Making the Statistical Case for SEO

News of the publicity about social media usage sometimes overshadows the actual numbers. For instance, comScore's Unique Visitor Table for June 2014 showed that Facebook (141.4 million unique visitors) had fallen behind Microsoft Sites (164.2 million), Yahoo! Sites (171.3 million), and Google Sites (189.7 million). The numbers fluctuate, but keep in mind that press accounts and reality aren't always the same.

And just because more than 864 million people worldwide (82 percent outside North America) were called daily active Facebook users in September 2014 doesn't mean they're all using it to search for information that might lead them to your company.

In fact, a study in June 2013 by Forrester Research ("How Consumers Found Websites in 2012") showed that the majority of adult Internet users in the United States still opt for search engines more than social media networks or other sources to find websites, as shown in Figure 5-1. To reach that majority, SEO remains the technique of choice.

REMEMBER

Sobering reminder: Older American audiences (over age 64) still gravitate toward print and television.

Enter your preferred SEO tools in your Social Media Marketing Plan and insert the tasks into your Social Media Activity Calendar.

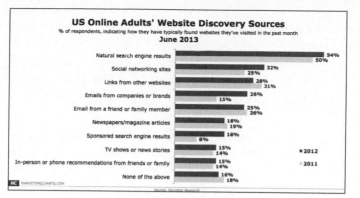

FIGURE 5-1:
In 2013, adult U.S.
Internet users still
favored search
engines over
social media to
find websites.

Reproduced with permission of Trackur LLC. Source: "How Consumers Found Websites In 2012,"
July 2013, Forrester Research, Inc.

At the moment, no social media alternative covers as wide a base of web pages or as commanding an algorithm for assessing relevance as search engines. What will happen in the future? Get out your crystal ball or watch eMarketer and other sites for more data. One thing about the web is for sure — like the world, it always turns.

Given these statistics, do you still need to bother with search engine optimization techniques for your company website, as discussed in Book 2, Chapter 2? Absolutely. Here's why:

>> Although the younger subset of Internet users is attracted to searching for trending topics on social media or relying on friends' recommendations of products, not all members of your target audience are active users of social media — especially if you have a business-to-business (B2B) company or target an older consumer audience.

>> After you optimize your hub website or blog, registered under your own domain name, you can quickly transfer the techniques, tools, and results to social media, especially to blogs and tweets.

>> Inbound links to a hub website remain a key to high ranking in search results, especially on Google. Your social media pages are a rich source of these links. Google treats social media channels, which are written in HTML, just like any other sites on the web for purposes of ranking and search.

Google can't review social media pages that have been set to private, no matter how much traffic or engagement those pages may have.

REMEMBER

>> Most social media services still aren't as flexible as a full-fledged website when it comes to handling e-commerce, database applications, forms, or other myriad features involving real-time data entry. Most third-party apps on social media that offer some of this functionality can't give you the same degree of control as you have on your website.

>> Your website or blog benefits from links to your site from social media pages. In particular, make sure your profile is public and contains links to your site.

>> SEO remains an essential, though not sufficient, method of ensuring site visibility based on a method other than the number of friends, fans, or followers you have. You're chasing profits, not popularity.

REMEMBER

SEO isn't an end in itself. The goal is to draw qualified visitors to your website so that you can turn them into customers and clients. A strong SEO foundation helps direct traffic to your full-featured hub from your social media presence.

For more information about search engine optimization, see the latest version of *Search Engine Optimization All-in-One For Dummies* by Bruce Clay and Susan Esparza (John Wiley & Sons, Inc.).

Thinking Tactically and Practically

The best results for SEO sprout from the best content — and so does the largest stream of qualified prospects. Though this chapter talks about many SEO techniques, none of them will work unless you offer appealing content that draws and holds the attention of your audience.

Two schools of thought drive SEO tactics for social media:

>> Optimize your website and all your social media for the same search terms, occupying the first page of results with one or more pages of your web presence.

>> Use your social media pages to grab a good position for some relatively rare search terms that your website doesn't use.

TIP

Get greedy. Go for the best of both worlds. Use your standard search terms on social media profiles and the more rarely used terms on individual posts, photo captions, or updates.

Use a free trial at sites such as http://seosuite.com, www.webseoanalytics. com/free/seo-tools/keyword-competition-checker.php, or http://moz.com/ tools to see how your site ranks on different search terms. Your tactical decisions about keyword selection may depend on those results, as well as on the goals and objectives of your social media campaign.

GRASPING SOME SEARCH ENGINE JARGON

Help yourself by mastering search engine terminology:

- **Natural or organic search** refers to the type of search results produced by a search engine's *algorithm* (set of rules) when indexing unpaid submissions.

- **Paid search results** are those for which a submission fee or bid has been paid to appear as sponsorships at the top of a search results page, in pay-per-click (PPC) ads in the right margin, or in some cases at the top of the list of search results.

- **Search engine marketing (SEM)** combines both natural and paid search activities.

- **Search engine optimization (SEO)** is the process of adjusting websites, web pages, and social media pages to gain higher placement in search engine results.

- **Social media optimization (SMO)** is the process of adjusting social media profiles and postings to gain higher placement in search engine results.

- **Spiders, crawlers, or robots (bots)** are automated programs used by search engines to visit websites and index their content.

In the later section "Choosing the right search terms," you discover how to select terms that people are likely to use and ones that give you a chance of breaking through to the first page of search results.

Focusing on the Top Search Engines

Ignore all those emails about submitting your site to 3,000 search engines. You need to submit only to the top two: Google, and Yahoo!/Bing (which share the same algorithm). When you submit to Bing, you're also listed on Yahoo! However, the results pages may not always be identical, particularly on local searches.

Table 5-1 tells where to submit your sites to those search engines.

According to comScore, these three search engines accounted for 96.7 percent of all searches in July 2014, with Google executing more than three times as many searches as Bing, its closest search competitor. All remaining search engines together accounted for the remaining 3.3 percent of searches. These primary search engines now send out spiders to crawl the web incessantly. You don't need to resubmit your site routinely. But you should resubmit your site to trigger a visit from the arachnids if you add new content or products, expand to a new location, or update your search terms.

TABLE 5-1   Submission URLs for Key Search Engines

Name	URL	Search % in July 2014	Feeds
Google	`www.google.com/webmasters/tools`	67.4	AOL, Ask.com
Yahoo!	`www.bing.com/toolbox/submit-site-url`	10.0	Lycos
Bing	`www.bing.com/toolbox/submit-site-url`	19.3	Same submission site as Yahoo!

Source: comScore July 2014 U.S. Search Engine Rankings report (`www.comscore.com/Insights/Market-Rankings/comScore-Releases-July-2014-US-Search-Engine-Rankings`)

Fortunately, you can ping search engines to notify them of changes automatically, as discussed in Book 2, Chapter 1. After receiving a ping, search engines crawl your site again. Different search engines use different *algorithms* (sets of rules) to display search results, which may vary rapidly over time. To complicate matters further, different search engines tend to attract different audiences. Optimize your site for the search engine that best attracts your audience. Here are some facts about the top search engines and their audiences:

>> About 72 percent of B2B buyers planning to purchase a product start with Google search.

>> Alexa data shows that users are somewhat more likely to use Yahoo! or Bing at school and Google at home.

>> More than 70 percent of 18- to 29-year-olds preferred search results branded as Google; this number dropped to 64 percent of 30- to 44-year-olds. Those over 45 generally favored Bing results.

>> People who search with Google tend to live in states with above-average median household incomes, above average college graduation rates, higher job growth rates, and older populations.

>> States that favor Bing for search appear to lean towards the right of the political spectrum.

>> Yahoo! users show a high correlation with very religious states but are found less often in areas with more Starbucks coffee shops or more college graduates. Because college graduation correlates to income, Yahoo! users also show a lower overall personal income.

>> Market share is not even across the country. Google dominates both the West Coast (with a market share over 80 percent) and the East Coast (with a market share around 85 percent in Massachusetts, New York, and the District of Columbia). Of states in the U.S., only Delaware has a Google market share below 70 percent.

Knowing the Importance of Search Phrases

Users enter search terms into the query box on a search engine, website, or social media service to locate the information they seek, particularly when the users are mobile and on the go. The trick to success is to identify the search terms that your prospective customers are likely to use.

REMEMBER

For good visibility on a search term, your site or social media profile needs to appear within the top ten positions on the first page of search results for that term. Only academic researchers and obsessive-compulsives are likely to search beyond the first page.

Fortunately or unfortunately, everyone's brain is wired a little differently, leading to different choices of words and different ways of organizing information. Some differences are simple matters of dialect: Someone in the southern United States may look for *bucket*, whereas someone in the north looks for a *pail*. Someone in the United Kingdom may enter *cheap petrol*, whereas someone in the United States types *cheap gas*.

Other differences have to do with industry-specific jargon. *Rag* has one meaning to someone looking for a job in the garment industry and another meaning to someone wanting to buy a chamois to polish a car.

Other variations have to do with spelling simplicity. Users will invariably spell *hotels* rather than *accommodations*, or *army clothes* instead of *camouflage* or *khaki*. And users rarely type a phrase that's longer than five words.

Longer search queries, which are sometimes called *long-tail keywords*, are more likely to land people on a specific page or post. Therefore, these long queries may be more likely to lead to conversions.

Choosing the right search terms

Try to come up with at least 30 search terms that can be distributed among different pages of your website (more if you have a large site). You must juggle the terms people are likely to use to find your product or service with the likelihood that you can show up on the first page of search results. Here are some tips for building a list of potential keywords:

>> Brainstorm all possible terms that you think your target audience might use. Ask your customers, friends, and employees for ideas.

>> Be sure your list includes the names of all your products and service packages and your company name. Someone who has heard of you must absolutely be able to find you online.

>> Incorporate all the industry-specific search terms and jargon you can think of.

>> If you sell to a local or regional territory, incorporate location into your terms: for example, *Lancaster bakery* or *Columbus OH chiropractor.* It's very difficult to appear on the first page of results for a single word, such as *bakery* or *chiropractor.*

>> For additional ideas, go to Google, enter a search term, and click the Search button. Then click the Related Searches option in the left margin. You may be surprised by the other search phrases that users try.

>> If you already have a website, look at your analytics results to see which search phrases people are already using to find your site.

>> Use one or more of the free search tools listed in Table 5-2 to get ideas for other keywords, how often they're used, and how many competing sites use the same term.

TABLE 5-2   **Keyword Selection Resources**

Name	URL	Description
Google Insights	`www.google.com/trends`	Research trending search terms
Google AdWords Keyword Planner	`https://adwords.google.com/keywordplanner`	Free keyword generator and statistics available to AdWords users
SEMrush	`www.semrush.com`	Research keywords used by competitors for Google and Bing organic search
Ubersuggest	`http://ubersuggest.org`	Free keyword suggestion tool
WordStream	`www.wordstream.com/keywords`	Basic keyword tools; 30 free searches
Wordtracker	`www.wordtracker.com`	Keyword suggestion tool; free 7-day trial

>> Figure 5-2 displays results and synonyms from the Google AdWords Keyword Planner (`https://adwords.google.com/keywordplanner`) for the phrase dog grooming. (Intended to help buyers of Google AdWords, this tool is also useful when you're brainstorming search terms.) To access this tool, you need to sign into an existing AdWords account or create a new one by clicking the links on the Keyword Planner page.

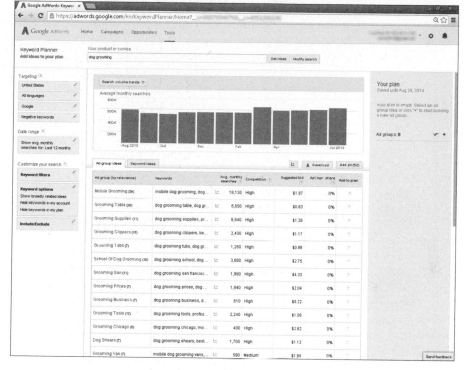

Source: Google Adwords

FIGURE 5-2:
The Google AdWords Keyword Planner displays the frequency of requests for related search terms and estimates the advertising competition for a term.

Alternatively, you can reach this page by signing into your Google AdWords account at `https://adwords.google.com` or at `http://google.com/mybusiness`. After you log in, navigate to the Tools tab and click Keyword Planner, which you can access without actually creating a campaign.

» Check your competitors' search terms for ideas. Visit your competitors' sites and right-click to view page source, or look in the browser toolbar for something like View > Source. The keywords are usually listed near the top of the source code for a page. If you don't see them, try using the Find command (Ctrl+F) to search for *keyword*.

» Not sure who your competitors are? Enter one of your search terms to identify similar companies appearing on the first page of search results. Then you can go look at their other keywords, too.

» Look at the tag clouds for topics on social news services or blog search engines such as `www.icerocket.com` or `www.blogsearchengine.org` to assess the relative popularity of different search terms. *Tag clouds* visualize how often keywords appear in specific content or how often they're used by searchers, with the most popular terms usually appearing in larger type. (You can find more on tag clouds in the section "Understanding tags and tag clouds," later in this chapter.)

>> Avoid using single words except in technical fields where the word is a term specific to a particular industry, such as *seismometer* or *angiogram,* with only hundreds of thousands, instead of millions, of competing pages. Not only will you have too much competition on generalized single words, but results for single words also produce too wide a range of options. People simply give up.

Crafting a page, blog post, or social media profile for more than four or five search terms is difficult. Break up your list of terms into sets that you think you can work into a single paragraph of text while still making sense.

TIP

Optimizing for search terms that real people rarely use doesn't make sense. Sure, you can be number one because you have no competition, but why bother? You will show up on these words anyway. The exceptions are your company and product names and terms highly specific to your business.

REMEMBER

Always test your selected search terms to be sure that sites like yours show up in the results for that term. For instance, entering *artificial trees* as a search term yields inexpensive artificial Christmas trees, especially at the holiday season, and perhaps some silk palm trees. However, that term doesn't produce appropriate results if your company offers $30,000 tree sculptures designed for shopping malls, zoos, or museums.

Where to place search terms on your site

Sprinkle your keywords throughout the content that visitors will see. Although Google searches the entire page, it's a good idea to include search terms in the first paragraph of a page.

Opinions vary, but some experts recommend generally constraining your use to three to five search terms per page, aiming for a keyword density of 2 to 6 percent. The longer your content, the more search terms you can include on a page. Just be careful that the language remains readable!

Naturally, your home page should include your most important search terms and your brand names; you may want to include as many as eight terms. As you drill down in the navigation, the nature of the search terms may change. For instance, give your *category pages* (additional pages in the top navigation), which have general overview information, two to four general, short phrases.

Detailed pages that describe your products or services generally appear at secondary or tertiary levels in your navigation. Keep the search terms on these pages focused on one topic per page, and optimize for one to three brand names or longer search terms related to your topic.

TIP

You generally don't get much mileage from search terms on boilerplate pages such as your Privacy Policy, Terms of Service, or Contact Us unless you modify the content to include relevant information.

Understanding tags and tag clouds

Tags are the social media equivalent of search terms (several keywords together, such as *New Mexico artists*). Tags are commonly used on blogs, social media, and content-heavy sites other than search engines to categorize content and help users find material.

REMEMBER

Tag clouds are simply a way to visualize either how often keywords appear in specific content or how often they are used by searchers. Keywords in a tag cloud are often arranged alphabetically or with common terms grouped and displayed as a paragraph. The more frequently used terms (minus common elements such as articles and prepositions) appear in the largest font, as shown in Figure 5-3.

Tag clouds can help you quickly grasp the popularity of particular topics, the terms that people most often use to find a topic, or the relative size or frequency of something, such as city population or usage of different browser versions.

FIGURE 5-3: This tag cloud from Wordle shows the frequency (popularity) of words used on Array Technologies' website.

Reproduced with permission of Array Technologies, Inc.

When you submit your site to social bookmarking or social news services, you're often asked to enter a list of helpful tags so that other people can search for your content. The first rule is to use tags that match your primary search terms and ensure that those terms appear within your text.

TIP

You can quickly generate a tag cloud for content by using a tool such as TagCrowd (`http://tagcrowd.com`) or Wordle (`www.wordle.net`). Simply paste in text from your website or enter the URL for your site and click to create a tag cloud. You can then enter the most frequently appearing words as the tags when you submit content to a social media service.

Some social media services display tag clouds created on a running basis to identify trending topics. Use these tag clouds on social media to help determine the popularity of various topics while you decide which content to post. You can also modify the tags you use to categorize your postings. Include or default to commonly used tags when you make your submission to increase the likelihood that your posting shows up in search results.

Maximizing Metatag Muscle

Search engines use the title and description metatags to help rank the relevance of a website, blog, or social media page to a search query. Historically, engines needed many types of *metadata* (data that describes a web page overall) to categorize a website, but now search engines need only the title and description metatags for that purpose. Search engines can automatically detect the rest of the information they need, and too many metatags just slow them down.

WARNING

The keywords metatag, though used more by human beings than by search engines, may be penalized by Yahoo!/Bing if the search terms don't also appear in the body copy for the page.

Title and page description tags have become even more important with the advent of social media. Facebook and some other platforms will pull content from these tags when a URL is shared.

REMEMBER

Don't confuse the term *metatags*, which refers to specific entries that appear in page source code, with the term *tags*, the label used to refer to assigned keywords in social media.

To view metatags for any website, choose View > Source in Internet Explorer; look for a similar command in other browsers. (You can also right-click a web page and choose View Source from the pop-up menu that appears.) A display appears, like the one shown in Figure 5-4, which shows the primary metatags for Array Technologies (`www.arraytechinc.com`).

FIGURE 5-4:
The page source for the home page of Array Technologies (top). Their home page is at the bottom.

Reproduced with permission of Array Technologies, Inc.

Note that the detail boxes shown in Figure 5-4 (bottom) are optimized with the same search terms that appear in the keyword tag. Note also the page title above the browser toolbar, which also includes three of the search terms. We talk more about this metatag in the section "Tipping the scales with the page title metatag," later in this chapter.

If you see no metatags in the page source for your own site, you may be in trouble. That could partially account for poor results in search engines.

You can usually insert metatags and <alt> tags for photos quite easily if you use a content management system (CMS) to maintain your website or if you use blog software. If you don't, you may need to ask your programmer or web developer for assistance.

Tipping the scales with the page title metatag

Perhaps the most important metatag, the page title appears above the browser toolbar when users are on a website. (Refer to Figure 5-4, bottom, to see where the title tag's output appears on the screen.) A good page title metatag includes one or more keywords followed by your company name. Select one or more search terms from the set of keywords you've assigned to that particular page.

Because browsers may truncate the title display, place the search term first. Although you can use a longer title tag, we suggest an average length for the title tag of seven to ten words and fewer than 70 characters. Some search engines may truncate title tags that are more than 55 characters long anyway. A long, long time ago, way back in the dinosaur age of the Internet, page names were used to index a website. That method is now unnecessary; it's an absolute waste of time to use a phrase such as *home page* rather than a search term in a page title. It's almost as big a waste of time as having no <title> tag. The <title> tag (*Commercial Solar Systems | Lowest Levelized Cost of Electricity | PV Trackers: Array Technologies. Inc.*) that appears in Figure 5-4 (top) is a good example.

Because longer, more descriptive title tags may work better for social sharing, don't obsess about length. It's always better to write a title tag that gets clicks!

Google and other search engines dislike multiple pages with identical metatags. Changing the <title> tag on each page is one of the easiest ways to handle this preference. Simply pull another relevant search term from your list of keywords and insert it in front of the company name in the <title> tag.

Pumping up page description metatags

The page description metatag appears as several sentences below the link to each site in natural search results. It's important to write an appealing page description because you may want to repeat this tag in all your social media profiles.

Some search engines truncate description metatags after as few as 115 characters. Historically, description metatags used to be 150 to 160 characters. Just in case, front-load the description with all the search terms from the set you've assigned to that page. Search engines display the first line of text when a page description metatag isn't available.

TIP

Why pass up a marketing opportunity? Just because your site appears near the top of search results, you have no guarantee that someone will click through to your site. Write your page description metatag as though it were ad copy, including a benefits statement and a call to action.

Figure 5-5 displays natural search results on Google with the page description for a category page of Array Technologies, Inc. Note the inclusion of search terms (for example, *PV trackers, commercial solar system*) from the keywords metatag in Figure 5-4 (top), the benefits statement *(easy-to-install)*, and the calls to action *(Become part of the energy movement. Contact us today)*.

Page description

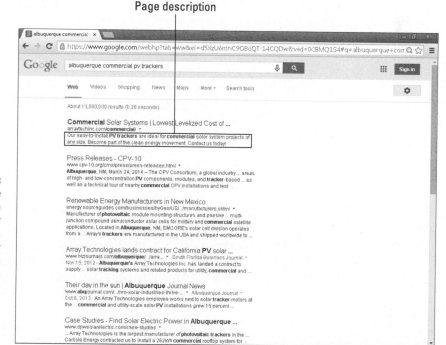

FIGURE 5-5:
The page description metatag for pages on the Array Technologies site appears in the natural search results for Albuquerque commercial PV trackers.

Source: www.google.com

Optimizing Your Site and Content for Search Engines

Optimization is the process of adjusting your site, blog, or social media profiles to play well with search algorithms. You optimize primarily by having plenty of relevant content, updating it often, and making sure that your web presence is easy for general and on-site search engines to discover with their spiders. The following sections cover a few of the most important tricks of the trade. For additional information on search engines and site optimization, check out some of the resources in Table 5-3.

TABLE 5-3 **Search Engine and Optimization Resources**

Name	URL	Description

Google Webmaster	`https://support.google.com/webmasters/bin/answer.py`
	
	`https://support.google.com/webmasters/answer/35291`
		Guidelines and suggestions for site optimization and SEO information for webmasters

Search Engine Guide	`www.searchengineguide.com/marketing.html`	Search engine articles, blog, marketing
Search Engine Journal	`www.searchenginejournal.com/seo-101-resources-learn-with-guides-tutorials-and-more/35740`	Best practices for URLs and SEO
Search Engine Land	`http://searchengineland.com`	Search engine news
Search Engine Watch (a publication of ClickZ)	`www.searchenginewatch.com`	Articles, tutorials, forums, blogs, SEO articles, and tips
Moz	`http://moz.com`	SEO learning resource with tools and community support
Urltrends	`www.urltrends.com`	Suite of SEO tools and reports

TIP

Because these changes will unfold over time, your best option is to watch your search engine results weekly and take action as needed. To stay up to date on Google's jitterbugs, waltzes, cha-chas, quick-step, and other dances, you might want to bookmark `http://searchengineland.com/library/google/google-algorithm-updates`. You can also monitor any of the sources in Table 5-3 for news.

Writing an optimized first paragraph

First and foremost, use the search terms you've assigned to each page in the first paragraph of text or the first paragraph of a blog posting. (See Figure 5-6.) Although most search engines now check the full pages of entire websites or blogs eventually, it's better to have search terms visible near the beginning of page text for faster indexing.

TIP

There's nothing like on-site social media, such as a blog or forum, to generate keyword-rich content for search engines to munch on. Best of all, other folks are helping you feed the beast! Generally speaking, keep your copy per page to 150 to 300 words for SEO purposes.

Figure 5-6 (top) shows a well-optimized posting and its source code (bottom) from the Changing Aging blog. Ecumen, a nonprofit organization specializing in senior housing and services, owns the blog. This entry (at www.ecumen.org/blog/seven-ways-pay-long-term-care) includes the phrase *long-term care* in its URL, post title, and text. Note all the social media chiclets above the post. The source code uses the same term in the title and page description metatags, and it indicates that the Ecumen Changing Aging blog has both an XML site map and an RSS feed.

TIP

Try to arrange your navigation so every page on your site is accessible with no more than three to four clicks from any other page.

Don't try to force more than a few terms into the first paragraph. If another phrase or two fits naturally, that's fine. Trying to cram more words into your text may render it unintelligible or jargon-loaded to human readers.

TECHNICAL
STUFF

No matter where the first paragraph of text appears on the page, place the text near the top of the source code. The text should appear above any tags for images, video, or Flash.

Updating often

Search engines, especially Google, love to "read" updated content. Regular updates are a sign that a website is loved and cared for, and easily updated content is one of many reasons for having a blog or content management system on your site. If changing content is simple and free, you're more likely to do it.

At least once a month, change a paragraph of content on your site. Include this task on your Social Media Activity Calendar (see Book 2, Chapter 4). If you can't commit to this task, at least ask your programmer to incorporate some kind of automatically updated material, whether it's a date-and-time stamp, a quote, or an RSS feed, for example.

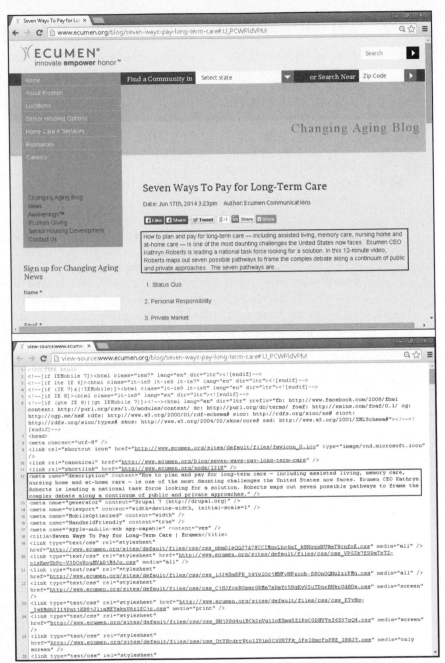

FIGURE 5-6:
Compare the blog post (top), which uses the keyword phrase long-term care in its title, page URL, and text to the source code (bottom).

Reproduced with permission of Ecumen

TIP

If you follow no other search optimization tips in this chapter, make sure that you follow at least these two: Update often, and optimize the first paragraph of text on every page.

Guess what? You score extra jelly beans in the relevance jar if your search terms appear in particular places on your website, in addition to your title and page description metatags. Follow these tips to optimize your web page or blog for your selected set of search terms (however, if they don't work naturally, don't force them):

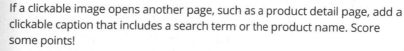

>> **Links:** Use the words from your set of search terms as *text links* or *anchor text* (words that form an active link to another internal page or external site). Link liberally within text, but don't waste valuable real estate on meaningless phrases such as *Learn more* or *Click here.* They don't do a darn thing for your search ranking. Make sure that internal links open in the same window, while external links open in a new window so users don't lose track of your site.

TIP

If a clickable image opens another page, such as a product detail page, add a clickable caption that includes a search term or the product name. Score some points!

>> **Headings:** Headlines and subheads help organize text and assist readers who are skimming your copy for the information they want. Headings that include your search terms can also improve your search engine ranking.

Onscreen, these words usually appear in bold and in a larger font size or different color (or both) from the body copy.

TECHNICAL STUFF

Headings must carry the <h1> to <h6> tags that define HTML headings, rather than appear as graphics. Search engines can't "read" words embedded in a picture.

>> **Navigation:** Search terms that appear as navigational items, whether for main or secondary pages, also earn extra relevance jelly beans. Like with headings, navigation must be in text form, not in graphic form.

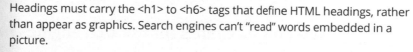

>> **URLs:** Include search terms in understandable URLs for your pages. URLs not only help with search engines, but also are often used as link text elsewhere on the web — for example, when shared on social media.

>> **Body text:** Use search terms intelligently in your content. Above all, make sure that the content makes sense to a human reader and is rich in information.

WARNING

Avoid *keyword stuffing:* Don't overload a page with repetitive search terms or a long list of different terms in an effort to juice your standing on search engine results pages. Not only do words out of context ring an alarm bell for Google, they make readers very unhappy. If you stick with well-written, natural English

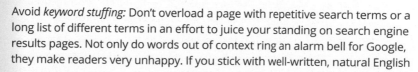

and useful content, you'll do just fine in both human and search engine results.

>> **Images and** *<alt>* **tags:** Not only may your images appear in image search results, they can also help with search engine results. The title, filename, caption, nearby text, and *<alt> tag* (the text that appears when hovering over an image on a PC) can contribute to a better ranking when they include a search term.

Sometimes you have to weigh the design considerations or limitations of your CMS or blog against search engine optimization needs. Some designers prefer the greater control and flexibility of font styles available in a graphic. Unfortunately, text in graphics is not readable by search engines. Ultimately, only you can decide what matters more to you.

WARNING

Under no circumstances should you implement *black hat* techniques, which are scams promoted as the search engine equivalent of a get-rich-quick scheme. For instance, don't even think about hiding search terms in the same color as the background, installing magic pixels, or any other shifty tricks. These techniques might get you blacklisted from search engines.

Making your site search engine friendly

In addition to trying the techniques in the preceding section, which apply at the page level, you can take specific actions to make your site, as a whole, friendly to search engines.

Avoiding elements that search engines hate

If you expect a search engine to rank your site or blog favorably, you have to give it something to work with. Computers may be getting smarter all the time, but they can't yet "read" pictures, videos, or soundtracks, let alone minds. They need to be fed a rich diet of words. The list of search engine "detestable content" is short, but they can all be avoided without harming your message:

>> **Graphics without descriptions:** As much as artists and photographers love pages without words, search engines hate them. Simple solutions can make your pictures search engine friendly: Provide an <alt> tag and/or caption; have text appear below the fold (as long as the text appears near the top of the code); or include a descriptive paragraph near the image. For an extra boost, include keywords in the filenames for photos.

>> **Flash animations:** Whether developers provide Flash animation because it's lucrative or because their clients demand it, not all search engines can index Flash content. (Not to mention that Macs and mobile phones detest it.)

Although Google can "read" Flash files, your best bet is to incorporate Flash much as you would incorporate a video — as an element on a page, not as an entire page.

» **Frames:** This old-fashioned (anything ten years old on the Internet is practically an antique) way of controlling the appearance of pages lets you modify content within a box. Unfortunately, search engines can't always see everything inside a frame or iFrame. Even Google can't guarantee that it will be able to associate content properly with the correct page URL. Many alternatives now exist, from tables to Cascading Style Sheets (CSS). If your developer insists on using frames, find a new developer.

» **Substantially duplicate content at different URLs:** The content may not be malicious; maybe it's just printer-only versions of your website. Be sure to delete old versions of pages that have been replaced. Even if they sit in archives, search engines may try to index these pages and reduce your page rank for duplicate information. Send your programmer to https://support.google.com/webmasters/answer/66359 for direction about how to handle this situation. On the other hand, if Google thinks the duplication is deliberate, your site may be penalized or removed from the index.

» **Splash pages:** This misguided attempt to design a website as though it were a book with a cover may do real harm to site traffic. Generally, a site loses half its audience every time a click is required. Why cut your prospect list in half before you even have a chance to explain your benefits? Splash pages often consist of beautiful images or animations that make a statement about a company but carry no content or navigation. If you use rich media on a splash page, make sure to include a regular HTML link to a text-based page for search purposes.

TECHNICAL STUFF

Often found on sites of companies specializing in entertainment, web development, architecture, arts and crafts, or graphic design, splash pages usually offer viewers an option to skip the introduction and an arrow cuing them to click to enter the "real" site. The simpler solution is to not include a splash page on your site. If you insist on having a splash or entry page, at least don't annoy your visitors. Direct the navigational link for Home to the main page of real content, not to the splash page. With a bit of clever naming, you may be able to get search engine spiders to crawl over the first page of content and ignore the splash page.

Configuring URLs

The best URLs are readable and might include one of your search terms or a descriptive title: www.yourdomain.com/social-media-small-businesses. Using a search term from your set of keywords for your web or blog page earns you another point for relevance and lets users know what to expect. At least try to keep the URLs as readable text, as in www.yourdomain.com/pages/socialmedia/article1234.htm.

If the content in this entire section makes your eyes glaze over, just hand this chapter to your developer.

Problems with page URLs tend to occur when they're automatically assigned by a content management system (CMS) or when the pages are created dynamically. Those URLs tend to look like gobbledygook: www.yourdomain.com/shop/AS-djfa-16734-QETR. Although search engines can review these URLs, these addresses do nothing for your search engine ranking and aren't helpful to users.

You can improve your URL configuration several other ways:

>> Use hyphens to separate words instead of using underscores, spaces, or plus signs.

>> Keep your URLs as short as possible. Make your URL easier to copy and paste by minimizing the number of words and trailing slashes.

>> Don't use database-generated URLs or pages created on the fly (called *dynamic URLs*) that include multiple non-alphanumeric characters: www.yourdomain.com/cgi-bin/shop.pl?shop=view_category=ASDFJ%20 &subcategory=XYZ%6734. Search engines are less fussy than they used to be, but many still have problems indexing URLs that have more than four non-alphanumeric characters. Some still have problems with only three such characters.

Be careful when redesigning a blog or website, especially if you're changing developers or platforms. If the existing site is already doing well in search engines, try to preserve its URLs. Not all transitions to a new platform accommodate this strategy. Ask your programmer before you begin.

A badly configured URL may simply not be indexed. This problem can become significant with product databases on e-commerce sites, especially when you want every individual product detail page to appear in search engines. Note that this doesn't apply to tracking ID numbers appended following a ? to identify the source of a link. (For more on tracking URLs see Book 6, Chapter 1.)

Indexing a site

You can easily create a virtual path to ensure that search engines crawl your entire site. A virtual path of links is especially important in two cases:

>> When the top and left navigational elements are graphics, making it impossible for search engines to know which pages are really on the site

>> When you have a large, deep, database-driven site without links to all pages easily available in the navigation

For a small site that has graphical navigation, you have a couple of simple fixes. You can create a parallel series of linkable main pages in the footer of your site or create a navigational breadcrumb trail at the top of the page, as shown in Figure 5-7. Either way can help both search engines and human beings know where they are within your site structure.

A *breadcrumb trail* (think Hansel and Gretel) helps users track where they are on a complex website. It typically consists of a series of page links that extend horizontally across each page, just above the content. Breadcrumb trails, which may either display the site structure or the actual navigation path a user has followed, usually look something like this:

> Home page > Main section page > Internal page > Detail page

TECHNICAL STUFF

Put these links in a Server Side Include (SSI) within the footer to ensure that links are displayed consistently on all pages. You then make future changes in only one place (other than in the site itself, of course).

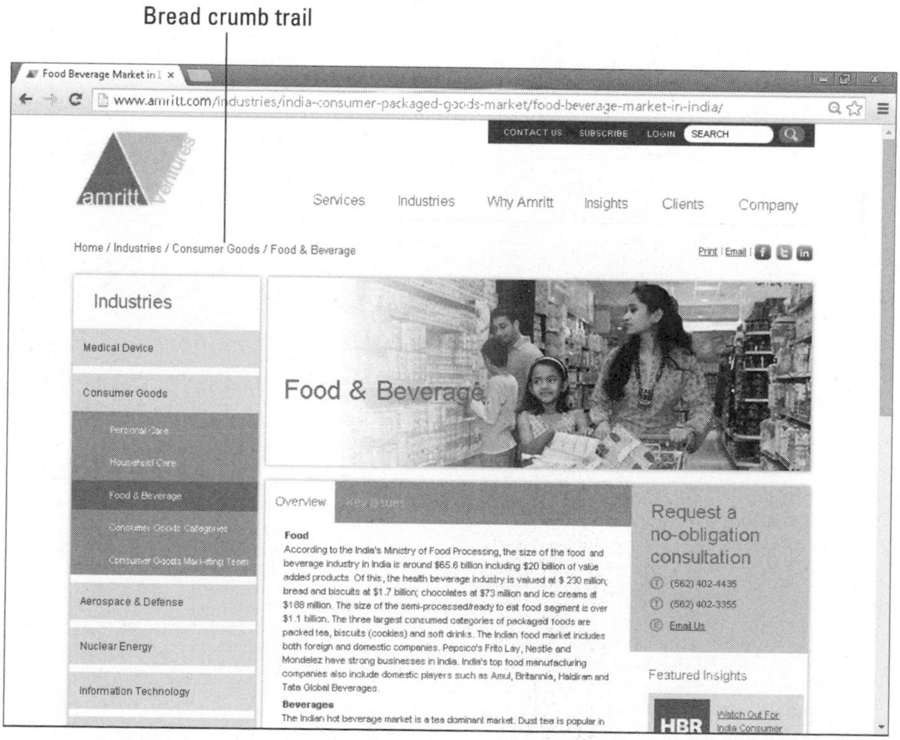

Bread crumb trail

FIGURE 5-7: Breadcrumb trails help both search-engine robots and real people navigate your site.

Reproduced with permission of Amritt Ventures, Inc.

For a site that has a significant number of pages, especially on several tiers, the best solution is to include a linkable site map or site index, shown in Figure 5-8. It looks a lot like a junior high school outline, which is a perfectly fine solution for both search engine friendliness and site usability.

Another solution exists for very large database-driven sites and large stores. Sitemap (XML) feeds that connect directly to Google or Yahoo!/Bing provide current content to all your pages. Direct your programmer to www.xml-sitemaps.com, https://help.yahoo.com/kb/yahoo-merchant-solutions/enable-sitemaps-sln19495.html, www.bing.com/webmaster/help/bing-xml-sitemap-plugin-f50bebf5, or www.google.com/support/webmasters/bin/topic.py?topic=8476 for more information. If content on your site doesn't change very often, you can update these feeds manually every month. If you have continually changing inventory and other content, have your programmer upload these feeds automatically, at least once a day, using RSS.

If you want to index your site to see what pages you have, try one of these free tools:

>> **Bing Webmaster Tools:** Use the Index Explore tool within the Reports & Data section to view how Bing sees your site (accessible in the top navigation after you log in).

FIGURE 5-8:
Page links on a site index provide easy access to all pages on the site.

Reproduced with permission of The Fat Finch

>> **Google Index Status page:** This tool provides stats about which URLs Google has indexed for your site over the past year. To get to this tool, sign in to Google Webmaster Tools at `www.google.com/webmasters/tools`.

>> **Xenu's Link Sleuth:** Download and run this link-verification program (at `http://home.snafu.de/tilman/xenulink.html`). In the results, click the link labeled Site Map of Valid HTML Pages with a Title.

Maximizing site speed

Google now includes download time in its methods for ranking websites in search results. Companies continue to post pages that take too long to download, testing viewers' patience and occasionally overwhelming mobile networks. Try to keep sites to less than 300KB to 500KB per page, especially now that 20 percent of website visits are from smartphones.

High-resolution photos are usually the main culprits when a page is too large. It isn't the number of photos, but rather the total size of files on a page that counts. A couple of tips can help reduce the size of your page:

>> When saving photos to use online, choose the Save for Web option, found in most graphics programs. Stick to JPEG or GIF files, which work well online, and avoid larger, slower-to-load TIFF and BMP files, which are intended for print.

>> Post a thumbnail with a click-to-view action for the larger version in a pop-up window. Be sure to save the larger image for the web. (Refer to the first bullet.)

TIP

Check the page speed and time for your home page for free at sites such as `https://developers.google.com/speed/pagespeed/`, `www.webpagetest.org`, or `www.websiteoptimization.com/services/analyze`, or check out `www.compuware.com/en_us/application-performance-management/performance-test-center.html`, which tests both mobile and web download times. Call your developer if changes are needed.

Optimizing for local search campaigns

Local search has obvious value for brick-and-mortar retail businesses using the web and social media to drive traffic to their stores. However, it's just as valuable for local service businesses such as plumbers, or even for non-local businesses seeking online customers from a particular region.

Local optimization is needed for your site to appear near the top of results in spite of geolocation devices on smartphones (not always turned on), geographic tagging of images on Flickr and other photo-sharing sites, or the localization settings on Google results.

Chances are good that your business is not the only one of a particular type in your city or neighborhood. Localization is absolutely critical for restaurants, tourism, hospitality, and entertainment businesses.

The concepts used for local optimization on websites apply equally well to social media:

>> **Optimize search terms by city, region, neighborhood, or even zip code.** Rather than use a locality as a separate keyword, use it in a search term phrase with your product or service.

>> **Include location in any pay-per-click ads.** This is equally true whether your ads appear on a search engine, Facebook, or other social media.

>> **Post your business on search maps such as Yahoo! Local, Google My Business, Bing Places for Business Portal, and MapQuest on Yext.com (which is a paid site).** Consider using one or more of your social media pages as site link extensions (additional links that appear following your page description in search engine results). Appearing on search maps is absolutely critical for mobile search, as discussed in the following section.

>> **Take advantage of local business directories, events calendars, and review sites to spread the word about your company and its social media pages.** In some cases, you might want to use one of your social media pages instead of your primary website as the destination link. Most directories are also excellent sources of high-value inbound links.

>> **Use specialized local social media with a geographic component.** These options include social channels such as Foursquare, Meetup, or Everplaces.

Optimizing for mobile search

There is no question that mobile is growing faster than a cake in a hot oven. There is also no question that more people are shopping in unconventional locations (yes, while using the bathroom) than ever before in the history of civilization.

Here is what you need to do to win:

>> **Make sure your site is responsive.** You site needs to look good on multiple resolutions, from iPhone 6 to iPad mini to Android. You either need an entire site rebuild or you can have your webmaster edit your CSS.

>> **Make sure the phone numbers on your website are clickable from a mobile phone.** Have you ever tried to contact a business from your phone and the number on the site is an image that you have to remember to dial on your phone? You know that it's annoying, so avoid making your prospective clients do the same.

>> **Make sure your site has less than five seconds to load.** For many users, cellphone Internet isn't as fast as their home computer, which is why you need to check your site speed and do what you can to make it faster. A lot of times, you can simply replace large images to improve the speed.

>> **Make sure users can find your address, phone number, or contact form in less than three seconds.** Otherwise you risk getting flushed down the drain!

Take the time to test your site on multiple mobile devices to verify that you've taken care of these points.

Building Effective Inbound Links

An *inbound link* from another site to your website, blog, or social media page acts as a recommendation. Its presence implicitly suggests that visitors to the original site might find useful content on yours. Testimonial links are particularly important for social media, where they are measured in rating stars, number of views, retweets, Likes, and favorites. These recommendations enhance credibility and build traffic because they encourage other viewers to visit your original post.

Conversely, an *external link* goes from your page to someone else's, providing the same referral function. All these links form a web of connections in cyberspace. A site may require a *reciprocal link* back to its site before it will post one to yours.

It sounds simple. However, identifying places that will link to yours and getting them to post the link can be quite time-consuming.

Why bother? Although all search engines track the number of sites that link to yours, Google (and only Google) uses the number and quality of these inbound links to determine your position on search engine results pages. In essence, Google runs the world's largest popularity contest, putting to shame every high school's search for a prom king and queen.

TECHNICAL STUFF

Sometimes companies link to `http://yourdomain.com` and sometimes to `http://www.yourdomain.com`. Search engines consider them separate pages and may not give full credit for your inbound links. Do a permanent 301 redirect from one to the other. (Google likes www domains better.) Alternatively, you can accomplish this task from Google Webmaster Central, but it applies to only Google. Similarly, use Webmaster Central to make your site more secure with HTTPS secure protocols instead of standard HTTP or SSL conventions. Google is so committed to user security that it has started using HTTPS as a signal worth a few extra points in search engine ranking.

Google PageRank

A popularity contest is truly an apt metaphor for PageRank because not all inbound links are equal in the eyes of Google. Links from .edu and .org domains carry extra credit, as do links you receive from other sites that Google ranks as having good content and good traffic. Think of them as votes from the in crowd.

Google factors hundreds of variables including link quantity, link quality, keyword use, content, social metrics, site traffic, and brand visibility into its proprietary PageRank algorithm.

The algorithm ranks pages on an earthquake-style scale from 0 to 10. (Google search and *The New York Times* both have a page rank of 9.) Empirically speaking, a Google PageRank (PR) of 5 is usually enough to place your site on the first page of search results — with no guarantees, of course. Because PageRank adjustments are made only a few times each year, the visible PR may be slightly out of date. TechRanger suggests these interpretations of PageRank:

- » **PR0 or ?:** Pages that haven't been ranked or have been penalized.
- » **PR1:** Pages that Google has indexed and checked for correctness.
- » **PR2:** A site is interesting and has potential.
- » **PR3:** A page is a good informational resource, such as many news or business pages.
- » **PR4:** Pages that are starting to break out from the pack as a noted authority.
- » **PR5:** Pages more likely to appear near the top of search results once they reach this score.
- » **PR6, 7, or 8:** Pages of clear and proven authority.
- » **PR9 or 10:** Only the *crème de la crème* (Google, YouTube, Twitter, and so on).

If you're serious about SEO, install the Google PageRank tool on your browser so that you can quickly check the PageRank of your site or blog, and that of your competitors. The PageRank display is built into Google's Chrome browser, or you can download it for Internet Explorer at www.google.com/toolbar/ie/index. html. (The Google toolbar may not work with all versions of all browsers; it is not supported on Firefox.)

To install PageRank on your Google toolbar, follow these steps:

1. **On most browsers, choose View > Toolbars > Google Toolbar, and if that option is not already checked, do so.**

   The Google toolbar should now be visible. If the PageRank tool isn't visible on the Google toolbar, you must enable it.

2. **From the Tools tab on most browsers, select the Page Rank check box and click Save.**

3. **If you're using Chrome, click the three-bar icon at the far right instead of following Step 2.**

4. **From the drop-down list that appears, choose Settings. On the next page, select Extensions from the left navigation.**

5. **If PageRank appears in the list, click the check box to enable it.**

   If PageRank doesn't appear, click the Get More Extensions link, which appears below the list, and search for PageRank Status. Alternatively, you can navigate directly to https://chrome.google.com/webstore/category/ extensions to search. Select an extension to enable from the list.

   You now see the PageRank tool on the Google toolbar. (See Figure 5-9 to see the Google PageRank tool in action.)

6. **To see the page rank for a website, enter its domain name into the address box on your browser and wait for the page to load.**

7. **Hover your mouse pointer on the PageRank tool until the pop-up box that displays page rank results appears in the toolbar.**

   For more information, see https://support.google.com/toolbar/ answer/79837.

TIP

To check page rank for multiple competitors' sites or potential inbound links at the same time, try the free tool at http://multipagerank.com.

Page Rank icon

Additional Page Rank information

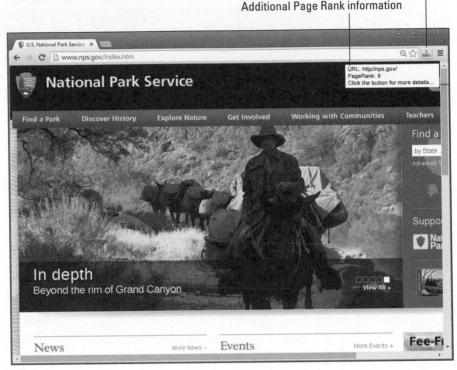

URL: http//nps.gov/
PageRank: 8
Click the button for more details...

Source: www.nps.gov

FIGURE 5-9:
The National
Park Service
has a Google
page rank of 8.

Knowing what makes a good inbound link

In a nutshell, good inbound links (sometimes called *backlinks*) come from sites that have these characteristics:

>> **Relevance:** The quickest way to determine relevance is to see whether the other site shares a search term or tag with your site. Use Google's search function to check, or view the source code on their pages.

>> **A decent amount of traffic:** Check www.alexa.com or www.quantcast.com to estimate traffic on other sites.

>> **Your target market:** Whether or not a link helps with PageRank, links from other appropriate sites help with branding and deliver qualified traffic to your site.

>> **A good Google PageRank:** Look for a score of PR5 or higher in the PageRank tool. Higher-ranking sites, which often have high traffic volume and good content value, are considered more credible references; they pass along *link juice* (share page ranking) from their site to yours.

Lists of inbound links differ on different search engines. Because Google counts only sites with a high PageRank, the list on Google is always the shortest.

TIP

To see your own or others' inbound links on a particular engine, enter link http://yourdomainname.com (where *yourdomainname*.com is replaced by your own domain name) in the search box for Google. For Yahoo!/Bing, you can check inbound links from their Webmaster tools at www.bing.com/webmaster/help/using-the-inbound-links-tool-a75f3640.

Hunting for inbound links

No matter how hard you try, it's difficult to find good sites from which you can request an inbound link to your own website or blog. Try link-checking tools such as the Link Popularity Checker (www.checkyourlinkpopularity.com) or Majestic (https://majestic.com, shown in Figure 5-10), as well as the tools listed in Table 5-4.

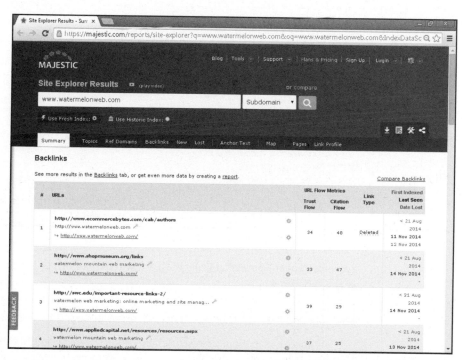

FIGURE 5-10:
For each site it indexes, Majestic displays a list of backlinks.

TABLE 5-4   # Free Inbound Link Resources

Name	URL	Description
Alexa	`www.alexa.com`	Link checker, related links, clickstream, and more; free version includes a site overview with global and U.S. ranks, demographics, audience, location, search traffic, top keywords, inbound links, and related links.
ClickZ	`www.clickz.com/search?per_page=20&date=this_year&query=linking`	Articles on link campaigns.
LinkPopularity	`http://linkpopularity.com`	Link checker for Google, Bing, and Yahoo!
Majestic	`https://majestic.com`	Check backlinks and history on other sites in bulk.
MultiPageRank Checker	`http://multipagerank.com`	Check Google PageRank and Alexa for multiple websites simultaneously.
Quantcast	`www.quantcast.com`	Audience Also Likes function.
Search Engine Colossus	`www.searchenginecolossus.com`	Directory of international search engines.
Search Engine Guide	`www.searchengineguide.com/searchengines.html`	Meta-index of topical search engines.
Search Engine Journal	`www.searchenginejournal.com/use-social-media-link-building-tool/80331`	Article on how to receive backlinks from social media.
WhoLinks2Me	`www.wholinks2me.com/`	Backlink analysis.
Yext	`www.yext.com`	Check which directories link to your website.

You can hunt for potential links with a few tried-and-true techniques. Try looking at the following:

>> Inbound links to other sites that rank highly in Google on your search terms.

Be sure that your company truly has something in common with the other site. Shared terms may not be enough — there's a big difference between companies that run a fish restaurant and those that sell lead-free weights for catching fish.

>> Inbound links to your competitors' sites.

>> If data is available, the Alexa sections What Sites Are Related To and/or Upstream Sites for your competitors' websites.

>> The resource lists of outbound links found on competitors' sites or other highly ranked sites.

>> Industry-based business directories.

>> Yellow Pages and map sites.

>> Local business directories.

>> Blog-specific directories.

>> Trade associations and other organizations you belong to or sponsor.

>> Inbound links to suppliers' websites, including your web development and hosting company.

>> Inbound links to sites owned by distributors, clients, customers, or affiliates.

>> The implementation of cross-links with all your social media sites (even though some of these don't help with PageRank).

>> Blogs you recommend in your blogroll from which you could request a link back.

>> Inbound links to related, but not directly competing, businesses that your target audience might also visit.

REMEMBER

Prequalify every potential link. Visit every link site to ensure that it accepts links, is truly relevant, has a Google PageRank of 5 or higher, and represents the quality and audience you want.

WARNING

Stay away from *link farms* (sites that exist only to sell links), *web rings* (a closed loop of companies that agree to link to each other), and *gray-market link sites* (sites that sell links at exorbitant prices and guarantee a certain result). Your site can be exiled from search engines for using them. Besides, they don't raise your PageRank!

Implementing your link campaign

You need to email requests for a link to each of the potential sites you identify. Try for at least 50 links and hope that 30 of them come through. There's no upper limit — the more, the better.

You might want to create a spreadsheet to track your link requests. Create columns for these elements:

>> Domain name

>> Appearance URL

>> Submission URL or email address

>> Submission date

>> URL of the landing page you asked others to link to

>> Reciprocal link requirement

>> Date you checked to see whether a link was posted

Don't be afraid to group spreadsheet rows by target market. For instance, if you sell products for toddlers, you might have a group of links for sites used by single parents and another group for sites used by day-care centers.

TIP

Break this task into bite-size pieces so that it doesn't become overwhelming. On your Social Media Activity Calendar (found in Book 2, Chapter 4), limit the search-and-submission task to only five to ten links per week.

After you qualify prospective links and add them to your spreadsheet, follow the directions on each site to submit your URL or email your request to the site owner.

Reaping other links from social media

Another easy way to build inbound links is by distributing (*syndicating*) content, as described in Book 2, Chapter 1. By repurposing content on multiple social media sites, you not only increase your audience, you also increase the number of inbound links.

Taking advantage of the many places to post links on social media pages not only drives traffic to multiple elements of your web presence, it also improves your search engine rankings in the process.

REMEMBER

Somewhere on your website or blog — at least on the About Us or Contact page — display a list of links to all your profiles on social media services, along with buttons for ShareThis and Google's +1. This form of passive link-building can pay off big-time with improved ranking in search results.

The more places these links appear, the better. You can also repeat text links to your social media pages in your linkable footer.

TIP

Don't be shy! Include calls to action to share your web page in the body copy of ads or e-newsletters. These links don't always have to hide their charms in the header or footer.

Here are a few other ideas for laying down a link:

>> Every profile on a social network has a place to enter at least your web address and blog address, if you have one. If possible, link to both. The links in profiles usually provide link juice, although the ones in status updates usually don't.

>> Include your web address when you make comments on other people's blogs, post reviews on recommendation sites, or submit someone else's news story. You may have to work it into the content. Use at least yourcompanyemail address@yourdomain.com for branding reasons.

>> Include your company name for branding and your web address for linking when you post to groups on any social networking site, as long as it's appropriate, relevant, and not too self-promotional.

WARNING

Read the terms of service on each site to be sure that you comply with requirements for use of email addresses, submissions, and links.

>> Post events on LinkedIn, Myspace, Facebook, and elsewhere with a link to your site for more information.

>> Include a share button to encourage additional distribution. People who receive content they like often pass it along or link to it from their own pages or blogs.

>> Be sure to post crosslinks on newsletters and on all your social media profiles to all your other web pages, including to your primary site and your blog.

REMEMBER

Now that social media are included in ordinary search results, using search terms consistently can help you occupy more than one slot in search engine results pages. You can see an example in Figure 5-11.

Creating a resource page for outbound links

One item to include when optimizing your site for search engines is a Link Resources page — by that name or any other — for external or outbound links.

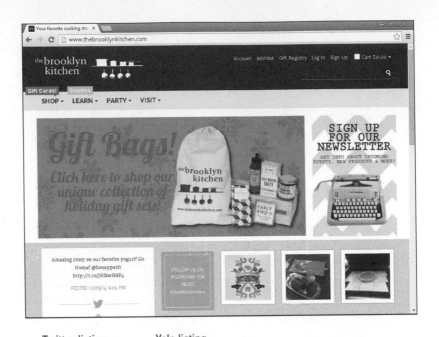

Twitter listing   Yelp listing

Google+ listing

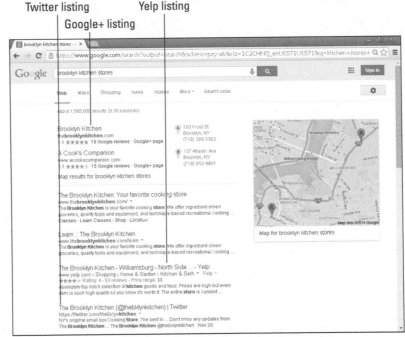

FIGURE 5-11:
The Brooklyn Kitchen (top) earns high placement in Bing search results (bottom) with postings from Yelp reviews, its Twitter feed, and its Google+ page.

You need this page in order to post reciprocal links to other sites, but also to help viewers find useful, neutral information on .edu, .gov, and .org domains. Nestling reciprocal links within an annotated list of informational sites makes reciprocal links less noticeable and less self-serving. Good ideas about places for neutral links to appear are described in this list:

» Sites with information about materials used in your products or how to care for them

» Educational sites discussing the services you provide, such as *feng shui* for offices, the benefits of massage, or tips on tax deductions

» Sites for trade associations and other business organizations to which you belong

» Local, state, and federal government sites whose regulations or procedures may affect your business or customers

» Nonprofit sites that share your values; for example, sites talking about recycling electronics or supporting entrepreneurs in developing countries

» Sites that talk about the history of your business or industry, or the local history of your brick-and-mortar storefront

» Other sites that may interest visitors to your site; for example, a hotel site that links to a local dining guide or events calendar

» HomeinSantaFeNM, for example, links to helpful sites at http://homes insantafenm.com/resources (see Figure 5-12)

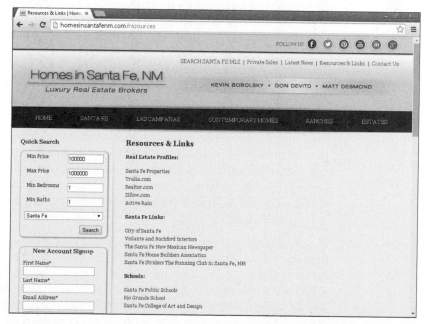

FIGURE 5-12:
Homesin SantaFeNM.com offers visitors helpful external links to related sites.

Reproduced with permission of Matt Desmond

A good starting place for neutral outbound links is to see inbound links for a high-ranked competitor. Enter its domain name into the search field on Alexa; then scroll down to the "What Sites Link To" section to see the total number of inbound links to that domain, and the top identity of the top five inbound links. Scroll down farther to the section "What Sites Are Related To" to see ten related links, and perhaps more importantly, a list of Categories with Related Sites, which you can use as a search string to find other potential links.

Optimizing Social Media for Search Engines

Here's the good news: Everything covered earlier in this chapter about using SEO for your website or blog applies to other social media, too. You still have to implement the techniques, but you can save time by reusing search terms, metatags, inbound links, and optimized text.

Every search engine has its own rules. You may need to tweak your terms for not only general search engines, but also internal search engines on specific social media services.

Placing your search terms on social media

Start by reviewing your research for keywords and phrases. Decide on a primary set of four to six terms that best describe your company. Because your search terms must still relate to your content, you may want to reuse other sets for individual posts from your SEO research, mix them up, or include additional terms not optimized on your primary site.

You can place these terms in many locations:

>> **Tags:** *Tags,* the social media equivalents of keywords, are assigned to specific content. Because many social media services place a limit on the number of tags that can be assigned to a given piece of content, pick a few from your primary set of search terms and select others (for example, brands, products, market, or competition) from your secondary list or elsewhere that are specific to your content.

If you're pulling tags out of thin air, remember to confirm which synonyms are most popular with the users of that service. For example, do people search for *Barack* or *Obama* or *president*? Use a keyword-selection tool for websites listed earlier in this chapter (refer to Table 5-2) or check a tag cloud (discussed in the section "Understanding tags and tag clouds," earlier in this chapter), if it exists, on the service you're using for the latest trends in tag usage.

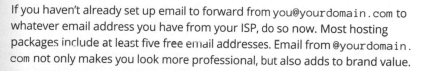
>> **Profiles:** Just about every form of social media asks you to establish an account. Most profiles ask for a brief description of your company and location, as well as the URLs for your website and blog. Work your primary set of keywords and brands into your profile and any other place you can comfortably integrate them, including featured products, department names, the marketing tagline, and staff bios.

Occasionally, a service requests only your email address. Of course, you use the one with your domain name in it.

**TECHNICAL
STUFF**

If you haven't already set up email to forward from you@yourdomain.com to whatever email address you have from your ISP, do so now. Most hosting packages include at least five free email addresses. Email from @yourdomain.com not only makes you look more professional, but also adds to brand value.

>> **Page content, status updates, and comments:** Obviously, you should include search terms in the first paragraph of text for each blog post. They don't need to be part of your primary set of terms, so you have some creative flexibility. Incorporate search terms in updates and comments, too, to increase the likelihood of being found in on-site search results.

>> **Metatags, titles, and headlines:** Use search terms from your list in the title of your blog or page name; in the title of your post; in <alt> tags, captions, or descriptions for images; and within metatags. Each service handles these elements a little differently, as we discuss in the later sections on individual services.

WARNING

If you use an automated service such as Hootsuite to update everything at one time, you may pay a bit of a penalty because Google considers automated, scheduled posts to be anonymous and doesn't index them. In addition, long, duplicate posts might set off warning bells. (There's no other evidence that search engines are penalizing third-party interfaces.) You should be okay if you combine scheduled posts through a service with personalized, spontaneous posts at other times. Facebook, and perhaps other social media platforms, may also see automated posts as spam; one study by HubSpot showed that Hootsuite posts got fewer Likes and clicks than manually posted ones, but that might have to do with the quality of the posts, not just the source. Only you can weigh the pros and cons based on your available time, staffing levels, and campaign objectives.

Optimizing blogs

Because blogs are basically websites in a different format, the same principles of site optimization and configuration apply, including the need for inbound links and cross-promotion on social media services. Hard-learned lessons and best practices truly pay off because search engines crawl frequently updated blogs at least daily.

Integrate your domain name with your blog URL (http://yourblog.yourdomain.com) or buy a separate, related domain name (http://yourcompanyblog.com), even if a third-party server hosts your blogs. For SEO purposes, you must own your own blog domain name. A blog at www.mycompanyblog.blogspot.com or www.typepad.com/mycompanyblog isn't acceptable.

Blogs are primo link bait. The casual sharing of relevant, text-based links within posts, the use of *blogrolls* (bloggers' linkable recommendations of other blogs), and related thematic material attract inbound links like black jackets attract white cat fur. With all that link juice, plus rapidly updated content, many blogs quickly zoom to Page One in search engine results.

Review all requests for inclusion on your blogroll or reciprocal link offers. Make sure that the requesting site is relevant, has a decent page rank, and is one that you feel good about recommending.

Different blog platforms operate somewhat differently, leading to some confusion on the part of bloggers trying to optimize sites for search engines. Whatever your platform, the same methods you follow for websites still apply, with a multitude of additions:

>> Include keywords from your primary list in your blog name, such as http://yourcompany.com/social_media_blog. The blog name should appear with an HTML <h1> tag on only the front page. On other pages of your blog, the heading level can be as low as <h3>.

>> Include keywords in individual titles for each post. Use these keywords in the <title> tag in the source code for that entry, as well as in the page URL. Put those titles at the HTML <h1> level.

>> Include primary keywords in the first sentence of content, which becomes the page description metatag by default, unless you write one manually. Use your secondary keywords in the body of your post.

>> Fill out the tag box with your keywords, but do so judiciously. You don't need to bloat your blog tags with synonyms or terms you don't need to rank on.

>> Incorporate search terms in anchor text for links on your blog.

>> Use <alt> tags, captions, and descriptions with search terms for any images or media you upload to your blog.

>> Post rich, appealing content with search terms regularly and often.

>> Make sure the search engine spiders can crawl your blog easily by including a side navigation column on all pages and by offering access to archives and previous posts from all pages of your blog.

>> Include a linkable breadcrumb trail that includes keywords without reaching the point of overstuffing.

>> Provide internal text links to your own related posts, especially to relevant ones that are already ranking well.

>> Submit your blog to blog directories and RSS submission sites. Two excellent lists are at http://web-marketing.masternewmedia.org/rsstop55-best-blog-directory-and-rss-submission-sites and www.toprankblog.com/rss-blog-directories.

>> Use your blogroll as a resource — just having a blogroll isn't enough. Contact other bloggers to request a backlink or offer a reciprocal appearance on your blogroll in exchange for a backlink. Just be careful that you don't inadvertently create a link farm. For more on blogroll links, see www.britmums.com/2014/07/blogs-sidebar-blogroll-yet.

>> Get backlinks to your blog with *trackbacks* (an automated way of notifying other bloggers that you've referenced their blog) or by posting comments on other blogs. Not all blogging hosts support trackbacks.

>> Create an XML site map and submit it to search engines, just as you would for your website.

>> Use *permalinks* (permanent links) to maintain blog URLs permanently.

>> Use analytics tools to monitor traffic and user behavior.

TIP

If you need quick suggestions for good blog keywords, install the Wordtracker Keywords Tool (it offers a free seven-day trial) at www.wordtracker.com/find-the-best-keywords. It sits next to your blog editor on the screen so that you can consider tag suggestions while you write. Alternatively, return to Google's free AdWords Keyword Planner, as described in the section "Choosing the right search terms," earlier in this chapter.

TIP

If you're an experienced blog writer, your posts are probably already written with one designated search term in mind. Review your top 10 to 15 most-viewed posts, make a list of the keywords you used for them, and use that list as input into the AdWords Keyword Planner.

TECHNICAL STUFF

Long blog pages with a lot of responses, including those from spammers, may end up with too many outbound links. Ask your programmer to place an HTML nofollow attribute in the code just before links from comments to discourage people from leaving fake comments that include links to their own sites in hopes of increasing their own search rankings.

Optimizing WordPress

Although plug-ins for WordPress templates can be set to automatically generate title and page description metatags, you may want to tweak the automated SEO results for important posts. Auto-generation is fine for mundane posts or when you're short on time.

For more flexibility and additional optimization features, try the Yoast plug-in at `http://wordpress.org/plugins/wordpress-seo` or the All in One SEO Pack at `http://wordpress.org/extend/plugins/all-in-one-seo-pack`.

Make your WordPress life easier by searching the list of WordPress plug-ins for items you need at `http://wordpress.org/plugins`. Compare plug-ins carefully — they're not all alike.

Here are a few things you can do to optimize your WordPress blog posts:

>> **Swap elements of the blog post title.** Reverse the WordPress plug-in default arrangement by putting the post title first, which contains keywords, followed by the name of your blog.

>> **Use a consistent format for keyword-rich page titles on all pages.** You can set up the format once in your template and apply it everywhere by using the Yoast or All in One SEO Pack plug-ins.

>> **Insert a longer title description, with more search terms, into the image title field.** WordPress automatically uses the title you give an image as its <alt> tag. Unless you insert a longer title description with more search terms into the Image Title field, WordPress uses the filename as the image title.

When you write a post and add tags, WordPress automatically adds your tags to its global tag system. The global system determines the WordPress list of hot topics in real time. Users can click any word in the real-time tag cloud to view the most recent posts for that tag.

WordPress, like other blogs, often duplicates content by showing the same posts on archive, author, category, index, and tag pages. To remove duplicate content, which can have a negative effect on SEO, create a robots.txt file. See `www.problogger.net/archives/2013/08/14/how-to-stop-your-wordpress-blog-getting-penalized-for-duplicate-content`.

Optimizing Blogger

Contrary to myth, Google doesn't necessarily give preference to blogs hosted on its own service, Blogger. However, Blogger poses some unique advantages and challenges:

>> Blogger templates place <h1> through <h6> tags into the source code through the What You See Is What You Get (WYSIWYG) interface, thereby helping with SEO. You can easily adjust page titles and blog names for the correct heading level in page templates.

>> Blogger lacks theme-related categories, which makes it a little more difficult for you and for theme-based SEO. To overcome that problem, create permalinks that include your categories or directory names. We discuss permalinks in the following section.

>> Because Blogger doesn't provide a related-links feature, create that list of related text links within or at the bottom of each post. These links should lead to your other postings on the same topic. Or take advantage of unlimited sidebar space to create a separate section for related links above your blogroll.

>> Use labels on Blogger to categorize your posts. On the page where you're writing a post, click the Settings tab in the right column. Select Labels from the drop-down menu. In the box that appears, enter the terms you want to use, separated by commas, and click Done. For future posts, just click Labels in the drop-down menu. All the terms in the box appear below your post when it's published.

>> Blogger defaults to weekly archiving, but the timeframes for archiving are malleable. Adjust the timeframe based on your volume of posts and comments to maintain good keyword density. If you post only weekly, it might make more sense to archive monthly. For an extremely active blog, you might want to archive daily.

>> Creating text links is easy, so use your keywords in links whenever possible.

Assigning permalinks

Because most blogs are created on dynamic, database-driven platforms, their posts don't have fixed web addresses. Links to individual posts disappear after the posting is archived and no longer available on a page. Obviously, that's bad news for inbound links and SEO.

Permalinks (short for *permanent links*) solve that problem by assigning a specific web address to each post. Then individual posts can be bookmarked or linked to from elsewhere, forever.

Most blog software programs, such as WordPress and Blogger, already offer this as an option; you just have to use it. If your blog doesn't offer it, you can generate permalinks at `www.generateit.net/mod-rewrite`, although you may need help from your programmer to install them. Try to avoid links that look like this: `www.yourblog.com/?p=123`. Instead, choose an option to use one or more keywords, such as `www.yourblog.com/contests/summer-travel-sweepstakes`.

If you prefer to customize your permalinks, use the Permalink option in the Post Settings box. On the page where you're writing a post, click the Settings tab in the right column. Select Permalink from the drop-down menu that appears. Then you can create a URL that's different from your title, which you might want for search term reasons.

TECHNICAL STUFF

To generate WordPress permalinks, open the Settings option in the Admin panel, which appears in the left navigation. From there, select Permalinks from the second tier navigation and choose either the Common Structure option or the Custom Permalinks option to enter your own structure. (For example, you might want to insert a category.) For new blogs, that's it; for existing blogs, you may need to use the Redirection plug-in, as well. For more information, see http://codex. wordpress.org/Using_Permalinks. For directions about creating permalinks on Blogger, visit https://support.google.com/blogger/answer/2523525.

Optimizing images, videos, and podcasts

Because search engines can't directly parse the contents of multimedia, you must take advantage of all opportunities to use your relevant search terms in every metatag, descriptive field, or <alt> tag.

Make these fields as keyword- and content-rich as you can. In these elements, you can often use existing keyword research, metatags from your website or blog, or optimized text that you've already created:

» **Title and** <title> **metatag for your content:** This catchy name should include a search term.

» **Filenames:** Using names such as image1234.jpg or podcast1.mp3 doesn't help with SEO; names such as PlushBrownTeddyBear.jpg or tabbycats-sing-jingle-bells.mp3 are much more helpful. Use terms also in category or directory names.

» **Tags:** Use relevant keywords, just as you would with other social media.

» <alt> **tags:** Use these tags for a short description with a search term; for example, *Used cat tree for sale*.

» **Long description metatags:** Follow this example: longdesc=for sale-gently used, gray, carpeted 6 foot cat tree with 4 platforms.

» **Content:** Surround multimedia elements with keyword-rich, descriptive content.

» **Transcriptions:** Transcribe and post a short excerpt from a keyword-loaded portion of your video or podcast.

>> **Anchor text:** Use keywords in the text link that opens your multimedia file.

>> **Large images:** Upload large versions, as well as the thumbnails that are visible on your blog or website.

>> **RSS and XML:** Expand your reach with media RSS and site maps.

For more information on indexing multimedia, see `https://support.google.com/webmasters/answer/114016`.

TIP

Even though search engines can't read watermarks, you may want to mark both videos and large images with your domain name and logo to encourage visits and for branding purposes, and to discourage unauthorized copying.

Optimizing Twitter

In addition to adhering to the standard admonishments about providing good content and using well-researched keywords, you can follow a few extra guidelines to improve your ranking in search results on both internal Twitter searches and on external searches:

>> **Your name on Twitter acts like a** <title> **tag.** If you want to benefit from branding and to rank on your own or your company name, you have to use it! If you haven't already done this, log in to your Twitter account and click the Settings link. Then change your name.

>> **Your username, or Twitter** *handle,* **should relate to your brand, company name, or campaign and be easy to remember.** It can include a keyword or topic area. Change it in the Settings area.

>> **Pack your one-line bio with keywords.** Your Twitter bio serves as the page description metatag and is limited to 160 characters. Use résumé-style language and include some of your primary search terms. Talk about yourself or your company in the third person.

From the drop-down list at the top-right of the page (under your profile icon), select View Profile. After you click on the Edit Profile button, you can edit your profile photo, header graphic, name, business description, location, website URL, and theme color. Remember to click the Save Changes button when you finish.

>> **On your Profile page, use your business address as your location.** Doing so helps with local searches. Remember to save your changes.

>> **Brand your Twitter cover (header) image.** Use your standard business logo, logotype, or a photo showing one of your products or services, resized to the current cover dimensions of 1500-x-500 pixels.

- **Include keywords and hashtags in your tweets and retweets whenever possible so you have more to offer search engines than a time stamp.** With the 140-character limit, Twitter might be a good place to use those single-word terms. Use keywords in your Twitter #hashtags, too.

- **Remember the importance of the initial 42 characters of a tweet.** They serve as the <title> tag for that post. Your account name will be part of that count. Search engines will index the full tweet, however, and Twitter will include the entire post in the title tag if users click on an individual post.

- **Format your retweets.** Keep them under 120 characters so there's room for someone to add his or her retweet information at the front. When you retweet, avoid sending duplicate content by changing the message a bit. Use the Retweet button to paste the content into a new Tweet box. Add the letters RT and the @*username* of the original author. You can insert your comment at the beginning of the message if you want. Finally, click Tweet to post the retweet.

- **Maximize retweets as a measure of popularity.** Write interesting content or share good articles, especially when the direct link to detailed content goes to your own site.

- **Increase your visibility.** When linking to your Twitter profile from other sites, use your name or company name rather than your Twitter handle as the anchor text for the link. (The @ in a Twitter handle, for example, @watermelonweb, isn't handled well by search engines.) If you happen to have a tweet with great keywords and hashtags, you can pin your tweet to the top of your timeline.

TECHNICAL STUFF

Because Twitter adds a nofollow attribute to links placed by users, linking to your site doesn't help with PageRank. Truncated URLs (such as the TinyURLs described in Book 2, Chapter 1) behave just like their longer-version cousins because they're permanent redirects.

However, links from Twitter still boost branding and drive traffic to your site. More traffic to your site improves your ranking at Alexa (www.alexa.com), which in turn improves one of the quality factors Google uses for setting PageRank. It's all one giant loop. For more information on Twitter, see Book 4, Chapter 1.

Optimizing Facebook

Take advantage of myriad opportunities to gain traffic from your Facebook pages by applying optimization techniques. Next to blogs, Facebook pages offer the highest number of opportunities to use SEO on social media to reach people who don't already know you. Fortunately, Facebook search engines can index all shared content on Facebook.

REMEMBER

Every social network has different rules for its account names and profiles. Though consistency is preferable for branding purposes, follow the rules carefully. When you first create a Facebook Page for your business, as described in Book 4, Chapter 2, try these techniques:

>> Use an easy-to-remember version of your business name alone or combined with a search term as your business's Facebook Page name. If possible, use the same username on both Twitter and Facebook for branding reasons. Facebook doesn't like generic names.

>> Under Websites on the About page, list all your relevant domain names, including your website, your blog, and other social media pages. Later, you can also place links to your website or blog or another type of social media within your posts. Generally, it's easier to use the actual URL than to implement anchor text.

>> Place keyword-loaded content in the first paragraph of each of the remaining boxes, which may vary depending on the type of page you elected to create. Include your contact information in the Company Overview box; address information also helps with local searches. Your page description metatag may work well in the Short Description box because it's already optimized for search terms. Be sure to include all your brand names and all the products or services that you offer in the Products box.

>> More search-term opportunities abound if you use iFrame-based solutions (customizable sections for your Facebook pages) to create HTML boxes or Facebook Page apps from third-party developers. These additional iFrame boxes or apps can display text, images, and more links. Be sure to use a good search term in your box app's tab name (which is limited to ten characters) and include text links in your content. It's a bit of a pain, but you can do this on your own.

>> If you're a page administrator, you can use the apps at `www.hyperarts.com/social-media/tabpress-facebook-app.html` or `https://apps.facebook.com/static_html_plus`, or find a list at `www.facebook.com/search/results.php?q=statichtml&init=quick&tas=0.6347709277179092`. For more information about one of the most popular iFrame apps, see `www.wildfireapp.com`.

For more information on creating a Facebook account and business Pages, see Book 4, Chapter 2.

Optimizing Google Business

Not surprisingly, the rules for optimizing Google Business Pages (`www.google.com/business`) track well with the principles for optimizing websites for Google.

To maximize your search engine visibility on Google Business Pages, SEO Hacker recommends the following:

- >> Include one of your essential keywords and company name in the title of your Google Business page, just as you would for a <title> tag.

- >> Claim your custom, branded URL. You need more than ten followers, a profile photo, and a page that's at least 30 days old. Go to `https://support.google.com/business/answer/6068603` for directions.

- >> Copy the page description metatag for your website into the Meta Description field on your Google Business page. You already optimized that tag for several of your important keywords.

- >> Because the Introduction section is the body of your Google Business page, you can use the same keyword-optimized content that appears as the first paragraph on your home page or on other essential pages of your site.

- >> Use search terms in the descriptive filenames for the five main photos that appear on your Google Business page.

- >> In the Recommended Links section, first link your website home page to your Google Business page; that link allows your Google Business page to appear in the right section of search results (the Knowledge Panel). Then add links to and from your blog, all your other social media pages, as well as any other web pages to which you want to drive traffic (for example, to your online store).

- >> Like with your main website, update your Google Business page every two to seven days to indicate activity. When appropriate for marketing reasons, linking to your Google Business page can help boost your search rankings. It's just another example of Google's self-love!

  - Publish to your Google Business page what you're already publishing to other social channels.

  - Get Your Story straight. You might want to re-use the About section from your website. Your Story should include your marketing tagline, an introduction to your business, what sets you apart, and of course, some search terms.

  - Optimize the first 45 to 50 characters of your posts — they become the post's page title in Google search results; in other words, include one of your prized search terms.

- >> Even on social media, pictures are worth 1,000 words, maybe more. Include a lot of photos, videos, graphics, or GIF animations.

>> Be sure that you and any other blog authors sign up for Google Business Authorship so that everyone's posts will be indexed. It helps your authors build their own personal credibility and following, as well. For more details about optimizing Google Business, see www.slideshare.net/HubSpot/8-tips-for-optimizing-your-google-page-posts-to-boost-seo.

Optimizing Pinterest

With its heavy use of visual content, Pinterest is perhaps the most challenging social media to optimize for search engines. Start by creating a business account or converting your personal one at www.pinterest.com/business/create, as described in Book 4, Chapter 3. Then take advantage of several tried-and-true techniques to give your Pinterest site some search oomph:

>> Verify your website by clicking the Verify Website button next to the Website Text field. Follow the directions in the pop-up window so that your site will show up on profile and search results. For more details, see www.pinterest.com/settings.

>> Optimize your user and/or Business Profile name to include your company name and a search term describing what you sell or what business category you're in (unless you're a well-known brand). For instance, instead of listing only *Pretty Puppy*, use *Pretty Puppy Play Clothes for Puppies*.

>> Use your four most important search terms and your page description metatag in the About You section of your company profile (under Settings).

>> Optimize for local search by including your city, state, and zip code in the Location field of the profile. Of course, include the URL for your website and or blog in the Website field.

>> Choose Settings > Business Account Basics and set the Visibility option to Off in your Profile; you *don't* want to hide your Pinterest profile from search engines. Choose Settings > Social Networks and be sure to select the cross-link options to Twitter, Facebook, and Google+. Also, upload your logo graphic under Settings > Profile.

>> Use a descriptive filename that includes a keyword for each of the images you pin from your website or blog. The source link for each image will go back to your website or blog to increase your inbound links and drive traffic to specific pages. If you have optimized images on Flickr or other photo-sharing sites, you can use your Flickr URL as the image source for a pin.

TECHNICAL STUFF

At the moment, Pinterest passes link juice only for an image description. Unfortunately, Pinterest has added the nofollow attribute to the originating URL for pinned images themselves, thus diminishing the value of those links as repins.

>> Include keywords in the title *and* description for each board and pin, whether the boards are employee headshots, photos of your company at tradeshows, or images also used on your blog. For local optimization, include your city. You might want to structure boards by customer type, product, service, or brand name to maximize the search terms you use.

If you create data charts or infographics, be sure to include keywords in the title for your charts or graphics. (Try the infographics tool at `http://piktochart.com`, which offers a limited free account.)

Remember to add the linkable Pinterest icon and link to your suite of social media buttons on your website, blogs, and other social media pages.

For more ideas, visit `http://blog.piqora.com/5-ways-to-increase-your-traffic-with-pinterest-seo-that-you-can-implement-immediately`.

WARNING

Use only images you own or have permission to use on Pinterest. You're liable for any copyright infringement. Respect the use of any credit lines required by Creative Commons or the owner of the image.

Like other social media, Pinterest is a back-scratching site — you like me, and I'll like you. To increase traffic to your Pinterest posts (and eventually to your website), follow other Pinterest users and boards related to your company, repin relevant images, and click their Like buttons.

For more information on creating and using Pinterest for marketing purposes, see Book 4, Chapter 3.

Optimizing LinkedIn

LinkedIn (discussed in Book 4, Chapter 4) doesn't offer quite as many options for SEO as other forms of social media do. Start by including search terms within your profile text, in the descriptions of any LinkedIn groups you start, and within postings to a group. Just keep it gentle and unobtrusive. Follow these steps to optimize your profile and to pass along some SEO credibility:

>> Use your name or company name in your LinkedIn URL (for example, `www.linkedin.com/in/yourcompanyname`). Because search engines look at keywords in URLs, this technique makes your company easier to find.

>> Use content similar to your page description metatag within the first paragraph of your LinkedIn profile. It should already contain some of your primary search terms.

>> Like links from Twitter, links from LinkedIn to other sites don't carry link juice. You can have as many as three links on your profile. Set one to your website

and another to your blog. Use keyword-based link text on a third link to drive traffic to another page on your site or to another of your social media pages. Nothing says that all links have to lead to different domains.

For more optimization ideas, see `www.linkedin.com/today/post/article/20140320151331-142790335-11-seo-tips-for-your-personal-linkedin-profile` or `www.socialmediaexaminer.com/make-linkedin-company-page-useful`.

Gaining Visibility in Real-Time Search

Needless to say, all the emphasis on social media has forced search algorithms to adjust accordingly. Search engines vary in how they handle social media services within natural search results. Google and Yahoo! note your social media presence but don't include individual tweets or posts in results because they're private. You may find that you need to resort to specialized search sites like `www.socialsearch.com` (shown in Figure 5-13) to see near real-time search results for Twitter, Instagram, and YouTube.

FIGURE 5-13:
Use tools like SocialSearch.com to find real-time posts on Instagram, Twitter, or YouTube.

Source: `www.socialsearch.com`

Bing offers two ways to see social content. First, it displays the results of topical posts from influencers and public figures in regular search results without users needing to connect to their social media accounts. However, if users connect Bing Social to Facebook on www.bing.com/explore/social, they'll see posts from their friends related to the search topic they've entered, such as their opinions on a movie or a recommendation for a Mexican restaurant.

Dedicated real-time search engines are available for different services, such as Facebook, Twitter, RSS feeds, and blogs. These engines, some of which are listed in Table 5-5, may also index comments and other elements found only on a particular social media service.

TABLE 5-5   **Real-Time and Specialty Search Engines for Social Media**

Name	URL	Description
48ers	www.48ers.com	Real-time search of news and social media across the web; includes Twitter and Facebook.
Bing Social Search	www.bing.com/explore/social	Near–real-time search includes Facebook and Twitter posts.
Facebook	www.facebook.com/search.php	Search Facebook People, Pages, Places, Groups, Apps, Events, and Web Results.
Google Plus	https://plus.google.com	Search for people, pages, or posts on Google+.
IceRocket	www.icerocket.com	Real-time search of Twitter, Facebook, or blogs, or a combination of all three.
LinkedIn	www.linkedin.com/search	Real-time search built-in for people, jobs, answers, groups, companies, universities, and posts.
Search Engine Land	http://searchengineland.com/the-social-search-revolution-8-social-seo-strategies-to-start-using-right-now-113911	Resource article on real-time and social search.
Sency	http://sency.com	Real-time search engine that searches micro-blogs; can search selected U.S. and international cities for places and companies that are trending at the moment.
Stinky Teddy	http://stinkyteddy.com	Real-time search that allows you to choose what type of results you get (web, news, video, real-time, and images).

Name	URL	Description
Topsy	http://topsy.com	Real-time search for the social web (primarily Twitter, blogs, images, video).
Twitter Search	http://search.twitter.com	Real-time Twitter search.
Yahoo!	http://search.yahoo.com	Real-time search from Yahoo! (includes Twitter, Yahoo! News, Yahoo! Shopping, several video channels, and more).

REMEMBER

You can't benefit from real-time search unless you're active on Facebook, Twitter, and other services. Looking for something to say? Add your twist on the latest trends in your market sector. For ideas on current topics, use Google Trends (http://google.com/trends) or the hot-topic searches on most social media services.

Gaining Traction on Google with Social Media

Sigh. Nothing ever stands still in the social whirl — or maybe social tornado is a better description.

Regular Google search results for the past hour may include near real-time results from Twitter, Facebook, Google+, or social media channels such as blogs and press release sites. (See Figure 5-14.) To view these, enter your search term on Google as usual. On the search results page, click the Search Tools tab > Any Time > Past Hour. If you're more concerned about time than content, switch from the default to Sorted by Date on Sorted by Relevance sub-tab that appears.

Although Google doesn't evaluate engagement on any social media platforms except Google+, it is aware of inbound links and search terms that appear in posts and profiles. Take action based on this information:

>> **Enhance your Google+ listing with frequent posts, shares, and participation in Google+ circles.** Google+ results show up in both social search and standard, natural search.

>> **Post early, post often.** Real-time search creates pressure to update frequently on social media so that you can stay near the top of the results stream. Multiple recent posts can tip the scale. Schedule times on your Social

Media Activity Calendar (found in Book 2, Chapter 4) to post to your blog, add to your Facebook Timeline, or send tweets at least twice a day. Use management tools like those in Book 2, Chapter 4 to make this process easier.

>> **Share and share alike.** Post a lot of appealing, keyword-rich content on social media, and explicitly invite others to link to it. Good content on social media may draw a lot of Likes, but it's the number of links to that content that pushes up search results.

>> **+1 +1 = 3, or maybe 30.** Put Google +1 buttons, as we describe in Book 8, Chapter 2, anywhere and everywhere — on your social media, your website, your newsletters, your forehead. . . . Google incorporates +1 buttons but doesn't evaluate engagement (such as Likes, follows, and comments) on other social media.

>> **Pin your hopes to Pinterest.** The Google spider now crawls pins and boards, looking for relevant keywords in descriptions. Use hashtag keywords for each pin for extra SEO-om-pa-pa.

>> **Add Pin It and StumbleUpon buttons to your content.** For referral traffic, these two sites offer special value.

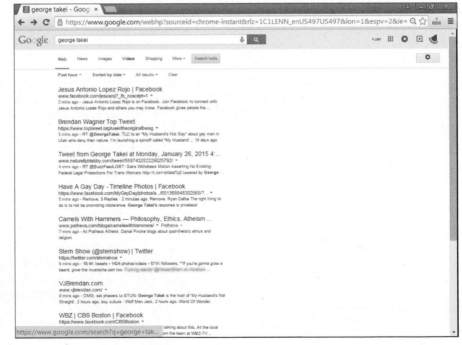

FIGURE 5-14:
Posts on Facebook, Twitter, and other social media are included in Google search results when you search by time.

Source: www.google.com

TIP

To view real-time results in Google+, enter your search term in the Search text box. When you see results, click the option for Most Recent at the top of the results list. From then on, relevant posts will appear in real-time.

Think about which messages are truly time-critical and save your real-time efforts for them. On your Social Media Activity Calendar, enter the times that you expect your target market might be searching, such as first thing in the morning or right before lunch. Make sure to ping all search engines with your updates.

TIP

Get some sleep! There's no point tweeting in the middle of the night when your customers are in bed (unless you're selling to insomniacs or international customers halfway around the world). Your tweets may be long buried by tweets from dozens — if not hundreds — of others by the time the sun rises. Better yet, schedule your tweets ahead of time with Hootsuite, Buffer, Netvibes, or other dashboard tools for specific social media channels.

Monitoring Your Search Engine Ranking

If you're serious about SEO, you'll want to monitor how well you're doing. Table 5-6 lists some search engine ranking software that shows where your site appears on search engines by keyword or page. Most ranking software carries a charge, but some either offer a free trial or will rank a limited number of pages, keywords, or engines for free.

TABLE 5-6   **Search Engine Ranking Services**

Name	URL	Starting Price
Rank Tracker	www.link-assistant.com/rank-tracker	Free download; licenses $125–$300
Search Engine Rankings	www.mikes-marketing-tools.com/ranking-reports	Free
Semrush.com	www.semrush.com	$69.95–$549.95; other tools also available

SEO is a long-term strategy to deliver solid traffic over time to your website or blog. It takes time for your investment in SEO to pay off, and results can vary unpredictably from one week or month to the next. Generally, after you have everything set up and running smoothly, monitoring once per quarter should be enough, except for exceptionally large and constantly growing sites.

REMEMBER

Enter your preferred SEO tools in your Social Media Marketing Plan and insert the tasks into your Social Media Activity Calendar.

3

Content Is King: Content Marketing

Contents at a Glance

Chapter 1

Growing Your Brand with Content

This chapter (and Book 3 as a whole) introduces you to the content marketing opportunity. Thanks to the free and open nature of the social Web, businesses can build brand awareness, develop relationships, and boost their profits in amazing ways. The trick is understanding the why's and how's of content marketing so you can produce and publish content that actually helps you reach your goals rather than creating the opposite effect — or no effect at all.

Before you dive into the world of content marketing, you need to prepare yourself by taking the time to find out how content marketing evolved and what you need to do to create content that drives traffic, conversation, sharing, and ultimately, purchases. In other words, there is more to content marketing than simply publishing words. Set yourself up for success from the start by mastering the fundamentals.

Understanding What Content Marketing Is

Content marketing encompasses all forms of content that add value to consumers, thereby directly or indirectly promoting a business, brand, products, or services. Content marketing occurs both online and offline, but the free and simple tools of the social Web have opened up the ability for companies of all sizes to compete alongside one another, not for market share but for voice and influence.

Marketing a business using content isn't a new concept; however, it has evolved in recent years to mean far more than creating a company brochure filled with overtly promotional messages and images. Today, content marketing focuses on creating content that is meaningful and useful to consumers with promotion taking a backseat to adding value, particularly adding value to the online conversation happening across the social Web.

These sections explain the ins and outs of content marketing and examine in plain English what you need to know.

Evolving from interruption marketing to engagement marketing

Nowadays, consumers actively try to avoid being interrupted by ads and marketing messages. While companies used to have to rely on catching the attention of consumers using tactics such as shock advertising and sexual innuendos, the same tactics aren't as effective today when consumers can simply click away from an online ad or skip commercials on their DVRs. Even the most attention-getting ads go unnoticed by consumers who fast-forward past them.

At the same time, consumers are now hyper-connected. They have access to enormous amounts of information, such as instantaneous access to real-time news, from their homes, offices, and mobile devices. In other words, simply interrupting consumers and delivering marketing messages won't get the job done anymore. Instead, companies have to quickly demonstrate the added value they can deliver, particularly if they're interrupting consumers in order to deliver that value.

To achieve success, companies need to engage consumers rather than interrupt them. Consider a pop-up ad appearing on a website today. It wasn't so long ago that pop-up ads were all the rage among marketers. Today, they're a sure-fire way to annoy customers and cause them to turn away from your brand. Rather than taking control of consumers' online experiences, businesses need to enhance those experiences, and they can do it with content that adds value and engages consumers.

Breaking through the online clutter

Given how cluttered the Web is with content, messages, spam, and so on, you're undoubtedly wondering how you can get consumers to notice you without doing something drastic to catch their attention. That's where you can apply the steps of brand-building to your content marketing strategy.

Just as a brand isn't built overnight, neither is an effective and influential content marketing plan quickly built. Start thinking of content marketing as an essential part of building your brand and online reputation. A powerful brand can lead a business to fantastic places. For example, the Disney brand adds immense value to the Walt Disney Company. You can build your own brand through content marketing and position yourself for success through long-term, sustainable growth.

You can apply the following three fundamental steps of brand building to your content marketing initiatives:

>> **Consistency:** All of your messages and activities must consistently communicate your brand image and promise, or consumers will become confused. They'll turn away from your brand and look for one that does consistently meet their expectations in every interaction.

>> **Persistence:** Brands are built over time and through continual efforts in spreading messages and meeting customer expectations.

>> **Restraint:** Brands must stay focused and resist extending into areas of business or activities that run counter to the brand promise.

REMEMBER

Just as a brand represents a promise that consumers can rely on to meet their expectations again and again, so should your content marketing. By publishing valuable content that consistently communicates your brand promise, consumers will develop expectations for your brand and become loyal to it. Loyal consumers talk about the brands they love. This is a marketer's dream come true. In other words, you can build your brand and your business through content with little or no monetary investment. Instead, you simply need to commit your time and effort. It's an opportunity that businesses would be crazy to pass up.

Understanding 21st century buying behaviors and purchase processes

Changes in the ways consumers make purchasing decisions is another reason content marketing has become a critical element of a business's marketing plan. No longer do consumers rely on television or print ads to get information about products and services; with the growth of the social Web, the pool of people and resources consumers can go to and get reviews and referrals has grown exponentially.

Research shows that prior to making a purchase, consumers conduct the majority of their research online. They read reviews from experts and everyday consumers. They search for comparison-shopping sites, and they publish questions on forums, blogs, social networking profiles, Twitter, and more. Consumers can learn about products and services and decide on which purchase is best for them in the privacy of their homes, either anonymously or otherwise. It's entirely up to each individual.

Within seconds, consumers can find honest opinions online through simple searches and by participating in conversations. Of course, not all reviews are created equal, but the fact is that this is where consumers do their research, and this is the stage on which they make the majority of their purchasing decisions, including where and what to buy. So, you not only need to represent your business in the online space, but also you need to monitor your business and industry across the Web conversations to ensure that they accurately reflect your brand, products, and services.

Again, you can achieve that goal with great content. However, as mentioned, that content can't consist entirely of promotional messages. The content must be interesting and engaging, or it will be ignored, simply because that's the type of interruptive content that consumers are *not* looking for online.

Being customer-centric

When companies first started creating websites, the sites were highly navigational, meaning they offered static information through one-way information delivery. As the Internet evolved, business websites became transactional, and consumers could actually make purchases online. Nevertheless, online communication remained primarily one-way until the evolution of the social Web, which changed the world of communication and business. Suddenly, businesses could participate in public two-way conversations. However, many businesses still haven't modified their websites and online destinations to focus more on consumers' needs than on the company's goals. In other words, business sites are still talking *at* people about topics that matter to the business and in a transactional manner rather than talking *with* people about topics that matter to those people and in a social manner.

Today, online communication trumps many traditional forms of communication, particularly as smartphones enable people to easily communicate via the tools of the social Web faster than they can via email, telephone, or in person. This fact doesn't mean a company should move all of its communications to the online space, but it does mean that the online space needs to be a priority in every company's marketing communications plan. The most successful business websites in the 21st century have evolved, too. Those sites are now customer-centric (or audience-centric), and the content published is created with consumers' wants, needs, and expectations as the top priorities.

Consumers are fickle and impatient. You need to give them information that makes them smarter consumers and that helps them in multiple aspects of their lives. Create a website and other branded online destinations that are customer-centric. In every branded interaction, give customers a reason to want to visit your website and engage with you and your content by adding value to the online conversation. A destination-centric content strategy that focuses more on your business than on your target audience won't get the job done anymore.

Comparing three types of marketing: online, social media, and content

Most people, including many marketers, are confused about the differences among traditional online marketing, social media marketing, and content marketing. These three forms of digital marketing overlap frequently, so making a distinction among them is challenging. However, you need to understand the underlying differences if you want to be successful in marketing your business with content.

The three primary forms of digital marketing are as follows:

>> **Traditional online marketing:** All forms of marketing related to the Internet are considered to be online marketing. Traditional forms predate the social Web and include all forms of online ads (such as banner, pop-up, flash, interstitial, video, and so on). Traditional forms of online marketing rely on "push" marketing strategies and are typically direct marketing efforts, meaning companies push messages at consumers with a specific action or response in mind from consumers.

>> **Social media marketing:** Social media marketing can include direct and indirect marketing efforts and includes all forms of marketing executed using the tools of the social Web. For example, writing a business blog providing tips or participating in a Facebook conversation related to your industry are both forms of indirect marketing through social media. Alternatively, publishing a discount code in your Twitter feed is a direct marketing tactic through social media. The tools of the social Web include all online publishing tools that enable people to publish any form of user-generated content such as articles, comments, videos, images, audio, and so on.

>> **Content marketing:** Content marketing is less social and more informational in nature than social media marketing (although great content can and should lead to conversations and sharing). All content that adds value and could market a business (directly or indirectly) is considered a form of content marketing. Content marketing can come in three forms:

- Long-form (such as blogs, articles, ebooks, and so on)

- Short form (such as Twitter updates, Facebook updates, images, and so on)

- Conversation and sharing (for example, sharing great content via Twitter or offering helpful information in an online forum)

As you may expect, an online article is a perfect example of content marketing. However, as consumers and audience members share and discuss the content, it becomes a social media marketing opportunity. In other words, content marketing involves understanding what consumers want and need, and then creating and publishing content that is relevant and useful. By publishing content that helps consumers, your brand and business become a part of their lives that they come to rely on and trust over time. As that content is discussed and shared across the social Web, what started as an indirect content marketing effort can become a powerful form of social media marketing. The opportunities are practically limitless.

Eyeing how different departments in an organization can use content marketing

Despite its name, employees from varied departments within an organization can participate in content marketing initiatives. Remember, content marketing doesn't have to include direct marketing messages at all, and that's where members of your organization outside the marketing department can get involved. The focus is on how content marketing can spread across an organization and become an organic part of employees' everyday responsibilities.

REMEMBER

Content marketing is all about publishing useful information that helps your target audience, which means your executives can write blog posts, ebooks, or presentations that offer their thoughtful leadership. Customer service team members can create answers to frequently asked questions or solutions to common problems, and the marketing team can create videos, conduct interviews, and publish tutorials. Figure 1-1 shows a breakdown of activities that different departments within a company can pursue via content marketing, as well as the social media marketing opportunities that evolve from great content.

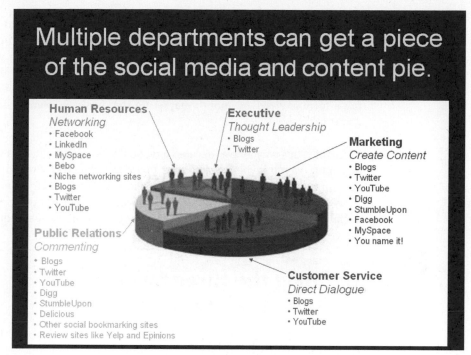

FIGURE 1-1:
Multiple
departments
can get a piece
of the content
marketing pie.

© John Wiley & Sons, Inc.

Of course, if you're a solo entrepreneur or have very few employees, you'll wear multiple hats and create varied content to leverage the multiple opportunities to connect with consumers. The trick is to publish varied content so your audience is continually engaged and its expectations are met again and again.

Discovering how you can benefit from content marketing

The primary benefits of content marketing are building brand awareness and developing relationships with your target consumer audience *and* online influencers. The idea, at this point, is to understand how content marketing can enable you to build your brand and business by putting you in front of audiences that matter.

By publishing content, you can put yourself on the map. As you build your business's online presence through consistent and persistent publishing of interesting and useful content, more and more people will find you or hear about you. If your content is relevant and interesting, they'll want more of it. They'll remember who you are, and they'll share your content with others. They'll want to talk about your content with you and with their own online (and offline) connections. In other words, your content opens the virtual door between your business and a global audience.

Your content helps people understand your brand message and promise, and it allows people to develop their own perceptions for your brand and business. They develop expectations for your brand based on the information you consistently share. They reach out and communicate with you via social Web conversations, and in time, they become loyal brand advocates who talk about your brand, creating a form of word-of-mouth marketing that business owners could only dream about years ago.

Think of it this way — two decades ago, business owners like you would have done anything (well, maybe not *anything*) to get together with an audience of engaged consumers to talk about products and services. Today, a larger engaged audience than you can imagine is available to you, thanks to the power and reach of the social Web. You just have to discover what they want to hear from you, and then deliver it again and again.

Defining the three forms of content marketing

Content marketing comes in three basic forms — long-form, short-form, and conversations. It's important to understand that content marketing is still a new form of marketing, and no one knows the recipe for success. Only a few rules and some loose guidelines are available for businesses and marketers to follow. In fact, you're really limited only by your creativity and dedication. Truth be told, any content that you make publicly available online and offline could be considered a type of content marketing, because all content is a reflection of your brand and business. Furthermore, all content opens up a potential talking point for consumers to consider, dissect, analyze, and debate. The social Web offers a perfect (and very public) place for them to do so.

Also, the forms of content marketing are constantly changing as new tools to create, publish and share that content are launched and others are shut down. Enhancements and new functionality are added to content publishing tools every day, which means the tools you're using to create, publish, and share content today might not be the tools you're using tomorrow.

The three forms of content marketing that you can create, publish, and share as part of your content marketing plan follow:

>> **Long-form content marketing:** Includes all published content that's longer than a few sentences and that offers deep value, such as blog posts, articles, ebooks, press releases, white papers, presentations, videos, podcasts, webinars, and so on.

>> **Short-form content marketing:** Includes all published content with no more than a few sentences and that communicates useful information, such as Twitter updates, Facebook updates, LinkedIn updates, images, and so on.

>> **Conversations and sharing content marketing:** Can happen through conversations about published content and through the sharing of published content, such as blog comments, forum comments, Twitter updates, link sharing via social bookmarking, comments on videos and images, and so on.

Each of the preceding forms of content marketing is described in detail later in this book. The important thing to remember is that you're likely to see overlap between the three forms as well as overlap with social media and traditional online marketing efforts. That's a good thing!

The best marketing plan is a fully integrated strategy where one piece connects to the next. For example, the phrase, "If you build it, they will come," doesn't apply to content marketing. Simply publishing content isn't enough. You also need to promote that content. You can do so through conversations and sharing as well as through social media and digital marketing efforts. In fact, you can even integrate your offline marketing efforts with your online content marketing efforts.

Understanding the Google Effect: How to Leverage the Power of Search

There has never been a better time in history for a small business to compete on a level playing field regardless of its budget. If you can spare even just an hour a day on content marketing-related activities, you'll see results in terms of increased word-of-mouth marketing, repeat business, and new business. But many people don't understand how to connect content marketing efforts with bottom-line business growth. If you're wondering how content marketing can help you build your business, you simply need to think of a single word — Google.

Ask yourself the following question — how do you find information about a type of product, service, or business? Do you pick up the local Yellow Pages or newspaper in search of an ad? Probably not, and it's fairly safe to assume that most people are just like you. When they need information about a product, service, or business, they turn on their computers or smartphones, open up their Web browser, and visit their preferred search engine. For the vast majority of Internet users, that preferred search engine is Google. Next, they type keywords related to the product, service, or business they need to find, and click the various links provided in the search results. In simplest terms, your business needs to be represented in keyword searches related to your products and services, and it's easier than ever to get there through content marketing.

Creating entry points

Consider the following scenario, which demonstrates how content marketing can help you ensure that you're represented on search engines and across the social Web. First, imagine that your business has a website. You invest in great design and copywriting and launch a ten-page website that looks fantastic and tells the complete story of your business and products. That site creates ten entry points on which Google or other search engines can find you.

Next, imagine that you connect a blog to your website and publish a new blog post every day for a year. Now, you have 365 *more* entry points to your website. Google and other search engines can find all these entry points and then deliver those pages to people searching for your type of business and products.

Now, imagine that the content you publish throughout the year on your business blog is interesting, useful, and meaningful content that meets your target audience's needs. Your audience will undoubtedly want to share that content with their own online connections. They'll tweet about it, post it on Facebook, blog about it, and more. When you write amazing content that people want to share, or *shareworthy content*, you're opening up the floodgates for even more entry points to your business blog and website. Suddenly your 375 entry points turn into hundreds or thousands more, all from the conversations and sharing of your shareworthy content.

This is the compounding effect of blogging, and it's a powerful thing. You simply can't buy that kind of access to consumers. By publishing amazing content that is relevant and useful to your target audience, your entry points will grow over time. Every day you wait is a missed opportunity to create those valuable entry points that every business needs in order to reach full potential.

Managing search engines reputably

There is more to search engines than keyword results. You can also use search engines to stay abreast of content and conversations related to your brand and business reputation. In this way, you can take the necessary steps to ensure those results are the ones you want people to see. In other words, when consumers type keywords related to your business into their preferred search engines, you need to know that the results they'll get not only point them in the direction of your business, but also point them to places that paint your business in a positive light.

You can use several tools to monitor your search engine reputation. Following are some easy tools that you can use free:

>> **Google Alerts:** You can set up Google Alerts (www.google.com/alerts) to send you email messages when content that uses your chosen keywords (for example, your business name) is published online.

>> **Google Advanced Search:** You can conduct daily or weekly Google Advanced Searches (www.google.com/advanced_search) using your chosen keywords (such as your business name) to find content that Google Alerts may have missed.

>> **Twitter alerts:** Twitter alerts work similarly to Google Alerts. You receive email messages telling you about Twitter posts that include your chosen keywords. TweetBeep (www.tweetbeep.com) is a good choice for automating Twitter alerts.

>> **Twitter Advanced Search:** You can conduct Twitter searches using very specific criteria to find tweets related to your chosen keywords using the Advanced Twitter Search form (http://search.twitter.com/advanced).

>> **Twitter apps:** A number of Twitter applications can help you monitor tweets and conversations on Twitter that are related to your business. Monitter (www.monitter.com) is a great Twitter app for keeping tabs on conversations using your chosen keywords.

Again, content marketing can't occur in a silo. You need to be aware of what's being said about your business, brand, products, competitors, and so on. In this way, you will be able to respond and create content that's even more relevant to your targeted audience's wants and needs.

Revealing the Broad Reach of Online Content

Your business operates in a truly global environment, and content marketing via the Internet has the ability to put your business in front of more people than ever. In fact, many small businesses have grown into global companies with millions of dollars in annual revenue simply through minimal efforts to build an online presence and by publishing valuable content. The nearby sidebar, "The success of Gary Vaynerchuk and Wine Library," describes one of the most popular examples of a small business expanding beyond anyone's wildest dreams, thanks to a blog and online video content.

THE SUCCESS OF GARY VAYNERCHUK AND WINE LIBRARY

Gary Vaynerchuk's father owned a small wine store in Springfield, New Jersey. As Gary grew up, he spent a lot of time at his father's store and developed a love of wines. One day, he asked his father if he could start a blog for the store. His father acquiesced, and Gary began publishing content about his love of wine, his unique ways of tasting wines and comparing the flavors of those wines to unusual objects like rocks. Soon, he added an online video element where he used his own video camera to record himself talking about wine to the Wine Library blog, and Wine Library TV (http://tv.winelibrary.com) was born.

Gary's passion for his subject matter and his enigmatic personality were contagious, and his audience grew and grew. Today, Wine Library is a $60 million-per year business with over half of those sales coming from the Internet. Gary is a sought after social media speaker, and he signed a multi-million dollar contract to author a series of books about social media marketing. And it all started from a blog.

It's amazing to think that people around the world can see the words you publish online instantaneously. Therefore, the question for businesses isn't "Why should you use content marketing?" but rather "Why *aren't* you *already* using content marketing?"

It comes down to earning a share of the online voice as mentioned earlier in this chapter. If you're actively participating in the online conversation (or at least being mentioned in that conversation), then you're earning valuable publicity without spending any money. The value of this *earned media* is incalculable.

Shifting from a Marketer to a Publisher Mindset

One of the first things you must do in order to be successful with content marketing is to forget everything you know about marketing. That's a scary concept for many people. For years, businesses have been following marketing strategies based on interrupting consumers. For your content marketing efforts to work, you need to put the aggressive marketing mindset on the backburner and focus on writing and publishing shareworthy content, as mentioned earlier in this chapter.

Therefore, as you're creating content, do so with your audience in mind, not your business goals. Deliver the content your audience wants and needs and then promote that content separately through your social media interactions. Inevitably, as mentioned earlier, your content and social media marketing activities will overlap, but your content should be able to stand on its own, separate from your social media marketing tactics. These sections offer some helpful suggestions to better enable you to separate your content marketing and content publishing thoughts.

Applying the 80-20 rule

In marketing theory, the *80-20 rule* states that 80 percent of business comes from 20 percent of the customers. There's a similar concept when it comes to content marketing and social media marketing. Remember, you have to think like a publisher to be successful with content marketing. If you apply the 80-20 rule to your content marketing efforts, 80 percent or more of the content you develop should *not* be self-promotional and 20 percent or less should be self-promotional. That means the vast majority of the time you spend on content marketing activities won't be directly related to marketing at all.

But hold on. Just because 80 percent of your efforts aren't directly self-promotional doesn't mean they're not indirectly marketing your business. In fact, it's indirect marketing that makes content marketing so powerful. Every piece of content you publish or share can add value to the online experience and further strengthen your relationship with your online audience of brand advocates who will talk about your content and share it with their own audiences. Don't think content that doesn't directly promote your business isn't helping drive revenues. It's just happening indirectly and might not be apparent immediately.

Adding value, staying relevant, and being shareworthy

If you're following the 80-20 rule, you know that 80 percent of your content should add value to the online experience, particularly for your target audience. This is how you build relationships and set expectations for your target audience and among online influencers who can help to spread your messages even farther across the global Web community. You need to take the time to research what type of information, messages, and content your target audience wants from a business like yours, and then deliver that content in a professional manner.

In addition, you need to offer content that your audience will share with others. Traditional publishers use this strategy to create content that not only sells newspapers or magazines but also offers a pass-along value that may convert secondary readers into subscribers. The same concept holds true for content marketing today. The difference is that today anyone, including you, can be a content publisher and use that content to lead to bigger and better things, such as brand awareness, business growth, and sales.

Never has there been such an exciting opportunity for small and mid-size businesses to stake their claims and position themselves for success — because now it's not necessarily the depth of your wallet that leads to success through content marketing but rather the depth of your words. Content marketing enables businesses to continually meet customer expectations and to add something extra to the consumer experience that helps develop trust, security, and loyalty.

Content marketing offers the perfect way for businesses to leverage the three S's of Customer Loyalty:

>> **Stability:** Customers become loyal to a product, brand, or business when it sends a consistent message they can trust and rely on.

>> **Sustainability:** Customers become loyal to a product, brand, or business when they believe it will be with them for a long time or at least for a specific amount of time with a predetermined end.

>> **Security:** Customers become loyal to a product, brand, or business when it gives them a feeling of comfort or peace of mind.

As you can see, consumers actively look for products, brands, and businesses that they feel they can trust and that won't abandon them. They become emotionally involved in the products, brands, and businesses that help them feel a sense of comfort. A well-executed content marketing strategy can offer the stability, sustainability, and security that consumers seek, and it can help them develop an emotional connection and relationship with a product, brand, or business.

Developing Content to Build Your Brand and Form Relationships

Content marketing, paired with social media marketing, is the single largest opportunity for individuals, organizations, and companies of any size to build their brands and build their businesses.

Content marketing offers a unique opportunity for you to engage with current and potential employees, position your brand as a brand of choice, develop an ongoing dialogue with consumers and influencers that ultimately creates brand advocates and brand guardians, and to learn an incredible amount about your target audience and competitors. What's not to love?

Understanding what a brand is

Branding is a difficult concept for many people to understand. That's because a brand isn't truly a tangible or quantifiable thing. Although a brand can be represented by tangible elements, such as a logo, color palette, and so on, intangible elements work with the tangible elements to create consumer perceptions, as illustrated in Figure 1-2. In other words, consumers, not companies, built brands. Companies might nudge consumers in a desired direction, but consumers create brands through experiences and emotions.

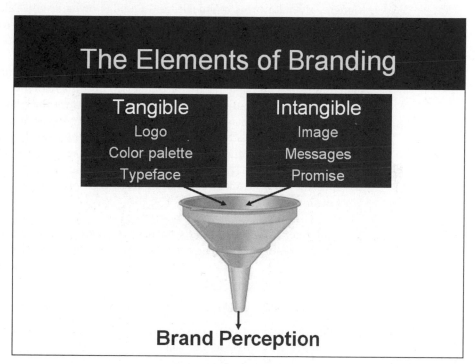

FIGURE 1-2:
The tangible and intangible elements of a brand.

The easiest way to think of a brand is as a promise to consumers. A brand sets expectations for consumers through that promise and meets those expectations in every interaction. Brands that don't meet those expectations fail.

As consumers experience brands and make them their own, the brands grow. The most powerful brands are relationship brands. These brands are typically shared by groups of people and provide opportunities for consumers to select how they want to interact with the brand they love through a wide variety of experiences. You can set the wheels in motion to turn your brand into a relationship brand by consistently and persistently publishing interesting, shareworthy content relevant to consumers' wants and needs, thereby adding value to their lives.

Positioning your brand

Before you can create content that sets brand expectations in consumers' minds, you need to determine where your brand is positioned in the marketplace relative to your competitors. The most powerful brands own a word in consumers' minds. For example, in the auto industry, Toyota owns *reliable* in the minds of U.S. consumers, Hyundai owns *affordable,* and Cadillac owns *luxury.* Take some time to determine where your business should be positioned relative to your competitors, and work on creating content that accurately reflects that position.

If you own a gourmet food store, for example, publishing content that shows consumers how to make meals for under $10 doesn't match your brand's position. Doing so will confuse consumers and could cause them to turn away from your brand in search of one that does meet their expectations based on the brand's promise. In other words, don't promise high-end, gourmet products and shopping experiences and then deliver low-end, cheap information and content experiences. That content doesn't add value to your target audience's lives, so they won't talk about it or share it with other people who might help your business grow.

You can determine your brand's position by taking the Brand Perception Snap Shot, which requires you to answer the following three questions:

1. What five words would you use to describe your brand today?

2. What five words would your customers use to describe your brand today?

3. What five words do you want customers to use to describe your brand in the future? What is your ultimate goal?

Be honest in answering these questions and then take some time to review your results. Find the gaps and opportunities and fill them. You can do this through your content marketing efforts and easily position your brand in consumers' minds. Your consistency and persistence will pay off over time as you continually develop audience expectations and perceptions of your brand.

Establishing credibility and becoming the go-to person for a topic

Your business is nothing if it's not credible. Your amazing content can help you develop an online reputation that is built on authority and that clearly demonstrates your knowledge and expertise in your area of business or topic. When you publish content, do so with the goal of always making sure the content helps to establish you as the go-to person for information related to your business.

The more you publish valuable content and the more people talk about that content, the more your reputation will grow and spread across the online community. One day you'll start getting emails or phone calls from people who want to use you as an expert for an article or interview. That's a sign your efforts are starting to pay off! Pat yourself on the back and keep publishing shareworthy content that helps to position your brand and yourself in the eyes of consumers and online influencers.

TIP

Just as Gary Vaynerchuk (see the sidebar earlier in this chapter) wasn't always the go-to person for social media marketing, you'll need time to establish your reputation and become a popular source for topics related to your own line of business. Don't give up too soon!

Determining the style and voice you want to use in your content marketing efforts is also important. That style and voice needs to be appropriate for your brand image and should match consumer expectations for your brand, but it also must be real and honest. If your personality and your passion for your business don't shine through, you're unlikely to retain an audience and build relationships based on that content.

Similarly, you need to be accessible to your audience. Communicate with them and respond to their questions, emails, comments on your blog, tweets, and so on. Content marketing and social media marketing go hand-in-hand. You can't publish content and then disappear. Instead, actively engage with your audience to deepen your relationships with them as well as their relationships with your brand.

Understanding the ARMS Theory of Brand Building

Four primary steps to brand building strategy can help you understand where you are on the path to building a successful brand and where you still have to go to reach the level of success you want and need. This is called the ARMS Theory of Brand Building, and it's broken down as follows:

>> **Awareness:** Consumers move from an unaware state to an aware state. They have heard of a brand but don't remember it without a prompt and can't remember any details about it.

>> **Recognition:** Consumers move from an aware state to a state of recognition where they remember a brand when they are prompted and know what it is and what it's for.

>> **Memory:** Consumers move from a state of recognition to a state of memory when they can recall a brand and what it's for without being prompted in any way.

>> **Spreading the word:** Consumers move from a state of memory to spreading the word when they have tried a brand, believe the brand promise, and want to share their knowledge and experiences with other people.

The ultimate goal of brand building is reaching the "spreading the word" stage where consumers aren't only loyal to your brand but also advocate it and defend it against naysayers. Therefore, it's essential that on the social Web you focus your efforts on building a band of brand advocates who will share your content, promote your content and your brand, and stick up for your content and your brand when it is questioned. You need to cultivate relationships with your brand advocates just as they cultivate relationships with your brand. Again, there's more to content marketing than simply publishing content. If you don't pursue the activities that can help the content thrive and work as indirect marketing tools, you won't get the results you want and need.

Committing to a Long-Term Strategy

As discussed earlier in this chapter, brands aren't built overnight and content marketing is a long-term strategy to build brands and businesses. You need to commit to pursuing content marketing initiatives for years to come in order to be successful. Remember the compounding effect of the blogging concept described earlier in this chapter (in the section "Creating entry points"). That kind of domino effect can't occur without a lot of dominos already in position (that would be your varied pieces of content). Each new piece of shareworthy content that you publish plays an important part in expanding the domino effect. Keep adding dominos.

Setting reasonable expectations for your content marketing success is also important. That's because your success is directly dependent on the amount of time you commit to content marketing. The more time you put into publishing great content and engaging with your audience online and offline, the better your chances are of seeing real results sooner rather than later. However, much of your content marketing efforts will rely on your willingness to experiment and tweak your efforts. That's because content marketing is still too new to have a defined roadmap to success. Instead, carve out your own roadmap. Just don't expect to become an Internet sensation overnight.

Perhaps one of the most important things to keep in mind as you're pursuing your own content marketing plan is . . . don't get too caught up in the numbers. When it comes to content marketing, quality trumps quantity.

Think of it this way: If you publish 1,000 pieces of poorly written content, they won't help you much. In fact, they could do more harm than good if they don't live up to consumers' expectations for your brand. However, if you publish 100 pieces of interesting, shareworthy content, the chances of that content spreading to your target audience and driving those people to visit your website, blog, or other branded online destination for more information are much greater.

Similarly, having 10,000 blog subscribers who don't share your posts or publish comments is far less helpful than having 1,000 blog subscribers who link to your posts, share them on Twitter and other social sites, join the conversation through comments, and so on. Quality relationships with your target audience can help you build your business far more effectively than can big numbers that are meaningless in terms of converting sales. It might be tempting to focus on numbers, but try to refrain.

Benchmarking Other Businesses That Are Doing It Right

Before you begin your own content marketing plan, it's helpful to look at other businesses that are doing great things in the online space. Of course, you don't have to do the same things that the businesses mentioned in this section are doing with content marketing, but you can get some ideas and implement some similar tactics if they're right for your business, brand, and audience. The key is to avoid reinventing the wheel. Take some time to research what other companies are doing well or mistakes they've made, and learn from those companies. If similar tactics might work for you, try them. Also, make sure you know what your competitors are doing so you can act appropriately to retain your brand's position in consumers' minds.

Following are several businesses that are doing great things with content marketing:

>> **Gary Vaynerchuk** (`http://tv.winelibrary.com`): As mentioned earlier in this chapter, Gary Vaynerchuk of Wine Library is a great person to follow to see how video content can help a business grow.

>> **Naked Pizza** (`http://twitter.com/nakedpizza`): Naked Pizza uses Twitter for both social media marketing and content marketing. The New Orleans-based pizza retailer publishes direct marketing messages such as discount offerings as well as newsletter content, all in 140-characters or less.

>> **Dell** (`http://en.community.dell.com`): Dell is a large company that has evolved into a content marketer to benchmark. The company effectively surrounds consumers with branded content through varied Twitter profiles, blogs, forums, social networks, and more, many of which can be found by visiting the online Dell Community site as shown in Figure 1-3.

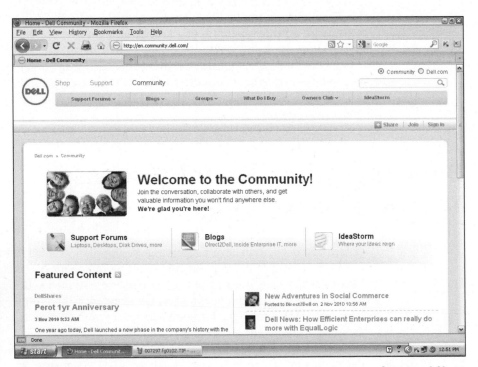

FIGURE 1-3:
The Dell Community provides access to a variety of content through blogs, forums, and more.

Source: `www.dell.com`

>> **Whole Foods Market:** Whole Foods Market publishes content that adds value to users' lives through a large number of national and local Twitter profiles, blogs, Facebook, Flickr, and more, all of which give Whole Foods a personality that matches the brand and a way of engaging with consumers. Many of these branded destinations can be found from the Whole Foods Market website map at www.wholefoodsmarket.com/sitemap.php.

As you spend time online, always be on the lookout for great content marketing examples and companies doing amazing things through content marketing. There is always something new to discover, and you never know when you might stumble upon an idea that will work perfectly for your own business!

Chapter 2

Creating a Content Marketing Strategy

When you fully understand how content marketing can help you build your brand and business, as discussed in Book 3, Chapter 1, you can begin to put together your own content marketing strategy. As with all marketing strategies, you need to analyze the market, competitors, and customers in order to find opportunities to effectively position and promote your company through content.

Your overall business marketing strategy should provide a clear direction for your business with content marketing efforts playing an important role in that strategy. When your strategy is defined, you can execute a marketing plan, as discussed in Book 3, Chapter 3, and pursue the various tactics you expect to use in order to achieve the goals defined in your marketing strategy. This chapter explains how to create the content marketing strategy within your overall business marketing strategy.

Researching Your Competition

Achieving higher levels of business success will be difficult if you don't know what your competitors are doing. In order to develop your content marketing strategy, you need to know your competition as well as you know yourself. Researching your competition allows you to react appropriately to their content marketing tactics and even to anticipate some of those potential tactics.

In other words, by knowing your competition, you can more effectively position your business in the minds of consumers and meet their needs and expectations. More specifically, competitive research enables you to find and exploit your competitors' weaknesses, position your brand as a brand of choice, establish your unique niche, and differentiate your business from other businesses. These sections focus on what you need to know about your customers and how you can go about discovering this information.

REMEMBER

Don't be tempted to assume that you already know everything about your competitors from years of experience. The Internet is a completely different space, and what worked offline through traditional marketing strategies and tactics is unlikely to work as effectively online. Consumers are actively looking for information. Give it to them, and know what your competition is doing so you can give consumers the information they're actively seeking better than your competition does.

Finding your competition online and monitoring their activities

The first step to researching your competitors is finding them across social media. However, you need to analyze more than your competitors' websites. Fortunately, a variety of tools are available to help you find your competition online. When you find your competitors, you need to analyze what they're doing on their branded online destinations as well as on sites they don't own but simply maintain a presence.

Following are a number of methods and tools you can use to conduct your competitive online research:

>> **Google Advanced Search:** Conduct a daily or weekly search on your competitors' names using the Google Advanced Search tool (www.google.com/advanced_search) to find content or conversations recently published about them.

>> **Google Alerts:** Set up Google Alerts (www.google.com/alerts) to send you alerts for your competitors' names.

>> **Twitter:** Follow your competitors on Twitter (www.twitter.com) and read their tweets. Use the Twitter profile search tool to find accounts (https://twitter.com/invitations/find_on_twitter). Note that you have to be logged into your Twitter account to use the Twitter profile search tool.

>> **Facebook:** Follow your competitors' profiles and business pages on Facebook and read their updates. You can use the Facebook People Search tool (www.facebook.com/search.php?type=users) to find profiles on Facebook, but if a profile is set to private, you can't view it unless you're "friends" with that profile owner. You can search for pages from the Facebook Page Directory search (www.facebook.com/directory/pages).

>> **LinkedIn:** Follow your competitors' profiles on LinkedIn (www.linkedin.com) and read their updates. If you know the names of your competitors' executives or employees, you can search for them on LinkedIn using the search tool found at the bottom of the LinkedIn home page or at the top of any page in your LinkedIn account. You can't view a private profile unless you're connected with that person. **Note:** Premium LinkedIn accounts allow users to see who is viewing them, so be aware if you don't want your competitors to know that you're checking them out.

>> **On-site searches:** Visit your competitors' websites and blogs and look for links to other online profiles or branded destinations such as YouTube channels, Flickr profiles, and so on. Companies that are implementing a social media marketing or content marketing plan should have links to their various branded online destinations prominently displayed on their websites and blogs. A good example is shown in Figure 2-1.

TIP

As you find your competitors' online destinations and conversations, analyze them to discover what kind of content they're publishing. Can you find any gaps or any opportunities to "borrow" a share of voice or to offer content that your target audience isn't already getting from your competitors? Is there a way to repackage the type of information they're publishing to make it more useful and interesting to consumers? What content are your competitors publishing that sparks conversations or sharing? Your findings can help you determine what kind of content to create and where to publish it.

Links to branded online destinations

FIGURE 2-1:
Look for links to your competitors' branded online destinations on their websites and blogs.

Source: www.wholefoods.com

Eavesdropping on your competitors' online conversations

Thanks to social media, you can read the conversations your competitors have with their customers and the online audience at large. Don't pass up this opportunity! Ten or twenty years ago, business owners would have done anything to be a fly on the wall and listen to their competitors' conversations, but there was really no way to do it legally. Many of those conversations are right at your fingertips now with social media. Look for them and listen to them! You can glean some important lessons that can have a significant impact on your marketing strategy.

You can start listening to your competitors' online conversations by analyzing their various online profiles and branded destinations as described in the previous section. However, other ways of listening in on your competitors' conversations can give you even more insight. Following are several tricks you can try to get the inside scoop on your competitors' messages and relationships with consumers:

>> **Friends and connections:** Review your competitors' profiles on Facebook, LinkedIn, and other social networking sites and find out who is connected to them as well as whom they're following. Follow those people, too, and keep track of the related conversations and sharing.

>> **Groups:** Review your competitors' profiles on Facebook, LinkedIn, Google Groups, and other social sites and find the groups in which they belong to and participate. Join those groups and monitor your competitors' conversations within those groups.

>> **Followers:** Review your competitors' profiles on Twitter and see both whom they're following and who is following them. Follow those people, too, and find out what content is being discussed and shared.

>> **Blog comments:** Read your competitors' blogs and pay close attention to the comments section on each blog post. Follow links within profiles, particularly the links that lead you to the site of the person who published a comment. Discover more about the people participating in these conversations and reach out to them. If your competitors accept and publish trackback links on their blog posts, follow those links to discover who else is writing about the content published on your competitors' blogs. If they're linking to your competitors' content, you need to connect with them so they'll link to your amazing content in the future. You can see an example of a trackback link published on a blog post in Figure 2-2.

Creating a Content
Marketing Strategy

FIGURE 2-2:
Trackback links appear in the comments section in blog posts that accept and publish them.

Trackback links are published within the comments section on some blogs providing an easy way for bloggers to see what other sites and blogs are linking to their content and potentially driving additional traffic to those sites and blogs from interested readers.

» **Incoming links:** Use a link checker tool like Google's to find out what sites and pages are linking to your competitors' websites and blogs. The owners of those sites and pages are actively discussing your competitors and sharing their content. You need to get a piece of that action, too, so reach out to those site owners and start building a relationship with them. To find incoming links to your website or blog, you can conduct a link search through Google by typing "link:*yourURL*" into the search box at www.google.com (where *yourURL* is the URL for your site, such as link:www.keysplashcreative.com). Google Webmaster tools also offer more comprehensive link research results (www.google.com/webmasters/).

Finding gaps and opportunities

As you monitor ongoing conversations and your competitors' involvement in those conversations and related content, look for opportunities to fill gaps and offer something different or provide similar information in a better way. In other words, don't market scared. Just because your competitors are publishing a specific type of content in a specific way doesn't mean those strategies or tactics are right for you and your audience. However, knowing what those strategies and tactics are can help you differentiate your business or better position your brand as the brand of choice.

Just as each piece of content that you publish becomes part of the larger compounding effect that can deliver long-term sustainable growth to your business, so do your research and analysis efforts. All together, your activities will enable you to drive organic buzz about your business that can be far more powerful than a simple banner ad.

Think outside the box and come up with new ways to offer content that your audience wants and needs. For example, if you sell customized gift baskets online, allow consumers to view those baskets through an online video so that they can see exactly what their money will buy and make changes on demand. This visual approach provides a creative way to add a tangible element to an online buying process. A business that once could thrive only offline can now thrive online, thanks to creative content marketing and communications via the user-generated content of social media.

If you own a business that can help customers by offering step-by-step tutorials, don't just provide in-person training classes or instruction manuals. Instead, add a content marketing aspect by offering webinars or screencast tutorials. You can even turn tutorials into videos that can be shared across social media to broaden the reach of your content and indirectly market your business. By offering useful information to consumers, you build a relationship with them based on appreciation and trust. In this way, you can deliver positive word-of-mouth marketing as well as tangible results to your business for years to come.

Identifying Your Audience

As you research your competitors, you also need to research your customers. Social media is an amazing market research tool that can give you an incredible amount of information about your existing customers, prospective customers, target audience, and audience segments. All you have to do is find your audience, pay attention to what they're doing online, read their content, and listen to their conversations. Sometimes you can even ask them questions.

Many of the tools and techniques that you use to find and research your competitors are the same ones you can use to find your audience. That's because competitors who are effectively using content marketing to build their businesses should already be present in the online destinations where your target audience spends time. However, simply finding your competitors and target audience isn't enough. You also need to evaluate what's happening on those destinations to determine which activities are truly right for you to invest your time and effort.

REMEMBER

As you discovered earlier, don't fall into the trap of marketing scared. Instead, create your own road map based on your own research and analysis of your market, competitors, and audience.

Determining your target audience and segments

The best content marketing strategy is to find your audience and publish the right kind of content to interest these people and add value to their lives. A combination of demographic and behavioral targeting is essential to creating a solid content marketing strategy.

Part of leveraging social media to market a brand or product involves changing your marketing strategy in terms of segmenting your customer base. Finding your best customers is a fundamental step in building a business. When you determine the customers you want to target, you need to define ways to find more people like your best customers in order to target that market with meaningful advertising, promotions, and so on — or in the case of content marketing, more useful and shareworthy content. The traditional way of taking this step is to segment your customers by focusing on similar demographic characteristics, such as age, income level, gender, and so on, and then to find similar people based on those demographics.

However, this approach is not necessarily the most effective way to segment and target your audience on the Internet. It's true that you need to know the primary demographic profiles of your best customer audiences and whether those profiles match sites where your audience may spend time; however, those factors aren't the only ones that matter — because the social media can be analyzed using behaviors in addition to demographics. In fact, behavioral targeting is often more powerful than demographic targeting because, while using the Internet for researching, communicating, shopping, building relationships, and more, people don't necessarily reveal personal demographic information. Furthermore, social media is filled with people who participate in conversations and publish content anonymously or by using pseudonyms, so actually compiling demographic information about these people can be very difficult.

Clearly, relying on demographic segmentation when building a content marketing strategy may lead your business down a path to failure. Instead, Internet users need to be segmented and targeted based on their online behaviors. What sites do they visit? What conversations do they join, and what do they say in those conversations? What content do they share with their own audiences? Those are just a few of the relevant questions marketers need to ask to understand their current and potential online audiences.

By continually evaluating online customer behaviors and adjusting the marketing strategy to address those behaviors, you can find similar people and introduce the best content, in the best places, and at the best time.

Finding your audience's hangouts

One of the most important steps you need to take before you launch your content marketing plan is to find where your target audience already spends time interacting and sharing online. You can use some of the tricks suggested earlier in this chapter by researching your competitors' followers and connections across social media. Chances are many of those people will be part of your target audience, too.

However, the first step is to use keywords to conduct Google searches (because that's the tool most people use to search for information online). In other words, pretend you're a potential customer looking for the type of business, products, or services you offer. Follow the links delivered in the search results just as a consumer would. As you follow the paths provided, you can follow your target audience. Inevitably, you'll find blogs, websites, forums, groups, and so on that your target audience is reading, participating in, and sharing with their own audiences. You need to get involved on those sites, too.

Begin by joining the conversations happening on those sites and offering useful information that adds value to the existing dialogue. Don't self-promote yet. Beginning to develop relationships with your target audience on the destinations where they already spend time is critical, and you can't do that if you're trying to sell. If you want to be a welcomed member to the party, you have to bring something to the table that is meaningful, or no one will want to hang out with you.

When you become a recognized part of the community on a specific destination where your target audience spends time, you can begin bringing those people back to your own branded online destinations, as discussed later in this chapter, where you can offer even more information through your amazing, shareworthy content and deepen your relationships with them. That's how you build lasting relationships that lead to brand loyalty, brand advocacy, and long-term sustainable growth.

Discovering what your audience wants and needs

If you're not delivering the type of content your target audience wants and needs, they won't read or view your content nor will they share it. In fact, they may even ignore you or publish negative responses to your content, which you don't want to happen.

Just as you need to determine what your audience wants and needs from your products and services to develop effective advertising, you need to determine what your audience wants and needs from content. Trying to think of new and amazing content to publish consistently and persistently can be intimidating. Don't worry. Every piece of content you publish doesn't have to be amazing. However, you don't want to dilute your value by publishing too much content that isn't discussion-worthy or shareworthy. The majority of your content should be meaningful, but everyone has days when they're simply not up to their full potential. It's acceptable to have off days when it comes to content marketing, and particularly if you don't have a large staff to cover for you. Just don't let it become a habit, or all of your hard work will have been for naught.

TIP

To find out what your audience wants and needs from your content, you can start by listening. In fact, listening is one of the most important parts of any successful content marketing strategy. You need to constantly be listening to the online conversation so that you can modify your content marketing strategy as necessary.

Consumers move quickly and change their minds even more quickly. If they find your content to be stale or outdated, they'll move on in search of another business or destination that offers the type of value-added information they want and need.

Use the tools suggested in the previous section to find your audience and listen to their conversations, just as you did to find and listen to your competitors. Furthermore, ask your customers both in person and online what kind of information they want and need. Publish a poll on your blog using a tool like Polldaddy (www.polldaddy.com) or SurveyMonkey (www.surveymonkey.com), or pose the question on a forum or group you belong to where your target audience spends time. Additionally, pay attention to your own website and blog analytics to see what content is driving a lot of traffic, comments, and incoming links.

REMEMBER

Your focus should be on long-term growth and trends. A few audience members will always be louder than others, and certain pieces of content may attract a lot of attention. It's up to you to pick out fluctuations that spell opportunities and anomalies that won't drive business in the long run. Pursue the opportunities aggressively, and put the anomalous traffic spikes on the backburner.

Finding and connecting with influencers

While you're researching your competitors and finding your target audience, you should also be looking for the online *influencers,* the people or companies who can help you drive more traffic and conversations around your content. For example, if you own a dating service company, you need to search for the top dating and relationship experts on Twitter and Facebook or the top dating bloggers. These people already have audiences that will be good matches for a dating service business, and if they're very popular, they probably have relationships with many of those audience members and have influence over them.

A number of search tools can help you find influencers across social media. Several options to get you started are listed here:

>> **Twitter apps:** Use Twitter apps such as WeFollow (www.wefollow.com) or Twellow (www.twellow.com) to find people by keyword or interest on Twitter. For example, as shown in Figure 2-3, a search using the tag *organicfood* on WeFollow delivered 88 results that a business selling organic foods would be wise to research. Look for people with a lot of followers and a lot of retweets and @replies to show they're truly engaged with their audiences.

>> **Blog searches:** Conduct a search for blogs by keyword by searching online for your topic and adding the search term *blog* or search a site like IceRocket (www.icerocket.com). Look for blogs that are updated frequently with

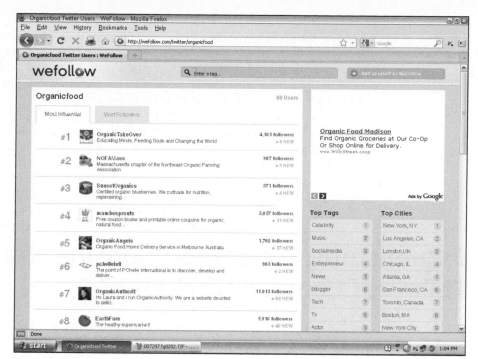

Source: www.wefollow.com

FIGURE 2-3:
Search for influ-
encers on Twitter
using an app such
as WeFollow.

quality content and have high subscriber numbers (if they're published on the site), Alexa rankings (www.alexa.com), and Compete rankings (www.compete.com). Though these ranking tools aren't 100 percent accurate, they can give you an idea of a blog's reach and influence.

>> **Video searches:** Many online influencers publish video content. You can conduct video searches on a number of Web sites, including the largest online video site, YouTube (www.youtube.com), or Google (http://video.google.com). Look for video publishers whose videos get a lot of views and comments and whose profiles link to their blogs and other branded online destinations so that you can get a better idea of their positions and influence in the online space.

>> **Groups:** You can search for groups on Facebook, LinkedIn, or Google (http://groups.google.com/). Not only will your target audience partici-pate in relevant groups, but group leaders also could be highly influential voices online. Look for groups with a lot of active members in order to find the best groups to target.

When you find online influencers who seem to have an engaged audience of people who match your target audience profile, work to get on those influencers' radar screens. Follow them on Twitter and retweet their content or send them @replies.

Friend them on Facebook, like their Facebook page if they have one, and converse with them. Read their blogs and publish comments. However, don't self-promote immediately. Instead, work to demonstrate your knowledge and ability to add value to the online influencers' conversations through social media marketing efforts before you share your own content with them.

An aggressive approach of self-promotion is unlikely to keep you in the good graces of online influencers. Instead, build a relationship first, and then when the time comes when you want to ask an online influencer to help you spread the word about your content or business through a tweet, guest blog post, or other tactic, that online influencer is more likely to be willing to help you.

Establishing Goals and Choosing the Best Forms of Content Marketing

As you develop your content marketing strategy, you need to do so with goals in mind. Because content marketing is a long-term marketing strategy, you must define where you want your business to be in the future. This strategy includes determining how much time you can devote to content marketing, the resources available to help you with your content marketing efforts, and the results you want to attain from those efforts.

You need to approach content marketing realistically, or you won't be satisfied with your results. Remember, content marketing success comes in the form of long-term sustainable growth through brand building and relationship development, which lead to loyalty and word-of-mouth marketing. You can supplement your long-term strategy with short-term tactics such as discount promotions, contests, and so on, but the power of content marketing comes from the organic growth it creates.

With that in mind, you need to move forward with a highly focused content marketing plan. You can't be all things to all people. In fact, trying to spread yourself too thin will reduce your own content quality and confuse consumers. If you can't meet their expectations through your content, they'll leave you behind and find someone who can. The most powerful brands are highly focused brands, so it makes sense that with all the clutter and competition for a share of voice online, niche-focused content can help you stake your claim in the online space. You can read earlier in this chapter about establishing credibility and being the go-to-person for information related to your business. Your brand, online reputation, and business will benefit immensely if you take the time to choose a specific area of focus and related keywords to *own*.

Your content marketing goals need to be realistic. For example, you may create a goal to develop three viable branded online destinations within the next three months, or you may create a goal to attract 1,000 quality Twitter followers over the next six months. Make sure your content marketing goals are always based on quality, not quantity, because if you publish quality content and focus on developing quality audiences, quantity will come organically in time. In other words, your content marketing strategy is successful when the compounding effect begins to truly work for you and you see your numbers growing simply because your content and conversations are meeting customer expectations.

Quality content and relationships help you increase your sphere of influence in the online space, which is a valuable intangible business asset.

Before you define your goals, you also need to think about the types of content marketing you can realistically pursue given the amount of time and technical savvy they require. The best part about content marketing is that the tools of social media that enable you to publish content are fairly easy to use. If you can use word-processing software and an Internet browser, then you can use social Web tools.

Take some time to create accounts on the most popular sites that enable you to publish content such as WordPress for a blog, Facebook for social networking, and Twitter for microblogging. Before you announce that you're joining social media or start reaching out to other people online, play around with the features and start publishing content to build up an archive of amazing content. Get an idea of which tools you enjoy or think you can stick with for the long term, and begin to define your marketing strategies using those tools as your top branded online destinations.

Creating a Core Branded Online Destination

When you pursue a content marketing strategy, you need to have some place to publish content online. In other words, you need to have a core branded online destination that serves as the centerpiece of your content marketing activities. Remember, not all of your content marketing efforts will happen on your own sites, particularly as your social media marketing activities overlap with your content marketing efforts. Your online conversations that happen across social media both on and off your own sites should all lead back to your core branded online destination.

These sections examine where you can build an online destination, how you can plan it, and how you can ensure that your customers find the information there valuable.

Where: Location! Location! Location!

You can use many tools to establish your core branded online destination. A blog is the best choice, because it gives you the most flexibility in terms of the type of content you can publish in one place. Blogs are also very search-engine friendly and are very powerful in terms of the compounding effect of blogging and building your online presence.

But what if blogging isn't right for you? What if the idea of writing even a single paragraph blog post sounds like a monumental effort? That's okay. Choose another tool that you do enjoy and make that your core branded online destination. Some of the most popular core branded destinations other than blogs are Facebook pages, LinkedIn profiles, YouTube channels, or Twitter profiles. You can make any social site your core branded destination, because the value comes from the content you publish there, not the name of the tool.

You can read the story of Naked Pizza told in Book 3, Chapter 1. It's the perfect example of a brick-and-mortar retailer that successfully uses Twitter as its core branded online destination. The most important thing that you need to do is to ensure that your core branded destination offers the most information to enable you to connect with and build relationships with your target audience. If Naked Pizza can achieve that in 140-character tweets, so can you.

Designing your central hub

If your core branded destination is the central hub for all your content marketing efforts to which all roads lead, then you need to make sure that central hub accurately reflects your brand image and promise. It needs to meet consumers' expectations for your brand both in content and visual appeal.

For example, a technical company positioning itself as expert in website development should have a core branded destination that looks great, loads quickly, and is designed with intuitive navigation with all the bells and whistles people expect from a top website development provider. If that company's core branded destination looks like an out-of-the-box, standard site that anyone could create with little technical knowledge, consumers will be confused and search for another site and company that meets their expectations.

TIP

Therefore, take time to make sure your core branded destination looks great, works well, and accurately reflects your brand. If you invest money in your content marketing strategy, then the design of your core branded destination should be at the top of your priority list when it comes to setting your budget.

Fortunately, you can find designers who can help you create branded blogs, Twitter backgrounds, Facebook pages, and more. Following are several sources to help you find affordable design help:

>> **Twitter backgrounds:** You can get custom Twitter background design help from many freelance designers.

>> **Freelance blog designers:** You can search for freelance blog designers on Google or check the footer in blogs you like to see if a link to the designer is provided. Alternatively, you can publish a design request opportunity on Craigslist (www.craigslist.org) or a freelancer website such as Freelancer. com (www.freelancer.com), Elance (www.elance.com), or iFreelance.com (www.ifreelance.com). Some of these sites require that you pay a fee to publish a listing, so be sure to read all of the site requirements.

Blog design doesn't have to cost thousands of dollars. Thanks to the many premium themes available for the most popular business blogging application, WordPress, you can purchase a premium theme and hire a designer to help you tweak it to match your brand and needs for anywhere from a few hundred dollars and up, depending on the extent of your customization requests and the designer you choose. To find out more about blog design and themes, check out *Blogging All-in-One For Dummies*, 2nd Edition, by Susan Gunelius (John Wiley & Sons, Inc.).

Adding value and making it easy to buy

Of course, your core branded destination should offer a wealth of content that adds value to your target audience's everyday lives so that they talk about it, share it, and come back for more. But there is more to creating your core branded online destination than publishing amazing content on a site that's well designed. You also need to make sure it's extremely easy for your audience to buy from you or perform the action you want them to do when they visit your site, such as submit an inquiry form.

No matter how important it is to publish amazing content and indirectly market your business through your content, you're still running a business, and you need to make money. Although you don't want to be overly aggressive through your content in promoting your business (review the 80–20 rule described in Book 3, Chapter 1), you do want to make sure that visitors can easily make a purchase or perform your desired action when they come to your core branded destination. You don't want to make them feel like they're being pushed to buy something, but you do want to make sure the option is always available and easy to do.

Therefore, make sure links to your online catalog or inquiry form (or other page or action you want visitors to follow) are prominently displayed on every page of your core branded destination. Don't interrupt the audience's experience as they read your content and engage with you. For example, a pop-up window that appears when visitors navigate around your site is a surefire way to annoy them. Instead, provide links for convenience in your blog's sidebar or core branded destination profile, so they're easily accessible but not overbearing and interruptive.

Surrounding Consumers with Branded Content

When your core branded destination is established and you're building an archive of amazing content on that central hub, begin spreading your tentacles across social media. Ultimately, you want to surround consumers with your branded content by creating branded online destinations that allow consumers to choose how they want to experience and interact with your brand.

Not everyone likes the same type of content or experiences, which is why companies like Disney offer varied ways for consumers to experience their brand. For example, a consumer can watch the Disney Channel, visit Walt Disney World, or shop at the Disney Store. Each experience is different and is likely to appeal to different audiences and consumers. In the online space, Disney offers varied branded experiences as well, including blogs, online games, a Facebook page, online shopping, forums, and more. Consumers can select how they want to experience the Disney brand online, too.

The more time you spend publishing content and engaging with your audience, the more you're likely to enjoy content marketing. In time, setting up multiple branded online destinations won't seem like an overwhelming task. If necessary, you can recruit employees or hire freelancers to help you maintain your varied online branded destinations without breaking the bank.

REMEMBER

As you build your branded online destinations, you must make sure that all of those destinations accurately reflect your brand, add value, and lead back to your core branded online destination. Never forget that all roads lead back to that central hub, and that's where you want to try to lead as many people as you can so you can share even more information and deepen your relationships with them.

Figure 2-4 shows a representation of a business using a blog as its core branded online destination with varied branded online destinations leading back to that central hub.

FIGURE 2-4:
All roads lead back to your core branded online destination.

Don't feel like you need to create numerous branded online destinations right away. Quality trumps quantity, so only pursue extending your brand to new online destinations if you're certain you can commit to them for the long-term with quality content and interactions. You don't want to focus on varied branded online destinations at the expense of your core branded online destination.

Comparing Free versus Premium Content Strategies

As you move forward with your content marketing strategy, you're likely to find some businesses that offer only free content and some that offer both free content and premium content that is available with a price tag. For example, premium content can come in the form of an ebook available for purchase, a newsletter available for a monthly subscription, a membership fee to a site that gives people access to more content, and so on. Businesses can get creative in how they package content in order to make money.

Before you can determine if putting a price tag on your content is right for your business, you need to review your content marketing goals. Ask the following questions:

>> Why are you offering content online?

>> What do you want to get from your content?

>> What do you want people to do with your content?

>> Who do you want to read or view your content?

Answer the preceding questions and compare them to the benefits that putting a price tag on your content can give you in terms of revenue. Would the money you could potentially make from your content mean more to you than the word-of-mouth marketing, brand loyalty, brand advocacy, and search engine optimization that free content gives your business?

A true content marketing strategy offers all content for free in an attempt to drive an online buzz, create entry points to your branded online destinations, surround consumers with branded experiences, engage consumers, encourage sharing, and indirectly market your business for long-term, sustainable, and organic growth. A content marketing strategy that includes a premium component adds a direct sales and revenue-generating element to the strategy that may run counter to the true purpose of content marketing. Again, only you can decide if the potential revenue outweighs the indirect marketing benefits of a true and free content marketing strategy.

Chapter 3

Long-Form Content Marketing: Blogging, Online Articles, Ebooks, and More

There is no time like the present to start thinking about the types of content you want to publish to both directly and indirectly promote your business and brand. Much of your decision depends on two factors — your writing abilities and your technical abilities. Fortunately, the tools of online publishing make it easy for even the most technically challenged individuals to become content publishers within minutes. If you know how to use a Web browser, email, and a word-processing application, then your learning curve for most online publishing tools will be short and painless.

The other factor related to pursuing a content marketing plan isn't as easy to master. If you're not comfortable writing more than a few sentences, then long-form content marketing will be more challenging. That's not to say long-form content marketing will be impossible, but you'll need to spend some time polishing your writing skills or find a writer to produce your content. The choice is yours, but don't skip long-form content marketing entirely just because writing isn't your strength. Many successful content marketers freely admit that writing isn't their top skill.

Understanding and Using Long-Form Content Marketing for Your Business

Book 3, Chapter 1 explains that long-form content marketing includes all published content that is more than a few sentences and that offers deep value, such as blog posts, articles, ebooks, press releases, white papers, presentations, videos, podcasts, webinars, and so on. In other words, any content you publish online or offline that takes a person more than a couple of minutes to read, listen to, or view could be considered a form of content marketing when that content is related to a business or brand and provides useful information.

The vast majority of business-related content you publish (even very loosely related content) that's more than a paragraph in length or that takes more than a couple of minutes to read could be considered content marketing.

Most long-form content isn't self-promotional. No one wants to read a 1,000-word marketing pitch. There is a reason infomercials are labeled as such — because to simply call them informational programming would be misleading when they are truthfully just a lengthy commercial.

TIP

Your content should not read like a marketing pitch or commercial even if it's intended for direct marketing purposes. While it's acceptable to include a brief promotional message or link within your long-form content, further self-promotion turns your content into an ad or marketing brochure rather than a useful content marketing tactic. There is a fine line between content marketing and advertising. Avoid crossing that line, or your target audience may perceive your content marketing efforts as nothing more than advertising.

The trick to creating successful content is ensuring that it's not about you. Always make sure your content talks more about your target audience than about you. For example, instead of writing a blog post announcing the freeze-and-serve meals available at your restaurant for takeout, write a blog post that explains how to make healthy meals in 30 minutes or less. End the post with a line that says, "If 30 minutes are more than you can spare, you can still eat well without breaking the bank with affordable premade meal solutions. For example, our healthy freeze-and-serve take-out meals are cheaper than dining out but faster than cooking at home." This way, you first provide shareworthy information (refer to Book 3, Chapter 2 for more on this topic), and second, for convenience (and to make a potential purchase easy), you suggest an appropriate alternative related to your business. In this way, your suggestion is perceived as a welcomed option rather than as an intrusive marketing message.

REMEMBER

Most long-form content marketing builds awareness of your business and establishes your brand's position relative to competitors. This type of marketing can help build trust and define you as the go-to person or business on specific topics. Therefore, try to publish long-form content that is well-written and copyrighted with a Creative Commons license so your audience can use it and share it with their audiences, thereby exponentially increasing your reach and awareness of your business.

Becoming a Blogger

In the simplest terms, a *blog* (short for *web log*) is a website where the author (called a *blogger*) publishes entries (called *posts*) that are typically displayed in reverse chronological order and stored in dated archives. Some blogging applications allow bloggers to publish *pages* that live outside the post chronology. Posts usually include a comment feature that allows readers to publish their own comments directly beneath the post. Blogs also include sidebar and footer areas where bloggers can display links to their additional branded online destinations and content, ads, and more.

Blogs are very flexible, which enables individual bloggers to set up their blogs exactly the way they want them. Blogs are also highly interactive and an amazing relationship-building tool, thanks to the comment feature and the ability to continually publish fresh content, including links to other relevant content across the social Web. In other words, you can use your business blog to build relationships with potential consumers as well as with other content publishers and online influencers.

Blogging is one of the best options for publishing long-form content. For example, blogs are very search-engine friendly and allow you to create numerous entry points (which live forever in your blog's archives) that search engines can index. People familiar with the social Web are familiar with the pass-along value of blog posts. By spreading links to their own online profiles and through blogging,

Long-Form Content Marketing

people quickly share valuable posts with their own audiences. In fact, blogs are probably the best option for a core branded online destination because they are flexible, easy to use, and offer so many ways that you can directly and indirectly promote your business. Therefore, this chapter offers a great deal of information about using a blog for content marketing.

Creating your blog

The first step to becoming a blogger is to create a blog for your business. If you're serious about using a blog to build your business, I highly suggest reading a book like *Blogging All-in-One For Dummies,* 2nd Edition by Susan Gunelius (Wiley, 2012), which offers specific instructions about all the tools and tasks you need to effectively join the blogosphere. Although there's not enough space in this chapter to fully cover the topic of blogging, you'll find some important basics to start you on the path to successful business blogging.

Choosing your tools

Before you can create a blog, you need to decide which blogging application you want to use. The three most popular blogging applications for businesses are WordPress, Blogger, and TypePad. Each offers pros and cons, but the self-hosted version of WordPress (available at www.wordpress.org) may be the best one for building your business blog. In fact, you can build your entire website using the application available at WordPress.org, which makes it very easy to manage your site and make changes on the fly without hiring expensive Web developers and designers to help you. You may still want to hire a freelance designer or developer to ensure that your blog is set up correctly, is professionally designed, and accurately reflects your business and brand. However, with very little technical knowledge or ability, you can manage the ongoing maintenance using the self-hosted WordPress application.

TECHNICAL STUFF

When you choose to use the self-hosted WordPress application from WordPress to create your blog, you must pay for your own Web hosting and your own domain name, but both fees are very affordable. The added flexibility that WordPress offers over other blogging applications makes the small fees related to hosting and domain registration worth it.

The self-hosted WordPress application (often referred to as *WordPress.org* because that is where it can be found for download) is an open source application that anyone can use. Simply download the WordPress application from WordPress.org and upload it to your Web hosting account. Then you can log into your new WordPress blog account online to create your blog.

Unlike WordPress.com, Blogger.com, and TypePad.com, you *must* obtain your own Web hosting account with a third-party hosting company such as Bluehost.com, GoDaddy.com, or HostGator.com to store your data and serve it to online visitors if you use the WordPress.org application. Doing so sounds harder than it actually is, and a book like *WordPress For Dummies* (John Wiley & Sons, Inc.) by Lisa Sabin-Wilson breaks down all the steps for creating your own WordPress site and blog.

WordPress.org users also have the ability to modify their blog designs in any way they want, because they have access to the code used to create those designs. That's a big perk that you're sure to use as you modify your own blog to suit your business' needs. Furthermore, developers create WordPress plug-ins that exponentially enhance the functionality of WordPress.org blogs and websites. For example, you can upload WordPress plug-ins to your blog that give your blog posts a search engine optimization (SEO) boost, create contact forms, back up your blog content, add related post links to all your blog posts, and more. The options are always growing as more plug-ins are released, mostly free of charge.

Selecting a theme

When you decide on your blogging application and create an account, you need to choose a layout for your blog. Most blogs are presented in 1-, 2-, or 3-column layout where the largest column takes up about two-thirds of the browser window and one or two smaller columns appear on the right or left or flanking the largest column. Blog posts appear in the largest column, and the one or two sidebars include extra information, links, and so on. Some blogs use a magazine-style layout, such as the one shown in Figure 3-1, which enables you to display a lot of information on the home page of your blog. This layout is popular for blogs that publish new posts frequently throughout the day and want to give new content more exposure on the front page.

Choose the layout that enables you to display your most important information above the fold, meaning visitors don't have to scroll to see it. Depending on how often you publish blog posts and how much extraneous information you want to draw attention to, your blog layout could be magazine, 1-column, 2-column, or 3-column. It's completely up to you.

TIP

Select a responsive theme, one that works great on both mobile and desktop. You can always change your blog layout at anytime, so don't feel like you have to commit to a layout forever. Just try to retain brand consistency in terms of color, header design (like the masthead of a newspaper, your blog's header spans across the top of every page and at the very least should include your logo), and so on. This way, even if the layout changes, return visitors will still know they've made it to the right place. You never want to confuse your audience by not meeting their expectations.

FIGURE 3-1:
A magazine layout displays snippets of many blog posts on the home page.

Source: www.newyork.cbslocal.com

If you choose WordPress as your blogging application, you can find many resources online with premade themes to give your blog a unique look. There are three types of WordPress themes: free, premium, and custom. Free themes are exactly what you would think. They are offered free for anyone to use. Premium themes come with a price tag (typically $50–100 for a single-use license) and can be modified to give your blog a unique look than free themes can provide. Custom themes are the most expensive (typically over $1,000). They are designed from the ground up specifically for the site they're built for.

Try using a premium theme that offers free support and has a reputation for being well coded. Here are some sites where you can find free and premium WordPress themes:

» **StudioPress:** Offers the popular Genesis premium theme, also called a framework (www.studiopress.com).

» **Theme Forest:** Offers more than 20,000 themes and website templates for $2 (www.themeforest.com).

» **WordPress Hub:** Offers themes handpicked for usability (www.wphub.com).

Designing your blog

When you know which blogging application and layout you want to use on your blog, you need to put the pieces together and design your branded online destination. Fortunately, blogging applications make the design process easy, but you can enlist the help of a professional designer or developer to make your blog work exactly the way you want it to. This is one of the few investments that you'll need to make as part of your content marketing plan, so invest wisely. For example, work with a developer to fully integrate your online storefront with your blog and website so that consumers will find the experience seamless and easy to navigate. This investment will deliver long-term returns because it makes the buying process easier. As mentioned in Book 3, Chapter 2, design is an important part of your content marketing strategy. Don't skimp.

At the very least, your business blog should prominently display your logo and links to your other branded online destinations, a well-written About page, integration with your website, a contact form, and easy-to-read content. You need to make sure your theme works well and your content is displayed neatly. For example, using a small font that is difficult to read damages the user experience on your blog and means fewer repeat visitors.

Some design problems are easy to notice and fix, while others are less obvious or more challenging. For example, if you don't know the coding languages used to create your blog, Cascading Style Sheets (CSS), and HyperText Markup Language (HTML), you may need a designer or developer to help you.

Publishing content to your blog

You can publish content to your blog several ways, and you should use all of them. For example, create pages (if your blogging application allows it) that provide static information about your business and publish posts to share your thoughts, breaking news, useful information, advice, and tips. Publish helpful links, videos, and so on within your posts and in your blog's sidebar. The space is there; use it to directly and indirectly market your business!

Don't be afraid to get creative with the content you publish on your blog. Although writing blog posts is a form of long-form content marketing, you can also republish your short-form marketing content on your blog. For example, display images from your Flickr profile in your blog's sidebar or publish your Twitter posts in your blog's sidebar. Both options are ways you can cross-promote your content and further deliver useful information to your audience.

The most popular blogs are updated frequently — as often as several times per day. To ensure your blog is persistently in front of your audience, try to publish new content at least three times per week. The more the better, but if you publish less frequently, it's easy to be forgotten. Remember, the online audience is fickle and quick to replace publishers who aren't meeting their expectations.

Furthermore, try to keep your blog posts succinct. Although blogging is a form of long-form content marketing, the information you deliver via your blog should be concise and easy for readers to skim through to determine if they want to read it in more detail. A good word count target for blog posts is 500–800 words, but more or less is fine as long as your post is interesting and conveys valuable information. If one of your posts gets to be longer than 800 words, consider breaking it up into a series (which is also a great use of tease marketing). Also, be sure to use headings, lists, and images, as appropriate, to break up text-heavy posts.

Using comments to generate conversations

After you publish a blog post, don't abandon it. If people submit comments to your blog posts, respond to them. One of the primary advantages of content marketing is the ability to build relationships with your target audience because relationships typically lead to sales, brand loyalty, brand advocacy, and increased business. Your chance to build relationships is lost if you ignore your audience. If a person leaves a comment on one of your blog posts, it's safe to assume that person is engaged in your content and open to hearing from you. You wouldn't ignore that person if you were in a face-to-face situation, so don't ignore them online.

Be careful of spam comments and *trolling* — comments that are submitted simply to incite arguments. Moderate comments submitted to your blog to ensure they aren't spam, don't include links to offensive websites, and don't include offensive language. While you want to allow free speech, your blog is *yours*, which means you can delete or edit comments that might damage the user experience on your blog and your reputation. However, that doesn't mean you can simply delete negative comments about your business on your blog. Chances are if a disgruntled customer submits a complaint on your blog and you delete it, that person will not go away quietly. Don't try to hide your mistakes. Instead, discuss the issue with the customer either through private email or by responding professionally to negative comments. Always consider the source and craft your response accordingly.

Comments don't happen only on your blog, though. You should also take time to read other blogs and submit comments on posts that interest you. Be sure to use the same name in the name field of blog comment forms and include your website (or blog) URL in the URL field in every comment you submit to any blog. This useful SEO trick can increase links to your branded online destination as well as traffic. If people like your comment, they just might click on the link to see what else you have to say.

Making it easy to share blog content

If you're taking the time to write shareworthy content on your blog, then you should also take the time to make it very easy for people to share that content with their own audiences on Twitter, Facebook, LinkedIn, Digg, StumbleUpon, and any other online profile or destination they choose. If you use WordPress as your blogging application, then you're in luck. A number of plug-ins make it easy to automatically add social Web sharing links and buttons to your blog posts. Even if you don't use WordPress, many tools can help you add some social sharing links to your blog posts in Blogger and TypePad. For WordPress.org, here are a number of WordPress tools and plug-ins that enable you to make sharing a snap for your audience:

>> **TweetMeme Retweet Button:** Add the extremely popular Retweet button so people can tweet a link to your blog post in their Twitter streams (`http://wordpress.org/extend/plugins/tweetmeme`).

>> **Facebook Share (New) Button:** Add a Facebook Share button so people can easily share a link to your blog post in their Facebook updates (`http://wordpress.org/extend/plugins/facebook-share-new/screenshots`).

>> **ShareThis:** Add links to share your blog post on a wide variety of sites (`http://wordpress.org/extend/plugins/share-this`). Similar plug-ins include AddThis (`http://wordpress.org/extend/plugins/addthis`) and Sociable (`https://wordpress.org/plugins/sociable/`).

This free plugin (`https://wordpress.org/plugins/wp-share-buttons-analytics-by-getsocial/`) performs what all of the three preceding options do.

TIP

Make sure visitors have the ability to easily share every post on your blog in order to boost exposure and traffic to those posts. It costs nothing, takes a few minutes to set up, and can have a significant effect on the performance of your blog posts in terms of directly and indirectly marketing your business.

Leveraging feeds and subscriptions

RSS (Really Simple Syndication) is the most commonly used Web feed format, which is the technology used to standardize Web content so people can read it via email or feed reader.

TECHNICAL
STUFF

Some companies actually aggregate Web feeds (including blog feeds) and make them available as part of larger content packages, which are sold to companies, websites, news organizations, and more.

You should set up your blog's feed using a tool like FeedBurner (www.feedburner.com) and prominently display an invitation for visitors to your blog to subscribe to receive your feed content via email or feed reader. Subscribers receive an email message with your new blog content on a daily basis, so they can keep up with your content without having to continually visit your blog looking for new content. Some people prefer to aggregate the feeds of the blogs they enjoy and access all those feeds in one place using a feed reader like Google Reader. You should invite people to subscribe to your blog via feed reader or email so that they can choose how they want to receive and consume your content. Figure 3-2 shows an example of a feed subscription invitation in a blog's sidebar.

FIGURE 3-2:
Prominently
display your
blog's feed
subscription.

Source: www.keysplashcreative.com

You can also use feeds to cross-promote your content. For example, you can publish the feed content from other blogs you write or enjoy in your blog's sidebar or footer using the RSS widget provided in WordPress. You can also feed your blog content to your Twitter, Facebook, or LinkedIn updates, and vice versa, using a tool like Twitterfeed (www.twitterfeed.com) and the tools built into

Facebook and LinkedIn. Check out the feeds displayed in a blog footer as shown in Figure 3-3 to see how it works.

FIGURE 3-3: Cross-promote your content by publishing feeds from your other blogs and social profiles on your blog.

Source: www.keysplashcreative.com

Feeds can do more to help you promote your varied content than just making it easy for people to know when you publish new blog content. Be creative with your feeds and let them automatically cross-promote your content.

Promoting your blog

As shown in the previous section, you can feed your blog content to your online profiles to give your blog posts more exposure. You should also include a link to your blog in your online profile biographies, in your email signature, in your forum signatures, on your business card, on your letterhead and invoices, and anywhere else you can think of. This is particularly important if your business blog is your core branded online destination.

Other promotional opportunities include guest blogging (discussed in the next section), feeding your blog updates to LinkedIn groups that allow the News feature (read more about LinkedIn groups in Book 4, Chapter 4).

Furthermore, do some keyword research and write blog posts with SEO in mind (see Book 2, Chapter 5 for more on SEO). Applying simple SEO tactics to your blog posts can help drive organic search traffic to your blog that can last for a long time!

Being a guest blogger

Guest blogging is a popular blog promotional tactic that you can use to build awareness of and traffic to your business blog. You can do guest blogging in two ways. You can either write blog posts as a guest writer for other blogs or publish blog posts by guest writers on your blog. Both options can help you build relationships with other bloggers and increase traffic to your blog.

For example, when other bloggers write guest posts on your blog, they are likely to share it with their audience of followers who might not already be reading your blog. On the flip side, when you write guest blog posts for other blogs, your content gets in front of new audiences who might like what you have to say and follow you back to your own blog to read and further interact with you.

Conducting blogger outreach

The first step to writing guest blog posts for other blogs is doing your research. You need to find blogs whose existing readers match your target audience. Conduct a Google search (www.google.com — and add *blog* to your search criteria) to find blogs about topics related to your business. Read your competitors' blogs and follow links from people who submit comments to your competitors' posts to see if they write blogs related to your business.

When you find blogs that you want to write guest posts for, begin to leave comments and join the conversations happening on those blogs so that you get on the bloggers' radar screens. Follow the bloggers on Twitter and connect with them on their various online profiles. This is particularly important for highly successful bloggers who get many inquiries each day. When you've established a relationship or at least gotten on a blogger's radar screen, send an email asking if you can submit a guest post. Explain that the post will be original content for that blog only and mention the topic so that the blogger understands your content will be useful to that blogger's audience.

TIP

Don't harass bloggers and don't send generic messages to them, or you'll be accused of blog blasting. Instead, send personalized email messages that demonstrate the value you can deliver to the bloggers' audience, and make it clear that your guest post won't be self-promotional.

Finding guest blogging opportunities

You can find guest blogging opportunities by searching Google for keyword phrases such as *guest blog submission* or *write for us,* but that can be time-consuming and hit or miss in terms of getting positive responses. To find more guest blogging opportunities, you can join a site such as HARO (www.helpareporter.com), which is great for blog exposure.

Tricks to make guest blogging work for you

For your guest blogging efforts to be successful, you need to choose blogs to write for that can enable you to get in front of your target audience. That means you need to do your research first. Next, you need to follow the suggestions provided earlier in this section related to effectively reaching out to bloggers for whom you'd like to write guest posts, and finally, you need to write amazing, shareworthy content in your guest blog posts.

REMEMBER

Be sure to include a brief bio at the end of your guest blog posts with a link back to your blog and website. Just make sure your bio is short (two to three sentences) and isn't written in a self-promotional tone. You don't want your post to be ruined when people get to the end of it and find themselves bombarded with marketing messages that leave a negative last impression of you and your business.

Writing Articles and Contributing to Websites

A number of article publishing websites allow you to publish your content free, providing another way for your target audience to engage with your brand. You can also reach out to websites that accept contributors and pitch your content for inclusion on those sites. Article publishing and website content contributions are typically a bit more formal in tone and formatting than blog content, so you need to approach this form of long-form content marketing with that in mind.

Guest posting your way to greatness

The best way to get your content out there is to give it to websites that need to feed readers who are interested in your topic. Website owners with a large following are always looking for good content to share with their readers. After you establish yourself as someone they can trust to deliver great content, other website owners will come and find you. You can also do the following tips:

>> **Seek out blogs that write about your product or service.** They don't need to be huge blogs. You can start small and get your name out there.

>> **Reach out to the blog owner.** Give her a free blog entry or five topics you can write about and ask if her readers would be interested in any.

Writing articles for the Web

When you write articles for the Web, you need to consider more than simply conveying useful information. Many article submission sites and sites that accept contributors have specific guidelines you have to follow or your content won't be published. Always search for writers' guidelines on sites you plan to submit articles or content to, and follow them to the letter.

You should also be sure to write with SEO in mind, because many article directory sites are very search-friendly. To get maximum exposure for your articles, you need to be sure that people can find them. It can also help to write your articles in HTML so that you can be confident they are published exactly how you want them to look.

TECHNICAL STUFF

You can find out more about basic HTML on a site like Dave's Site (www.davesite.com/webstation/html) or w3schools.com (www.w3schools.com/HTML/default.asp).

Finally, take some time to read other articles that have already been published on sites where you want to submit your content and be sure to format your articles similarly to other articles related to your topic that perform well. Many article publishing sites allow you to sort content by topic or view popular articles. Find out what top performers are doing on each site, and then write and format your articles similarly.

Republishing and retooling

When you're submitting content to article publishing sites, you need to remember that those sites aren't your own branded online destinations. Therefore, your content appears alongside content from a lot of different people and businesses. Make sure the sites you choose match your brand promise, but also make sure your efforts match the site where your content will appear.

For example, article directory sites are perfect places to retool and republish your existing content. As long as you don't republish the exact same article in more than one place, you can derive benefits from it. A content marketing trick is to *repurpose* your content so that it's not exactly the same but conveys similar concepts on multiple sites. Save your hard work and efforts for crafting original, amazing content on your own branded online destinations, and use repurposed or retooled content on article directory sites as a supplement to your online presence.

Promoting your articles

Articles are perfect for supplementing your content marketing efforts, but don't lead with them. For example, instead of linking to your articles on article directories, link to similar content on your blog or other branded online destination. Articles should serve a primary purpose of capturing the attention of people who might not find your content otherwise and directing them (through a link within your content) to your core branded online destination where they can discover more about you, read more of your amazing content, and further interact with you.

TIP

With that said, don't spend time promoting your content on article directories. Instead, let those articles pick up extraneous traffic and send it your way, but don't drive traffic to those articles. It's far more beneficial to spend your time driving people to your branded online destinations. That's why article directories are the perfect place for your repurposed content.

Becoming an Author: Ebooks

Ebooks are a highly popular form of long-form content marketing. They can deliver a lot of information in an easy-to-read, easy-to-share, and easy-to-produce manner. It seems like ebooks are available on about any topic you can think of, but the well-written, authoritative ebooks stand far above the rest in terms of popularity and pass-along value. Furthermore, the promotional opportunities are plentiful.

Choosing an ebook topic

When you decide to write an ebook as part of your content marketing plan, you need to choose a topic that is directly related to your business. An ebook isn't a direct marketing tool. On the contrary, an ebook should be highly informational or educational with little or no direct marketing messages included. In fact, the most effective ebooks in terms of content marketing success include little more in terms of direct marketing messages than a line of copy at the beginning or end that says, "for more information contact us at XYZ or check out our blog at ABC. com." If the information is useful enough, that ebook will drive interest, conversations, and traffic without a direct and repeated request.

Consider writing about a topic that you're passionate about or that you receive a lot of questions about. Either approach ensures that your ebook will be interesting and useful. Always put your target audience first. Although you may have marketing message you'd like to deliver, if your ebook doesn't meet your audience's wants and needs, your message will be ignored. The content of the ebook in terms of its consumer appeal should be your top priority. The trick is ensuring that you can link that ebook topic back to your business in some way so that readers are likely to look to you for more information and great content.

Considering length

Ebooks should be fairly short. If you type your ebook draft in a word processing program like Microsoft Word, set your margins to one inch, your font to 12-point Times New Roman, and your line spacing to double space. Your target length could be as short as approximately 20 pages or 5,000 words. Of course, the most important thing is that your ebook is concise, clear, and informative. Don't agonize over length. Just make sure that your ebook is long enough to be useful, and you'll be okay.

You don't want your ebook to be just a few pages, or it's not an ebook at all. It's a long article. On the other hand, you don't want your ebook to be too long, or you run the risk of rambling and losing readers before they finish (or before they even start) reading. Write with 20–40 pages or 5,000–10,000 words in mind for best results.

Writing your ebook

Your ebook should be written like a short book. That means you need a title, copyright page, table of contents, and chapters. You need to write original content and cite sources for information that isn't your own original content. Get started by determining what you want readers to walk away understanding after they read your ebook. When you determine that end goal, you can create an outline that shows how you're going to get there throughout your ebook's chapters.

REMEMBER

Make sure you use headings, lists, callouts, and images in your ebook. Many people read ebooks online, so it's important that yours is easy to scan on a computer screen. Remember, ebooks should be short and easy to read. Your tone and style should be less formal than a research paper or encyclopedia but more formal than a blog post or Facebook conversation. You need to demonstrate your expertise in your ebook or no one will read it, but you also need to seem human and accessible or no one will read it. Try to find a balance between exuding authority and exuding arrogance and your ebook will have a greater chance for success.

TIP

When you're done writing your ebook and think it's perfect, show it to colleagues, friends, family, and even existing customers to get their feedback. Their suggestions are likely to make your ebook even better and you might even be surprised at the spelling and grammatical errors they find. Always have someone else proofread your own work. You're too close to it and you'll miss typos and other errors no matter how many times you read it.

Designing your ebook

When your ebook is written, it's time to make it look great. Design can really give an ebook a boost, because great design makes an ebook look more professional and makes it easier to read. Following are ten ebook design suggestions that can help you develop a better final product:

>> Format your ebook in a landscape orientation since many people read ebooks online.

>> Use a font size and type that's easy to read both online and offline, such as Georgia or Verdana, with a size no smaller than 14 points.

>> Use a white background with black text for the body of the ebook to ensure maximum readability online and offline.

>> Test your ebook on different monitors and in printed form to ensure that the colors and layout look good everywhere people might view them.

>> Use web-friendly colors and fonts.

>> Use a lot of white space for maximum readability.

>> Use images to break up long blocks of text.

>> Invest in royalty-free images that readers are not likely to have seen on other Websites, blogs, or ebooks.

>> Save your ebook in PDF format so that it's easy (and free) for people to download, print, and share.

>> Hire a designer to make sure your ebook looks great and that it is saved optimally for download and sharing.

No matter how great your content is, if your ebook looks terrible, is difficult to view, or impossible to download, no one will read it. Don't waste the time and effort writing your ebook by trying to design it on the cheap.

Long-Form Content Marketing

Making it easy to share your ebook

One of the best things you can do to ensure that your ebook is a successful component of your content marketing plan is to remove the gateway and allow anyone to access it. Second, publish your ebook with a Creative Commons Attribution license so that anyone can share it, republish it, and use it in their own work as long as they cite you as the owner and source. You can include information on your copyright page that explains the Creative Commons Attribution license and even request that attribution be provided in a specific manner, such as a link to your website or core branded destination.

TIP

Make sure that your ebook includes a footer so that your name and website link are displayed at the bottom of every page. This way, even readers see only a single page of your ebook, your name and URL will be available to them.

Publish the link to view and download your ebook on your core branded online destination along with a message that describes the Creative Commons Attribution license and make it clear that readers are welcome to share the content with their own audiences. Many people skip the copyright page, so you want to be certain they understand they can pass along your ebook freely. The goal is for your ebook to get maximum exposure, so you want everyone to understand the Creative Commons Attribution license and what it means to them. Check out `https://en.wikipedia.org/wiki/Creative_Commons_license` for more on the Creative Commons license.

Promoting your ebook

After your ebook is uploaded to your website and core branded destination and is available for the world to see, it's time to start spreading the word about the ebook:

1. Begin by publishing a blog post about your ebook and be sure to include a link to read or download the PDF file along with a note assuring readers that it's okay to share the PDF file with their own audiences.

2. Use a service like bit.ly (`http://bit.ly`) to create a trackable link that goes to the page where your ebook can be found online. Tweet that link along with a note about your ebook and share it on Facebook, LinkedIn, and on all your other online profiles and destinations.

3. Include links to your ebook in your forum signatures, email signature, and business card. You can even upload your ebook to SlideShare (discussed in the "Publishing Presentations" section, later in this chapter) or make it available through Amazon's Kindle eReader device using the Amazon Digital Text Platform (`https://kdp.amazon.com/signin`). The key is getting your ebook

included in Amazon searches, which can really increase exposure for your ebook, you, and your business.

WARNING

To offer your ebook on the Kindle, you do have to put a price tag on it, but you can use the lowest price, $0.99, and offer some of your content for free preview.

Bottom line, if you take the time to write and design a great ebook that your target audience is likely to find very useful, don't be afraid to shout it to the world.

Writing Press Releases

Press releases are different from other forms of content marketing because they should not include marketing language at all. Instead, press releases should be written in a journalistic style and about truly newsworthy events that are likely to be of interest to wide audiences. Try to make your business newsworthy so that you can create press releases to indirectly market your business. You can turn a lot of events related to your business into news. For example, events such as launching a new product or website, taking on a new client, attending an event, hosting a training session, or hiring a new employee could all be turned into newsworthy press releases.

In order to use press releases as a content marketing tool, you need to learn the correct way to write press releases and how and where to publish them online in order to generate exposure for you and your business.

Writing and formatting press releases

Press releases should be written in the following way:

1. Start by writing a headline that explains the news being released and includes your company name.

2. Lead with the town, state, and date for the release.

3. Quickly get to the point of your news release by addressing the who, why, when, where, what, and how questions of journalism.

   The key is to write so that all the critical information about your release can be communicated within the first paragraph.

4. Include supporting details and quotes from you or key individuals related to the press release.

5. End with a boilerplate paragraph about your company that includes your website URL and a contact name, an address, a phone number, and an email address for media inquiries.

Long-Form Content Marketing

Press releases should be written in the third-person style and should not include any kind of promotional messages. They should be completely factual and devoid of hype. Write press releases with a target word count of no more than 500 words. Try to write with keywords in mind, particularly within the first 250 words of your press release and within any links used in your press release. If the sites where you upload your press release allow you to include keyword tags, be sure to do so to maximize the number of people who can find your release in searches.

Distributing press releases

There was a time when press releases could be distributed only through large wire services used by news organizations. Today, you can distribute press releases through a wide variety of services and websites offering varying costs and reach. Following are a number of options to choose from:

>> **PR Newswire:** Varied price levels with different distribution for each (www. prnewswire.com). Small business packages are available.

>> **PRWeb:** Different price levels for different types of distribution (www.prweb. com).

>> **Free Press Release:** Offers free and paid distribution options (www.free-press-release.com).

>> **openPR:** Offers free press release publishing (www.openpr.com).

>> **PR.com:** Offers free and paid press release publishing (www.pr.com).

>> **Small Business Trends:** Offers free press release publishing (www. smallbiztrends.com).

>> **WomenOnBusiness.com:** Offers free press release publishing (www. womenonbusiness.com/submit-a-press-release).

It's perfectly acceptable to submit your press release to multiple sites and services. Just be aware of the costs and overlap in distribution audience to ensure that you don't spend more money than necessary to reach the same people.

Promoting your press releases

Press releases aren't necessarily content that you can promote. Instead, press releases are a supplement to your content marketing strategy that allows you to get your name, URL, and information in front of audiences who might not see it otherwise. Be sure to publish your press releases on your own website and blog, and link to them from your Twitter, Facebook, and LinkedIn profiles and branded destinations to share your news with your existing audience. If you belong to groups on Facebook, LinkedIn, and so on whose members might find value in your news, share the link in those groups, too. Some of those people might even share your news further with their own audiences.

TIP

Don't spend time promoting your press releases that can be found on distribution sites and services. Instead, drive that traffic to the version on your own website or blog where they just might click around to read more of your fine content.

Publishing Presentations

SlideShare (www.slideshare.net) is a tool that enables you to upload your PowerPoint, OpenOffice, or PDF presentations to your own branded channel. After you upload your presentation, people can easily view, print, download, share, and embed your presentations into their websites or blogs. SlideShare makes it easy for you to share your sales presentations, training presentations, and more with a broad audience, and because people can embed and share your uploaded presentations, the pass-along value is huge.

Understanding the value of sharing your presentations

At first glance, you might think sharing your presentations is like giving away all your trade secrets, but that's not the case at all. Imagine being able to pitch your sales presentation in a room filled with hundreds or thousands of people who've already expressed interest in what you're going to present to them. That's exactly what you get when you publish that same sales presentation on SlideShare; however, instead of pitching a room full of people, you're pitching a global audience via the Web. That's an opportunity businesses would be crazy to miss.

You might be tempted to upload your presentations to SlideShare but not enable the functions that allow people to print, download, share, or embed those presentations elsewhere online. Doing so significantly limits the exposure and reach of your presentations. Remember, content marketing works from the sharing and word-of-mouth marketing that your amazing content elicits. Don't stop your content from doing what it was meant to do. Instead, remove the gateway and let it spread for maximum success.

Long-Form Content Marketing

Using SlideShare

You can create a free account with SlideShare, customize your own SlideShare channel, and begin uploading presentations immediately. Be sure to create a complete profile, including links to your core branded online destination, and make your profile public so that people can find your content. You can see an example of a free SlideShare page in Figure 3-4. When you upload presentations, make sure you set them up so people can print, download, share, and embed them.

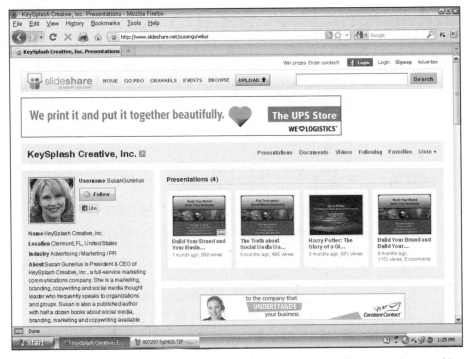

FIGURE 3-4:
A free SlideShare page can look very professional.

Source: www.slideshare.net/susagunelius

TIP

SlideShare does offer professional packages with price tags attached to them. Paid accountholders get access to analytics and can remove ads from their videos and channels. Start with a free account and upgrade to a professional account in the future if SlideShare becomes a vital component of your content marketing strategy.

Promoting your presentations

Of course, you should blog about your presentations when you upload them (be sure to embed them in your blog post), and share links to them on Twitter, Facebook, LinkedIn, and so on. You can even add a SlideShare tab on your Facebook Page and a SlideShare widget on your blog to further promote your presentations.

When you upload presentations to SlideShare, be sure to name them with keywords in mind and include a description and tags that are keyword rich to boost the number of people who find your presentations through SlideShare searches. SlideShare also enables you to include a text transcript of your presentation, which is great for SEO — use it. You can even create collections of presentations and join groups on SlideShare, which can give your presentations more exposure.

4

Using Social Media

Contents at a Glance

Chapter 1

Marketing and Communicating with Twitter

This chapter covers some of the essentials of using Twitter for marketing in your business, explains what some other businesses have tried, and points you in the right direction to get started yourself.

Understanding the Business of Twitter

Twitter has the potential to filter into every possible aspect of business as a versatile communications platform and problem-solving tool. It has uses way beyond the marketing and customer-engagement layer. Twitter can affect pretty much everything, from the way enterprise software works to how project status is shared. It can fundamentally change communication and problem-solving, as well as match resources, accommodate human-resources challenges, and lower expenses.

Twitter can have powerful effects on personal and professional networks. Sales professionals can use it to generate leads, journalists can locate sources, publishers can discover new content, and any business can create better relationships with customers. You can listen to and harness the massive flow of ideas and information passing through Twitter so that you can advance your business objectives.

You can use Twitter to create ad-hoc communities, organize and publicize live events, or extend an experience to a remote audience. You can sell directly — if you do it right — or you can just develop an inexpensive listening and conversation post among the very people whose problems your business solves. You can use Twitter to generate traffic to your business's website. You can use it to solicit feedback. It can even make your company and brands easier for users to find on search engines such as Google.

To get started, let's take a look at some ways Twitter might fit with your brand.

Putting Your Best Face Forward

Businesses can use Twitter to talk to their customers and potential customers, and generally increase brand recognition. Given that Twitter has so many potential uses that are so diverse, how can you get started?

You can probably guess that your *profile* is your business's face on Twitter. Even though many people use Twitter through a service on their phone or desktop rather than through the web page itself, assume that most everyone will at least look at your profile page — if not the web URL that you provide within that profile — before deciding whether or not to follow what you're doing on Twitter.

TIP

Dress nicely on Twitter: Fill out the whole profile page when you set up your business's Twitter account, and upload an avatar. (In most cases, your company logo is appropriate, but in others, a photo of your team or customers could be better.) Link back to your main website, and link to your Twitter account from your website. You need to verify that the business account is actually yours and promote the availability of the Twitter stream to all your customers. With a Twitter stream widget embedded on your site, you can even tweet to your customers (keeping freshly updated content front and center) without their even logging into Twitter.

Make sure that the Twitter bio section, short though it may be, tells Twitter users about your business. Also, the content of your business's tweets needs to honestly, transparently show what you're doing on Twitter. Perhaps you'd like to introduce the people behind your business's Twitter account; they're the people your Twitter readers and connections actually talk to, so you could let the individuals behind the keyboard shine through.

After you create a great profile page, what do you do? Here are a few simple ways to get out of the Twitter background and into public awareness:

>> **Listen.** Pay attention to what's going on around you on Twitter. Twitter users have fascinating things to say about pretty much everything, but more important for you, they may already be talking about you and your business. You're going to want to find as many ways as you can to tune in. You can get useful information from Twitter in many ways, from Twitter Search to sophisticated social media listening tools. If you think of Twitter as a giant consumer sentiment engine, you can start to understand its potential. You can learn a lot by listening.

>> **Balance.** For the average business Twitter account, you need to have a good ratio of personal (or conversational) tweets to business (or promotional) ones. This ratio depends, in part, on how much you interact on Twitter and what you hope to accomplish — not to mention the nature of your business and your target audience or customer base.

   You may want to come up with an approximate numerical ratio that accomplishes your balance goals. You could decide, for example, that you want to make only one or two of every ten tweets personal. Alternatively, you can opt to put a particularly personal or original slant on promotional tweets, making them notably funny, valuable, or interesting to your readers.

   If you have a more conversational Twitter account that you still want to connect to your professional life, make about half your tweets personal, fun, or off-topic, and the other half about your business. If you prefer to deliver business value all the time, set up your account to curate and cultivate links about events, blog posts, news, and ideas that are relevant to your field. You can also sprinkle in some self-promotional tweets, but make sure it's not the only thing you do. Even when you share things about your company, make an effort to show how what you're sharing relates to your readers. Whatever you do, be useful. Offer value. You want to keep people engaged, which is what Twitter is all about.

>> **Engage.** While you listen and talk on Twitter, be sure to interact with other Twitter users. Twitter is a communications tool, and although it's based on a one-to-many concept, it works best when you make friends and have real conversations right in the Twitter stream. Sometimes when you find people talking about subjects relevant to your business, you can offer helpful contributions to their conversations. When it comes to business, public relations, and customer service (which we talk about in the following sections), you absolutely need to engage other people on Twitter.

>> **Connect.** Use the ability to take conversations offline and into the real world via tweetups, events, and meetings to your business's advantage. Twitter makes finding ways to meet and engage with customers in real life easy, and therein lies its largest business value. Take your business's conversations and connections beyond the 140-character limit.

Public relations

You can use Twitter as a fantastic public relations (PR) channel, whatever kind of business you work for. It offers global reach, endless connections, networking opportunities, a promotion platform, and immediate event planning and feedback. Best of all, if you float your ideas out there in genuine, valid, and interesting ways, others can pick them up and spread them around. Many Twitter users — from individuals to large corporations — report scoring numerous press opportunities as a result of engaging other Twitter users and sharing on the Twitter platform.

Some traditional public relations firms may be intimidated by Twitter's potential to connect stories, sources, and journalists. Many of them don't yet see the opportunity, or they're thinking about it too narrowly. Twitter is just one more tool — albeit a powerful and efficient one — to add to your arsenal if public relations is important to your business. Twitter simply gives you a way to make what you do more accessible to people who might otherwise not hear your message.

Twitter has introduced a revolutionary new way that journalists can report on the news in real-time. One New York City–based startup called Muck Rack (`http://muckrack.com`) realized this early and jumped on the Twitter bandwagon, taking real-time news and allowing you to filter and analyze that news. The platform includes a tracking tool that emails you when a journalist tweets about a specific or relevant term. This means that instead of your searching the Internet to find a specific story, that story now comes to you.

It's possible that you heard about Twitter in the first place in the context of a mainstream news story about an event of global importance that was first reported via citizen journalism on Twitter. One of the most famous examples of this occurred in January 2009 after the emergency landing of a commercial airplane in the Hudson River (`https://twitter.com/jkrums/status/1121915133`). Indeed, Twitter is an exceedingly powerful tool for detecting breaking events. You don't always get in-depth analysis (at least, not until links to longer writings about the story begin to spread), but you do frequently find yourself way ahead of the game when a story breaks if you're on Twitter.

Another noteworthy example of news breaking on Twitter was during the Boston Marathon bombings in April 2013 (see Figure 1-1). The *Boston Globe*

(@BostonGlobe) was the first to tweet an accurate update about the news (`https://twitter.com/BostonGlobe/status/323873235949207552`). Then, several other marathon attendees and participants followed by tweeting images of the mass chaos that broke out, including photos and videos of police helping wounded victims. It wasn't before long that the Boston Police Department (@bostonpolice) tweeted a picture of the bombing suspects from their own account (`https://twitter.com/bostonpolice/status/325002310369542144`) and asked for help with identifying them. All this real-time tweeting and live footage actually led to successfully identifying and capturing the suspects.

FIGURE 1-1:
The *Boston Globe* breaking news about the Boston Marathon bombings over Twitter.

Source: Twitter

It's not every day that you see news stories such as the airplane in the Hudson River or the Boston Marathon bombings. However, even on a regular day, journalists and PR practitioners are among some of Twitter's most avid users, and they do some pretty interesting things with it. On Monday nights, professionals from both fields gather to talk about current stories, their professions, and the future of media simply by tagging their tweets with the word #journchat. Because #journchat is an agreed-on tag and a longstanding event, people know to point their search tools (or `https://twitter.com/search-home`) to that word and watch the conversation scroll by.

It was Twitter innovator @prsarahevans who came up with the idea for #journchat, and the community she built catapulted her from obscure community-college public relations practitioner to an extremely well-known social media innovator.

National Public Radio (@NPR) implemented a similar standing event that used #NPRWIT to extend its voice beyond radio broadcasts.

Because Twitter usernames are short and frequently easy to remember, they can be a powerful way to introduce people and pass along contact information. In an interview, a reporter was surprised how easily Laura could rattle off half a dozen sources that the reporter might like to talk to. Armed with these Twitter handles, the journalist used the profiles behind those usernames to get a quick snapshot of those users' interests, abilities, and points of view, plus links to further detailed information about them and easy ways to make contact.

Here are some tips to make your Twitter-based public relations more user-friendly and successful:

>> **Keep it real.** The "Be genuine" Twitter rule applies at all times, even when you're embarking on a publicity campaign (often *especially* when you're attempting to drive sales or awareness to your product, service, or site). Twitter's users can be very turned off by empty marketing banter.

>> **Remember your balance.** Just because you want to see fast results doesn't mean that you should bombard your Twitter followers with *link spam* (numerous tweets that contain links to your business) or constant nagging about whatever you're trying to promote. Remember to space it out. On Twitter, overly aggressive promotions can slow your progress and reduce your audience. Tread with respect.

>> **Give your idea wings.** Come up with a pithy or witty statement about your promotion that inspires people in your network to share and pass it along (to *retweet* the statement, or *RT*) to their own networks. Getting your message retweeted is much more effective than hammering your point home on your own.

>> **Be genuinely helpful.** Watch for conversations about topics relevant to your company or product, and provide unselfish solutions, ideas, and help to those conversations.

>> **Listen to feedback.** If someone asks you a question, answer it in your own public feed so that you can continue to generate organic interest in your promotion. Answer others who happen to tweet related questions, but make sure that your answers aren't selfish or too pushy. How can you tell? Pay attention to how effective your efforts are.

>> **Measure effectiveness.** Do people click your links? Do they retweet your messages without your having to ask? Do they complain that you're being promotional — or, worse, do they not say much at all? Use trackable link shorteners such as Bitly so that you can see which of your tweets people

are bothering to click or retweet (passing your messages along for you). Sometimes, you may need to tweet a little less frequently to avoid letting spamminess make you less effective. Want to really dig into some data about your effectiveness? Cruise on over to https://analytics.twitter.com and have a look around. By exporting your data, you can even see in great detail which tweets get the most impressions, engagement, favorites, retweets, click throughs, and more.

>> **Offer incentives.** Not giveaways or money, but value. Give people an unselfish reason to pay attention to you. It takes more than just promotions. Followers listen to you for the value you add, and if you consistently add insightful and worthwhile thoughts to their Twitter streams, they'll be there for you when the roles reverse and you need them.

Twitter provides all users access to influential journalists, bloggers, writers, and people from all walks of life. If you use it consistently and well, you can find powerful, inexpensive ways to share messages that help solve people's problems and gain visibility for your work.

Customer service

Big-name companies such as Comcast, Nike, and JetBlue use Twitter as part of an overall strategy to reinvent their reputations for poor customer service and turn things around for their brands.

How did they do it? More important, how can *you* do it? Comcast has a few Twitter accounts that are specifically designed to receive customer service inquiries: @comcastcares and @ComcastWill are both run by Will Osborne, and @ComcastBill is run by Bill Gerth, both Comcast employees specializing in customer service. Although these accounts don't schedule or tweet any broadcast messages, all three are very active in the Tweets & Replies section of their accounts, where they have many 1-1 conversations going on with frustrated or confused customers.

Another example of a brand that has a separate Twitter handle for support-related inquiries is Nike at @NikeSupport. In the Twitter bio you'll see that this Nike account supports seven different languages (English, Spanish, French, Dutch, Italian, German, and Japanese), which truly makes this account a global source of help for anyone having trouble with a Nike device or product.

Although many brands create separate Twitter accounts for support-related matters, JetBlue has chosen to use its main account for both marketing and support. The company simply vows to always respond quickly and use humor when it's appropriate (see Figure 1-2 as an example). The benefit of using your main account is that customers won't get confused as to which Twitter handle they should be tweeting to when a question or issue comes up. This also means that any praise or positive messages will come directly to the @JetBlue account instead of only negative problems.

All three of these brands got in the trenches of social media through Twitter and engaged their customer bases, facing criticisms and complaints head-on, and showing a desire to help and respond quickly without making excuses or shifting blame. Twitter users around the world can witness this transformation and watch the companies respond to others' complaints, which improves the companies' images for even more people.

By listening diligently for mentions of their companies and quickly extending a helping hand, Comcast, Nike, and JetBlue have generated substantial goodwill (not to mention press coverage). Even when the products and services sold under those brands elicit unpleasant reactions from the public, having a real person reach out to help in a public forum can do a lot to prevent or dissipate consumer anger. Used artfully, one-to-one contact via Twitter instills a sense of hope that the people behind the company walls aren't leaving customers hanging. A presence and timely responses on Twitter can make the difference between a firestorm of complaints and a quickly managed situation.

FIGURE 1-2:
JetBlue using humor to engage and appeal to its audience.

Source: Twitter

WARNING

Customer service on Twitter allows businesses to catch consumers in their moments of frustration and help them right away. But Twitter alone can't fix back-end customer-service infrastructure problems such as overloaded call centers or poorly trained representatives who have no real power to help.

You don't need to be a huge company (and you certainly don't need to be suffering from a bad reputation) to create an effective business presence on Twitter. Twitter provides a great customer-service channel for small and medium-size businesses, too. If you're at a small company, Twitter can broaden your ability to reach out widely and listen carefully at almost no expense (only some time and possibly tools) while saving you the cost of having an entire customer-service department. Having a Twitter account for your business can make your business more accessible, not to mention let you help people who have real problems in real time, and see instant improvement in how consumers perceive your business.

When you first dive into Twitter for customer service, you may see negativity about your company, particularly at first. Keep going. The best part about Twitter as a customer-service channel is how you get feedback when a customer leaves satisfied. Many satisfied customers send out thank-you tweets that all their contacts see, which gives you instant good public relations buzz — and that kind of buzz is priceless. Letting go of control (you don't necessarily have control anymore anyhow) of your brand and engaging publicly with dissatisfied customers can really get that goodwill going.

Networking on Twitter

Whether you do it via Twitter or an old-fashioned card file, your business, personal, and career success depends heavily on a little thing called your network. If you're looking for ways to network more effectively — or you want to find interesting, valuable people efficiently — Twitter can help you build up a genuinely interesting, astonishingly relevant, and powerful network. Entire new horizons of opportunity can open up when you finally connect with the people who are right for you. Building a network comes naturally on Twitter. The platform makes it easy to interact and connect with people and businesses that share your interests and goals, and because of @replies and other links between Twitter networks and Twitter users, to randomly interact with and discover interesting new people along the way.

The more you interact on Twitter, the more your network increases. You can build almost any specific type of network on Twitter, too. Twitter offers access to all levels of people and businesses, from those seeking work or a better social life to CEOs and national politicians. It even offers a level of transparency that erases normal boundaries and rivalries.

Twitter can also help business networking in the employment sector. It's a fantastic way to meet and evaluate new employees, and also to find new work. This Twitter job-hunting movement creates a more open and flexible hiring environment for all kinds of companies. You can observe potential employees while they talk about what they know, get referrals from people who know them, and introduce yourself — all in real time. Twitter also efficiently harnesses networks of loose ties — the friends of friends who are more likely to know about job opportunities and job candidates.

Freelancers who network and collaborate on projects can use Twitter to find former colleagues from past companies with whom they lost touch, and to get to know their existing employees and customers. In so many ways, Twitter acts as a portable business-networking event that you can pop into when the time and availability suit you. Bonus: You don't have to talk to anyone you don't want to talk to.

Building Brand Awareness

If you're planning on using Twitter to help grow your business, one of your goals might be to simply increase awareness of your brand's existence. By building up your brand's reputation on Twitter, you're fostering a space for your followers to find entertainment or helpful information. It's important to give folks passing by a reason to actually click Follow, so they come back and keep reading, and eventually might want to pass a mention of your brand along to their friends.

Three examples of consumer products making waves on Twitter are @OldSpice, @Charmin, and @Skittles. These three brands tend to take a more humorous and likeable approach in order to build brand awareness and grow their following. These brands are constantly getting retweeted due to their non sales-oriented tweets that include funny pop culture references, clever use of trending hashtags, or seemingly risqué interactions with other brands.

Take Figure 1-3 as an example of two brands interacting with each other on Twitter. Here, you'll see that Old Spice tweeted a funny thought that its target audience would enjoy. Notice that this tweet is just for fun and doesn't include a 140-character sales pitch. Taco Bell comes back with an equally humorous thought to keep the conversation going, and Old Spice follows up once more. This quick exchange on Twitter, although seemingly "just for fun," helped both brands gain visibility, new followers, and generally become more loveable due to the high number of times the thread was retweeted and the fact that the interaction became "news" that was picked up by blogs and other publications.

Similar to the Old Spice and Taco Bell example in Figure 1-3, Old Spice was involved in another brand-on-brand Twitter interaction with Oreo in December

2013 — just in time for the holidays (https://twitter.com/Oreo/status/413852283651510272). This interaction helped show product function and versatility in a humorous way.

Building up a reputation and a following like @OldSpice, @Charmin, and @Skittles might take some time, but with the right strategy in place you could certainly get there. Remember that you don't need to build a giant audience; you just need to build a well-targeted and engaged one. A smaller scale example of using humor to build a following is @CrapTaxidermy, an account that started by posting pictures of taxidermy gone wrong.

FIGURE 1-3:
Old Spice and Taco Bell communicating for visibility on Twitter.

Source: Twitter

Offering Promotions and Generating Leads

If you represent a company that has something to sell, you can find a unique home on Twitter. You may need to adjust your messages a bit so that you can shift from a hard-sell philosophy to an attitude of interaction and engagement that doesn't necessarily follow a direct path to a sale. But after you find and flip that switch from "talking at" to "talking with" potential customers, people on Twitter can interact with and respond to your company's information ideas and products in ways that often lead to benefits for both sides.

You can sell-without-selling just about anything on Twitter. Whether you want to sell something large (such as used cars) or something small (such as shoes), you can probably find people on Twitter who need and want them. These potential customers have questions for you about your item, your company, your staff, and *you*, and you can let them talk to you on Twitter about their concerns. You're in business because you solve problems and fulfill needs for people. Spend your time on Twitter being useful and informative about the types of problems you solve, and the rest really does follow.

Some brands "sell-without-selling" by using Twitter as a point of entry to a long buyer's journey, rather than trying to earn immediate action. One example of this is @Lowes on the business-to-consumer (B2C) side. Of course Lowes tweets last-minute deals such as "Get $100 off a Dyson vacuum — today only!" but they also post creative photos and Vine videos that lead users to helpful blog articles for home remodeling or even the Kitchen Planner Guide. If you're looking to turn your Twitter account into a return on investment (ROI) engine, take a page from Lowes' book.

On the business-to-business (B2B) side, a great example of entering a long buyer's journey through Twitter is @HubSpot. Because this is a B2B company, the term generally used here is "lead generation." Let's walk through an example of how HubSpot might generate leads using Twitter. First, the account tweets a helpful blog post, possibly including an eye-catching photo or additional media. After a Twitter user clicks the link in the tweet, she's led to a helpful blog post such as "How to Use Twitter for Business." When the reader scrolls through the post, she sees a call-to-action (CTA) to download a free e-book. This e-book generally expands on the blog post topic. When the reader clicks the CTA and reaches the landing page for the free e-book, she sees a form to enter her contact information in exchange for free information. From here, HubSpot follows up with relevant emails and other forms of helpful communication in hopes of "nurturing" her as a lead and building a relationship until she is closer to being ready to buy.

If you'd prefer to stick to Twitter-only promotions, take a page from the @DunkinDonuts book. This account hosts endless contests and sweepstakes, including #DunkinAppSweeps, #PumpkinatDunkinSweeps, and #DDCaptionThis. Often, these contests are quite simple: unscramble a phrase, caption a photo, and tweet your answer to the hashtag. Prizes include gift packs, free food products, or even cash. What Dunkin' Donuts gets out of these contests are new followers, awareness to the company's Twitter account and hashtags, loads of engagement, devoted fans, and ultimately more sales.

Running a contest isn't the only way to offer promotions on Twitter. @JetBlueCheeps is an account dedicated to posting limited-time deals for last-minute flights. Because Twitter is such a fast-moving, real-time network, this is the perfect place to post deals on the fly for avid and spontaneous travelers. Suddenly, this Twitter account feels like an exclusive all access ticket to peek at

JetBlue's best-kept secret. People following this account can even receive SMS text updates to their phones whenever JetBlue posts a new deal.

You can replicate these companies' successes by keeping these tips in mind:

>> Be interesting.

>> Be accessible.

>> Be genuine (mean what you say).

>> Be yourself.

>> Don't hard-sell.

>> Don't link spam.

>> Follow the 90/10 rule: 90 percent unselfish tweets to 10 percent promotional tweets.

Promoting Bands and Artists

If you're in any way in the business of creating, whether it's art, music, film, photography, or what-have-you, Twitter can become a home away from home. Twitter users are incredibly receptive to creative people who tweet. Just ask Miley Cyrus (@MileyCyrus). The former teen idol turned racy pop singer had a childish image. She'd been the star of *Hannah Montana* on the Disney Channel, and nobody was taking her seriously as a young adult. But she joined Twitter around the same time that she drastically changed her look and dropped her album and tour called Bangerz. Throughout this transformation, she shared updates (bizarre photos included) with her followers on Twitter to let the world see another side of her.

Cyrus is a pretty drastic example of how you can use Twitter for rebranding, marketing, and self-promotion as an artist, but Twitter can also help relatively unknown people make it to the top for the first time.

Twitter also helps artists such as Natasha Wescoat (@natasha) increase their prominence in the art world. Wescoat's work is finding a home in art galleries, movies, and more, and she can attribute some of that increasing reach to contacts that she made on Twitter.

How can you (as an aspiring musician, artist, photographer, or other person who makes a living in the creative industries) find success on Twitter if you aren't already on the level of Miley Cyrus (@MileyCyrus), MC Hammer (@MCHammer),

Taylor Swift (@taylorswift13), Lady Gaga (@LadyGaga), and Justin Timberlake (@jtimberlake)? Here are some simple tips that you can follow:

>> **Surround yourself with successful people.** Not just others in your profession or field who are more successful than you — people in other fields or areas of creativity who inspire you, too. You can start to find them by finding out which of your real-world contacts in the industry are on Twitter or by doing a few Twitter searches to find like-minded people while you build your network.

>> **Take it offline.** Take the connections that you make on Twitter and organize events and get-togethers that bring the experience offline. You can also find out about other members' tweetups that are relevant to your business. In creative industries, the talent is what counts, and so real-world connections can really lead to new opportunities, fan segments, and opportunities to build your loyal fan base.

>> **Share your content.** You don't have to give away all your hard work, but put your music, art, videos, or other work out there for people to sample and play with. Start a SoundCloud (https://soundcloud.com) channel, upload a short video to YouTube, offer free MP3s on your website, or set up a page that features a few Creative Commons–licensed photos. Whatever you do, give people a way to take a look or have a listen so that they can get to know you and what you make.

TECHNICAL STUFF

Creative Commons (http://creativecommons.org) is an organization that makes it easy for people to license their work so that they retain their copyright but allow it to be shared. For more information on how Creative Commons works, go to http://creativecommons.org/about.

>> **Tweet on the go.** Give your fans and potential fans a look backstage, in the van, behind the canvas, on tour, or behind the lens. Take them with you by tweeting while you travel with your music, art, film, or other creative medium. Also, let them know where you are. Many fellow Twitter users would love to hang out with you if you happen to be in town.

>> **Engage your fan base.** Don't just post static links to content or schedule changes. Talk to your fans and respond to them through Twitter. They probably want to ask you about the thoughts behind your work, your experiences, and you. Let them. Answer them. Engage them in good conversation, and watch as they spread the word about your work to their friends and followers.

>> **Be yourself.** Put a good face forward, yes, but don't try too hard to project a persona that really isn't authentically you. Twitter is a medium that rewards authenticity, candor, and transparency. Try too hard to put your best face forward, and you may lose yourself and stop being genuine. Twitter people notice if you aren't being real. Don't worry about impressing people. Just do what you do and be yourself, and the fans will follow.

TIP

Check out some of the most-followed people in each category on user-generated Twitter directory Wefollow (http://wefollow.com). Categories include musicians (http://wefollow.com/interest/music), TV personalities (http://wefollow.com/interest/tv), actors (http://wefollow.com/interest/actor), comedians (http://wefollow.com/interest/comedy), and other celebrities (http://wefollow.com/interest/celebrity).

Sharing Company Updates

If you have a new or growing company that you want to introduce to the world through Twitter, start a separate account for the company. You may find balancing traditional corporate professionalism with the level of transparency that Twitter users have come to expect to be a little tricky sometimes, so keep these guidelines in mind when you start your new account:

>> **Provide value to the Twitter community.** Your company account can become a source of news, solutions, ideas, entertainment, or information that's more than just a series of links to products and services. Educate your Twitter followers. Reach out to people whom you can genuinely and unselfishly help. You can even offer sales incentives for products, in the way that @DellOutlet does, as long as what you offer has genuine value. Establish your company's leadership in providing ideas, solutions, and innovation.

>> **Be human.** Most brands use their company logo as their Twitter avatar to keep things official, but they'll add a little personality to their header photo or individual tweets. A commonly favored approach is to let your followers become familiar with who's behind the company voice; it makes them feel more engaged. Take photos of your company during team outings to show off the culture, or tweet a dorky industry joke here and there. Humans like to talk to other humans, so make sure your brand doesn't feel robotic.

>> **Don't spam.** Don't flood the Twitter feed with self-promotional links or product information that don't deliver genuine value to readers. Whether self-promotional or not, you never want to clog up people's Twitter streams with irrelevant information. You might not talk about your cat or your marriage on a company account, but you can still make it personal. Profile an employee, talk about milestones for employees, or talk about what's going on in your office. You can even hold tweetups at your office and invite your followers to stop by, as Boston's NPR news station WBUR (@WBUR) does. This approach gives people a peek at what makes your company run.

Before tweeting in earnest for your company, it's a good idea to openly discuss your plans to demonstrate that you're taking a productive, innovative approach and to prevent any misguided fears that joining Twitter means you will somehow suddenly start to leak sensitive company information or otherwise break reasonable corporate policies. As with any public communications platform, you do need to consider just how much you can say about what goes on inside your business. Transparency is key, but you don't want to disclose industry secrets in a public forum. Every company has a different style. It helps to have a good plan in place and make sure that the employees assigned to the company Twitter account are trustworthy and have solid judgment.

Building Community

Community-building sometimes suffers from a "Kumbaya" perception that devalues the importance of using tools such as Twitter to connect with people. But building a truly engaged community is extremely valuable.

Apple is an example of a company that benefits tremendously from its engaged community in terms of promotion, sales, and even customer support administered from one Apple fan directly to others. Apple built its community by building great products people get passionate about, not by worrying about any particular tools. So as you approach the Twitter opportunity, remember how powerful and engaged community can be and remember what people actually engage around — the things they really and truly care about.

At its best, the community concept of sharing and connecting can help you spread a positive image and good comments about your company; done wrong, it can veer into feel-good, self-help banter that's ultimately empty. Again, don't fuss too much about Twitter as a tool. Think more strategically about the community and what they care about and engage them with substance and real contributions.

Building a community is not necessarily the same as building a network:

>> **Network:** Your network is there for you and your business, a kind of foundation for concrete professional growth.

>> **Community:** Building a community means inspiring the people who follow you on Twitter to embrace your brand and create a feeling of solidarity around your business, service, staff, or product.

With a community, you can build a loyal corps of evangelists: people who are passionate about your brand, even though they have no professional or financial stake in the company. If you can engender the community feeling through your use of Twitter and how you interact with your customers, your customers begin to feel emotionally invested in your success online.

You can see this community feeling with JetBlue. The Twitter users who follow the airline are so dedicated that they act like they're legitimately invested in the brand's success. JetBlue fosters this effect by staying on top of what people on Twitter are saying about them, or about flights and traveling in general, through the use of monitoring tools. Then they jump in with help, as needed. If you tweet about having trouble finding a flight, for example, you can expect a JetBlue employee to send you a direct message (DM) or @reply in less than a day that includes links to the proper pages on the JetBlue site. Plus, JetBlue has spent so much time building a strong community that Twitter members who don't even work for JetBlue will routinely pass along information they see or hear and will even reach out on behalf of the company and connect potential customers with JetBlue.com.

@TheEllenShow's #Oscars SELFIE

Talk about a brand leveraging Twitter to build a community! Samsung may have pulled off the most remarkable Twitter marketing stunt of all time. During the 2014 Academy Awards, host Ellen DeGeneres (@TheEllenShow) was running around the event with her Samsung smartphone, taking hilarious selfies (a self-portrait photograph taken with a smartphone or digital camera) as she navigated the televised event.

The reason DeGeneres was doing this was not for comedic relief alone, but also because Samsung had sponsored the entire event and needed a representative. The #Oscars hashtag already had a significant amount of user-generated buzz coming from the live television event, but Samsung wanted to make it epic.

Samsung gave DeGeneres a Galaxy Note 3, which she connected to Twitter's mobile app. She then proceeded to run into the celebrity audience and announce that she was attempting to break the record for most retweeted tweets ever while being on live television. Until that point, the winner was President Barack Obama's "Four more years" tweet (https://twitter.com/BarackObama/status/266031293945503744), with more than 770,000 retweets.

Gathering stars such as Bradley Cooper, Jennifer Lawrence, Meryl Streep, Julia Roberts, Brad Pitt, Angelina Jolie, and Kevin Spacey, DeGeneres took a selfie that will go down in the history books (https://twitter.com/TheEllenShow/status/440322224407314432). With more than 3.4 million retweets, this tweet will be a difficult one to surpass.

(continued)

(continued)

Source: Twitter

Community is also a huge aspect of the Twitter experiences of many musicians and artists, such as Imogen Heap (`@ImogenHeap`) and John Mayer (`@JohnMayer`). Heap uses Twitter to interact more directly with her fan base, which increases the loyalty of her listeners, who have come to see a more human side of her and feel like they've even come to know her. If someone tweets something about Heap that her Twitter followers don't like, you can watch the community leap to her defense. At the same time, tweets from her Twitter community usually reflect the tone of her own calm tweets, remaining mellow and not shrill.

Musicians, actors, and other celebrities are really personality-based businesses, and bringing forth those personalities on Twitter by asking questions and sharing parts of their lives cements a valuable engagement between the artist and fans.

You can build community through

>> Offering genuine interaction

>> Asking questions

>> Being honest and transparent

>> Following people back who follow you

>> Not overautomating

» Being more than a link list

» Providing value

Conducting Research

Twitter is an excellent tool for crowdsourcing and focus-group research. You can easily get the answers you seek after you establish a relationship with your followers that encourages participation, conversation, and sharing. Larger corporations are continually diving in to conduct their own research and build their own tools that can make sense of the tremendous amount of data being generated on Twitter all the time.

If you're willing to experiment with different ways to watch the Twitter stream, you can collect *passive data* (what people happen to be mentioning), do *active research* (asking questions and conducting polls), and even engage actual focus groups and ad-hoc communities in live events.

GROWING YOUR NUMBERS NATURALLY

Although effective questions and good tagging can help your research spread beyond your direct network, to do most kinds of research on Twitter, you need a healthy following first. This network will have much more value in the long run if you grow your numbers through natural conversational methods and organic back-and-forth follows. (Note: Don't post "Please follow this account," the way that actor Ashton Kutcher did when he was trying to race CNN to 1 million Twitter followers.) When you know that you have a diverse crowd of intelligent people following you on Twitter, including those who are both fans and critics of your brand, you can feel relatively comfortable starting to ask them for feedback and insight.

Take it slow, and wait for a solid, engaged, relevant network to build up. Your business and you can begin to thrive on the real-time feedback about your products, services, and staff. Twitter can, among other things, help you find out before it's too late that a new flagship product is flawed, spread the word about your excellent customer service directly from the customers that were involved, and invite interested customers to come to real-life tweetups to find out more about your brand. Any forward-thinking business that has transparency on the mind or wants to remain on top of brand perception at all times has started to use Twitter.

As you build your network and start gaining more followers on Twitter, it becomes a very useful tool for informal conversational research. If you ask a really good question and send it into the world with a #hashtag to make the answers easier to find, you can even do research with a very small following, because the tag attracts curious bystanders who may later become new followers. As you ask questions, you can use any number of polling tools or even a simple manually generated tracking system (such as a Microsoft Excel spreadsheet) to collect the answers and data that you receive.

Twitter can be thought of as a global, human-powered, mobile phone–enabled sensing and signaling network. What Twitter knows about the world is pretty incredible, and when businesses understand how to work with that information, the combination can contribute toward closing some pretty important gaps in our economy between supply and demand.

Going Transparent

Transparency is a crucial marketing buzzword for some businesses and a scary reality for others. Lest you think we're asking you to live out that unpleasant dream in which you forget to wear your pants to school, relax. Transparency doesn't require exposing company data to corporate spies or baring your soul for the Internet. More than anything else, it simply means being honest, disclosing your biases, admitting to mistakes, and not trying to force your message and spin on everyone all the time.

Although many Twitter users find themselves becoming more casual in their use of the service over time, you need to find your own personal comfort level between acting like a real person and oversharing. After you find that line for yourself, your business, and your employees, being genuine and transparent on Twitter becomes second nature. Transparency fosters trust and relationships. It's no secret that people like to work with people they like.

Here's how to achieve transparency:

>> **Release control.** Stop worrying about what might happen to your brand. Instead, listen to what your customers are trying to tell you and respond to that feedback. The truth is, you haven't been able to control your message for a while now; you just may not have known it.

Look at the hashtags #McDStories and #AmazonFail. In the former example, McDonald's attempted to start a cute hashtag sharing warm and fuzzy stories about the brand; it failed spectacularly when stories about poor restaurant conditions and pictures of questionable food started surfacing.

McDonald's customers used Twitter to express their anger and ultimately got the campaign suspended. The Amazon Fail incident happened when books pertaining to gay and lesbian themes were suddenly pulled from the online retailer's bestseller lists. Again, Twitter users smelled something fishy and instantly started spreading the word. Both companies learned from going through this process that a better Twitter listening practice would have helped them address concerns early and prevent a conflagration.

» **Admit to problems.** When you acknowledge that your business and you occasionally have rough patches, you can form stronger, more genuine connections with your community. That kind of open disclosure has limits when it comes to some professions. Obviously, people in the legal and medical professions, as well as government agencies, have to restrict and curtail their Twitter use because of privacy issues. But for most businesses, honesty is the best policy.

» **Reach out continually.** Don't stop seeking out the customers who are talking about you and reaching out to them. That personal touch goes very far in establishing and maintaining a positive perception of your business or brand.

» **Be proactive.** If you're engaged with the community in a genuine way, people forgive most mistakes. Twitter's community is pretty cooperative, and if you embrace it, you can be rewarded with unexpected benefits such as loyalty; advocacy; and even organic, voluntary promotion of you and your work.

Advising Employees on Tweeting

Business owners often feel some uncertainty and concern about how to manage employees so that they don't waste time or make costly mistakes when using Twitter. Remember to apply common sense and manage based on behavior and results, not just specific tools. Your existing guidelines about email, blogs, commenting on message boards and forums, and even conversations with outside individuals cover any concerns that you have about your employees' use of Twitter.

That said, it's important to remember that information spreads fast on Twitter, and that Twitter is a very open and searchable public forum. Errors can — and will — go farther, faster, so the exercise of common sense is in order.

Before you start using Twitter for your business, provide staff guidance on how to use it and what to be cautious about. Twitter is extremely new to many people, and they may not be familiar with just how public and open it is. Definitely set a few ground rules to help prevent common mistakes. You can simply write a one- or two-page set of reminders or direct employees' attention to the parts of your existing human-resources policy that cover public communications.

Make the guidelines basic, clear, and easy to follow. Here are some thoughts to get you started:

» If you wouldn't say it in front of your parents, kids, or boss, perhaps you shouldn't say it on Twitter.

» If you do something confidential at a company, keep private information under wraps. Respect clients' privacy as well as your company's.

» Respect the company brand when you're out at *tweetups* (Twitter-based meetups) and events. Anyone can get quoted at any time.

» Perception is reality. Even if the complaint you tweet right after a client phone call wasn't about the client, it can be misconstrued that way.

» Manage your time on Twitter well so that it doesn't interfere with your workload.

Unless your business has other issues that come into play (if you work for a law firm or government agency, for example), these basic rules should be enough to keep people from abusing their time on Twitter. Customize them however you want.

TIP

Twitter can be an extremely valuable tool for building your professional team and bringing them together. You can set up meetings, tweet notes, meet customers, and more, and your staff can connect more easily by using Twitter as well. The more of a team you can build, the better you can weather any economic buffering.

Sharing Knowledge

You can use Twitter to share knowledge, collaborate inside the company and out, and gather business information and research. After you start to build a healthy network, you need to send out only a few tweets about your project, problem, or issue before people come out of the woodwork to try to help your business and you. If you haven't been building your Twitter network, you may have to wait a while for this aspect of Twitter to become useful for you.

Suppose you come up with a major presentation about what your company does or sells, but you need something to complete it, such as a chart or a link to a relevant study. Twitter can probably help you find that missing piece. People on Twitter usually offer a helping hand when it comes to knowledge sharing, collaboration, and information gathering, especially if you spend time interacting on Twitter and building your network. Avid Twitter users are all aware of the same thing: By helping others, they can get a hand when they need it.

Chapter 2

Building a Following and Running a Facebook Marketing Campaign

Social media is about connecting with friends and followers. When marketing a business in the Facebook world, people often focus on how many friends and followers they have. The fact is, if you have friends and followers but have no influence over them, you might be wasting your time and marketing dollars.

Success on Facebook is about building an audience that is listening. Better yet, it's about building a network of influence, in which you influence not just the people in your own audience but their friends and connections as well. In the following sections, we give you practical advice on how to increase engagement with your current customers and how to attract new customers.

Although this chapter focuses on building your business using your business page, much of the advice here is useful for individuals who are just looking to up their game on Facebook and have a more popular personal timeline. Of course, if you're promoting your business or branding your business on Facebook, you should abide by the Facebook terms of service and create a business page instead of using your personal timeline for your business.

When starting your Facebook marketing, you'll probably find out how to build your audience, make connections with your audience, and nurture those connections so that they become loyal friends and followers.

After you've built a foundation with your business page audience, you likely need to give it a boost to take things to a higher level. A little shaking of the trees is required to let people know that it's worth connecting with your company on Facebook. Social marketing campaigns are a great way to do this. A social campaign enables you to reach people who you will not likely capture the attention of through daily interaction.

Campaigns tap into *crowdsourcing*, or using the resources that the public (the *crowd*) can provide to accomplish more than what you or your team can do with the resources you have. The word is a play on the word *outsource*, which is to look for a service provider outside your organization to deliver a service.

In this chapter, you find out how to start a social marketing campaign. You also discover how to build your business page to best show off your campaign and draw in fans to enter your promotion.

Understanding the Importance of Engagement

When people *Like* your business page, they value a connection with your company, at least to some degree. That connection has to have some meaning. The more you can humanize your brand, the more value you will get out of your marketing efforts. This is achieved through engagement.

You can't build engagement without some human effort behind your Facebook marketing. You can automate a lot, but at the end of the day, people are looking to connect with other people. When customers feel that your company values the personal connection to them, they are more likely to do business with you.

Don't forget about being top of mind. If customers have several choices when buying a product or service, all things being equal, whoever they remember gets the business. This is one big reason why engagement on your business page is so important. Consumers tend to have a higher level of trust for a brand if they're more familiar with it by name or experience. This certainly presents a good case for having a presence on Facebook, but all the more for having an active presence where you engage with your consumers. Figure 2-1 shows an example of how Amy's Kitchen reached out to its customers to meet a need. Customers commented and felt connected to the brand.

Facebook and other social media sites have fostered a social media–driven world where people expect to be able to interact with their favorite brands. Some of this will happen automatically if you have wide enough name recognition. Some will happen only as you nurture your customer connections. When you nurture those customer connections, they become better customers and recommend you to their friends.

Building friends and followers for your business

You won't have a successful experience with Facebook for your business if you don't make the effort to build an audience. Building an audience starts with inviting people to Like your business page. The next steps are to get some interaction from the people that Like your business page and turn them into loyal followers who will tell their friends about you.

Here are a few ways to start building a following for your business:

>> **Start in house:** When you first launch your business page, one of the most important things to do is get the ball rolling. People like to be where the party is, and having a starting group helps! Look to the people already involved with your company. Start by inviting everyone in your company to Like the business page. From there, each employee or partner can ask their personal friends to Like the business page as well.

Amy's Kitchen
September 27

Tomorrow is Good Neighbor Day. We help get regular food deliveries to our neighbor, COTS (Committee on the Shelterless, in California), a nonprofit that cares for the homeless in our town. Any good deeds happening in your neighborhood?
http://pinterest.com/pin/135319163777135273/

BE KIND TO OTHERS

Like · Comment · Share   👍 138 💬 2 ↪ 31

👍 138 people like this.   Top Comments ▾

Write a comment...

Joy Lynette ▓▓▓ Yep! Tomorrow at our county fairgrounds (at Girard, KS) is a day-long benefit for a friend's child who has a congenital heart defect. To accommodate the medical equipment she requires, the family has to remodel their home - not cheap! Lots of local businesses donated raffle prizes, local bands are donating their time, and members of the community are volunteering to staff the gate and booths. Live music all day, a bake sale, t-shirts and games for kids and adults. Free-will donation admission. It is going to be a great time, for a great cause! There is rain in the forecast but it is a rain or shine event.
Like · Reply · 👍 2 · September 27 at 11:49am

Jane ▓▓▓▓▓▓▓ ♡
Like · Reply · September 27 at 2:35pm

FIGURE 2-1:
Creating
meaningful
connections.

Source: Facebook

>> **Ask and invite:** No one is going to find your business page if they don't know to look for it, so it's a good idea to take every opportunity to share Facebook with your customers. It seems too easy, but a simple "Please Like our business page" really does work. Incorporate a link to your business page in your e-newsletter reminding your customers to Like your business page on Facebook. You'll get a good number of people who are happy to click the Like button and be the first among your Facebook audience. If you hand customers a receipt, put your Facebook address on the receipt, or hand them a card

with your Facebook address. At the very least, remind them verbally to find you on Facebook and be sure to Like the business page.

TIP

Keep the ticker in the back of your mind, too. When you have several people Liking your business page at the same time, the ticker shows more Facebook Like activity, increasing the chance that a friend of someone who Likes your page will also Like your business page.

>> **Use custom tabs:** A custom static HTML iframe tab enables you to have content that is only for people who Like your page. When you create a custom iframe tab, you have the opportunity to create more incentives for becoming a friend or follower. For example, you can create a tab that invites potential fans to Like your business page and then download a coupon, a white paper related to your niche, or even a short e-book. Giving potential friends and followers a reason to Like your business page is easy with a custom tab.

>> **Use contests and sweepstakes:** By giving something away, or asking a question with the winner receiving a prize, or using games or any other creative way to get engagement, your friends and followers feel more involved with your brand and business. And those who don't already Like your page may be drawn in when they see the activity of their friends who do Like your business page in their news feed or ticker.

WARNING

Facebook has strict guidelines for hosting contests and sweepstakes on its platform. You can check out the guidelines at www.facebook.com/page_ guidelines.php - promotionsguidelines. Breaking the rules could mean losing your business page!

>> **Make a difference:** A business was launching a business page for the first time. In an effort to create some buzz and get a burst of new followers, the customer launched a campaign to donate a dollar to a local charity for every Like on its business page within a certain time. The charity was promoting the campaign, and so were all the company's employees. The customer increased his Facebook audience by giving potential followers a compelling reason to Like his business page.

Connecting with your friends and followers

You need to connect with your friends and followers, but how do you keep up if you have a large audience? You can connect with your Facebook friends and followers in many ways; you're not just limited to making comments and posts.

The following list provides a few ideas that you can use to connect with your friends and followers:

>> **Ask questions.** It's not about you; it's about your audience. The best thing you can do for your Facebook engagement is to ask questions of your Facebook friends and followers. When you give them a chance to talk, not only do they take a step in engaging with you, but their activity shows up in their friends' ticker. When their friends see that activity, they may be more likely to check out your business page and become a follower.

>> **Encourage them to check back later.** You want your friends and followers to be repeat visitors. Sometimes it's just a matter of letting your fans know that more is coming tomorrow. How about posing a riddle of the day, and offering the answer the next day, along with a new riddle? With your business page's Pin feature, you can pin the daily riddle, question, or discussion to the top of your business page. Or you could create a new cover photo each week with a new question. If your fans come to expect a new cover photo on a certain day each week, you encourage them to visit your business page regularly.

>> **Comment on other business pages as your business page.** A one-sided conversation isn't much fun, is it? It's important to remember that if you want people to interact with you, you also need to interact with them. You can even comment as your business page rather than your personal timeline.

Figure 2-2 shows how someone commented on another business page's status update as his company Crowdshifter. By commenting as his business page instead of himself, he's introducing his brand to potential followers.

REMEMBER

You can't comment on personal timelines when you're using Facebook as your page; you can interact only on another business page.

The value of commenting as your business page is making mutual connections by connecting with other businesses and building connections with some of their followers. This may lead to some of their followers choosing to check out your business page to find out more about your business.

>> **Be a real person.** It's okay to let your personality shine through on your business page. Be funny, be serious, be professional. You know your goals and your audience and know what they can handle. Bring a little of yourself to your business page!

If you have multiple people in your office who update the business page, have them sign their updates with their name. Your followers will start to recognize your employees (and their personalities) and will feel a stronger connection with your entire company.

Source: Facebook

FIGURE 2-2:
Commenting as a
business page.

TIP

If you have a large audience, you can't always talk one-on-one with them all. Start by focusing on the influencers and those who are most engaging. You'll still project a human brand to your audience, even to those who aren't commenting directly with you.

Integrating Facebook in Marketing Campaigns

If you own a business, you know that finding and increasing your audience is essential for long-term success because those connections are the ones that lead to repeat business and referrals. As your Facebook audience grows, take advantage of the opportunity to build loyalty with those who connect with your company.

With a successful Facebook marketing strategy, you still use traditional marketing tactics. If Facebook proves to be a strong platform for your company, use outside marketing campaigns as a tool to drive new connections to Facebook. Do this by making Facebook the ultimate call to action. If your primary goal is to build an audience for long-term sales and customer loyalty, a call to action that leads them to Facebook is ideal.

Promoting Facebook via traditional advertising

You can advertise your company or product in many ways. With traditional advertising, your goal is to be seen by potential customers so that they know who you are and will choose to buy your product. Advertising is always more memorable if the person you reach takes some kind of action.

TIP

In addition to creating a memory, creating a database is important too. Advertising can be expensive. Not only do you want customers to buy your product today, you want them to buy again tomorrow. For example, after a car dealership sells a car to a customer, the next challenge is to get the customer to refer new customers to the dealership. And the next challenge is to get the customer back for service on his or her vehicle. If you can convince this loyal customer to connect with your business page, the person becomes part of your database from which you can ask for repeat business or encourage referrals. This is why promoting your business page within your traditional marketing is so valuable.

The following list gives tips to promote your business page using traditional marketing:

>> **Billboard ads:** If your marketing campaign is going to reach a broad audience in a concentrated city (or several cities), a billboard may be part of your marketing strategy. Driving people to your business page from a billboard is challenging. Billboards only allow for a simple message, and a long URL might be difficult. If your company name is unique, it might be more effective to invite people to find you by searching your company name. Do this by telling people, "Search for us by name on Facebook." A more common name may make that difficult though. For example, Blazefly might be fairly unique and therefore easy to find in a search. On the other hand, something like Bob's Car Care may be the name of several places and it may be difficult to find the correct one in a Facebook search.

TIP

Keep in mind that Facebook search is literal. If you search for *blaze fly* instead of *blazefly,* you won't find the business page. The capitalization isn't important, but the spaces are. As a business page owner, you want to be sure to title your business page in the way that you think people will search for it.

>> **Print ads and handouts:** Someone who discovers your company in a favorite magazine or receives a handout has a little more time to read your message. Print ads and handouts are perhaps the easiest ways to get a message across because you can provide ample information. Often times, incorporating the Facebook logo and colors helps to make it more clear that your business page can be found on Facebook.

>> **Free samples:** People love getting free samples before they decide to make a purchase. One really powerful way to build a database is by offering a free sample to anyone who requests it. You can create an iframe tab that hosts a contact form where people submit their contact information to receive a free sample.

REMEMBER

Make sure that the actual form is just in the Like-only section, so that people have to Like your business page to access it.

>> **The secret password:** If you've found a website that makes sense for you to advertise on, driving people with a good call to action is critical. You don't just want them to see the ad; you want them to click and take action. Imagine your company is a credit counseling service, and you're offering a free initial credit evaluation session. Your advertisement could say, "Click to go to our business page and get the secret password to redeem your free initial session." With this, you have the opportunity to use a fans-only iframe tab that provides the password. You get people who are interested in your services, and they become Facebook followers at the same time.

Having a memorable URL

When you share your Facebook URL as a call to action, it needs to be memorable. For example, if you're advertising on a billboard, your audience has a few seconds to read your ad. If the URL is a long destination, you may not get any traffic.

TIP

Get a custom Facebook username (also called a vanity URL) for your business page. You can read up on how that works at www.facebook.com/notes/equine-calculator/how-to-claim-your-vanity-url-for-your-facebook-page/474147772600069. After you have a vanity URL for your business page, it's a lot easier to tell people where to find you. If your company name is not conducive to being memorable in the form of a Facebook URL, try a typical web URL and redirect it to your business page. You can even redirect the URL to a specific tab, because Facebook tabs each have a unique URL.

You can buy a URL from NameCheap (www.namecheap.com), among other places. These services always have a simple function to allow you to direct your web address to any other page.

REMEMBER

When creating your marketing materials, use the proper URL address. Make sure it's the URL you see when looking at your business page the way your fans view it, not your home screen where you look at your news feed.

Using apps to build influence

Using third-party apps can help strengthen your engagement with your friends and followers because you can customize specific functions and characteristics into your business page. Apps can provide a variety of functions if you have the resources to develop them. For example, if you provide efficient heating and air equipment, you could build a home efficiency calculator app that allows users to find out how they can lower their heating bills. The idea with this is to generate more influence with your fans by providing value.

Apps should, of course, be relevant to your business and the people you want to attract. For example, if your business is an arcade, how about having a game that fans can play right on your business page? If you aren't ready to invest in developing (or even repurposing) a customized app, you can use several simpler apps to customize your business page and provide value.

Outsourcing your Facebook management

When running a business (especially as the owner), you have to balance your many tasks and determine the best use of your time. The question comes up frequently, "Is it okay to outsource social media to an expert?" You will always be best at serving your customers, but there are arguments for both sides of this conversation.

Outsourced social media marketing

When you outsource your social media (such as content creation and daily management), your biggest benefit is that you can hire someone who is familiar with the tools and how to effectively use them. Social media consultants usually end up in the business because they enjoy social media and are natural at executing social networking and communications.

The negative is that they are likely serving several clients at the same time and can't spend all their time on your company. Another negative is that they may not be fully familiar with your company, its culture, and its goals. It may take an outside resource weeks or months to learn the nitty-gritty of your business and your audience the way you do.

Finally, be sure you're working with a person or agency that truly understands the space. Many agencies say they can handle a social media campaign but either aren't aware of Facebook's basic terms of service or ignore them because they've seen others ignore them. If you're building a reputation on Facebook, you want to be sure the people helping you aren't hurting your brand's integrity.

In-house social media marketing

In-house people often find that their jobs can call them to many different activities. It's rare when someone can direct his or her full attention to just social media engagement, especially if the responsible party is the owner of the business. A business owner almost always has more immediate "fires" to put out, so social media management gets put on the back burner. For this reason, in-house Facebook management needs to come with discipline.

The connections and influence you build yield great long-term value. The biggest benefit of managing social media in-house is that you are always your best advocate and the best person to connect with your customers.

Comprehending What Makes Social Marketing Campaigns Work

The goal of a social marketing campaign is to increase your business page engagement, followers, and awareness. The most successful campaigns are interesting enough to your followers that they're willing to do more than just read your status updates in their news feeds. Both Fanta (`www.facebook.com/fanta/posts/285086828227700`) and Red Bull (`https://apps.facebook.com/red-bull-tt/`) used their business pages to create complicated but fun scavenger hunts that rewarded interaction. We want to point out, though, that the rewards weren't always physical prizes. Often just completing a task — if it's interesting or challenging enough — is enough. In the case of Fanta, fans worked together to help a cartoon character find her way through the business page time warp. Red Bull followers had to follow intricate clues to win prizes. Both companies were promoting awareness about their brand by enticing friends and followers to explore their business pages, but the tasks kept followers' attention.

Another type of campaign that businesses often use on Facebook is a *promotion* (this is what Facebook calls contests and giveaways). Facebook has specific guidelines in place for promotions. You can find them at `www.facebook.com/promotions_guidelines.php`.

Regardless of the type of campaign you choose to run, here are some of the defining characteristics that make a social marketing campaign work:

>> **Interactivity:** In many instances, the audience you want to reach isn't the audience you already have; it's their friends. To reach that audience, you need to entice your current friends and followers to share your content with their friends. Most Facebook users share only funny, useful, or interesting content. Regardless of the type of campaign you intend to implement, the content associated with it must be worth sharing.

Another interactive option is to include a voting component in a promotion. For instance, if you host a contest that requires each contestant to get votes to win, they are incentivized to invite people to your business page to help them win. You should note that contests should always be hosted on a third-party application.

>> **Incentive:** Giving people an incentive to take action is a must. As we said earlier, if your campaign is engaging enough, the act of completing a task or solving a problem may be enough. On the other hand, your friends and followers will likely be motivated if they have the opportunity to win something exciting.

The nature of the prize can depend on the type of campaign, your goals for the campaign, and your desired reach. For example, invite your followers to submit a video of themselves interacting with your product. You aren't likely to get people to create their own dramatic video (and edit it) if there is only a chance that they could receive a prize worth $250. However, people would certainly upload a simple picture for such a prize. As with everything, it's important to know your audience. The value of the prize varies with different types of product industries and people.

>> **Followers-only content:** When you offer followers-only content, you require that the visitors Like your business page before they can access the content, for example, a video or a white paper. For example, Figure 2-3 is a Welcome page you see if you haven't Liked the Microsoft business page. After you click Like, an animation plays.

>> **Datacapture:** One of the most important goals from a business perspective is to capture data. That data may simply be Likes or more specific information such as a name, an email address, or demographics. The purpose of acquiring this information is to understand your current audience and build a larger audience with whom you can continue to connect. When you know your audience and can cater to their needs and interests, you can build the relationship.

Just click Like. We'll do the rest.

FIGURE 2-3:
Invite friends and
followers to Like
your business
page.

Source: Facebook

Identifying Types of Facebook Campaigns

When you decide that you want to conduct a Facebook campaign, the next step is to determine the campaign's structure. If your sole goal is to earn space in the mind of current and potential customers, just about any form of campaign might work. A more specific goal requires a particular campaign concept.

TIP

Consider lead ads to collect leads and connect with the people who want to hear about your business without leaving Facebook. Check out `www.facebook.com/business/news/lead-ads-launch`.

Here are some of the most common features of Facebook campaigns:

>> **Voting contests:** A voting contest is based on people entering a contest — usually by producing something — and getting votes for their entry. Photo contests are a common, time-tested concept for voting contests. Facebook requires that you use a third-party app to conduct this contest.

Facebook's terms of service state that you can't require anyone to take a specific Facebook action to participate in the contest. For example, you can't define Liking a post as a form of voting.

>> **Sweepstakes:** In a sweepstakes, participants enter the sweepstakes and a winner is determined by a random drawing. The downside is that the sharing component is not as strong in this format. With other sorts of contests (especially voting contests), you often rule out some participants simply because they aren't confident that they have a chance to win. In a sweepstakes, each

contestant has an equal chance of winning in most cases. For this reason, you could attract more entries, even if you don't get as much voting traffic to your business page.

>> **Fundraisers:** A fundraising campaign is not necessarily a competition. Fundraisers promote the opportunity to do good by giving to a charity and inviting others to do the same. For example, you might offer to donate $1 for every Like your business page receives in a certain period of time. Fundraising through Facebook campaigns helps you spread the word in a lot of the same ways that contests do. Sometimes charities will form teams to encourage a little friendly competition in raising funds.

>> **Facebook as a landing page:** Almost any marketing campaign benefits from having a landing page. A *landing page* is where you direct people with your call to action. For instance, you could direct visitors to a page where they can request free samples or sign up for your email newsletter. Because the web is such a critical part of marketing, a landing page should be part of any campaign. Email marketing messages often have a corresponding landing page (or several, depending on the content of the message).

Using Facebook as a landing page simply puts the leads or customers you attract with your advertising in the path of your business page. This technique could be a simple way to increase your Facebook audience while targeting another goal. The best way to execute this is by directing a customized web address directly to your Facebook page tab. Create a unique URL that you place in your advertising message (something like "Find out more at www . ourlandingpage.com"), and then direct that URL to your page tab. Each page tab has its own web address (something like www . facebook.com/mypagename? sk=app_7146470129).

Implementing Sharing Contests

Facebook contests have many variations, but one thing they all have in common is an *ask*, or a call to action. The call to action might be to complete a form, upload a picture, or nominate a charity. If your ask is only to complete an entry form for the contest, implementation of the campaign might be easy. If participants must create a video, complete the form as they upload, and promote the contest to their friends and ask them to vote, your ask is clearly more complicated. If the latter is the case, you face the potential of *abandonment*, when people begin to enter your contest but then abandon the process, presumably because the effort to enter outweighed the potential reward.

Photo and video contests are popular forms of contests. People often love to share their photos and videos, especially when they might win something. Here are some of the things you need to know about photo and video contests:

>> **Get a third-party app to host the contest.** Facebook has strict rules about not using any Facebook features (such as clicking Like or commenting) as a means of entry. Third-party apps allow you to manage the entry and hosting of the contest. A well-known third-party app that follows the Facebook rules is Offerpop (www.offerpop.com), which allows you to implement a video or photo contest for your business page.

REMEMBER

Because Facebook requires that promotions be run within third-party applications, promotions can be run only on business pages and not on personal timelines. All third-party applications are installed on a page tab (also called an *application page*). Page tabs display content through iframes, which means that the content itself (like the contest app and images) is hosted on a separate site, and your page tab displays that content.

>> **Include clear instructions for how to participate.** Demonstrating visually always helps, so use some visual aids. You could even make a video describing how easy it is to enter.

>> **Market to the right crowd.** Video contests are more complicated than photo contests, because putting together a video is more work than taking a photo. Be sure that the people to whom you market are likely to have a video camera and are comfortable producing a video. Many can shoot some video with a smartphone; however, some people are still intimidated by the idea of shooting a video. Video contests also work best when you clearly describe what you want in a video. You don't want people to be overwhelmed with the challenge of scripting.

Photo contests, although simpler by nature, require the same clear concept as video contests. A cutest puppy contest is a simple concept. Make sure that your concept is something that people can easily understand.

>> **Compare voting versus judges to select the winner.** Gathering votes is a great way to incentivize friends and followers to invite people to see the entries and select their favorite. This method is a great way to attract new followers; however, in some cases, it may not be the ideal method. Do you want people to vote by clicking a button or by entering information? If you ask for information (such as a nomination or an email address), you're likely to get less traffic but more engaged traffic. Make your decision based on the goals of your contest.

Both Wildfire and Offerpop support all the preceding features.

Getting a good response

One of the biggest fears you may have at the beginning of a Facebook contest is whether you will get a good response. When you've invested a lot of time and effort (and sometimes money) in a Facebook campaign, it would be a big letdown

Building a Following and Running a Facebook Marketing Campaign

if it falls flat. You never know what is going to be a bang-up success and what isn't, but if you follow some best practices, you can certainly start with confidence.

Consider the balance of effort versus reward. More appropriately, consider the *perceived* effort versus *perceived* reward. It doesn't matter how easy it is to enter your contest or how exciting you believe it is; if entering appears too difficult, you won't have a successful response. If the incentive or reward doesn't interest the people that you reach, you may not have the success you desire.

The following tips will help you find the right balance so you can be sure to get a great response for your contest:

>> **Private information:** People are often willing to give their home address, phone number, email address, and so on if there is context for doing so. For example, if you ask people to enter your promotion to have their profile pictures featured as the face of your company, and you also ask for a home address, you may have a lower response because people feel that the information you're asking for isn't necessary. If capturing home addresses is important, offer a prize that must be sent in the mail.

>> **Relevant messaging:** When determining your contest concept, be sure that your contest message and your business message align. For example, if your company prides itself on providing the highest quality to discriminating buyers, any message that enforces discounts or free products is inconsistent with your business message.

Contests can be a great way to reinforce a brand message. The components of that message are often embedded throughout the entire contest and its marketing materials. Use contests to enforce a message you want to get across to your customers. For example, if you make paper products and want to position yourself as a company committed to green products, consider a contest that asks people to show how they too are green. In a photo contest, for example, you may ask participants to "upload a picture of you wearing all green" or "show us your best tips on being green."

>> **Easy entry:** Instructions for entering the contest should be clear. Use a simple call to action and limit what activities you ask participants to perform. Every barrier you put in place has a potential of eliminating entries. For example, if you host your contest through a third-party Facebook contest application that requires users to allow the app access to their Facebook accounts, and then they have to complete an entry form, you will have fewer participants than you would if you eliminate one of those steps.

As a general rule, the best first action (other than clicking to your contest landing tab) should be filling out a basic information form. On this form, include fields for only the minimum amount of information that you need.

If additional steps are necessary, make the steps something participants can do after they've submitted the form. If you give participants a percentage of completion, they are more likely to complete the steps because it feels unfinished.

>> **Simple messaging:** Share a clear message that leaves nothing to conjecture. The longer your contest description, the fewer people will bother to read it. Be aware that some of your audience is going to find out about the contest through someone sharing it on a Facebook status update or other channel (such as Twitter). Make sure that your concept is something that can be summed up in as few words as possible.

Avoiding a flopped contest

Sometimes, no matter what you do, you just don't get people to participate as quickly as you would like. One of the best ways to avoid this situation is to make sure that you don't launch a contest without a strong network to invite to participate. Sometimes personally asking your customers to enter is a great way to get the ball rolling. For example, an HVAC service company asked every one of their technicians to invite their customers to enter their Facebook contest after each appointment. Putting a little extra attention on promoting your contest at the beginning makes a big difference.

Some people feel that it's okay to ask a few customers or friends that you know personally to enter a contest to get things started. Others feel that this gives people an unfair advantage or otherwise less genuine entries. Regardless of your feelings on the matter, be sure that you never seed a contest with falsified entries to make it seem like there's lots of interest.

Marketing a Facebook Contest

Initially, you might think that posting status updates telling people about your Facebook contest is enough. It isn't. The primary reason to conduct a Facebook contest is to increase the interaction that you get from your friends and followers, as well as increase your audience by attracting new followers. A Facebook marketing campaign in most cases involves more than just Facebook to make it happen.

Facebook works well with other forms of digital marketing. Sure, sometimes if you have a strongly engaged and interested audience, you might be able to post one status update and see it turn into a major success. Most times, however, you have to use other resources as well.

The following list provides advice on how to market your campaign and make it a success:

>> **Announce your campaign to your email list.** Suppose that you send out a monthly newsletter. The content of that newsletter should highlight your Facebook contest and drive people directly to it. The cross-promotion of email to Facebook and Facebook to email makes your connection to your audience much stronger and more effective.

   Some best practices include putting a graphic right at the top of the email and linking it to the desired landing page. Note that you can link directly to the page with its unique URL. Find this in your browser address bar when you view the tab on which your contest is hosted. You may have made it your default landing page, but that applies only for followers.

>> **Pass out cards at the counter.** If your business is in retail or any other business in which you see customers' faces, give them a small card that promotes the contest. Include a hook that gets them interested in checking out the contest. They have to be interested enough to remember to check out the contest later.

   Alternatively, you can place a QR code by the register so customers can scan it with their smartphones.

>> **Post your campaign on your website.** Make sure an invitation to join the contest obviously stands out on the home page of your site, and remember to link directly to the contest page on Facebook. When people visit your website, the first thing they see should be a contest announcement. This way, you can convert some of your web traffic into engaged Facebook followers.

>> **Find a partner.** Finding a partner (also called *comarketing*) is perhaps the most powerful method in promoting a Facebook contest. If you sell custom wheels and another company sells customized car parts, you can be pretty certain that you have nearly the same type of people in your target audience — people who take pride in their cars and may want to make their cars ready for show. You're lucky, because this audience is already interested in sharing with friends. The winner of the contest might get his or her car fully outfitted with the two companies' products. By doing this, you promote the contest on both business pages, both email lists, and so on. You'll likely expand each company's following just by cross-promoting.

Eyeing the Power of Crowdsourcing

One of the greatest reasons to conduct social media campaigns is because of the power of crowdsourcing. Crowdsourcing can yield great ideas and help to expand your reach.

Using crowdsourcing to create a new product

Suppose a company that sells T-shirts with clever puns wants to introduce a new design. However, the company doesn't have a new design to announce. So they put together a Facebook contest with the following two stages:

1. Invite Facebook friends and followers to help determine the new slogan for the T-shirt.

2. Invite Facebook friends and followers to help create a concept for the new shirt's graphic.

The new T-shirt is released in a few weeks at a big event that many customers attend. The contest was a grand success for a number of reasons:

>> The company uncovered many new ideas for the new T-shirt design. Ultimately, the company was able to simultaneously test the design's popularity before printing the T-shirts.

>> The company increased its Facebook following because it gave people a compelling reason to visit the business page.

>> The new T-shirt design sold better because Facebook fans already had a vested interest in the shirt. The new product raised specific awareness and attracted new buyers.

>> The crowd was part of the creation of a new product, which sent the message that the company values its customers.

Using crowdsourcing to determine your Facebook content

One of the greatest challenges is keeping your Facebook followers interested and engaged in the content that you provide on a daily basis. Discussion keeps people interested. Let your Facebook followers tell you what they're interested in, and allow them to lead the conversation. This is where crowdsourcing comes in. A contest or campaign can help you attract the interaction that will launch that sort of activity with your Facebook followers.

People like to be valued, and people tend to like the idea of being featured or recognized. One way to do this is to ask your Facebook fans to start a conversation about your company on your business page. Maybe you could ask your fans for a new slogan for your company or what they like best about your business. This invitation to engage in conversation might prompt participation from your audience without requiring that you award a prize.

Preparing Your Business Page for the Campaign

Make sure your business page is ready for any contest or campaign that you implement. Campaigns can be simple or structured. Regardless, the most important aspect is making sure that people know that you have a campaign. The following sections describe how you can prepare for your campaign.

Your cover photo

If possible, the theme of your business page should match your branding. When you conduct a campaign, you may want to tweak the cover photo design to highlight a theme, but you'll still want to keep your branding. For example, a Christmas photo of the week contest might feature holiday colors or other images to give the campaign a holiday theme, but keep your brand's logo or other defining characteristic on the photo as well.

The cover photo is a great way to highlight your campaign while still branding the look of your business page. For example, you might include bells and holiday colors for a holiday campaign, or pictures of dogs and cats for a cutest pet photo contest. Remember that your cover photo is 851 pixels wide by 315 pixels tall. (Facebook prohibits calls to action on the cover photo, such as "Enter Now," so be sure to use the photo only for branding and design aspects.)

A custom tab

You host your contest on an page tab. It's best to have a custom page for the contest that shows only a preview to nonfollowers and the full version to followers (refer to Figure 2-3). When visitors click Like, they see another view of the tab. You can utilize this setting when you create a custom Facebook tab.

By setting up separate tabs for followers and nonfollowers, you save some content for followers, thereby giving nonfollowers one more reason to become a follower. More importantly, when your campaign attracts tons of traffic, you can gain more of those visitors as followers. It's important to note again that you can't have the entry come by way of visitors Liking your business page; the entry must happen in the third-party app.

Contact forms

Using a contact form extends your lead capture beyond only people Liking your page. Facebook contests are a great way to increase your email list as well.

You embed a contact form in your Facebook tab in the same way you embed HTML on most websites. Using the Static HTML app, you can simply place your code in the fields. You don't have to know how to create a form — several services offer easily built forms. We recommend Formstack (`www.formstack.com`) because its service has many functions that enable you to create lead capture forms, including database storage for the data, and connect it to your favorite email marketing services.

Canvas apps

Canvas apps are different than the common page tabs that are part of your business page. A canvas app enables the owner of the page to occupy the entire screen in the context of the application. This screen includes the ticker, which updates with activity from the application, as well as other similar applications.

Canvas apps are 760 pixels wide, which allows for a reasonable amount of content; however, it's just shy of the 810-pixel width of the page tabs in your business page.

Setting up a canvas app can enable an interactive experience between users. This feature is most useful when your contest involves a game or something that can display real-time activity in the app. One distinct disadvantage is that canvas apps redirect your fans to an alternative URL, such as `http://apps.facebook.com/wordswithfriends` instead of `www.facebook.com/wordswithfriends`. This means your visitors may have a few seconds of wait time as the canvas app loads.

Canvas apps are great when more page space is necessary (or when you need to enhance the quality of your campaign). Offerpop (`http://offerpop.com`) is a great third-party tool for setting up a canvas app–based campaign. Figure 2-4 shows the Scrabble canvas app. (Most games are hosted on a canvas app.)

The ticker

One big benefit of a Facebook campaign is the additional visibility created through the activity feed. Specifically, the Facebook ticker, shown in Figure 2-5, displays your friends' activity on the top-right side of your home screen.

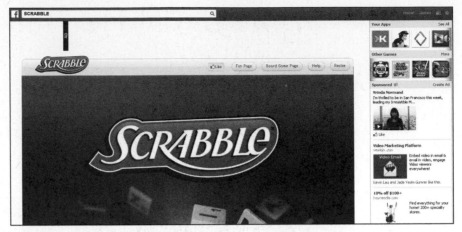

FIGURE 2-4:
A canvas app.

FIGURE 2-5:
The ticker.

Expect the following activity in the ticker:

- **Status updates:** If your contest encourages people to post a status update, people will see it in their news feed, but it appears also in the ticker.

- **New business page Likes:** Often, contests result in new Likes for your business page. These appear in the ticker as well.

- **Likes and comments:** When people Like or comment on a post in your contest, the ticker displays it.

- **Real-time data:** All the data you see in the ticker can be seen elsewhere on Facebook. The ticker just displays the data as it happens in real time. This factor might encourage you to carefully time your campaign launch. When you launch a Facebook campaign and everything (your Facebook tab and profile picture) goes live at the same time as your email announcement and Facebook status posts, you may attract more activity through the action showing up in people's news feeds.

Chapter 3

It's All in Your Image: Instagram and Pinterest

Have you ever noticed how people tend to react more to imagery than text on the social networks? That's because they see photos before they read text. So it's always in a brand's best interest to accompany great text with a great photo. Many times, though, the photo speaks for itself, and few words are needed. In fact, brands can find their community is very receptive to hanging out with them on a more visual platform, and that's where Instagram comes in.

Instagram is a social network based on photos, not words. Although Instagram allows hashtags, likes, and comments, you won't see text-heavy updates or link sharing. Instead, both individuals and brands alike let their photographs do the talking. In fact, many people prefer Instagram to other social platforms because there's less chatter.

Instagram gives you an opportunity to show your brand's creative side and think outside of the proverbial box. Instead of attracting people with viral videos or discount codes, you're using color and light. This chapter talks about how to set up an Instagram account and share photos with your community.

Pinterest is more than a social network for people who like to share recipes or photos of their latest home improvement projects. On Pinterest, the marketing element is subtle — you can tell your brand's story and direct traffic to your business without using a single marketing term — but effective. Viewers don't see promotional copy or a sales spiel; instead, their eyes are drawn to images, and if the images are compelling, the viewers will want to learn more. In this chapter, you find out how to effectively share content to drive traffic.

Promoting Your Brand on Instagram

Instagram is a mobile platform. Although you can view Instagram photos online via your regular web browser, you're very limited with what you can do. The majority of people using Instagram to view photos and interact are doing so with smartphones and tablets.

TIP

To reach your customers with photo, video, or carousel ads, consider the ad network https://business.instagram.com/advertising/. (*Carousel ads* allow prospective customers to swipe to see additional images and a call-to-action button that takes them to your website.)

WARNING

You can't set up an Instagram account or upload photos to your Instagram account from your computer; you can only view and like photos from your computer. If you want to sign up for an Instagram account or share photos with your community on Instagram, you must use a mobile device.

Here are a few examples of how brands use Instagram in creative ways, while still staying within their comfort zones:

>> The Starbucks account shares images of their customers, their baristas, and even members of the executive team trying new flavors and blends.

>> Red Bull Energy Drink uses their Instagram account to appeal to adrenaline junkies by posting photos of skydivers or skateboards high in the air.

>> Nike shares photos of athletes doing what they do best.

TIP

Be creative with your Instagram photos. The best Instagram strategy is to keep it simple. Oftentimes, the best photos are the ones closest to home. You don't need to take a trip to Europe in order to take photos to share with your community, because your brand has enough interesting things going on in your own backyard.

Almost every brand can present a more visual side to its community by using Instagram, although you might not immediately see what your brand should highlight. The section "Determining What Is Photo-Worthy for Your Brand," later in this chapter, throws out some suggestions for photogenic moments.

Creating and Using Your Instagram Account

Is your mobile device in hand? Good. The following sections discuss how to set up an Instagram account, upload photos, and control notifications.

Setting up your account

Follow these steps to set up an Instagram account:

1. **Locate the Instagram app on iTunes or Google Play and download it to your mobile device.**

2. **Choose to register either with your Facebook account or with your email account, as shown in Figure 3-1.**

3. **If you elected to register with your Facebook account, enter your Facebook login information.**

   If you elected to register with your email account, enter your email address and the password you want to use for the site and select Next.

4. **Create your username, fill out your profile, and upload your profile shot. Also, you have the option to enter your full name and phone number. After you enter all the desired information, tap Done.**

   Now you're ready to take and share photos.

Source: Instagram

Sharing photos

You can share photos on Instagram by following these steps:

1. **Open the Instagram app on your mobile device and select the Camera option.**

2. **The Camera option looks like a square with a circle inside.**

3. **Either select a photo from the photo album or tap the blue button to take a photo.**

4. **When you have the photo you like, tap Next.**

5. **You see the photo you want to display, along with various filters, as shown in Figure 3-2. The filters are fun ways to highlight your photo — for example, with different borders and tones, or even in black and white.**

   (Optional) Choose a filter, if you want.

FIGURE 3-2:
Instagram comes
with a variety of
filters you can
use to enhance
your photos.

Source: Instagram

6. **If you like the photo as-is, don't worry about a filter. However, do take some time at some point to familiarize yourself with Instagram's different filter options because you might find some that make your photos look awesome.**

7. **Tap Next.**

8. **Write a caption and add hashtags, if needed.**

   For more on hashtags, see the later section "Using Hashtags in Your Instagram Posts."

   (Optional) Tap on Facebook, Twitter, and other social networks to share, as shown in Figure 3-3.

   You can upload your Instagram photos to both Facebook and Twitter at the same time you're Instagramming. Your photo gets increased visibility when you share it on multiple channels, which means more opportunities for others to like, share, comment, and recognize your brand.

WARNING

When you post the same content on every platform, people may not feel the need to follow you on every platform. You may gain more Instagram followers if you don't share the same images on Facebook, Twitter, and other platforms.

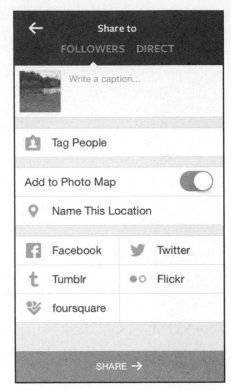

FIGURE 3-3:
You can upload
photos to Face-
book and Twitter
from Instagram.

Source: Instagram

9. If you're not logged into these social networks, you may be taken to a screen
   at those social networks so you can log in.

10. Tap Share, located at the bottom of the screen.

Controlling notifications

You can set your account up so that you can receive Instagram notifications on
your mobile device, even when you're not using the app. To do so, follow these
steps:

1. Select Options in your profile account.

2. You can find your profile at the lower-right corner of your Instagram screen.
   It looks like an ID card — a rectangle containing a circle and three lines.

3. At the top-right of the profile screen that appears, tap the wheel to open a
   drop-down list.

4. **Scroll down and, below Preferences, select the Push Notification Settings option you want.**

    You can choose to turn on notifications from friends or everyone, or to turn them off completely.

TIP

If you find your phone is always beeping and buzzing because you're receiving Instagram notifications every time someone likes or comments on a photo or sends a friend request, you can turn the notifications off in your smartphone's notification center. Look for the Instagram app in the notification center and select your desired notification settings.

TIP

If you received a like, you were tagged in an image, or someone new followed you, a red heart notification appears on the lower-right of your Instagram app screen.

Determining What Is Photo-Worthy for Your Brand

You may be thinking your brand isn't as visual as an energy drink or coffee brand. The truth is, very few brands can tell their stories in photos. Most, however, *can* find some ways to present photos while staying true to their brand's focus and mission.

Here are some of the ways brands can share on Instagram:

>> **Teamwork:** Fans love to see the behind-the-scenes workings of a brand. Don't shy away from showing the team at meetings, in the cafeteria, or chatting it up in the hallway. It shows your community that your team is human.

>> **Test kitchens and factories:** Who doesn't love to see how products are made or served to the public? Taking the mystery away (without giving away company secrets) will endear you to your fans.

>> **Products and ingredients:** Show what goes into a product. For example, if yours is an organic food brand using only wholesome ingredients, share photos of some of your suppliers, like farms and farmers markets. Showing what goes into a product is also a great tool for selling. People like to know what they're eating.

>> **Outings:** Share photos of the team picnic or conference.

- » **Ideas for using the product or service:** What are some of the things people make with your products? Share how others use what you do.

- » **Sightings "in the wild":** If you spot people using your products on the street, share photos on Instagram — but do get permission first.

With Instagram, the possibilities are endless. You don't need expensive equipment or a degree in photography. You only need the ability to understand what your community responds to.

TIP

Before taking photos, do a search and see how other brands and individuals are using Instagram. If you tap the Explore button, shown in Figure 3-4, random images from Instagram users appear in a grid on your screen. A search bar also appears, which you can use to search out other brands that are on Instagram and see how they're doing it. You're sure to get inspiration from others, and you also can see how the brands are interacting.

FIGURE 3-4:
Use the Explore button to view random photos or search for other Instagram accounts.

Explore

Source: Instagram

Using Hashtags in Your Instagram Posts

Hashtags help make a photo searchable. For example, if you post a photo of shoes on Instagram, and use the hashtags #shoes, #style, and/or #fashion, that photo will show up in the streams of others who are looking for items by using that same hashtag. When someone clicks on that hashtag, it will bring up public images that have been labeled with that hashtag.

REMEMBER

Your content has a limited shelf life when hashtagged, especially with a popular hashtag. So if it's a trending or popular topic, it may be visible at the top of the search for only a few minutes or hours. Sometimes an image will have longer visibility on a less popular hashtag because it's not pushed to the bottom of the search by more current entries. Play around with both popular and less trendy hashtags to see where you receive the most engagement.

Here are some hashtag best practices:

>> **Use two or three hashtags at most.** Using too many hashtags makes a post too busy. Sure, your post appears on many different searches now, but most people prefer to look at photos with less clutter.

>> **Make up your own hashtag.** Make up a hashtag that suits your brand and share it with your community. Now when they use your product or take part in a related activity, they use your brand's hashtag, giving you more visibility and prompting others to try the same.

>> **Keep an eye out for trending hashtags.** Hashtags don't have to be brand related. Plenty of hashtags relate to holidays, current events, and television shows. Don't spam a hashtag with irrelevant content, but if you have an image appropriate for trending hashtags, don't be afraid to use it.

>> **Think of popular things people like to do or buy.** Some hashtags that are popular on Instagram are #food, #shoes, and #cats. Familiarize yourself with popular hashtags but keep in mind that your content won't stay at the top of a very popular hashtag for long.

>> **Take part in hashtag memes.** Try having fun with your Instagram account by taking part in a meme. For example, you can use #ThrowbackThursday or #TBT to share photos of your business in its early stages or #outfitoftheday to show what your staff is wearing.

>> **Hashtags work best with public accounts.** Brands shouldn't have private accounts because it limits the brand's audience: Hashtags are seen only by people who have access to the account. If yours is a private account with 50 followers, it has the potential to be seen by only 50 people. If your account is public, your image has the potential to be seen by hundreds, if not thousands.

If you want to make your account private so only people you choose to be friends with can see your photos, follow these steps:

1. **On your profile screen, select Edit Profile.**

2. **Scroll down to the bottom of the page to the area where it says Posts Are Private.**

3. **Flip the little toggle switch to the right.**

Keep in mind that with a private account, you have to manually approve any friend request. With an account that is public, anyone can follow and view your photos.

People come to Instagram for the visual. Although you should give the photo a little caption or description, don't write an essay or you'll lose people.

Finding Friends and Fans on Instagram

What good is having an Instagram account if you have no friends to share your photos with?

To search for people or brands to follow, follow these steps:

1. **Tap the Explore button.**

2. **In the search text box, shown in Figure 3-5, type the person's or brand's name or Instagram handle.**

    You can also search hashtags for topics related to your business. For example, if you restore classic cars, you can use hashtags #classiccars, #classiccarspotting, and #classiccarsdaily, which are the most popular hashtags in that topic. Now you can see who some of the classic car enthusiasts are on Instagram. Follow them, and they may follow you in return to see photos of your restorations.

3. **When you find an account you're interested in, click the Follow button to follow that account.**

4. **Unless you follow people or brands that have private accounts, after you click the Follow button, their photos automatically appear in your feed. However, if you want to follow someone who has a private account, you have to request permission to follow her. Many of the people you follow will follow you in return.**

FIGURE 3-5:
The search text
box enables
you to search
both users and
hashtags.

Source: *Instagram*

WARNING

Don't follow random people just to get followers. Make sure you're following the right people. Online communities are made up of like-minded people. It's a waste of time to follow people who have no interest in what you do. Find people with whom you have a common interest for a mutually beneficial relationship.

Make sure to tell your Facebook, Twitter, and blog communities that you're now on Instagram. If people follow you on one social media site, they'll likely follow you on another.

Getting Going with Pinterest

Signing up on Pinterest is quite simple. Just point your browser at www.pinterest. com, enter your email and a password, and click Sign Up.

If you're running your account yourself for a small company you own, setting up your account is pretty self-explanatory. For large companies with typical staff turnaround and those who outsource their social media work, you need to do a few other things:

>> **Make it very clear you are hiring the person or asking the staff member to use Pinterest on the company's behalf, and that the account will be owned and controlled by the company.** You do not want a profile to build a following and get wildly popular, and then have a staff member (or firm) get fired and take it with him or claim the account belongs to him.

>> **Control access to the account by using a company-based email for signup.** If you let someone use their own personal email account to sign up, you will have no way to get back into the account if they quit or leave.

TIP

If you will have staff members or firms handling Pinterest or any social media accounts, consider creating a social media email in your business domain. Then if someone quits in a huff, gets fired, or simply is unreachable, you can easily get into that email account to recover a password or change the profile.

>> **Keep a master copy of the password and any other pertinent access details.** It is always a good idea to ensure anyone in the company can use the Pinterest account if need be. This can be especially important if your account is hacked and someone is sending out spam or inappropriate pins. This hasn't been reported as a major issue, but there have been isolated incidents of Pinterest account hacking. If the person who maintains the account is on an island vacation off the grid, you need to be sure someone can get into the account.

>> **Be careful about whose Twitter and Facebook accounts are integrated into the Pinterest account.** If you have a business Twitter account to connect to your Pinterest profile, that is not as big of an issue. As of this writing, however, you can only integrate a personal Facebook account with Pinterest. Although there are many benefits to doing that, especially to gain followers, this hands over access to the staff member or firm representative whose personal Facebook profile is connected.

Once you click a few feed topics to get started, you're officially a member of Pinterest — congratulations! Continue reading the next section to find out how to complete the setup of your new Pinterest profile.

Having a profile picture is a must-do on most social networks, and this is the case with Pinterest. People tend to ignore, not follow, and not interact with members who have no avatar. If you are creating a business profile, a logo or image of a product works well. If you are creating a personal profile, a close-up headshot is ideal. Cartoon characters, pets (unless your business is pet-related), and children's faces instead of your own can be off-putting to other members who are looking to engage with either you or your brand.

To edit your profile, log in to Pinterest and click Edit Profile. From there you can choose a photo on your computer to upload, fill in more info about you, such as a short bio, your location, and website URL.

REMEMBER

An ideal profile image is square. Also, it must at least be 200 x 200 pixels in size, or it may appear pixelated and distorted on your profile page.

A bio helps tell others on Pinterest about you. When someone visits your profile page, your bio is displayed just below your profile picture in the left column.

TECHNICAL STUFF

The bio is text only. You can't use HTML coding in your bio to, say, place sections in boldface or to add a link to your site.

Do you want Pinterest to notify you of all activity related to your profile by email alert? Or do you dislike emails and prefer to get your updates when you go directly to the site? Pinterest Settings allow for a variety of preferences (click the Settings icon, which looks like a gear).

REMEMBER

Email alerts are handy for keeping track of activity, such as when people repin (or share) your pins, follow you, or comment on your pins.

Understanding social etiquette for businesses on Pinterest

On every social network, as in life, no one likes people who only talk about themselves all the time. This is just as true on Pinterest as other sites, and perhaps even more so. Many members have come to view Pinterest as a place of beauty and inspiration. People don't like spam and excessive self-promotion.

Still, if you want to market on Pinterest, you can't exist as a martyr on the site, right? There is no doubt that people are self-promoting there. What you want to avoid, just as you would in a real-life conversation, is overdoing it. Share a little about yourself, and then share other members' content and pins.

Here are some general guidelines to following Pinterest etiquette:

>> **Don't just horde followers, but follow people back.** This is especially true if your purpose is marketing. No one likes to feel snubbed. When a member sees a favorite brand is followed by a million but is only following ten people, they get irritated.

>> **Share about others more than you share about your company.** Yes, of course, if you have a great post or an exciting new product, pin it. But you should follow an 80-20 rule: Make sure no more than one in five pins is self-promotional. You can share less about yourself than that, but don't share more. Don't be that guy at the party that everyone avoids.

>> **Pin images from their original source and credit properly.** A big source of the copyright controversy and issues is related to people pinning images from places that are not the source (Google image search and Tumblr, for example). Avoid creating original pins that don't properly connect to the source, and also avoid repinning poorly sourced pins. You can always click through a pin to see where the original pin leads before you repin.

Understanding Pinterest lingo

These terms come up in the world of Pinterest, so it's a good idea to become familiar with them:

>> **Pinboard:** A group of pins organized on your Pinterest profile by a topic set by you. They are also called *boards*.

>> **Pin:** As a verb, it is to share an image on a pinboard. By pinning an image you either upload or find on the web, it will appear on your Pins page, in the stream of those who follow you, and on your board page. As a noun, it is an image you have shared on Pinterest.

>> **Repin:** When you see another member's pin that you like, you can add it to one of your own boards and share it with your own followers by clicking Repin. It is similar to a retweet on Twitter or Share on Facebook.

>> **Like:** When you see another member's pin you like, you can click Like to indicate it. This places you on a list of people who like the pin on the pin's page, and it shows this pin on your personal profile's Likes page. Liking an image does not repin the image — it won't show up in one of your pinboards.

>> **Hashtag:** You can include a tag in a pin's description by prepending a word with the number sign using the common social media format #keyword (no spaces or other characters). When you do this, the word becomes clickable. Clicking it takes users to search results for that term.

>> **Follower:** On your profile, your list of followers includes people who follow all of your boards.

>> **Following:** On your profile, your following list includes the profiles for which you are following all boards.

- **Mention:** When you are following someone and they are following you back in return, you can mention them in a pin description by typing the @ symbol. This brings up a pull-down list as you type a member's name. When done, the name becomes linkable to the person's profile.

- **Pin It Button:** This is a browser add-on that allows you to pin an image directly from the web page where you found it.

- **Pin It Button for Web:** This is a button you can place on your own web site or blog to allow people to pin an image directly from your site with a click of the button.

Sharing on Pinterest

Many marketers who were skeptical about Pinterest at first now admit it's a great source for sharing information about brands, products, and services. With the right image and the right descriptive text, a picture really is worth a thousand words.

Here are just a few of the ways brands are sharing their content on Pinterest:

- Wedding planners: Use Pinterest to pin images of flowers, gowns, table settings, and limousines in order to catch the attention of brides-to-be.

- Catering companies: Pin recipes with mouthwatering images of food.

- Yarn suppliers: Pin images of scarves, hats, and sweaters, as well as supplies such as needles and knitting bags.

- Travel agencies: Pin images of island getaways, luggage, and luxurious hotel suites.

- Interior designers: Share photos of finished rooms and individual design elements.

- Home contractors and supply brands: Show off finished rooms done with their products and services.

- Fashion brands: Pin images of complete ensembles, including accessories and shoes.

- Businesses: Create boards featuring team members.

- Book publishers: Highlight books and authors.

What all these types of brands have in common is that they're not using their boards to post logos or product sales and information. In fact, many times, their pins come from external sources. They're providing an appealing look into what they do. This is what helps them to gain more followers, more interest, and greater brand recognition.

Choosing what to share

What to share isn't a decision to take lightly. If you repin only the most popular pins, pins that everyone on Pinterest has already seen ad nausea, you're not giving any incentive for anyone to follow you. If you share only obvious sales ploys, people are going to consider you a spammer. However, if you're known as someone who posts interesting, intriguing, shareable content, you'll have followers galore.

What sort of things you should share depends on your goal with Pinterest, the type of business you run, and who your customers are. Consider your brand and your message, and then brainstorm unique ways to share your brand's story. Before posting anything, ask yourself, "Is this image representative of my brand?"

Here are a few things to consider:

>> Make your content shareable. Find images people will enjoy and talk about.

>> Images should appeal to the senses. Make them mouthwatering, thought-provoking, funny, or the stuff that inspires fantasy.

>> Try to find images no one else is sharing. The more unique your pins and boards, the more followers you will have for those pins and boards.

>> People prefer images to text. Funny sayings and infographics are fun from time to time, but they can get old if that's all you post.

TIP

If you run a product-based company, consider putting a price tag on some of the items you sell, which places the items in the Gifts section.

Sharing other people's pins

When you share another person's pin in your feed, you *repin* it. Similar to a Facebook share or Twitter retweet, a repin tells the original pinner you liked what she posted so much, you also wanted to share.

To repin a pin that you like, follow these steps:

1. **Hover your mouse pointer on the pin that you want to share and click the red Pin It button that appears in the top-left of the pin.**

   The Pick a Board window pops up with the pin on the right, as shown in Figure 3-6. The Description section automatically populates with what the original pinner wrote.

2. **From the Boards drop-down list, select the board you want to repin the image to.**

   You have the option to select a board you already have or create a new board. If you want to change the description, you may do so at this time. If it's helpful information, such as the name of a particular food dish, you may want to leave it as-is.

3. **Click the Pin It button.**

   The pin gets added to the board you selected and it shows up in your feed and in the feeds of all the people who follow your board.

FIGURE 3-6: Click the Pin It button to share someone else's pin with your community.

Source: Pinterest

Note: You can also click the pin, which takes you to the pinner's page and to the pin itself. You can like the pin from there in the same manner. Click the pin image one more time to be taken to the original website where the image came from.

Using share buttons

Ultimately, you want others to share your content on Pinterest. The ideal situation is for other people to read your blog or view one of your photographs and pin it, inspiring dozens of repins. But you have to make it easy to do so.

Most people who read content online won't share the same content if sharing isn't made easy for them. Though it doesn't take more than a few seconds to cut a link and paste it into the Pinterest Add function, the truth is, it's too much trouble for most. They want to be able to share at the click of a button and not have to leave their current page.

Share buttons enable the people who consume your content to share it without even visiting Pinterest. All the user does is click the Pin It button, fill in the description, and choose a board, and then the content is pinned to his board. If you're not logged in to Pinterest already, you're taken to the login screen so you can do so first.

Here are a few features and plug-ins to look into:

>> **Pin It:** Available from Pinterest at `http://pinterest.com/about/goodies`, the Pin It button enables you to embed code on your blog or website so that others can pin your content. Pin It is available for WordPress blogs and even Flickr so that you can share your photos with others.

>> **Widget Builder:** You can add a Follow Me button and more to your blog or website. Grab the code for that button, for example, at `https://developers.pinterest.com/tools/widget-builder/#do_follow_me_button`. Most people like pasting the code into their right sidebars at eye level. Buttons should never be difficult to find.

>> **DiggDigg Alternative:** This WordPress plug-in at `https://wordpress.org/plugins/aas-digg-digg-alternative/` features share buttons for Twitter, Facebook, Google+, and many other social networks, including Pinterest. When you install this plug-in, the share buttons appear on the side of your content so readers can share the content if they're so inclined.

>> **ShareThis:** Another plug-in that enables social share buttons. When you activate this plug-in, share buttons appear at the top or bottom of the page. You can find it at `https://wordpress.org/plugins/share-this/`.

Although DiggDigg Alternative and ShareThis aren't specific to Pinterest, these popular share buttons are used to share content on Pinterest and other social networks. People who use one of these plug-ins, such as the ShareThis plug-in, shown in Figure 3-7, have the option to tweet, pin, post on Facebook, and so on. Because DiggDigg Alternative and ShareThis feature all the social networks, the majority of bloggers who use share buttons on their content use these plug-ins rather than installing a bunch of individual ones.

FIGURE 3-7:
Use Pinterest share buttons on your content.

Source: Pinterest

Driving Traffic with Pinterest

Did you know that Pinterest drives more traffic to individual blogs and websites than YouTube, Google+, and LinkedIn combined? That's a force to be reckoned with, and it's why Pinterest, unlike some of the other emerging social networks, is something anyone marketing a brand needs to take seriously.

Here's how the traffic flow works. If you're following proper Pinterest etiquette, you're sharing a good mix of content (which can be both images and video). Some of that content is from your own sources, such as your blog or website. The rest of your content is from other content, including repins and other people's blog posts or videos. In fact, most of the items you pin shouldn't be your own content. Unless an image is uploaded directly, most images are links from external sources. Most people who are marketing with Pinterest do so because they want pinners to click their links.

However, it isn't as simple as sharing a link and hoping people visit your website; you have to be strategic about it.

Here are a few things to consider when creating and sharing content on Pinterest:

>> **Select images with Pinterest in mind.** Your most important goal when creating pin-worthy content is to select an image that represents the article and entices others to click through to the originating site. Don't go through the motions and select some random stock photo. Use colorful, thought-provoking, and awe-inspiring photos. Pinterest automatically gives

image options when you're preparing to pin something from a site, so take advantage of that opportunity to select the best pin! Photos that tell a story will inspire others to click to learn more.

» **Be descriptive.** On Pinterest, brevity is essential. With that said, you should write a description worthy of the image. It's not exactly a headline but, similar to a headline, you want to use the description to capture attention. Share one or two sentences describing the image but leave most of the details to the imagination.

» **Tag when at all possible.** There's really no reason to tag all your friends every time you post a pin; that gets kind of annoying. However, if a pin reminds you of someone or if you want to give credit to a particular pinner, do tag. The person being tagged, more often than not, will like or share your pin, and that helps get your brand on other people's radars.

» **Give others the opportunity to pin your content.** Use share buttons on your blog posts, articles, images, and videos so that others can share with their friends.

» **Take advantage of the Gifts feed.** The Gifts feed is a way to sell without annoying people with spam or a sales pitch. You can add a price tag to a sales item, and it will appear on the Gifts page. Check out `http://socialnewsdaily.com/27172/pinterest-gifts-feed-makes-platform-shopping-a-breeze/` for more on the Gifts feed.

» **Use keywords and search terms.** In your descriptions, use the words and phrases that people are searching for. People also search for images online, so optimize your photos for search to help others find them.

» **Grow your community.** Keep finding new people to follow and interact with. While you grow your Pinterest community, you also grow traffic. The "Building Your Pinterest Community" section later in this chapter talks more about this.

» **Be consistent.** Pin on a regular basis. If people never see anything new from you, they have no reason to continue to follow your pins.

» **Get nichey.** Cater to your niche. Appeal to the people who are most likely to use your products or services.

» **Use humor.** People love to share funny pins, and humor is a great way to break up the themes of your regular pins now and again.

» **Pay attention to your board categories.** Don't be generic. Your boards should be as eye-catching as your images. Take special care with the names you use for your boards. Pinterest suggests names, but those are only suggestions. Don't be afraid to change them. Be creative and imaginative, and explore how other brands are using boards.

> » **Be strategic when arranging your boards.** Don't have a random mishmash of boards. Arrange them in an order that puts the most important boards first. If your goal is to sell, place the board with pins relating to your products or services first.

REMEMBER

Not every pin has to be your content or from you. You can use other people's content on your boards and in your pins.

Being descriptive but brief

The descriptions you include with pins are just as important as the images. It's not the image that brings in search traffic, but the words you use to describe the image.

If you're a travel agent and are posting a photo taken in Bora Bora, for example, you should let the viewer know where the image was taken, but you also need to tell the viewer that you can arrange vacations there. Write a description such as, "This gorgeous vista is Bora Bora. Now doesn't it make you want to plan your next tropical getaway there?" With this description, you also appear in searches for *Bora Bora*, *tropical*, and *getaway*. Did you notice that we didn't state directly that we can plan the vacation for the viewer, though? Drive traffic with your pin but avoid appearing too "selly" to the viewer. You want the viewer to come to you.

Pinterest doesn't allow descriptions to break text into paragraphs, which means descriptions can become one long-winded block of text if you're not careful. Make sure your message comes across in a few clear, concise sentences.

Because you're using Pinterest as a sales or marketing tool, you want to be visible to search engines. You also want to create a description so enticing that pinners click through to your website when you pin your own items.

What follows are a few best practices for creating the best descriptions for your pins:

> » **Use search engine optimization (SEO).** It's important to catch the attention of the search engines. By all means, use search terms in your pin descriptions, but don't make it obvious. The terms you use should flow naturally. Think about what words people use, or words you want them to use, to land on your brand in Pinterest. Use those words or terms in a way that doesn't look silly. Book 2, Chapter 5 talks more about SEO.

- >> **Use words that paint a picture.** A description should, well, describe. If you pinned an image of a hen holding a flag, avoid stating the obvious. *This is a hen holding a flag* is descriptive but kind of boring. Calling the hen *patriotic* is less boring and describes the hen without insulting the intelligence of the reader.

- >> **Use words that stimulate discussion.** Try to string together words so they're open ended. When you ask questions, request more information, or make a statement that leaves room for interpretation, you're more likely to receive comments.

- >> **Use titles if they benefit you.** If you're pinning from a link to an article or a blog post, there's nothing wrong with using the original title as your description. However, there's also nothing wrong with *not* using the title and instead describing the image using words that benefit your brand and bring searchers to your board or pin.

- >> **Let your personality show.** Don't be afraid to be funny, perky, or anything else that helps you and your brand shine. Avoid bland, general terminology and Internet slang. Use words that show your personality instead.

- >> **Avoid negativity.** Don't use words that evoke negative images or connotations. Always go for a positive point of view. But it's important to be appropriate and authentic. If your business sells Goth items, for example, "dark" words might be expected by the audience.

Finding pinners to emulate

You can get help from the top pinners in your community to see which pins are receiving the most attention. Just click the categories button at the right side of the Search box. In the categories page that appears, some of the top pinners for that category are displayed. Or simply look closely at your feed. Each pin shows how many likes and repins it receives. If a pin is going viral — you see the pin more than once — look for its original source.

TIP

Note the types of posts getting the best reactions in terms of the most repins and positive comments, too.

Using keywords

After you find the top pinners (discussed in the preceding section), read a sampling of their pins. Think about the descriptive words and phrases you would use to find them. Are they using the same keywords? For example, if a bedroom set has gone viral, read the description to note if it's a *girl's bedroom set* or a *blue bedroom set*. Those descriptive terms are keyword phrases. Consider the words and phrases people are using to find pins and use those words and phrases in your own pins.

Here are some best practices when using keywords on Pinterest:

>> **Make sure the keywords and phrases sound natural.** People don't type information into search engines in the same way they speak. For example, they might type *wet iPhone* instead of *How to dry a wet iPhone*. When pinning, use phrases that sound natural. Pinterest is a visual platform, but the words should be as pleasing as the photos.

>> **Avoid creating pins with keywords in mind.** Write for the people, not the platform. Definitely use keywords in your pins, but don't put up any old photo just because you want to use a keyword.

>> **Match the keyword or phrase to the pin.** Don't use a keyword unless it describes the pin. You'll lose followers if you're known to bait and switch.

>> **Use keywords for board titles.** Rather than using Pinterest-suggested titles for your boards, use your own titles that include keywords. This way, both boards and pins will appear in a search.

>> **Research keywords within your niche.** Use a keyword tool to see what the popular keywords are for your niche. There are some free tools you can use — for example, Google's keyword suggestion tool located at `https://adwords.google.com/KeywordPlanner`.

TIP

Do some Pinterest searches within your niche and see what keywords are being used in the most popular results. This information gives you a good idea of keywords to use for your own pins.

Chapter 4

Marketing Yourself and Your Business with LinkedIn

When LinkedIn first launched, it grew primarily through invitations — you joined only if someone who was already a member invited you and encouraged you to join. However, membership is now open to anyone 13 years or older (as long as the user hasn't previously been suspended or removed from LinkedIn, of course). You can have only one active account, but you can attach multiple email addresses, past and present, to your account so that people can more easily find you.

You're presented with some configuration settings during the signup process that you might not know what to do with until you get more familiar with the system. In addition, based on your initial settings, LinkedIn recommends people to invite to your network.

This chapter discusses how you can use LinkedIn for marketing purposes.

Joining LinkedIn

If you haven't gotten an invitation to join LinkedIn, don't let that turn you into a wallflower. You can join LinkedIn directly, without an invitation from an existing user.

Open your Web browser and go to www.linkedin.com. You see the initial LinkedIn home page, as shown in Figure 4-1. When you're ready to join LinkedIn, just follow these steps (bear in mind that websites change all the time — the steps you encounter may be different):

1. **In the Get Started section in the middle of the page, provide your first name, last name, email address, and a password in the boxes provided, as shown in Figure 4-1.**

Source: LinkedIn

FIGURE 4-1: Join LinkedIn from its home page.

2. **Click the Join Now button.**

   You're taken to the next step, where LinkedIn starts to build your professional profile by asking about your current employment status and location, as shown in Figure 4-2.

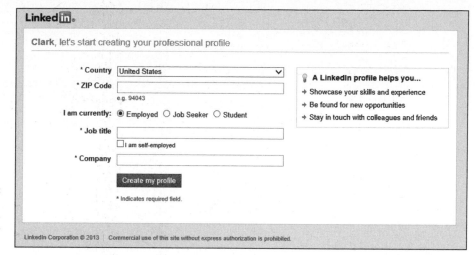

Source: LinkedIn

FIGURE 4-2:
Tell LinkedIn a
little about your-
self to create your
account.

3. **Complete the fields regarding your current employment status and location.**

Specifically, you need to provide the following information:

- **Country and zip code:** LinkedIn won't display your zip code, but it does use it to assign a Region to your profile so others know the general area where you reside.

- **I am currently:** Indicate whether you're employed, a job seeker, or a student.

- **Details about your status:** Depending on your status, LinkedIn asks for a Company, Job Title, and Industry if you're employed, or asks for your most recent job title and company, if you're looking for work, as shown in Figure 4-3.

TIP

If you find it difficult to choose an industry that best describes your primary expertise, just choose one that's closest. You can always change the selection later. If you're employed but looking for another job, you should still pick the industry of your current profession.

4. **Click the blue Create My Profile button to continue.**

LinkedIn then offers to import your contacts from your email program, as shown in Figure 4-4. LinkedIn walks you through the steps of importing your address book and offers you the chance to connect with existing members of LinkedIn. You can also do this after you create your account by clicking the Skip This Step link.

5. **LinkedIn asks you to confirm the email address for your account.**

Depending on the email account you used to register the account, LinkedIn may be able to log directly into that email account and confirm your email

Marketing Yourself
and Your Business
with LinkedIn

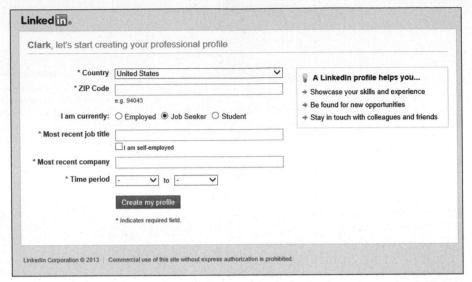

FIGURE 4-3:
Depending on your work status, LinkedIn asks for different information.

Source: LinkedIn

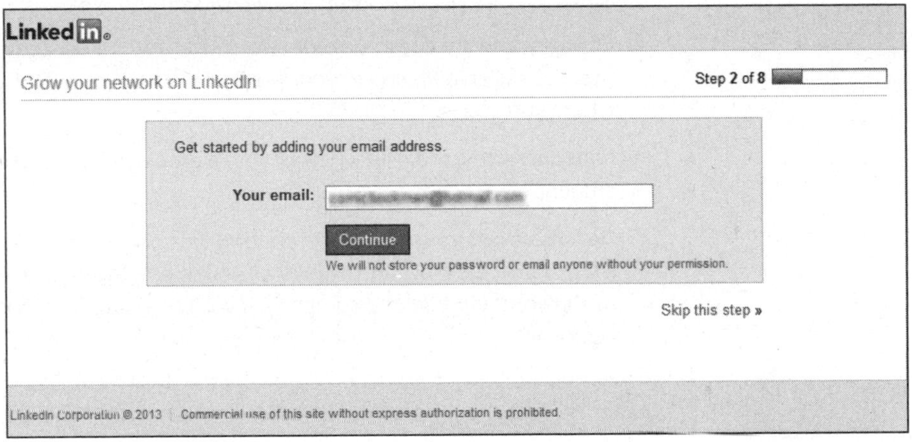

FIGURE 4-4:
LinkedIn can help you identify who to add to your network.

Source: LinkedIn

address. (For example, clicking the Confirm My Hotmail Account button illustrated in Figure 4-5 confirms the sample account being created.) Otherwise, LinkedIn emails you a confirmation, which you can choose to receive instead of using LinkedIn to log directly into your email account.

If you choose (or have) to receive a confirmation email, open your email program and look for an email from LinkedIn Email Confirmation with the subject line. Please confirm your email address. When you open that email, you should see a request for confirmation, as shown in Figure 4-6. Either click the Confirm Your Email Address button or copy and paste the URL provided in the email into your web browser.

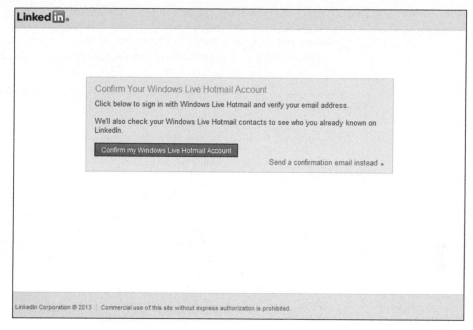

FIGURE 4-5:
LinkedIn may be
able to confirm
your email
address directly
with your email
provider.

Source: LinkedIn

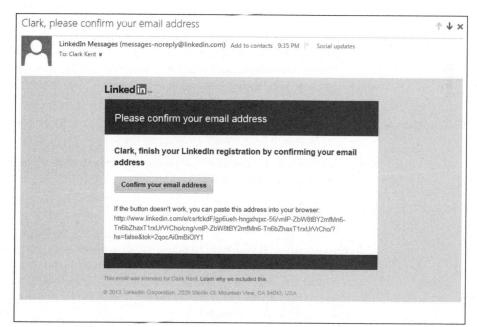

FIGURE 4-6:
Confirm your
email address
with LinkedIn.

Source: LinkedIn

Marketing Yourself
and Your Business
with LinkedIn

When you click the button, you're taken back to LinkedIn and it confirms your address, as shown in Figure 4-7. You may be asked to log in to your account, so simply provide your email address and password when prompted.

FIGURE 4-7:
LinkedIn confirms your email address.

You are asked to connect your email account to look for new contacts, prompted to install the LinkedIn mobile application, and offered the chance to upgrade your account to a paid account. You can always click Skip This Step to move along the account creation process and save those tasks for later.

WARNING

If you skip this step of confirming your email with LinkedIn, you won't be able to invite any connections, apply for jobs on the LinkedIn job board, or take advantage of most other LinkedIn functions.

6. **Your account is created, and you're now free to start building your network and updating your profile.**

   You're taken to your home page, as shown in Figure 4-8, where LinkedIn asks for information to help build your profile.

In the meantime, if you want to take a break to check your email, you'll find a nice Welcome to LinkedIn! message there from LinkedIn Updates, assuring you that you're now a registered LinkedIn user. The email encourages you to connect with people you may know and offers to take you back to the website to search for more people to add to your network.

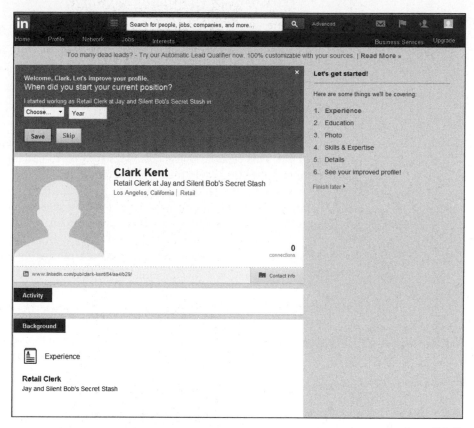

FIGURE 4-8:
Welcome to
LinkedIn!

Source: LinkedIn

Marketing with LinkedIn

When it comes to maximizing the benefit you receive from LinkedIn, you are your biggest advocate. Although your network of connections is instrumental in helping you grow, much of your marketing happens without your being involved. After you create your profile, that and any other LinkedIn activity of yours are read and judged by the community at large — on the other members — own time and for their own purposes. Therefore, you want to make sure you're creating a favorable impression of yourself by marketing the best traits, abilities, and features of you and your business. Because of the nature of LinkedIn, this marketing occurs continually — 24/7. So, you should look at LinkedIn as something to check and update on a continual basis, like a blog. It doesn't mean you have to spend hours each day on LinkedIn, but a little bit of time on a consistent basis can go a long way toward creating a favorable and marketable LinkedIn identity.

Marketing Yourself
and Your Business
with LinkedIn

The following sections look at the different ways you interact with LinkedIn, and what you can do to create the most polished, effective LinkedIn identity possible to further your marketing message.

Optimizing your profile

Your professional profile is the centerpiece of your LinkedIn identity and your personal brand. This section focuses on ways for you to update or enhance your profile with one specific goal in mind: marketing yourself better or more consistently. As always, not every tip or suggestion works for everyone, and you might have already put some of these into action, but it's always good to revisit your profile to make sure it's organized the way you intended.

To make sure your profile is delivering the best marketing message for you, consider these tips:

>> **Use the Professional headline wisely.** Your Professional headline is what other LinkedIn users see below your name even when they're not looking at your full profile. Some users stuff a lot of text into this field, so you should have enough space to communicate the most important things about yourself. If you have specific keyword phrases you want associated with your name, make them a part of your headline.

A standard headline reads something like "Software Development Manager at XYZ Communications," but you can write entire sentences full of great keywords for your headline.

>> **Make sure you use keyword phrases that match popular keywords for you or your business.** The first step, as mentioned, is to put these phrases in your headline. The second step is to make sure these phrases are reflected in your Summary, Experiences, and Interests.

Be careful not to overuse your main keyword phrases. The search engines call this practice *stuffing,* which means cramming as many instances of a phrase into your site as possible in hopes of achieving a higher ranking. If the search engines detect this, you'll experience *lower* ranking results.

>> **If you're available for freelance work, make sure to identify at least one of your current positions as freelance or self-employed.** Remember, people aren't mind readers, so you need to let people know that you're a freelance writer, website designer, dog walker, or whatever. If you look at Cynthia Beale's profile in Figure 4-9, you can see that she's listed her current position as self-employed.

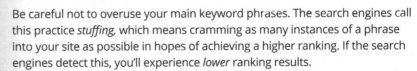

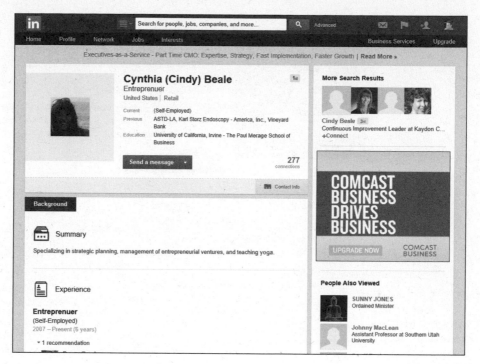

FIGURE 4-9:
Make sure to
note if you are
self-employed or
freelance.

>> **Use the additional sections in your profile to include any relevant information that reinforces your marketing message.** For example, if you want to be seen as an expert in a given field, add the SlideShare application to upload presentations you've given, or update the Publications section of your profile to include the articles or books you've written, articles you've been quoted in, focus or advisory groups you belong to, and any speaking engagements or discussions you've participated in. LinkedIn has created sections like Projects, Patents, and Certifications for you to display specific accomplishments that are an important part of your professional identity.

>> **Make sure your profile links to your websites, blogs, and any other part of your online identity.** Don't just accept the standard "My Company" text. Instead, select the Other option, and put your own words in the website title box, such as "Joel Elad's E-Commerce Education website."

For an example of effectively linking your profile to other areas of your online presence, take a look at Scott Allen's profile, shown in Figure 4-10. His three website links replace the bland My Company, My Blog, and My Website with his own text — Momentum Factor, Linked Intelligence, and Social Media Is My Middle Name. Not only does this give more information to someone reading his profile, but search engines have a better idea of what those links represent.

Marketing Yourself
and Your Business
with LinkedIn

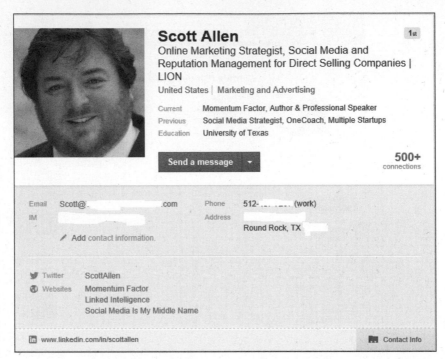

FIGURE 4-10:
Give your website
links meaningful
names.

Marketing yourself to your network

Optimizing your profile in the ways described in the previous section is one of the best ways to market yourself effectively using LinkedIn. Another is to be alert to how well you're communicating with your LinkedIn connections. Whether it's automatic (like when you update your profile and LinkedIn automatically notifies your network through a network update) or self-generated (when you use LinkedIn InMail or introductions to send a note to someone else), this communication becomes your ongoing message to the members of your network and keeps you in their minds and (you hope!) plans.

The most effective marketing occurs when people don't realize you're marketing to them. After all, the average American sees all kinds of marketing messages throughout their day. Your goal is to communicate often but not be overbearing about it so your message subtly sinks into people's minds.

So when you're contemplating how to effectively communicate with your network connections, keep these points in mind:

>> **Update your profile when appropriate.** Updating your profile means that you're sending an update of your newest projects to your network so that your connections can consider involving you in their own current or future

projects. You don't need to update your profile as often as you update a blog, but you certainly don't want to leave your profile untouched for months on end, either. Useful times to update your profile include

- Getting a new job or promotion

- Starting a new freelance or contract job

- Launching a new company or venture

- Adding a missing piece of your Experience section, such as adding a new position, updating the description of an existing job, or clarifying the role of a group or interest on your profile

- Receiving an award or honor for your professional, nonprofit, or volunteer work

- Being appointed to a board of directors or elected to a professional association board

- Taking on new responsibilities or duties in any of your endeavors

» **Take advantage of the Network Update feature.** When you specify your current endeavors, several things happen. Your profile reflects what you enter here, your network connections see what you enter here when they read their network updates about you, and you start to build your own microblog, in a sense, because people can follow your natural progression.

TIP

A similar example of a microblog is Twitter. As you update your Twitter profile with 140-character messages, other people can follow your activities and even subscribe to these updates. Tie your Twitter updates to your LinkedIn account, so if you tweet on Twitter, those updates are automatically reflected on your LinkedIn profile.

Some people use the Network Update feature to let people know that "Joel is getting ready for his next project" or "Joel is finishing up his first draft of *LinkedIn For Dummies.*" Other people use the messages to show progression of a certain task, like "Joel is currently conducting interviews for an Executive Assistant position he is trying to fill," then "Joel is narrowing down his choices for Executive Assistant to two finalists," and finally "Joel has made an offer to his top choice for Executive Assistant."

» **Search for, and join, any relevant LinkedIn Groups that can help you reach your target audience.** It's a good idea to participate in these groups, but whatever you do, don't immediately download a list of all group members and spam them with LinkedIn messages. When you join the group, you're indicating your interest in that group because your profile now carries that group logo. Membership in such groups gives you access to like-minded people you should be communicating with and adding to your network. Spend some time every week or every month checking out LinkedIn Groups and networking with group members to grow your network.

>> **Participate on a regular and consistent basis.** The easiest way to ensure a steady stream of contact with as many people as you can handle is to dedicate a small but fixed amount of time to regularly interact with the LinkedIn community. Some members spend 15 to 30 minutes per day, sending messages to their connections, reading through the Groups and Companies or Influencers page, or finding one to two new people to add to their network. Others spend an hour a week, or as long as it takes to create their set number of recommendations, invite their set number of new contacts, or reconnect with their set number of existing connections. You just need to establish a routine that works with your own schedule.

Marketing Your Business Through LinkedIn

LinkedIn can play a significant role in the effective marketing of your business. LinkedIn's value as a marketing tool gets a lot of buzz from most companies' finance departments, especially because they see LinkedIn as a free way of marketing the business. Although you don't have to pay anything in terms of money to take advantage of most of LinkedIn's functions, you do have to factor in the cost of the time you put in to manage your profile and use LinkedIn to the fullest.

Currently, LinkedIn offers your company promotion through its Company pages section. LinkedIn ties status updates, job titles, and other pertinent information from company employees' profiles directly into the Company page. From each page, you can see those people you know in the company, open career positions, recent updates from their employees, and other pertinent facts.

If you're a small business, you can create your own Company page. You need to have your company email address in your LinkedIn profile and be established as a current employee/manager/owner of that company in your profile as well. Click the Interest link from the top navigation bar, and then click Companies from the drop-down list that appears to learn more.

Using online marketing tactics with LinkedIn

Marketing your business on LinkedIn involves working through your own network, employing both your current list of contacts as well as potential contacts in the greater LinkedIn community. Your efforts should also include making use of links from your online activities to your LinkedIn profile and promoting your business online from your LinkedIn identity. Here are some things to keep in mind as you develop your LinkedIn marketing strategy:

>> **Encourage every employee to have a LinkedIn profile and to link to each other.** Extending your network in this way increases your exposure outside your company. And if anybody in your organization is nervous about preparing her profile, just tell her that LinkedIn can be an important asset in their professional or career development. You can mention that even Bill Gates has a LinkedIn profile. That should do the trick.

>> **Make sure your business websites and blogs are linked to your LinkedIn profile.** By offering your website visitors a direct view to your LinkedIn profile, you're allowing them to verify you as an employee of the company because they can see your experience and recommendations from other people. They may also realize they share a bond with you and your business that they never would have discovered without LinkedIn.

>> **Make sure your LinkedIn profile links back to your business website and blog.** You not only want your visitors and potential customers to be able to verify who you are, but you also want them to go back to your website and do some business with you. Make sure that you, and every employee of your company who's on LinkedIn, includes a link to your business's website and, if there is one, the company blog.

WARNING

If you have a search engine expert working for you, that person may complain about something called a *two-way link,* which is a link from your LinkedIn profile to your website and a link from your website to your LinkedIn profile. This practice, known as *reciprocal linking,* hurts your search engine ranking. If so, have that person identify which of the two links is more important and implement only that link.

>> **Make sure that your most popular keyword phrases are in your company or personal profile.** Use sites such as Wordtracker (www.wordtracker.com) or Good Keywords (www.goodkeywords.com) to find the hottest keyword phrases in your field. If your business is doing any online ad campaigns, make sure those keyword phrases are the same as the ones in your profile. Presenting a consistent image to potential customers makes you and your company look more professional.

>> **Develop relationships with key business partners or media contacts.** When you search for someone on LinkedIn, you can be precise about who you want to reach. So, for example, if you know that your business needs to expand into the smartphone market, you can start targeting and reaching out to smartphone companies such as Apple, Samsung (maker of the Galaxy and Note), and HTC (maker of the One). If you want to increase your visibility, start reaching out to media members who cover your industry.

Promoting your services through a recommendation

Now, you may ask, "What if I *am* my business?" If you provide a professional service, such as consulting or freelance writing (to name just a few), be sure to take advantage of the fact that LinkedIn can classify you as a service provider. Some categories and subcategories of service providers range from computer-related consultants to attorneys, accountants, and real estate agents. Although you can no longer search exclusively for a service provider, your recommendations for any service position still show up in your profile, which can be visible when people search LinkedIn, making it a potentially valuable addition to your business.

To request a recommendation from someone, just follow these steps:

1. **Click the word Profile in the top navigation bar, then click Edit Profile from the menu that appears.**

2. From your profile page, scroll down to the Recommendations section and click the Edit link (the pencil icon) to open up that section.

   You see an expanded view of your recommendations, as shown in Figure 4-11, along with the Ask to Be Recommended link on the right side of the screen.

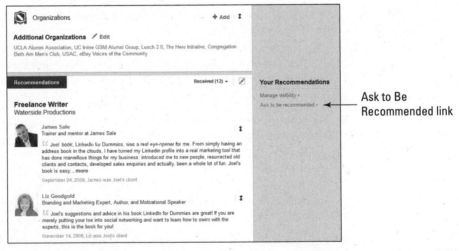

FIGURE 4-11: Start by editing the Recommendations section of your profile.

Source: LinkedIn

3. **Click the Ask to Be Recommended link to bring up the Ask for Recommendations page, shown in Figure 4-12.**

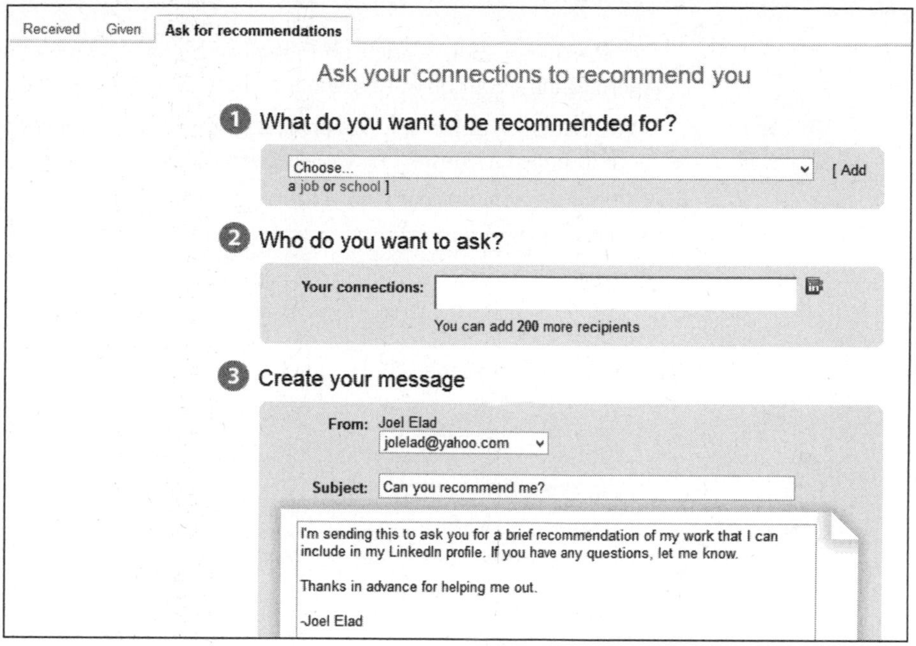
Received
Given
Ask for recommendations
Ask your connections to recommend you
1 What do you want to be recommended for?
Choose...
[Add a job or school]
2 Who do you want to ask?
Your connections:
You can add 200 more recipients
3 Create your message
From: Joel Elad
jolelad@yahoo.com
Subject: Can you recommend me?
I'm sending this to ask you for a brief recommendation of my work that I can include in my LinkedIn profile. If you have any questions, let me know.
Thanks in advance for helping me out.
-Joel Elad

FIGURE 4-12: Start your service provider recommendation request.

Source: LinkedIn

4. **In the What Do You Want to Be Recommended For section, click the arrow for the drop-down list to find the position you want someone to recommend you for.**

   If you want your Services recommendation to be tied to a specific role, pick one of your positions that indicates the service, such as Freelance Writer or Website Designer. If you don't see an appropriate position in your list, click the Add a Job or School link to add a new position to the Experience section of your profile.

5. **In the Who Do You Want to Ask section, start typing the names of people to ask for a recommendation.**

   As you type those people's names, LinkedIn prompts you with the full name of that person. Click that prompt to have LinkedIn add that person to the list.

6. **Repeat Step 4 until you add all the people you want to ask for a recommendation.**

7. **In the Create Your Message section, type a note to send to each person you selected, similar to the example shown in Figure 4-13.**

   Although LinkedIn fills in this box with canned text (as shown in Figure 4-13), you should personalize this text to make it sound as though it's coming from you. Most importantly, you should use this message to emphasize to the recommenders what areas you're hoping they'll comment on regarding your service. It's not about feeding them a speech to say about you, but pointing them to the areas you want mentioned in their recommendation.

TIP

Make sure the Subject line is appropriate, too, to help your chances of getting your intended requesters to actually open the email and respond.

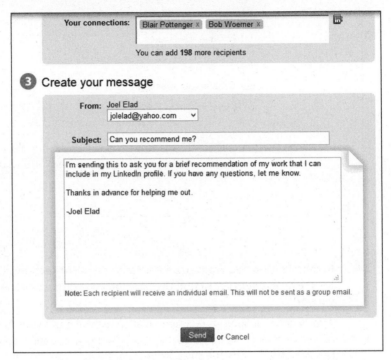

Your connections: Blair Pottenger x Bob Woerner x

You can add **198** more recipients

3 Create your message

From: Joel Elad
jolelad@yahoo.com

Subject: Can you recommend me?

I'm sending this to ask you for a brief recommendation of my work that I can include in my LinkedIn profile. If you have any questions, let me know.

Thanks in advance for helping me out.

-Joel Elad

Note: Each recipient will receive an individual email. This will not be sent as a group email.

Send   or Cancel

FIGURE 4-13:
Ask your network connections for a recommendation.

8. **Click Send.**

    Your request is sent, and your selected connections receive a message from LinkedIn asking them to come to the site and complete a recommendation for you.

That's it!

TIP

The best business etiquette involves a combination of online and offline methods, so don't be afraid to follow up with your recommenders through a phone call, email, or face-to-face interaction after you send the request to make sure you can answer any questions they have and help them complete the process.

Chapter 5

Being Prepared for What's Next

Without a doubt, Facebook, Twitter, LinkedIn, and Google+ are the elephants in the social marketing zoo, at least in terms of the largest number of visits per month. But this is one big zoo, as shown in Figure 5-1, which displays only 35 of more than 300 significant social sites. Among these sites, you'll find lions and tigers and bears, and more than a few turtles, trout, squirrels, and seagulls.

You have to assess your business needs, research the options, and select which (if any) of these minor social marketing sites belongs in your personal petting zoo. The first part of this chapter looks at methods for doing just that.

Social media is no longer confined to a standard computer of any size. The proliferation of smartphones and apps, 4G networks, more affordable data plans, built-in web browsers, and mobile-ready websites have all contributed to the growth of mobile social activities. Most devices (except old feature phones) can use either a cellular network or Wi-Fi for wireless Internet access.

The integration of social media with mobile devices creates more opportunities to reach your target audience in addition to challenges for managing and integrating your marketing campaigns.

As a social media marketer, try to tap the potential that these mobile devices offer: incredible marketing opportunities to reach both retail and business prospects at the moment they seek information about the product or service you offer, wherever they are. You don't have to wait for them to get back to their desktop computers. Of course, the social media marketing techniques you select may depend on the platforms that your target market uses. The second half of this chapter looks at how rapidly advancing mobile technology allows you to use social media to reach people on the go.

REMEMBER

Mobile social marketing gives you many new ways to reach with your message. The challenge, of course, is that everyone else is trying to do that, too. Your efforts have to cut through an increasing amount of clutter.

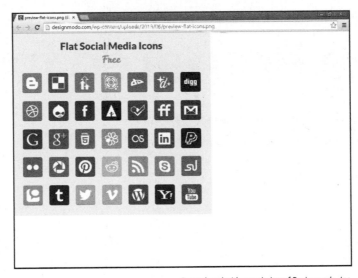

FIGURE 5-1:
The zoo of social media sites is vast. Your time, however, is limited.

REMEMBER

With the exception of the community-building site Ning and free-standing blogs (which can become your primary web presence if you use your own domain name), these smaller sites are best used to supplement your other social marketing efforts.

Reviewing Your Goals

Book 2, Chapter 3 suggests that you develop a strategic marketing plan. If you haven't done so yet, there's no time like the present. Otherwise, managing your social networks can quickly spin out of control, especially when you start to add multiple smaller sites for generating or distributing content.

REMEMBER

Marketing is marketing, whether offline or online, whether for search engine ranking or social networking. Obviously, your primary business goal is to make a profit. However, your goals for a particular marketing campaign or social media technique may vary.

Social media marketing can serve multiple goals. It can help you

>> Cast a wide net to catch your target market.

>> Brand.

>> Build relationships.

>> Improve business processes.

>> Improve search engine rankings.

>> Sell when opportunity arises.

>> Save money on advertising.

Your challenge is to decide which goal(s) apply to your business and then to quantify objectives for each one. Be sure that you can measure your achievements. You can find additional measurement information in the other chapters in Book 4.

Researching Minor Social Networks

Doing all the necessary research to pick the right mix of social networks may seem overwhelming, but, hey, this is the web — help is at your fingertips. Table 5-1 lists many resource websites that have directories of social networking sites, usage statistics, demographic profiles, and valuable tips on how to use different sites. The selection process is straightforward, and the steps are quite similar to constructing an online marketing plan, as described in Book 2, Chapter 3.

TABLE 5-1 Social Network Research URLs

Site Name	URL	What It Does
Alexa	`www.alexa.com/siteinfo`	Ranks traffic and demographic data by site
Display Planner by Google	`https://adwords.google.com/da/DisplayPlanner/Home`	Compiles traffic data, demographics, and device use by site; requires a Google account
Google Toolbar	`www.google.com/toolbar`	Installs Google Toolbar with Google PageRank (not available for all browsers)
HubSpot	`http://blog.hubspot.com/blog/tabid/6307/bid/33663/7-Targeted-Social-Networks-Niche-Marketers-Should-Try.aspx`	Describes seven attractive niche social media sites
Mashable	`http://mashable.com`	Presents social media news and web tips
	`http://mashable.com/category/social-media`	Lists stories and resources about social media
	`http://mashable.com/category/social-network-lists`	Lists of older social media sites by topic
Quantcast	`www.quantcast.com`	Compiles traffic and demographic data by site
Social Networking Watch	`www.socialnetworkingwatch.com/all_social_networking_statistics`	Aggregates social net news and stats
Wikipedia	`http://en.wikipedia.org/wiki/List_of_social_networking_websites`	Directory of more than 200 social networking sites

Follow these general steps to get your research under way:

1. **Review the strategy, goals, and target markets for your social marketing campaign, as described in Book 1.**

   If your B2B business needs to target particular individuals during the sales cycle, such as a CFO, buyer, or project engineer, be specific in your plan.

2. **Decide how much time (yours, staff's, or third party's), and possibly budget, you want to commit to minor social networking sites.**

   WARNING

   Don't underestimate how much time social media marketing can take. After you're comfortable with Facebook and (if they fit) Twitter or LinkedIn, it's okay to start with just one or two minor sites and slowly add services over time.

3. **Skim the directories and lists of social media in (refer to Table 5-1) to select possibilities that fit your goals.**

    For more ideas, simply search using terms for your business area plus the words *social network* or *social media* (for example, *fashion social network*).

4. **Review the demographics and traffic for each possibility by using a site such as Alexa, Google's DisplayPlanner for ads, or Quantcast (as discussed in Book 2, Chapter 3), and then cull your list to keep only those that fit your target market and marketing objectives.**

    Figure 5-2 displays the relative market share, according to StatCounter Global Stats (`http://gs.statcounter.com/#all-social_media-US-monthly-201406 201408-bar`), for the seven top-ranked social media services in the United States from June 2014 to August 2014. Market share is ranked not by traffic to the sites themselves, but rather by the amount of traffic they refer to other sites. This approach may be valuable for business analysis because it discounts personal users who stay on social media sites to communicate with their friends. The Other category in this figure encompasses LinkedIn, Delicious, Digg, Google+, and many more sites.

5. **Review each network (see suggestions in the following bullet list) to make sure you feel comfortable with its web presence, user interaction, Google PageRank, features, ease of use, and ability to provide key reports.**

    Prioritize your sites accordingly.

6. **Enter your final selection in your Social Media Marketing Plan (described in Book 2, Chapter 3), and set up a schedule for implementation and monitoring on your Social Media Activity Calendar (see Book 2, Chapter 4).**

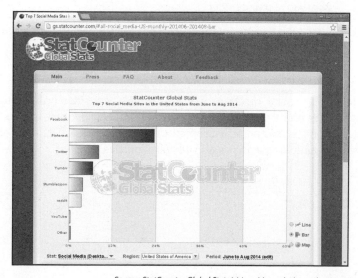

FIGURE 5-2:
Factor in relative market share, using data such as that from StatCounter Global Stats.

Source: StatCounter Global Stats `http://gs.statcounter.com`

7. **Implement your plan.**

   Modify it as needed after results come in. Wait at least a month before you make changes; gaining visibility within some social network sites can take time.

TIP

For leads to other social networks that appeal to your audience, look for a section named Other Sites Visited (or similar wording) on one of the statistical sites.

Keep in mind these words of caution as you review statistics for various minor social networks in Steps 3 and 4 of the preceding list:

>> **Not all directories or reports on market share define the universe of social media or social networks the same way.** Some sources include blogs, social bookmarking sites such as Delicious, or news aggregators. Small social networks may come and go so quickly that the universe is different even a few months later.

>> **Confirm whether you're looking at global or U.S. data.** What you need depends on the submarkets you're trying to reach.

>> **Determine whether the site displays data for unique visitors or visits.** A unique visitor may make multiple visits during the evaluation period. Results for market share vary significantly depending on what's being measured.

>> **Repeat visits, pages per view, time on site, and number of visits per day or per visitor all reflect user engagement with the site.** Not all services provide this data, whose importance depends on your business goals.

>> **Decide whether you're interested in a site's casual visitors or registered members.** Your implementation and message will vary according to the audience you're trying to reach.

>> **Check the window of measurement (day, week, month, or longer) and the effective dates for the results.** These numbers are volatile, so be sure you're looking at current data.

TIP

Regarding social media or everything else, consider online statistics for relative value and trends, not for absolute numbers. Because every statistical service defines its terms and measurements differently, stick with one source to make the results comparable across all your possibilities.

Assessing the Involvement of Your Target Audience

After you finish the research process, you should have a good theoretical model of which minor social networks might be a good fit for your business. But there's nothing like being involved. Our advice in the preceding section recommends visiting every site to assess a number of criteria, including user interaction. If you plan to engage your audience in comments, reviews, forums, or other user-generated content, you *must* understand how active participants on the network now interact.

Start by signing up and creating a personal profile of some sort so that you can access all member-related activities. The actual activities, of course, depend on the particular network.

Lurking

Spend time watching and reading what transpires in every interactive venue on the site, without participating. In the olden days of Internet forums and chat rooms, you were *lurking*. You can make a number of qualitative assessments that can help you determine whether this site is a good fit for you:

>> **Quality of dialog:** Do statements of any sort float in the ether, or does interaction take place? Does a moderator respond? The site owners? Other registered members? Is there one response or continual back and forth? If you intend to establish an ongoing business relationship with other participants on the network, you want to select a site where ongoing dialog is already standard practice.

>> **Quality of posts:** Are posts respectful or hostile? Do posts appear automatically, or is someone reviewing them before publication? Do they appear authentic? Because you're conducting business online, your standards may need to be higher than they would be for casual, personal interaction. Anger and profanity that might be acceptable from respondents on a political news site would be totally unacceptable on a site that engages biologists in discussion of an experiment.

>> **Quantity of posts compared to the number of registered users:** On some sites, you may find that the same 20 people post or respond to everything, even though the site boasts 10,000 registered members. This situation signals a site that isn't successful as a social network, however successful it might be in other ways.

Responding

After you have a sense of the ethos of a site, try responding to a blog post, participating in a forum, or establishing yourself as an expert on a product review or e-zine listing. Assess what happens. Do others respond on the network? Email you off-site? Call the office?

Use this side of the lurk-and-response routine to gain a better understanding of what you, as a member and prospective customer, would expect. Will you or your staff be able to deliver?

TIP

If a site requires more care and feeding than you have the staff to support, consider dropping it from your list.

Quantifying market presence

In addition to assessing the number of unique visitors, visits, and registered members, you may want to assess additional components of audience engagement. Sites that provide quantitative information, such as Quantcast, help you better understand your audience's behavior, learn more about their lifestyles and brand preferences, and target your message. You can learn about these concepts:

>> **Affinity:** A statistical correlation that shows the strength of a particular user behavior, such as visiting another site, relative to that of the U.S. Internet population as a whole — for instance, whether an Instagram user is more or less likely than the general Internet population to visit YouTube

>> **Index:** The delivery of a specific audience segment, such as women or seniors, compared with their share of the overall Internet population

>> **Composition:** The relative distribution of the audience for a site by audience segment, such as gender, age, or ethnicity

>> **Addict:** The most loyal component of a site's audience, with 30 or more visits per month

>> **Passerby:** Casual visitor who visits a site only once per month

>> **Regular:** A user partway between Addict and Passer-by; someone who visits more than once but fewer than 30 times per month

Choosing Social Sites Strategically

It may seem ridiculously time-consuming to select which minor social marketing sites are best for your business. Why not just throw a virtual dart at a list or choose randomly from social sites that your staff likes to visit? Ultimately, you save more time by planning and making strategic choices than by investing time in a social media site that doesn't pay off.

TIP

If you're short of time, select sites that meet your demographics requirement but on which you can easily reuse and syndicate content, as described in Book 2, Chapter 1. You can replicate blog postings, for instance, almost instantly on multiple sites.

If you truly have no time to select one of these sleek minor critters, stick to one of the elephants and add others later.

Somebody's Mother's Chocolate Syrup, shown in Figure 5-3, uses multiple social media channels to achieve its marketing goals.

REMEMBER

Even the smallest social network sites can be valuable if they have your target market. All the averages mean nothing. It's about *your* business and *your* audience. Niche marketing is always an effective use of your time. Fish where *your* fish are!

FIGURE 5-3:
Somebody's Mother's Chocolate Sauce generates traffic to its website from a variety of social media, as shown by the chiclets in the lower-right corner.

Understanding the Statistics of Mobile Device Usage

To understand why mobile social marketing is so important, you must first acknowledge the explosive growth in the use of mobile devices. StatsCounter Global Stats estimates the usage of mobile devices for Internet access ballooned by 67 percent worldwide between August 2013 and August 2014.

Overall, the rate of use of mobile platforms and apps has already surpassed the use of desktops and laptops for web access, as shown in Table 5-2.

TABLE 5-2 **Changes in Platform Usage for Web Access in the United States**

Device Usage	March 2013	March 2014
Desktop	53%	40%
Mobile	47%	60%
Mobile App	40%	52%

Source: www.comscore.com/Insights/Presentations-and-Whitepapers/2014/The-US-Mobile-App-Report (page 5)

Smartphone penetration in the U.S. market by population continues to grow. Consumers are increasingly using smartphones to search for local information, research products, and make purchases, as shown in Figure 5-4.

Exploring mobile use of social media

According to *Business Insider,* more than 60 percent of the time users spend on social media is now on mobile devices, not desktops. *Salesforce's* research shows that 75 percent of consumers access social media at least once a day on their smartphones, as do 64 percent of tablet owners.

As you would expect, the increased use of mobile devices means that social media channels are seeing significant growth in mobile usage. According to ComScore, Facebook and Twitter enjoy majority usage on mobile platforms, while newer social networks like Vine, Snapchat, and Instagram are used almost exclusively on mobile platforms (see Figure 5-5). Only LinkedIn and Tumblr are still used primarily on desktops.

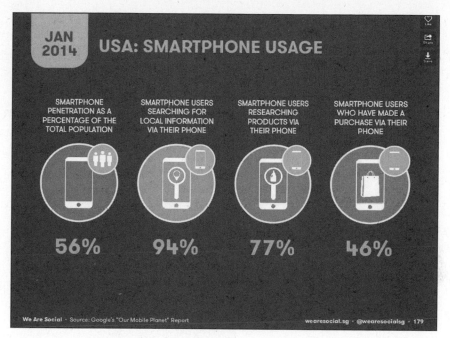

FIGURE 5-4:
How people in the United States used their smartphones in January 2014.

Reproduced with permission of We Are Social

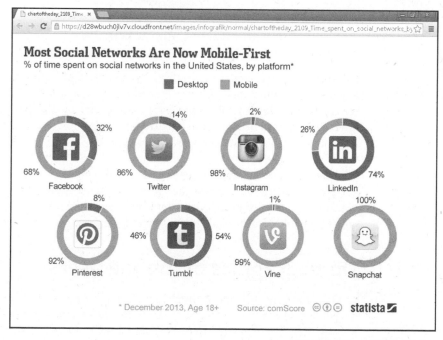

FIGURE 5-5:
Users spend more time on social media channels in the United States from their mobile devices than from desktops.

Reproduced with permission of Statista

Generally speaking, Apple's iOS and Google's Android operating systems are highly competitive. Android led with a 52.5-percent market share April 2014, as shown in Figure 5-6.

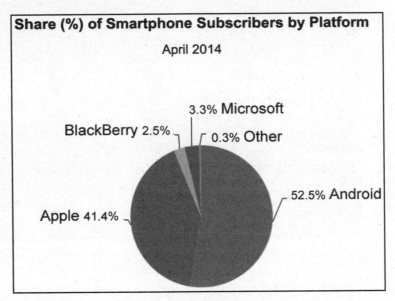

Share (%) of Smartphone Subscribers by Platform

April 2014

3.3% Microsoft

BlackBerry 2.5%

0.3% Other

52.5% Android

Apple 41.4%

FIGURE 5-6:
Market share for smartphones by operating system.

Source: https://www.comscore.com/Insights/Press-Releases/2014/6/comScore-Reports-April-2014-US-Smartphone-Subscriber-Market-Share

REMEMBER

In terms of social media marketing, the question of platforms affects only the development of mobile apps, which need to be created for specific operating systems. Mobile sites, mobile advertising, and social media channels are generally operating-system neutral from a marketer's point of view (unless you're marketing your own app to users of a specific platform).

Why bother your marketing head with all this mobile information? You need to get your social media message across on the specific social media channels that your target audience uses, no matter how they access those channels. Your social content should be optimized visually and for ease of use on mobile platforms.

Demographics of mobile users

A 2014 study by the Pew Center showed that 61 percent of U.S. adult men and 57 percent of women owned a smartphone as of January 2014. The report also showed that the smartphone user population is racially diverse: 53 percent of whites, 59 percent of blacks, and 61 percent of Hispanics now use smartphones.

The biggest variation in smartphone use is by age, with 83 percent of those age 18 to 29 using smartphones; 74 percent of 30- to 49-year-olds; 49 percent of those ages 50 to 64; and 19 percent of those 65 and older.

Household income is a second differentiator: Only 47 percent of households earning less than $30,000 annually have a smartphone, but 53 percent of those earning $30,000 to $49,999 have one, as do 61 percent of those earning $50,000 to $74,999 and 81 percent of those earning more than $75,000.

Getting a handle on mobile activities

Mobile users check email, weather, traffic, maps, directions, and headlines. They also search for companies and products (especially local ones), compare prices, review entertainment schedules, access social media sites, watch videos, check review and ratings sites, sign up for alerts and coupons, and play games online. In other words, they are avid users of just about every social media channel.

Going Mobile: Create A Mobile Responsive Version Of Your Site

With the rapid growth in the use of mobile media, you need a mobile version of your website. As you can see by comparing the regular website for HoardingNJ.com (see Figure 5-7) with its mobile version (see Figure 5-8), the regular website is too wide to navigate on a small screen. The mobile site has a different layout and focuses on fast, easy navigation.

Here are the two best practices for creating a mobile version of your website:

>> Reformat an existing website so that it automatically resizes to fit various mobile platforms using a process called responsive design.

>> Build a new website that's designed from scratch to work on desktops as well as on multiple mobile platforms of various sizes.

>> Develop a unique mobile app for your site.

TIP

Check out http://blog.hubspot.com/marketing/responsive-design-list for more information about why having your site viewable on mobile devices is important and what you can do.

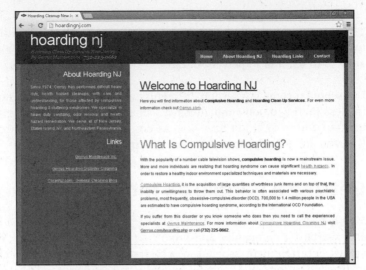

FIGURE 5-7:
HoardingNJ.com's
standard website
as it appears
in a desktop
environment.

FIGURE 5-8:
The dedicated
mobile website
for http://m.
HoardingNJ.
com.

TIP

You can have your web programmer or developer build a mobile site or app from scratch, but many template-based sites allow you to build a mobile site yourself, or they will automatically convert your site into responsive design at a much lower cost than custom development. Some of these tools are listed in Table 5-3.

TABLE 5-3   **Tools for Building Mobile Sites, Apps, and Ads**

Name	URL
AdMob (mobile app promotion run by Google)	www.google.com/ads/admob/index.html
bMobilized (mobile site creator)	www.bmobilized.com
Call Loop (SMS service)	www.callloop.com
DudaMobile (mobile site creator; free and low-cost template and responsive design versions)	www.dudamobile.com
goMobi (mobile site creator; free seven-day trial)	http://gomobi.info
InMobi (mobile advertising network for games)	www.inmobi.com
Mobify (mobile shopping platform)	www.mobify.com
MoPub (mobile ad network owned by Twitter)	www.mopub.com
Webhosting Search (mobile website tools and resources)	www.webhostingsearch.com/articles/30-best-tools-to-create-mobile-website.php

To decide the best type of mobile presence for your business, you must first decide the goals for your mobile site, just as you establish goals for any other marketing effort. Conduct some basic research to see whether content, content length, writing style, calls to action, navigation, and/or user behavior should be different in a mobile environment compared to desktop use to meet those goals.

Making the choice for responsive design

Responsive design makes the most sense when the content and functionality of your primary site and your mobile site will be basically the same. All you need to do is re-arrange the layout a bit. For example, if your site is compatible with it, responsive design may be a quick, first answer to obtaining a mobile presence. And it's inexpensive if you use one of the automated conversion sites.

Responsive design works particularly well when you have a small, information-based site. Keep in mind that some sites designed for desktop use don't convert well to responsive design. Carefully test sites like these:

>> Text-intensive sites with long scrolling pages

>> Image-intensive sites with graphics spread out around a page

>> Sites with so many images that it may take too long to download to a smartphone

>> Sites with many tables, which generally need to be reformatted

>> Sites supported by banner advertising

>> Sites with multiple columns of information

On the positive side, when you change content on a primary site built with responsive design, it changes on the mobile platform, as well. With responsive design, you don't need to set up redirects; people on a mobile environment automatically see the mobile version.

Making the choice for a new mobile site

Creating an entirely new mobile site has some distinct advantages:

>> You can break free from older technologies you used to build your website long ago or that you selected to remain compatible with older versions of desktop browsers.

>> Users generally have a better experience with newer technologies, and those technologies reduce your maintenance costs.

>> Third, you can reduce the download time by reducing the amount of content, such as using fewer, smaller images.

Mobile-only sites are particularly valuable when you want to create a teaser advertisement, using only a few screens to tell your story and drive people elsewhere online for additional activity.

There are some downsides to a mobile-only site, of course:

>> Depending on the application, some users will prefer a consistent experience between their desktop and mobile environments.

>> Whenever you have two separate sites, you need to update both.

>> With two sites, you must offer obvious ways to link between them, and you must insert simple code so that mobile users are automatically redirected to your mobile site.

Making the choice for a mobile app

An app is a different animal altogether. Apps, by definition, involve more than the presentation of information with simple links; they require programming so that users can enter information or must supply information in response to a query, as the Foursquare app does in Figure 5-9.

Most apps are done with custom programming. Generally, this custom programming makes an app more expensive to develop than a mobile site, and it will take longer to launch. Because new versions of operating systems are released frequently, apps usually don't have as long a lifespan as a mobile site or one with responsive design; they will need to be updated and tested to keep pace with changes in operating systems. And because apps are platform-specific, they don't have as broad a reach as mobile sites that can be seen on any smartphone.

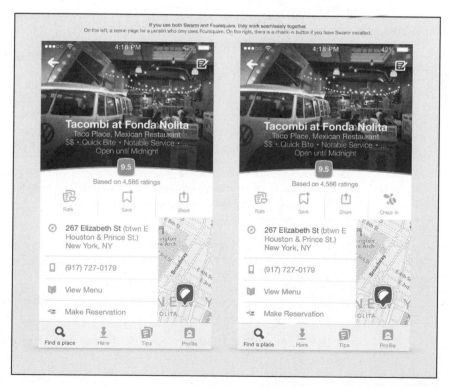

FIGURE 5-9:
Foursquare, a location-based social media channel, exists as an app in a mobile environment.

Source: Foursquare

TIP

Table 5-3, earlier in this chapter, includes some sources for less expensive, automated app-development services. Sometimes these apps work, sometimes they don't. Test thoroughly!

Choosing the app route

An app is the preferred solution if your mobile activity involves

>> Interactive gaming

>> Frequent, personalized usage, requiring that the app pull up specific records

>> Inserting entered data into calculations, reports, or charts, such as financial records

>> Accessing functionality that isn't mobile-specific, such as a separate camera or additional processing power

>> Accessing content or functions without a wireless connection

Like with responsive design and mobile sites, apps have some downsides. Consider these drawbacks:

>> Users can't instantly access apps via a browser on multiple devices; they must download and install each app (and each new update) from an app store such as iTunes or Google Play.

>> Apps aren't compatible across platforms the way mobile sites are; you must create separate versions for each platform and make them available for each type of device. This incompatibility extends to ongoing support issues because you'll need to do upgrades and testing on multiple platforms over time.

>> Mobile sites are more practical than apps for public communications or marketing because they're easier to change. Updated content or features are immediately available on mobile sites, but changes to apps require that users download new versions.

>> You can more easily integrate mobile sites with other mobile technologies, such as GPS and QR codes, than you can integrate apps with these technologies.

>> Search engines can't find apps (you have to publicize them to users), nor can search engines index the content of apps.

>> Users can't share apps with a simple link, the way they can share a mobile site.

Reaching People on the Move with Social Media

Almost all social media services now automatically reconfigure their sites for mobile devices (responsive design). However, most also have their own app optimized for mobile usage (both smartphone and tablet), as shown in Table 5-4.

TABLE 5-4   **Mobile Apps for Social Media**

Name	URL to Download App	Mobile Site (Responsive Design)	Vanity URL
Digg	https://itunes.apple.com/us/app/digg/id362872995?mt=8 https://play.google.com/store/apps/details?id=com.diggreader&hl=en	http://m.digg.com	None
Facebook	https://itunes.apple.com/us/app/facebook/id284882215?mt=8 https://play.google.com/store/apps/details?id=com.facebook.katana	https://m.facebook.com	www.facebook.com/mobile
Flickr	http://itunes.apple.com/us/app/flickr/id328407587?mt=8 https://play.google.com/store/apps/details?id=com.yahoo.mobile.client.android.flickr	https://m.flickr.com	www.flickr.com
Foursquare	http://itunes.apple.com/us/app/foursquare/id306934924?mt=8 https://play.google.com/store/apps/details?id=com.joelapenna.foursquared	None	https://foursquare.com/download
Google+	http://itunes.apple.com/us/app/google+/id447119634?mt=8 https://play.google.com/store/apps/details?id=com.google.android.apps.plus	None	www.google.com/mobile/+
LinkedIn	http://itunes.apple.com/us/app/linkedin/id288429040?mt=8 https://play.google.com/store/apps/details?id=com.linkedin.android	https://touch.www.linkedin.com	www.linkedin.com/mobile

(continued)

TABLE 5-4 *(continued)*

Name	URL to Download App	Mobile Site (Responsive Design)	Vanity URL

Pinterest	`http://itunes.apple.com/us/app/pinterest/id429047995?mt=8`
	
	`https://play.google.com/store/apps/details?id=com.pinterest`
		None	None

Twitter	`https://play.google.com/store/apps/details?id=com.twitter.android`	`https://mobile.twitter.com`	`https://twitter.com/download`

In either case, you don't have to worry about the mechanics of changing your page or post. But you do have to think about how you can benefit from reaching people who are using mobile devices and how your posts and profiles will appear in these formats.

For example, the mobile version of Facebook focuses on interactivity. Users can view their News Feeds and post their own updates, comments, videos, and images.

Even Twitter, which has cellphone DNA in its genes, has revamped its mobile appearance with an app. The app offers an easy-to-use layout, with navigation that allows you to visit your Timeline, discover trends or people, view your own profile, search for people or tweets, and of course, send out a tweet.

So what does all this mean for your business while you develop social media messages for users who are always on the run? Keep in mind the following points:

» Pin your posts to the top of the newsfeed stream because only the first several posts will be displayed on mobile screens.

» Use analytics to make sure your posts are relevant to the demographics and behavioral patterns of the users of that particular social channel.

» Before publishing, always double-check the appearance of your posts and other content on smartphones and tablets to be sure everything looks right.

» If you have links, be sure they go to mobile-friendly pages; links to your website should go to a mobile-specific site or to a page built with responsive design.

» Make it easy for users to share your content from their mobile devices via text, email, and/or share buttons.

Compare the mobile app version of The Lodge at MSL Resort's Facebook Page in Figure 5-10 with the desktop version of that Facebook page in Figure 5-11.

FIGURE 5-10:
Compare the
mobile app
version of the
Facebook page
for the Lodge
at MSL Resort
with the desktop
version in
Figure 5-11.

Reproduced with permission of Mountain Springs Lake Corp.

FIGURE 5-11:
The desktop
version of the
Facebook page
for the Lodge at
MSL Resort.

Reproduced with permission of Mountain Springs Lake Corp.

TIP

Also check your Facebook Page, LinkedIn profile, and Twitter stream on various smartphone and tablet operating systems to see how they appear; adjust as needed.

Harvesting Leads and Sales from Social Mobile

You can find as many applications for marketing via mobile social media as you can imagine. Keep in mind the areas described in this list, whatever the device or market segment you target:

>> **News and updates:** Distribute this type of information to your Twitter, Facebook, and LinkedIn followers, as well as to people on your prospect list and your newsletter subscribers. (See Figure 5-12 for an example of news updates distributed on the mobile version of Twitter.)

>> **Emergency information:** Warnings range from product recalls to weather hazards.

>> **Comparison-shopping:** Provide information so that Facebook, Twitter, and Pinterest shoppers can compare by price and feature and learn about sales.

>> **Local business announcements:** Announce coupons, deals, and special offers across all your social media channels.

>> **Customer service improvements:** For instance, use Twitter to let customers place a pickup order and find out when their order is ready. Use QR codes so people can quickly determine your competitive products, features, and prices.

Able to hold about 350 times more information than a bar code, QR codes usually appear in print or online as a square or rectangle with black-and-white dots. Viewers can use their smartphones to scan a QR code, which then links them directly to a web page with additional information.

>> **Event publicity:** On Twitter and Facebook, consider providing real-time logistical information.

>> **Integration of mobile marketing and social media:** Post updates on the fly and use geo-marketing services, such as Foursquare, especially if your business targets younger, local customers. (Refer to Figure 5-9, earlier in this chapter.)

Don't let the obvious business-to-customer (B2C) value of mobile devices blind you: Mobile marketing has a place in business-to-business (B2B) strategies, as well. For example, sales people are using the technology for competitive research, tracking sales calls, and demonstrating their products and services to prospective customers. In fact, according to the 2013 AT&T Small Business Technology Poll, 98 percent of small businesses have already incorporated some form of wireless devices into their operations.

FIGURE 5-12:
Distributing news updates on Twitter's mobile version makes a lot of sense for the Strand Bookstore.

Reproduced with permission of Strand Bookstore, Inc.

Measuring Your Mobile Marketing Success

As with all analytics, which elements you measure depend on your goals and objectives. Of course, your choices depend on whether you're measuring intermediate performance indicators (for example, the number of Likes on your Facebook Page from mobile versus desktop users) or your return on investment in a mobile advertising campaign, a new mobile app, or increased foot traffic to your brick-and-mortar store.

You can segment mobile visitors by using the available tools within Google Analytics to track behavior on a mobile site or on your regular website (or both). You might want to set up a separate conversion funnel for mobile users. Watch for variations between mobile and web visitors on traffic to your social media pages, links to your mobile website, qualified prospects, and leads that turn into sales.

Counting on Tablets

Use of e-readers, iPads, and other tablet computers is exploding. Given the convergence of high technology with usability, portability, mobility, and affordability, it may represent a true paradigm shift in computing.

By January 2014, roughly 44 percent of U.S. consumers owned tablet computers, and 69 percent of small businesses were using them. Social media channels are now omnipresent on both Apple iPads and Android-based tablets.

Like with smartphones, tablet owners use their devices for many purposes: research, shopping, news, customer reviews, and yes, social media. Once again, the Pew Research Center Internet & American Life Project comes through with essential insights:

>> Tablet use doesn't differ much by gender or by race and ethnicity any more. The percentage of American adults hovers at roughly one-third in each group.

>> The highest adoption rate is by users ages 30 to 49 (52 percent), followed closely by the younger cohort of 18- to 29-year-olds (48 percent). Both have significantly higher usage than 50- to 64-year-olds (37 percent) and those over 65 (25 percent).

>> As you might expect, the higher their education level, the more likely it is that adults own a tablet: 59 percent of college graduates, 45 percent with some college, and 29 percent of those without any college education.

>> Also quite predictably, ownership rises with household income, ranging from 25 percent of those with less than $30,000 in annual income, to 45 percent with annual income in the $30,000-to-$50,000 range, and 65 percent for those with a household annual income of $75,000 or more.

TIP

As smartphones become larger and tablets become smaller, the challenge of developing sites that will work in both environments may become moot.

Obviously, larger high-resolution tablets make viewing videos on tablets more appealing than viewing them on smartphones, leading to even greater popularity for video-sharing sites like YouTube and Vimeo. Figure 5-13 shows a YouTube site on a tablet.

FIGURE 5-13:
The YouTube
page for Moun-
tain Springs Lake
Resort displays
well on a tablet.

Although many social media channels have apps that work for all mobile devices, regardless of size, others have versions designed specifically for tablets. Some of these apps appear in Table 5-4, earlier in this chapter.

5

Incorporating Traditional Marketing

Contents at a Glance

Chapter 1

Creating Marketing Communications

C reative. The very word turns confident people queasy and rational people giddy. It prompts marketers to say such outrageous things as, "Let's dress up like chickens," or such well-intended but pointless things as, "Let's cut through the noise" or "Let's think outside the box." Far less often will you hear the conversation turn strategic, with statements like, "Let's talk in terms that matter to our customers" or "Let's define what we're trying to accomplish."

This chapter helps you set communication objectives and steer past the mistakes that shoot too many ad efforts into the great abyss, where wasted dollars languish.

Note: The first three sections of this chapter help *all* marketers, whether you present your marketing communications in person, online, with print or broadcast ads, or through direct mail. If you place ads in traditional mass media outlets such as newspapers, magazines, and broadcast stations, stick with this chapter to the end for information on scheduling and evaluating your ads. Then turn to Book 5, Chapters 2 and 3 as you make media selections and produce your ads.

Starting with Good Objectives

Copywriters and designers are talented and creative, but they're rarely tele-pathic. They can't create marketing materials that meet specific objectives if their instructions don't include what they're expected to accomplish.

So who is supposed to define the objective, set the strategy, and steer the creative process? Well, get ready, because that task falls to the person responsible for marketing, which is probably, well, *you.*

Defining what you want to accomplish

You can hit your marketing target almost every time if you take careful aim. Consider the following examples of creative instructions and note the differences:

> **Example 1:** "We need to build sales. Let's run some ads."

> **Example 2:** "We need a campaign to convince teenagers that by shopping after school on weekdays they'll enjoy our best prices in a club atmosphere because we feature live music, two-for-one cafe specials, and weekday-only student discounts."

Example 1 forces those creating the ad to guess what message to project — and toward whom. It'll likely lead to round after round of revisions as the creative team makes best guesses about the target market, promotional offer, and creative approach.

Example 2 tells the ad creators precisely which consumers to target, what message and offer to project, and what action to prompt. It guides the project toward an appropriate concept and media plan — probably on the first try.

REMEMBER

As the chief marketer for your business, your job is to give those who produce your marketing communications the information they need to do the job right the first time.

WARNING

An old saying among marketers concludes that half of all ad dollars are wasted, but no one knows which half. You can move the dividing line between what works and what doesn't by avoiding three wasteful errors:

>> **Mistake #1:** Producing marketing materials without first defining your marketing objectives, leading to materials that address neither the target prospect nor the marketing objective.

>> **Mistake #2:** Creating messages that are too "hard-sell" — asking for the order without first reeling in the prospect's attention and interest.

> **» Mistake #3:** Creating self-centered communications that focus more on what your business wants to say about itself than on the benefits that matter to a prospective customer.

A good ad can inform, persuade, sell, or connect with consumers, but it can't do all those things at once, nor is it likely to move the right target audience to the desired consumer action if the audience and objective aren't clearly established before ad creation begins.

REMEMBER

Before you undertake any marketing effort, define the audience you aim to influence, the action you're working to inspire, the message you want to promote, and the way that you'll measure effectiveness, whether by leads, web or store traffic, inquiries, social media likes or follows, or other actions you can prompt and monitor.

When setting the objective for your marketing communication, use the following template by inserting the appropriate text in the brackets.

> ***This*** [ad/brochure/sales call/speech/trade booth display] ***will convince*** [describe the target market for this communication] ***that by*** [describe the action that you intend to prompt] ***they will*** [describe the benefit the target audience will realize] ***because*** [state the facts that prove your claim, which form the basis of the message you want the communication to convey].

Putting creative directions in writing

Your communication objective defines *what* you're trying to accomplish. A *creative brief* provides the instructions for *how* you'll get the job done. These sections address some questions to ask as you communicate with your ad design team.

Who is your target audience for this communication?

Start with everything you know about your prospective customers (see Book 1, Chapter 2 for more information) and then boil down your knowledge into a one-sentence definition that encapsulates the geographic location, the lifestyle facts, and the purchasing motivators of those you want to reach.

EXAMPLE

The target audience is composed of Montana residents, age 40+, married with children living at home, with professional careers, upper-level income, and an affinity for travel, outdoor recreation, status brands, and high levels of service.

What does your target audience currently know or think about your business and offering?

Use research findings (if available), your own instincts, and input from your staff and colleagues to answer the following questions:

>> Have prospects heard of your business?

>> Do they know what products or services you offer?

>> Do they know where you're located or how to reach you?

>> Do they see you as a major player? If they were asked to name three suppliers of your product or service, would you be among the responses?

>> How do they rate your service, quality, pricing, accessibility, range of products, and reputation?

>> Do you have a clear brand and market position or a mistaken identity in their minds?

Be candid with your answers. Only by acknowledging your real or perceived shortcomings can you begin to address them through your marketing efforts. If your prospects haven't heard of your business, you need to develop awareness. If they're clueless about your offerings, you need to present meaningful facts. If they hold inaccurate impressions, you need to persuade them to think differently. Here's an example:

EXAMPLE

The majority of those in our target audience aren't aware of our existence, but among those familiar with our name, we're known to provide an experience competitive with the best contenders in our field. We need to reinforce the opinions of our acquaintances while also developing awareness and credibility with prospective customers and especially with opinion leaders whose recommendations are most valued by our affluent and socially connected target market.

What do you want your target audience to think and do?

Don't get greedy. In each communication, present one clear idea and chances are good that you'll *convey* one clear idea. If you try to present two or three messages, you'll likely communicate nothing at all.

REMEMBER

Four out of five consumers read only your headline, absorb no more than seven words off of a billboard, and take only one idea away from a broadcast ad — provided they don't tune out or skip over the ad altogether.

What single idea do you want prospects to take away from this particular marketing effort? As you answer, follow this process:

1. **Step out of your own shoes and stand in those of your prospect.**

2. **Think about what your prospect wants or needs to know.**

3. **Develop a single sentence describing what you want people to think and what motivating idea you want them to take away from this communication.**

EXAMPLE

Here's the desired outcome for a computer retailer targeting senior citizens:

> We want senior citizens to know that they're invited to our Computer 101 open houses every Wednesday afternoon this month, where they can watch computer and Internet demonstrations, receive hands-on training, and learn about our special, first-time computer owner packages.

WARNING

Be careful what you ask for. Be sure that you're prepared for the outcome you say you desire. If you aren't geared up to handle the online traffic, answer the phone, manage the foot traffic, or fulfill the buying demand that your ad generates, you'll fail strategically even though you succeeded — wildly — on the advertising front. Consider this example:

EXAMPLE

A one-man painting company decides to rev up business by placing a series of clever, small-space newspaper ads touting impeccable service, outstanding quality, affordable estimates, and prompt response. The ads win attention, action, and advertising awards. The problem is that the painter can't keep up with the phone calls, the estimates, or the orders. Prospects — who had been inspired by the great ads — end up signing contracts with the painter's competitors instead.

The moral of the story is to expect a miracle from good advertising and to be prepared to get what you ask for.

Why should people believe you and take the proposed action?

To be believable, your marketing materials need to make and support a claim.

>> **The easy way** is to list features — the oldest moving company in the East, under new management, the only manufacturer featuring the X2000 widget, the winner of our industry's top award, yada yada yada.

>> **The effective way** is to turn those features into benefits that you promise to your customers. The difference between features and benefits is that features are facts and benefits are personal outcomes.

Table 1-1 shows you exactly what this crucial difference means.

TABLE 1-1 **Features versus Benefits**

Product	Feature	Benefit	Emotional Outcome
Diet soda	One calorie	Lose weight	Look and feel great
Flower arrangements	Daily exotic imports	Send unique floral presentations	Satisfaction that your gift stands out and draws attention
Automobile	Best crash rating	Reduce risk of harm in accidents	Security that your family is safe
Miniature microwave	1.5 cubic feet in size	Save dorm room space	Make room for the floor's only big-screen TV

REMEMBER

Every time you describe a *feature* of your product or service, you're talking to yourself. Every time you describe the *benefit* that your product or service delivers, you're talking to your prospect. Consumers don't buy the feature — they buy what the feature does for them. Here are some examples:

>> Consumers don't buy V-8 engines. They buy speed.

>> They don't buy shock-absorbing shoes. They buy walking comfort.

>> They don't buy the lightest tablet computer. They buy the freedom to get online wherever they want.

TIP

Follow these steps to translate features into benefits:

1. **State your product or business feature.**

2. **Add the phrase "which means."**

3. **Complete the sentence by stating the benefit.**

For example, a car has the highest safety rating (that's the feature), *which means* you breathe a little easier as you hand the keys over to your teenager (that's the benefit).

What information must your communication convey?

Be clear about your must-haves. Those who create ads, websites, mailers, and other communications call it "death by a thousand cuts" when marketers respond to every creative presentation with, "Yes, but we also have to include. . . ."

If you know that you need to feature a certain look, specific information, or art-work, say so up-front — not after you see the first creative presentation. And keep the list of requirements as short as possible. Here are some guidelines:

>> **Must-have #1:** Every communication has to advance your brand image. Provide your image style guide whenever you assign a staff person or outside professional to help with the development of marketing materials.

>> **Must-have #2:** Be sparing with all other "musts." Every time you start to say, "We have to include . . ." check yourself with this self-test:

- Is this element necessary to protect our brand?

- Is it necessary to protect our legal standing?

- Is it necessary to prompt the marketing action we want to achieve?

- Is it necessary to motivate the prospect?

Let necessity — not history — guide your answers. Any ad designer will tell you that less is more. The more stuff you try to jam into an ad, the less con-sumer attention it draws. Include no more information than is necessary to arouse interest and lead people to the next step in the buying process.

How will you measure success?

Small business leaders are critical of their marketing efforts — after the fact. Instead, before creating any marketing communication, set your expectations and define your measurement standard in your creative brief.

After an ad has run its course, you'll hear such criticism as, "That ad didn't work, it didn't make the phone ring, and it sure didn't create foot traffic." Yet if you examine the ad, you'll often find that it includes no reason to call, no special offer, a phone number that requires a magnifying glass, and no address whatsoever.

What's your time frame and budget?

Know the specifications of your job before you start producing it, especially if you assign the production task to others. Remember the following:

>> **Set and be frank about your budget.** Small business owners often worry that if they divulge their budgets, the creative team will spend it all — whether it needs to or not. But the never-reveal-the-budget strategy usually backfires. If suppliers *don't* know the budget, they *will* spend it all — and then some — simply because no one gave them a not-to-exceed figure to work within. The solution is to hire suppliers you trust, share your budget with them (along with instructions that they can't exceed the budget without your prior approval), and count on them to be partners in providing a cost-effective solution.

CHAPTER 1 **Creating Marketing Communications** 423

>> **Know and share deadlines and material requirements.** If you've already committed to a media buy, attach a media rate card to your creative brief so your designer can obtain the specifications directly rather than through your translation.

>> **Define the parameters of nonmedia communication projects.** For example, if you ask for speechwriting assistance, know the length of time allocated for your speech. If you request materials for a sales presentation, know the audio-visual equipment availability and the number of handouts you want to distribute.

WARNING

What the creative team doesn't know can cost you dearly in enthusiasm and cost overruns if you have to retrofit creative solutions to fit production realities. Communicate in advance for the best outcome.

TIP

Whether you're creating an ad, writing a speech, making a sales presentation, planning a brochure, posting on an online network, or composing an important business letter, start by running through the questions on the creative brief to focus your thinking. For all major projects — or for any project that you plan to assign to a staff member, freelance professional, vendor, or advertising agency — take the time to put your answers in writing. Pass them along so they can serve as a valuable navigational aid. Then monitor success by counting inquiries, click-throughs to landing pages, coupon redemptions, or other measurable actions prompted by your communications — and share your findings so your creative team can benefit from the knowledge of what worked well.

Developing Effective Marketing Communications

Whether delivered in person, through promotions, or via traditional media, direct mail, or email, all marketing communications need to accomplish the same tasks:

>> Grab attention.

>> Impart information the prospect wants to know.

>> Present offers that are sensitive to how and when the prospect wants to take action.

>> Affirm why the prospect would want to take action.

>> Offer a reason to take action.

>> Launch a relationship, which increasingly means fostering interaction and two-way communication between you and your customer.

Good communications convince prospects and nudge them into action without any apparent effort. They meld the verbiage with the visual and the message with the messenger so the consumer receives a single, inspiring idea.

Creative types will tell you that making marketing communications look easy takes a lot of time and talent, and they're right. If you're spending more than $10,000 on an advertising effort or developing a major marketing vehicle such as a website, ad campaign, or product package, bring in pros to help you out.

Steering the creative process toward a "big idea"

After you establish your objectives and prepare your creative brief (see the earlier "Putting creative directions in writing" section), it's time to develop your creative message.

No matter which target audience you're reaching out to, the people in that audience are busy and distracted by an onslaught of competing messages. That's why great communicators know that they need to project big ideas to be heard over the marketplace din.

REMEMBER

The *big idea* is to advertising what the brake, gas pedal, and steering wheel are to driving. (See why they call it *big?*) Here's what the big idea does:

>> It stops the prospect.

>> It fuels interest.

>> It inspires prospects to take the desired action.

EXAMPLE

"Got Milk?" was the big idea that juiced up milk sales, and "Smell like a man" worked like magic for Old Spice.

But big ideas aren't just for big advertisers. Portland, Oregon's quirky Voodoo Donut's big idea that "The magic is in the hole" gained international appeal for an enterprise that has now expanded to six locations.

Big ideas are

>> Appealing to your target market

>> Attention-getting

>> Capable of conveying the benefit you promise

>> Compelling

>> Memorable

>> Persuasive

WARNING

An idea qualifies as a big idea only if it meets *all* the preceding qualifications. Many advertisers quit when they hit on an attention-getting and memorable idea. Think of it this way: A slammed door is attention getting and memorable, but it's far from appealing, beneficial, compelling, or persuasive.

Brainstorming

Brainstorming is an anything-goes group process for generating ideas through free association and imaginative thinking with no grandstanding, no idea ownership, no evaluation, and definitely no criticism.

REMEMBER

The point of brainstorming is to put the mind on automatic pilot and see where it leads. You can improve your brainstorming sessions by doing some research in advance:

>> Study websites and magazines for inspiration. Pick up copies of *Advertising Age, Adweek,* or *Communication Arts* (available at newsstands and in most libraries) for a look at the latest in ad trends. Also include fashion magazines, which are a showcase for big ideas and image advertising.

>> Check out competitors' ads and ads for businesses that target similar audiences to yours. If you sell luxury goods, look at ads for high-end cars, jewelry, or designer clothes. If you compete on price, study ads by Target and Walmart.

>> Look at your own past ads.

>> Think of how you can turn the most unusual attributes of your product or service into unique benefits.

>> Doodle. Ultimately, great marketing messages combine words and visuals. See where your pencil leads your mind.

>> Widen your perspective by inviting a customer or a front-line staff person to participate in the brainstorming session.

REMEMBER

If you're turning your marketing project over to a staff member or to outside professionals, you may or may not decide to participate in the brainstorming session. If you do attend, remember that a brainstorming session has no boss, and every idea is a good idea. Bite your tongue each time you want to say, "Yes, but . . ." or, "We tried that once and . . ." or, "Get real, that idea is just plain dumb."

At the end of the brainstorm, gather up and evaluate the ideas:

>> Which ideas address the target audience and support the objectives outlined in your creative brief?

>> Which ones best present the consumer benefit?

>> Which ones can you implement with strength and within the budget?

Any idea that wins on all counts is a candidate for implementation.

Following simple advertising rules

The following rules apply to *all* ads, regardless of the medium, the message, the mood, or the creative direction:

>> Know your objective and stay on strategy.

>> Be honest.

>> Be specific.

>> Be original.

>> Be clear and concise.

>> Don't overpromise or exaggerate.

>> Don't be self-centered or, worse, arrogant.

>> Don't hard sell.

>> Don't insult, discriminate, or offend.

>> Don't turn the task of ad creation over to a committee.

WARNING

Committees are great for brainstorming, but when it comes to developing head-lines, they round the edges off of strong ideas. They eliminate any nuance that any committee member finds questionable, and they crowd messages with details that matter more to the marketers than to the market. An old cartoon popular in ad agencies is captioned, "A camel is a horse designed by committee."

Making Media Selections

Even back in the day when advertisers chose from among three TV networks, a couple of local-market AM radio stations, and a single hometown newspaper, deciding where to place ads was a nail-biting proposition.

Now add in cable TV channels, dozens of radio stations in even the smallest market areas, 7,500 consumer magazines (and another 7,500 online magazines), countless alternative newspapers, and constantly emerging online advertising options, and you can see why placing ads sometimes feels like a roll of the dice.

These sections help tip the odds in your favor with an overview of today's advertising channels and advice about how to select the best vehicles for your advertising messages.

Selecting from the media menu

Marketing communications are delivered in one of two ways:

>> *Mass media* channels, which reach many people simultaneously.

>> *One-to-one marketing* tools, which reach people individually, usually through direct mail or email. (Book 5, Chapter 4 is all about direct mail.)

When people talk about *media*, they're usually talking about mass media, which traditionally has been divided into three categories, with a new category recently added:

>> **Print media:** Includes newspapers, magazines, and print directories.

>> **Broadcast media:** Includes TV and radio.

>> **Outdoor media:** Includes billboards, transit signs, murals, and signage.

>> **Digital media:** A mere few years ago, the digital-media category was usually called *new media,* but it's not new anymore, and its usage, popularity, and effectiveness increase almost by the moment. Exactly as its name implies, digital media includes any media that's reduced to digital data that can be communicated electronically. That means Internet advertising, webcasts, web pages, mobile and text ads, and interactive media, including social media networks.

Each mass-media channel comes with its own set of attributes and considerations, which are summarized in Table 1-2.

TABLE 1-2 **Mass Media Comparisons**

Media Channel	Advantages	Considerations
Newspapers, which reach a broad, geographically targeted market	Involve short timelines and low-cost ad production.	You pay to reach the total circulation, even if only a portion fits your prospect profile.
Magazines, which reach target markets that share characteristics and interests	Good for developing awareness and credibility through strong visual presentations.	Require long advance planning and costly production; ads are viewed over long periods of time.
Directories, which reach people at the time of purchase decisions	Increasingly available for free in digital versions; good for prompting selection over unlisted competitors.	Print versions are impossible to update between editions and increasingly eclipsed by digital directories.
Radio, which reaches targeted local audiences (if they're tuned in)	Cost is often negotiable; good for building immediate interest and response.	You must air ads repeatedly to reach listeners; airtime is most expensive when most people are tuned in.
TV, which reaches broad audiences of targeted viewers (if they're tuned in)	Well-produced ads engage viewer emotions while building awareness and credibility.	Ad production is costly; reaching large audiences is expensive; ads must be aired repeatedly; options such as DVD, Tivo, and Hulu erode effectiveness.
Digital media, which reaches people on-demand via any digital device	Allows two-way communication with customers; allows convergence of content by linking among digital sources; low cash investment.	Requires targeting of customers and keywords and a significant time investment to create, monitor, and evaluate online visibility and interaction.

Deciding which media vehicles to use and when

Sorting through pitches from local newspapers, local radio stations, daily-deal coupon sites, and industry-specific publications can consume entire days if you let it. Plus there's the elephant in the room: Social media.

Your media options are seemingly infinite, but your time and budget aren't. So before considering media proposals for any given communication or campaign, answer the following questions:

>> **What do you want this marketing effort to accomplish?**

REMEMBER

If you want to develop general, far-reaching awareness and interest, use mass-media channels that reach a broad and general market. If you want to talk one-to-one with targeted prospective customers, bypass mass media in favor of targeted online communications and direct mail or other one-to-one communication tools.

>> **Where do the people you want to reach turn for information?**

When it comes to purchasing ad space and time, trying to be all-inclusive is a bankrupting proposition. The more precisely you can define your prospect (see Book 1, Chapter 2), the more precisely you can determine which media that person uses and, therefore, which media channels you should consider for your marketing program.

TIP

When in doubt, ask customers how they like to be reached with marketing messages. Ask whether they read the local newspaper, tune in to local broadcast stations, or notice transit or outdoor ads. Ask whether they use social media networks and which ones. Ask whether they like or dislike marketing messages sent by text message or email. Talking directly with customers is your great advantage as a small business. Ask directly if you can or use the free survey tools available through sites like SurveyMonkey (www.surveymonkey.com) and Newlio (www.newlio.com) to poll customers.

By finding out the media habits of your established customers, you get a good idea of the media habits of your prospective customers because they likely fit a very similar customer profile (see Book 1, Chapter 2 for more on this topic). After you're clear about who your customers are and how they use media, you'll know which media channels to target.

>> **What information do you want to convey, and when do you want to convey it?**

TIP

Be clear about your message urgency and content, and then refer to Table 1-2 to match your objectives with media channels. For example:

- If you're promoting an offer with a close deadline, such as a one-week special event, you obviously want to steer away from monthly magazines that are in circulation long after your offer is history.

- If you want to show your product in action, you want to feature video in TV ads or on your website or YouTube channel, to which you can lead customers by including the link in your promotional materials, ads, and social media posts.

>> **How much money is in your media budget?**

Set your budget before planning your media buy. Doing so forces you to be realistic with your media choices and saves you an enormous amount of time because you don't have to listen to media sales pitches for approaches that are outside your budget range.

The Making of a Mass Media Schedule

When advertising on all mass media except digital media, the amount of money you spend and how you spend it depends on how you balance three scheduling considerations: *reach*, *frequency*, and *timing*.

Balancing reach and frequency

Your ad schedule needs to achieve enough reach (that is, your message needs to get into the heads of enough readers or viewers) to generate a sufficient number of prospects to meet your sales objective. It also needs to achieve enough frequency to adequately impress your message into those minds — and that rarely happens with a single ad exposure.

>> *Reach* is the number of individuals or homes exposed to your ad. In print media, reach is measured by circulation counts. In broadcast media, \ gross rating points measure reach (see Book 5, Chapter 3 for information on broadcast ad terminology).

>> *Frequency* is the number of times that an average person is exposed to your message.

TIP

If you have to choose between frequency and reach — and nearly every small business works with a budget that forces that choice — limit your reach to carefully selected target markets and then spend as much as you can on achieving frequency within that area.

The case for frequency

Ad recall studies prove that people remember ad messages in direct proportion to the number of times they encounter them. Here are some facts about frequency:

>> **One-shot ads don't work, unless you opt to spend millions of dollars to air an ad during the Super Bowl.** Even then, part of the audience will be away from the tube, replenishing the guacamole dish or grabbing a beer from the refrigerator.

REMEMBER

>> **On most broadcast channels, you need to place an ad as many as nine times to reach a prospect even once.** That means you need to place it as many as 27 times in order to make contact three times — the number of exposures it takes before most ad messages sink in. If your ad airs during a program that people tune into with regular conviction, the placement requirement decreases, but especially in the case of radio ads, the 27-time schedule generally holds true.

Why? Because each time your ad airs, a predictably large percentage of prospects aren't present. They're either tuned out or distracted, or maybe your creative approach or offer failed to grab their attention.

>> **Multiple exposures to your ad results in higher advertising effectiveness.** By achieving frequency, you increase the number of people who see your ad, resulting in increased recognition for your brand, increased consumer reaction to your message, and increased responsiveness to your call to action.

REMEMBER

Reach creates awareness, but frequency changes minds.

The case for limiting reach by using only a few media channels

Frequency and limited-reach, concentrated ad campaigns go hand in hand. A *concentrated campaign* gains exposure using only a few media outlets.

EXAMPLE

Instead of running an ad one time in each of six magazines that reach your target market, a concentrated campaign schedules your ad three times each in two of the publications. Or, instead of running a light radio schedule and a light newspaper schedule, a concentrated campaign bets the full budget on a strong schedule that builds frequency through one medium or the other.

REVERSING THE FORGETTING CURVE

Here's some information to remember — if you can.

In the late 1880s, German researcher Hermann Ebbinghaus quantified the rate at which people forget. You may not need formal statistics to confirm that most people forget 90 percent of what they learn in class within 30 days.

Get this: Most of the forgetting takes place in the first hour after contact with new information, and by the time two days have passed, people retain only 30 percent of the information.

This *forgetting curve* is why ad repetition is so important to marketers. Through schedule frequency, prospects encounter your message and just when they're about to forget it, they encounter the information again . . . and again.

A concentrated ad campaign offers several benefits:

>> It allows you to take advantage of media volume discounts.

>> It can give you dominance in a single medium, which achieves a perception of strength and clout in the prospect's mind.

>> It allows you to limit ad production costs.

>> It ensures a higher level of frequency.

Timing your ads

No small business has enough money to sustain media exposure 52 weeks a year, 24/7. Instead, consider the following mass media scheduling concepts:

>> **Flighting:** Create and sustain awareness by running ads for a short period, then go dormant before reappearing with another *flight* of ads.

>> **Front-loading:** Announce openings, promote new products, and jump-start sales by running a heavy schedule of ads before pulling back to a more economical schedule that aims to maintain awareness.

>> **Heavy-up scheduling:** Synchronize ad schedules with seasonal business or market activity using schedules that include heavy buys several times a year during what's called *ad blitzes.*

>> **Pulsing:** Maintain visibility with an on-and-off schedule that keeps your ad in media channels on an intermittent basis with no variations.

After setting your schedule, leverage your buy by using email and social media to alert customers to watch for your ads, or post the ad on your website and pages to make your investment go further.

Evaluating Your Efforts

Armchair quarterbacking is a popular and pointless after-the-ad-runs activity. Instead, set objectives and plan your evaluation methods early on — not after the play has taken place.

The quickest way to monitor ad effectiveness is to test a couple of great headlines online and measure the clicks they generate. The next-easiest way to monitor ad effectiveness is to produce ads that generate responses and then track how well they do, following this advice:

>> Give your target audience a time-sensitive invitation to take action, a reason to respond, and clear, easy instructions to follow. For example, if you're measuring phone calls, make your phone number large in your ad and be ready for call volume; if you're measuring website visits, present an easy-to-enter site address that leads to a landing page tied to your ad message.

>> Measure media effectiveness by assessing the volume of responses that each media channel generates compared to the investment you made in that channel. Also measure ad effectiveness by tracking the volume of responses to various ad headlines.

>> Produce your ads to make tracking possible by including a *key,* which is a code used to differentiate which ads produce an inquiry or order. Here are ways to key your ads:

- Direct calls to a unique phone extension keyed to indicate each medium or ad concept. Train those who answer the phone to record the responses to each extension so you can monitor media and ad effectiveness.

- Add a key to coupons that you include in print ads and direct mailers. For direct mailers, the key may indicate the mailing list from which the inquiry was generated. For print ads, the code could match up with the publication name and issue date. For example, BG0214 might be the key for an ad that runs on Valentine's Day in *The Boston Globe.*

- Feature different post office box numbers or email addresses on ads running in various media channels. When receiving responses, attach the source as you enter names in your database so you can monitor not only the number of responses per medium but also the effectiveness of each medium in delivering prospects that convert to customers.

>> Test headline or ad concepts by placing several ads that present an identical offer. Track responses to measure which ads perform best.

>> Compare the cost effectiveness of various media buys by measuring the number of responses against the cost of the placement.

Chapter 2

Generating and Placing Print and Outdoor Ads

W hen was the last time you opened the yellow pages?

If your answer is typical, it tells just how much directory advertising has changed over a few years. The year 2011 was a tipping point, when more people got their information from the Internet than from newspapers and when online advertising got most of the ad dollars as well.

Yet even though the numbers are declining, four out of ten people say they still get their news from newspapers — so you'd better know your customers before you abandon traditional advertising altogether (turn to Book 1, Chapter 2 for help in defining your customers). If you're advertising to an older age group, putting ink on newspaper is still an essential way to get your word out.

If your target audience is younger — especially 18 to 29— you're pretty safe ruling out traditional newspapers in favor of messages delivered via web-connected devices and TV. Even then, there's plenty in this chapter for you because the younger audience is a primary target for out-of-home ads (covered at the end of this chapter) and ads in highly targeted publications where your message can catch them while they're flipping through one of some 7,500 special-interest magazines.

This chapter points out the ins and outs of creating and placing more traditional ads in print and outdoors to help your small business reach the customers that you want.

Writing and Designing Your Print Ads

In the best print ads, the headline, copy, and graphics work together to capture attention, inspire the target market, promote the product's benefits, prompt the desired consumer action, *and* advance the brand of the business that placed the ad.

Whether you create ads yourself with aid from someone experienced in the fields of copywriting, design, and ad production or you turn to pros who create ads for a living, use these sections to understand the key steps in the print ad production process. From writing headlines and copy to making design decisions to preparing materials for reproduction by print media outlets, the upcoming pages highlight what you need to know.

Packing power into headlines

A *headline* is a print ad's major introductory statement. It's the large-type sentence or question that aims to stop readers in their tracks, target the right prospects, and pull them inside the ad to read more.

Four out of every five people who see your ad will read only the headline. Here's where they go:

>> One reader sees your headline and moves on because he doesn't have time to study the details at the moment.

>> A second reader sees the headline and rules herself out as a prospective customer because she doesn't want or need your product or service or because she can't afford what you're offering at this time.

>> A third one finds your headline all that's needed to reinforce an existing (hopefully positive) opinion.

>> A fourth one (should you be so lucky) finds the headline powerful enough to trigger the desired consumer action.

>> A fifth one is stopped by your headline and inspired to dive into the ad copy to find out more. Oh lucky day!

Knowing the attributes of a good headline

Your headline has to pack marketing power. It's your only chance to communicate with 80 percent of your prospects, and it's your hook for baiting the other 20 percent into your ad. If a headline doesn't grab and inspire, your body copy doesn't stand a chance. Here's what your headline needs to do:

>> Flag your prospect's attention by saying, in essence, "Stop! This message concerns you."

>> Appeal to your target prospect individually and immediately.

>> Promote an answer or solution to a problem.

>> Convey a meaningful benefit.

>> Advance your brand image.

As if the preceding weren't already a heavy load, the headline has to accomplish those things in words that people can read and grasp in five seconds. But even within that limitation, you have some creative elbowroom:

>> Headlines can be short or long, as long as they're irresistibly compelling.

>> They can sit at the top, in the middle, or along the bottom of the page.

>> They can be a single word, a phrase, a complete sentence, or a question.

Crafting your headline

Whether you write your headlines yourself or call on the talents of a professional copywriter or advertising agency, follow these tips:

>> **Lead with your most powerful point.** Too many ads use a clever come-on for a headline and then divulge the benefit somewhere toward the end of the copy, where few people see it. Flip the sequence. Create a headline that conveys a benefit or asks a question that'll stop people in their tracks. Then use your copy to fulfill the interest you pique.

- >> **Turn features into benefits.** If you say that your product works at double the speed of competing products, you've stated a feature. If you say that the consumer can save the equivalent of two days of vacation, you've stated a benefit. If you add that the extra vacation days are a free bonus with every purchase, you've fuel-injected the message.

- >> **Make your headline easy to read at a glance.** Choose very legible typeface and think twice before using all capital letters, which are harder to read and, as a result, easier to overlook.

- >> **Don't end your headline with a period.** The last thing you want is to encourage the reader to stop at the end of the headline.

- >> **Be believable.** An old line about advertising goes, *If it sounds too good to be true, it probably is.* Beyond that, media ad departments screen ads and reject ones that advance deceptive messages.

Adding power to your headline language

As you take a critical look at the language you use to develop your headlines, consider the following advice:

- >> **Positive statements carry power.** Figure out the pain your customers want to eliminate and use your headline to promote a solution. For example, if your customers want to save time, tell how your product allows them to work less. Offer an answer to their nagging problems.

- >> **Use compelling language.** After you settle on a headline, see whether you can push more impact into the words. For example, if your headline says *stomach,* ask yourself whether *guts* would pack more punch.

- >> **Find words that prompt mental images.** Instead of saying *reduce fear,* paint a picture by saying something like *eliminate white knuckles.*

- >> **Replace technical terms with words that most people understand.** Keep your headline simple, clear, and free of jargon.

- >> **Use the word *you.*** It's the most magnetic word in advertising. Every time you get ready to write *we,* turn the spotlight to the consumer by using *you.*

- >> **Tell *how.*** People are attracted to the feeling of interaction conveyed by the word *how.* Write a headline that includes *how to . . .* or *how you . . .* to draw prospects into your ad copy.

- >> **Use power words.** A widely cited study by the psychology department at Yale University found that the most powerful English words include *you, results, health, guarantee, discover, love, proven, safety, save,* and *new.*

Writing convincing copy

Copy is the term for the words that fill the body of an ad. Good copy talks directly to the reader. Its point is to connect and persuade. Instead of following the standard rules of grammar, copy is usually written to sound like people talk. It's conversational yet crisp and, above all, convincing.

REMEMBER

The first sentence of your ad copy only has to do one thing: Make the reader want to continue to the second sentence. The second sentence needs to lure the prospect to the third sentence. And so good ad copy goes, carrying consumers through your ad, building credibility and trust, and convincing readers of the merit of your message until, finally, the ad makes an irresistible offer and tells exactly how to respond.

As you lead prospects through your ad, aim to accomplish the following points:

>> **Tell your basic story.** Provide enough information to convey what you're offering, the benefits that a buyer can count on, and information that backs your claim.

>> **Sweeten your offer.** Add a guarantee, special financing terms, trade-in opportunities, a promotional price or package, special options, a free or limited-time trial, or other incentives to increase consumer responsiveness.

>> **Convey urgency.** Consider limited-time offers, promotions that reward only the first 100 respondents, or statements such as *while supplies last.*

>> **Explain what to do next.** Don't assume that prospects know how to reach you or how to find your business, whether in person or online. Explain when and how to respond.

TIP

As you review your copy, imagine that your prospect is saying, "Well, let me think about it; right now I'm just shopping." Then add statements of value, action inducements, or other ideas to overcome prospect hesitation. But for each statement you add, look for one to delete. The cleaner you can keep your ad, the better. Flip through a magazine or newspaper to see for yourself. Does your eye linger on the ads crammed full of text or those with strong headlines, bold graphics, and short blocks of copy?

If your ad includes prices, see Book 1, Chapter 2 for advice on how to convey costs while inspiring readers.

Making design decisions

Advertisers, ad agencies, and media outlets have spent enormous amounts of time and money to determine what does and doesn't work in the design of print advertisements. There's no pat formula — life in the marketing world isn't quite that easy — but when readers are asked which ads they remember positively, the following design traits emerge.

Adding visual appeal

Whenever you can, include an attention-getting visual element in your ads, following these tips:

>> **Use art.** Ads with stopping power nearly always have a photograph, an illustration (a drawing, cartoon, or other art), or both. The art may present the product, show the product in use, or relate to the product by reflecting its characteristics through what's known as *borrowed interest,* delivered by art that serves as a metaphor for the product.

For example, a restaurant ad may feature art of the entryway (the product), a photo of diners (the product in use), or an illustration of a sprig of rosemary or a bundle of herbs (borrowed interest reflecting the natural elegance of the restaurant and its recipes).

>> **Let your visual *show* what your ad is about.** You don't have to be literal. An ad for housekeeping services could feature a mop, broom, and vacuum cleaner. The ad may be more effective, however, if it communicates the benefit of more free time by showing a person in a bubble bath, feet propped up on the rim, open magazine in hand, in an immaculately clean setting.

Commissioning original photos or artwork assures that your ads feature one-of-a-kind images. Another option that's often more affordable though usually nonexclusive is to purchase rights to use what are called *stock images,* which you can locate through an online search for "stock photos and images."

As you invest in artwork, consider buying rights to feature the image not only in ads but also in direct mail, on your website, and in other venues that together leverage the image into a campaign symbol for your business.

Keeping it simple

Streamline your design to help readers focus on your ad's important points. Here are two ways to keep your ad design uncluttered:

>> **Frame the ad with open space.** Isolate your ad from those around it while providing the visual relief toward which the reader's eye will naturally gravitate.

> » **Make the ad easy to follow.** If you imagine a big letter "Z" placed over your ad space, you'll get a good idea of the path of most readers' eyes as they view ads. Design your ad accordingly, so readers grasp your message and see your name and logo before exiting your ad space. If your ad lacks an obvious focal point or if two design elements compete for dominance, the reader is apt to pass over the ad altogether.

You may notice ads that break these basic rules, but unless your ad is in the hands of an accomplished designer, you're wise to keep its design clean and simple.

Designing every ad to advance your brand

Small businesses have small budgets. Don't reduce your investment's impact by changing the look of your ads from season to season or, worse, from week to week. Here are some ways to advance your brand:

> » **Find an ad look and stick with it.** Settle on a recognizable format that readers can link to your name and brand. A consistent ad design gains you marketplace awareness and impact and also saves you time and money by eliminating the need to redesign every new ad.

> » **Prominently present your name.** Huge advertisers can get away with postage stamp-sized presentations of their logos because their products and ad looks are so familiar. Small business budgets don't allow for that level of awareness, so make your name apparent in every ad.

TIP

> » **When in doubt, leave it out.** This adage is good advice for do-it-yourself ad designers (and all other designers, too). As you consider tossing in an additional type font, different type size, ornamental border, or any other design element, remind yourself that good design is usually the result of subtraction — not addition.

Translating ad production terminology

Even if you pay the pros to produce your ads, it helps to know the language of print ad design and production:

> » **Ad proof:** This copy of your ad is the last thing you see before the presses run. When you review ad proofs, look closely at type set in all capital letters, which is where many typos slip through. Read your phone number twice and double-check your address. See that mandatory information (copyright lines, trademarks, photo credits, and so on) is in place. Then hand the proof to the best proofreader in your organization for a second review before you initial your approval.

KNOWING YOUR TYPE

Choosing the right type is an art that makes a tremendous difference in how your ad looks and, more important, how easy your message is to read. As you work on ad designs, you may find the following terminology helpful.

A *typeface* is a particular design for a set of letters and characters. For example, Garamond is a typeface. Helvetica is a typeface. Times New Roman is a typeface.

A *type family* is the full range of weights and styles available in a typeface. For example, you can stay within the Helvetica family and select bold, italic, and light versions in a great number of sizes. Helvetica, **Helvetica bold,** and *Helvetica italic* are all part of the Helvetica type family.

A *font* is the term used for a full set of characters (letters, numbers, and symbols) in a particular typeface and size. For example, This font is 10-point Garamond. **This is 10-point Garamond bold.** *This is 10-point Garamond italic.*

Limit the number of typefaces and sizes that you use in an ad, unless you're intentionally trying to achieve a jam-packed or cluttered look (which may be the aim of a carnival promoter or a retailer announcing a giant warehouse clearance event). Additionally, follow this advice:

- **Headlines** need to be attention grabbing, so designers usually choose typefaces that are capable of standing out while also communicating clearly. Choose *sans serif* typefaces, which have no decorative lines at the ends of the straight strokes in the characters. Probably the most popular sans serif typeface is clean-cut Helvetica.

- **Body copy** needs to be easy to read, so designers often opt for *serif* typefaces such as Garamond, Century Schoolbook, or Times New Roman because they have flourishes (serifs) that serve as connectors to lead the eye easily from one letter to the next. Avoid any font that's overly stylish or hard to read, avoid combining more than two type fonts in an ad, and definitely avoid using type in sizes too small for aging eyes.

>> **Display advertising:** Print ads that combine a headline, copy, art elements, and the advertiser's logo in a unique design are called *display* ads. All-word ads are called *classified* or *directory* ads.

>> **Four-color:** This is the term traditionally used to describe full-color printing, because (flash back to second-grade art class) you can create all colors from the primary colors of blue, red, and yellow (or, in printer terms, cyan,

magenta, and yellow). Before digital production, full-color printing involved separating a photo into these three colors and then reproducing it by laying one ink over the next until the image matches the original. Black (the fourth "color") is used for type and other details

>> **Spot color:** Color used to highlight an otherwise black-and-white ad.

Making Sense of Print Media Rates

Publications that accept print ads have a *rate card* that specifies pricing, deadlines, and production requirements. Here are definitions of key terms:

>> **Bulk or volume rate:** A reduced rate offered to businesses that commit to placing a certain amount of advertising over a contract period. Increased volume results in decreased rates.

>> **Cash discount:** A discount for prompt payment. Reduce the cost of your media charges by up to 2 percent by settling your bills quickly.

>> **Closing date or deadline:** The date by which you must submit ad material to a publication if your ad is to appear in a certain issue.

>> **Column inch:** A column inch is 1 column wide by 1 inch high. Most newspapers measure ad space in column inches, though once in a while you'll see ad rates quoted in *agate lines,* which equal $\frac{1}{14}$ of an inch. Just multiply by 14 to arrive at the price per column inch.

>> **Combination rate:** A discounted rate offered to advertisers who buy space in two or more publications owned by the same publisher or by affiliates in a syndication or publishing group.

>> **Cost per thousand (CPM):** The cost of using a particular medium to reach a thousand households or individuals. (The "M" stands for the Roman numeral designation for one thousand.) CPM also allows you to compare the relative cost of various media options.

The CPM formula: Media rate ÷ circulation or audience × 1,000 = CPM.

If a full-page newspaper ad costs $2,200 and the circulation is 18,000, the CPM is $122.22 ($2,200 ÷ 18,000 × 1,000 = $122.22).

>> **Earned rate:** The rate that you pay after all discounts are applied.

>> **Flat rate:** The cost of advertising with no discounts.

>> **Frequency discount:** A reduced rate offered to advertisers that run an ad a number of times within a given period.

>> **Local or retail rate:** A reduced newspaper ad rate offered to local or retail businesses. If you place ads in an out-of-town paper but sell your product through or in connection with a local business, see whether the business can place your ad or whether you can receive the local rate by mentioning the local business in your ad.

>> **Make-good:** A no-charge repeat of your ad, which you can request if your ad ran with a publisher error or omission.

>> **Open rate:** The highest price you pay for placing a particular ad one time with no discounts. Also called the *one-time rate* and the *basic rate*.

>> **Pick-up rate:** A discounted price that many newspapers offer for ads that are rerun with no changes within a five- or seven-day period.

>> **Short rate:** The amount you owe to the publisher if you don't earn the rate for which you contracted. If you sign a contract to run a certain amount of advertising but over the contract period you run less advertising than anticipated, you owe the publisher the difference between the contract rate and the rate you actually earned.

Placing Newspaper Ads

There are more opinions about what works in newspaper advertising than there are newspapers, and that adds up to a lot of differing ideas. Some advisers tell you to avoid the Sunday edition and the day that the grocery store ads appear because those papers are crammed with ads and your ad will get lost in the chaos. Others counter with the fact that those big and busy issues are crammed with ads because they're the best-read papers of the week. Some people tell you to place clever, small-space ads with high frequency, and others advocate dominating the paper with big-format ads, even if you can afford to run them only on a few carefully chosen dates.

Most of the advice you hear is absolutely right — but only some of the time. So how do you proceed?

>> **Know your target prospect** so that you can make an educated guess about which days and sections of the paper that person is likely to read.

>> **Know your objectives** (see Book 5, Chapter 1) so that you can select and time your ad placements accordingly.

>> **Know how newspaper advertising works** so that you can prepare a schedule that takes advantage of media discounts. That's what the upcoming sections are about.

Scheduling your placements

Myths are rampant about which days get the most newspaper readership. The fact is, from Monday through Friday, the number of people who open their papers varies only a few percentage points, with Tuesday's paper outpulling the others because in most markets it carries the food ads. If you want your ad to generate results, heed these tips:

>> **Place your ad on the day that makes sense for your market and message.** Here are some examples:

- If your target prospect is an avid price shopper, don't miss the issues full of grocery ads.

- If your target is a sports fanatic, advertise in Monday's sports section, where your prospect will be reading the weekend recaps.

- If you're promoting weekend dining or entertainment, advertise in the Thursday and Friday papers and in entertainment sections — unless you're trying to influence prospects in out-of-town markets, in which case you'd better run your ad Tuesday and Wednesday to allow time to make weekend travel plans.

- If your ad features an immediate call to action *(Call now for a free estimate),* don't choose the weekend papers if you're not open to handle the responses.

>> **Advertising in the Sunday paper usually costs more — and delivers more.** The number of single-copy sales is 10 to 40 percent higher on Sundays than on weekdays. What's more, readers spend up to three times as long with the Sunday paper as they do with weekday papers, and Sunday's paper tends to have a longer shelf life. Even if your newspaper charges a premium for Sunday ad placements, calculate the cost per thousand and you're likely to find that the cost of reaching readers is cheaper on Sunday than on any other day.

Using small-budget, small-size ads

Even though more readers note full-page ads than half-page ads, and more note half-page ads than quarter-page ads, small-budget, small-size ads still pull their weight. They're the only way to go if you don't have the budget to run larger ads multiple times, because a one-time ad is incapable of building the awareness or recognition you need your marketing efforts to achieve.

Though partial-page ads pull fewer readers, the number of readers doesn't drop as fast as the cost of the space. For example, though a full-page ad pulls about 40 percent more readers than a quarter-page ad, the quarter-page ad costs roughly a quarter of the price. As you work out a small-budget ad plan with your advertising salesperson, here's some general advice to follow:

TIP

>> **If you have to choose, opt for placement frequency over ad size.** Plan the largest ad that you can afford to run multiple times and don't worry if the most you can afford is only a partial page.

>> **Match your ad size to your message.** If you're opening a major new location, go for the biggest ad you can afford. But if you're promoting a $5.99 product, a big, splashy ad is likely overkill.

>> **Aim to dominate the page.** Even partial-page ads can have a page-dominating effect. Span the width of the page with a 1/3-page horizontal ad. Or run a half-page vertical ad, which echoes the shape of a full-page ad and dominates the page as a result. Long, skinny, one-column ads that run all the way down the page also draw attention, especially if they're placed along the paper's outer edge.

TIP

>> **If you're not the biggest, be the most consistent.** Ask your newspaper representative about a top-of-mind awareness (TOMA) program that offers outrageous discounts in return for running your ad — however tiny — several times a week, 52 weeks a year.

Requesting your ad placement

Right-hand page, as far forward as possible is repeated like a mantra by print advertisers. But there's no solid proof that an ad on the right page of an open publication does any better than one on the left page, and the same can be said for other hallowed rules about ad placement. In fact, research shows that newspaper ads placed above the fold pull no more readers than those placed below the fold, and ads next to editorial content pull the same as those next to other ads. An ad's success depends on its content, not on its placement.

Create a strong ad, *then* decide whether you'll reach your prospects if your ad runs anywhere in the paper (called a *run of paper* or *ROP* placement) or whether you need to request — and possibly pay extra for — a *preferred position*. The following advice can help you make your placement decisions:

>> **Make an "if possible" request with your ROP ad placement.** Most papers do their best to honor reasonable placement requests that accompany ROP orders, at no extra charge but on a space-available basis. Ask for placement in the front section, sports section, business section, or any other preference. But be willing to settle for what you paid for, which is placement anywhere in the paper. Most readers flip through nearly all the paper on a daily basis, and that's why most advertisers are confident rolling the dice with ROP ads.

>> **Ask about special rates** for display ads placed in the real estate and classified sections, as well as in special interest supplements that target your specific market.

>> **If your ad has a coupon, tell your ad representative in advance.** Request placement on an outer edge of the page for easy clipping and in a position that isn't up against a coupon on the flip side of the page.

>> **Leverage your budget.** Work with your newspaper to arrive at a contract rate based on the nature of your business and your advertising volume. Ask about a contract addendum assuring that a certain percentage of your ROP placements will be in a preferred placement.

Finding value in the classified section

The classified section is the bargain basement of the newspaper, and it just keeps getting smaller as more and more marketers move their classified ads online. (See the nearby sidebar, "The great ad flight to Craigslist and other online classified sites.") Still, if your market isn't Internet-savvy, classified ads can still pay off. Here's what to know:

>> **Small-print classified ads** are typeset by the newspaper and arranged into interest categories.

>> **Classified display ads** feature headlines, illustrations, special typestyles, and advertiser logos. They're available in sizes smaller than those accepted in the rest of the paper, and they stand out on the otherwise all-type pages of the classified section.

Classified ads follow many of the same guidelines as other print ads:

>> Use a short headline set in boldface capital letters to draw readers in.

>> Write your ad to talk directly and personally to a single target prospect.

>> Avoid abbreviations unless you're certain that most people will understand them.

>> Place your ad in a number of classified categories if it appeals to more than one interest area.

>> Include your contact info and give the reader a reason to call — to request an estimate, learn the price, view the product, schedule an appointment, or take some other action.

Placing Magazine Ads

When a full-page color ad in a major national magazine costs hundreds of thousands of dollars, you may wonder why your small business should even bother considering magazine advertising. The reason is that thousands of special-interest, small-circulation (and vastly more affordable) magazines exist, and many of the best-known magazines print regional or even city editions in which you can place an ad for a fraction of the full-edition price.

The following sections outline what you need to know about using magazines in your marketing.

Selecting magazines

The only magazine worth your ad investment is one that's consistently read by people in the target audience you aim to reach. Find out which publications your customers, prospective customers, and those who influence your customers subscribe to or read regularly.

Beyond conducting customer research, also look into which magazines serve your industry or those in your target audience. A good reference is the *Standard Rate and Data Service* (SRDS) advertising sourcebook, which is available on the reference shelves of many public libraries.

Suppose that your business sells software to small banks, and you want to run ads in magazines that small-institution bankers read. Go to the *SRDS Business Publication Advertising Source* and turn to the Banking section, where you'll find a list of magazines ranging from the *ABA Banking Journal* to *U.S. Banker*. Each entry lists the magazine's editorial profile, editorial personnel, ad representatives, page dimensions, deadlines, and rates, including commissions, discounts, and color charges.

Scheduling placements

As you schedule magazine ads, consider the following:

>> **Frequency matters.** Be sure that your budget is big enough to place your ad in the same magazine at least three times over a three-to-six-month period. Or, if you want to advertise during a single month, choose three magazines with similar readership profiles and run your ad in each one, building frequency for your message through *crossover readership* among publications. One way or the other, you need to reach your target audience multiple times to make an adequately strong impression.

>> **Magazines have long lead and response times.** For example, if you're trying to inspire spring vacation business, you need to run your magazine ads well in advance of the March and April vacation months in order to allow prospects time to read your ad, request information, and make plans. Unlike newspaper and broadcast ads, response to magazine ads builds slowly and continues for months and even years.

>> **Full-page ads dominate, but partial-page ads compete well.** Partial-page ads frequently share the page with other ads and end up toward the back of the magazine, but they also share the page with editorial content, which means that readers often spend more time on the page than they do with a full-page ad.

>> **Concept and design make or break your ad.** If you're advertising in a high-quality magazine, *definitely* invest in professional copywriting, design, and production to create an ad that represents you well in the highly competitive ad environment.

>> **Success stories are built on frequent placements of small, well-designed, black-and-white ads.** If you can't afford the production and placement of a full-color ad, run a small black-and-white or classified ad instead. Use the

space to invite readers to *Request our color catalog, Visit our website,* or other invitations that lead readers of your small-space ad to a larger presentation of your business.

>> **Work with magazine ad reps.** Explain your business, your desire to reach the magazine's circulation, and your budget realities. If you have an ad that's produced and ready to go, ask to be contacted when *remnant space* (last-minute, unsold ad space) is available — usually at a fraction of the regular cost. Also inquire about regional editions or any other means of placing your ad at a reduced rate.

TIP

>> **Take advantage of merchandising aids available to advertisers.** The magazine may have a *bingo card* that invites readers to circle numbers for additional information from advertisers. All you have to do is offer a brochure or other free item. You'll receive labels for all respondents — a great way to gather inquiries and build your database.

Also, ask for *tear sheets* mounted on boards reading *As Seen in XYZ Magazine* for display in your business.

>> **Reprint color ads for use as posters or direct mailers.** Maximize the cost and leverage the credibility of being a major magazine advertiser by turning the ad into promotional material.

>> **Consider including a QR code.** Turn print media into an interactive tool that allows readers to scan and click to reach your website home page, landing page, online video, or other content referenced in your ad. See the nearby sidebar, "QR codes: Let customers point and shoot to reach your business online." Check out *QR Codes For Dummies* by Joe Waters (John Wiley & Sons, Inc.) for more details, including how you can create and place QR codes.

Considering Yellow Pages, Directories, and Their Digital Alternatives

If your customers lug the phone books that hit their driveways or doorsteps through the front door (and not straight to the recycling bin), then traditional Yellow Pages listings are important to your business. If your customers have moved their direc-tory searches online, you should, too. The decision is really that easy. When it comes to phone book listings and other directory ads, go where your customers go.

But one way or another, be darned sure your business shows up in whatever directories your customers use. Otherwise, they won't find you at the very time they're most ready to buy.

Research conducted by the Local Search Association found that

>> Search engines are the top choice for consumers seeking local information, but Yellow Pages — in print or online — are most trusted.

>> Consumers under age 34 are more likely to use online searches, while those older than age 55 use print phonebooks and other traditional sources, such as newspapers, for local information.

>> Rural residents and those with lower incomes tend to use print Yellow Pages more than suburban and urban consumers.

REMEMBER

Most experts conclude that future usage will continue to slant even further toward online directories over print directories. And all agree that, regardless of how consumers seek information, being found in searches is absolutely essential, because after looking up a business, the majority of consumers make a business contact, and after contact, eight of ten make a purchase.

Creating and placing print directory ads

Before buying ads in the printed phonebook or any of the independent directories pitching for your business, take two steps:

1. **Find out which books your customers use — if any.**

Simply ask callers how they found your number. Admit that you're seeking their input as you determine which directories customers prefer.

2. **Ask the directory salespeople for proof of how their books are distributed and then do your own research to confirm that the books are reaching and being used by consumers.**

If you know owners of companies with ads in the directory, call to ask how well the directory worked. Or get old copies of the directory and compare ads in your category. If your competitors were in the book a few years ago and are either out of it this year or in with reduced-size ads, the ads probably pulled less-than-impressive results.

If you decide to place ads, you have a few decisions to make:

>> **Choose the right classifications.** Each category you add costs more money, so limit entries to sections your prospects are most apt to check.

>> **Select the right size.** If you don't have many local competitors, you hardly need a large ad to stand out in your field. Also consider the nature of your competitive arena. In some business categories, the most established and respected firms run the smallest and most subdued ads.

>> **Decide whether to add color.** Study the section where your ad will run to see whether color is necessary to compete on the pages. If you opt for color, read the rate card carefully because color charges vary from one directory to another but always mount up quickly.

>> **Write the right ad.** Research shows that directory readers look for two things: a solution and a business they can trust. They also appreciate information, business hours, and directions to listings of products or brands and professional endorsements and affiliations. But in a tight space, what you really need to present is your business name, an easy-to-read phone number and web address, and how to reach your street location. If your customers are tech-savvy, a QR code can lead them to additional information.

>> **Keep your ad simple.** Then use a border to set it apart.

REMEMBER

Don't accept the first directory ad price you're given. Directory ad prices are based on size, ad placement history, and whether the ad you're placing is larger than in previous years. Tell the rep that you need to compare rates with other directory offers, and chances are good that your comments will be met by a better price. After you agree to a price, be sure to get it in writing, and *always* insist on a proof of your ad before the directory prints.

Getting found in online directories

To place free (and sometimes paid) ads with some of the big-name directory sites, start with the following websites:

>> www.dexknows.com

>> www.google.com/local

>> www.graphiq.com

Using Billboards and Out-of-Home Ads

Out-of-home ads include billboards, transit displays, waiting bench signs, wall murals, building or facility signs, vehicle signs, movie theater billboard–style ads, digital kiosk ads, and even flyover signs. Wherever prospective customers are apt to be standing, sitting, or waiting, you'll probably see an advertising opportunity, usually accompanied by the name of the company to contact for advertising information.

For small businesses, the most frequently used form of out-of-home advertising involves billboards, and usually for directional purposes. Nearly every town (except those in billboard-free Alaska, Hawaii, Maine, and Vermont) has one or two companies that own most of the boards. Contact them to find out about available locations, costs, and contracts. Or, when you see a billboard in a desirable location, look along the bottom of the sign for the owner's name and then call for availability and cost information.

In scheduling billboard ads, a few key terms apply, including:

>> **Circulation** is measured by the number of people who have a reasonable opportunity to see your billboard or sign message.

>> **A full showing** or *#100 showing* describes the number of boards necessary to reach 100 percent of the mobile population in a market at least once during a 30-day period. A *half showing* (or *#50 showing*) reaches 50 percent of the mobile population. Anything less than a *#25 showing* isn't considered adequate for an advertising campaign, although the placement of one or two boards may be useful as directional signage.

In placing and creating billboards, two truths prevail:

>> **Location is everything.** Before buying an outdoor ad, drive by the ad site to be sure that it's in an area that reaches your prospects and enhances your image and that the sign is lit for nighttime visibility. Then, after your ad is posted, drive by it occasionally to confirm that lights are working, the installation is correct, and it's free of graffiti.

>> **Ads must pass the at-a-glance test.** Most viewers look at a billboard for five seconds, read seven words, and take away two ideas — your name and the reason to buy your product. Use large, legible type with adequate spacing between letters, words, and lines; strong color contrasts; and graphics that people can see and understand in a flash.

For more affordable outdoor ads, look into tourist-oriented directional (TOD) signs available through state transportation or tourism departments, vehicle signage (including magnetic door placards), and posters, which are becoming more and more affordable to produce. Just search for "digital poster printing" to reach links to resources.

Finally, a walk down any Main Street confirms that sandwich boards and sidewalk signs are making a comeback. If you choose to go this route, be sure you're in compliance with local sign ordinances and follow this advice:

>> Create a sign that reflects the brand and quality of your business image.

>> Use colorful graphics, with highly contrasting colors to pull attention.

>> Put a border around the sign so it doesn't meld into its surroundings.

>> Highlight a special or a promotional offer to invite people inside.

Chapter 3

Broadcasting Your Message

With at least one TV set in 99 percent of U.S. homes and radios in almost all cars, your customers are unquestionably tuned in to the broadcast world. Whether they're tuned in to broadcast ads is another question. More than half of all new cars feature a trial of commercial-free satellite radio, and nearly all TV viewers skip the ads at least some of the time.

Still, research confirms that TV ads are the most memorable form of advertising. And few advertising channels can beat radio for delivering an immediate message to a targeted and often captive audience.

The drawback is that low-budget broadcast ads — especially TV ads — air alongside ads by mega-marketers who spend millions on slick productions that make locally produced ads look as cheap as, in comparison, they are. Furthermore, even the most frugal TV ad and schedule can break a small business marketing budget, and for that reason many small businesses rightfully cross TV advertising off the list of possible marketing channels.

Yet others — especially restaurants, retailers, campaign and event organizers, and those seeking to reach local audiences in small, relatively affordable market areas — consider broadcast advertising essential to success. If broadcast advertising is important to your small business, this chapter helps translate the lingo, guide production and placement decisions, and leverage broadcast investments through website and social media placements.

Buying Airtime: Your Helpful Guide

If you're placing ads on a few radio or TV stations in your hometown market, you can probably handle the task on your own. But if your marketing reaches into multiple areas or if you're spending more than $10,000 on your media schedule, use a media buyer to wheel, deal, apply clout, and bring the kind of muscle that comes from experience in the field. You'll pay an hourly fee or a percentage of your overall buy, but you'll save time and confusion, and you'll almost certainly obtain a better schedule and price. If you use an advertising agency to create your ad, media planning and buying is usually part of the service.

If you're doing it yourself, begin by requesting a rate kit from each station you believe will reach your target market. The *rate kit* contains the following:

>> Audited research data, including statistical profiles of the age, gender, and consumer-buying patterns of the station's audience

>> Descriptions of network affiliations

>> Summaries of advertising success stories

>> Sample advertising packages

>> Rate cards

Use the rate kit to confirm that the station reaches your target audience and also as a cost guideline. In broadcast, prices vary depending on airtime availability, what times of day and year you air an ad, and the size schedule you buy. To win advertiser commitments, many stations throw in added-value enhancements and bonus schedules. Ask and you just may receive.

These following sections examine what you need to know about buying airtime, all explained in plain English.

Knowing some station and ad-buying terminology

Get acquainted with the following terms before talking with broadcast media representatives:

>> **Area of dominant influence (ADI):** The area that a station's broadcast signal covers.

>> **Availability:** Often referred to as an *avail,* an advertising time slot that's open for reservation. Except during holiday and political seasons, most stations have plenty of avails, even at the last minute.

>> **Call letters:** A station's identification; for example (borrowing from the old TV sitcom), WKRP.

>> **Dayparts:** Segments of the broadcast day.

Radio time is generally segmented into the *morning drive time* (6 to 10 a.m.), *midday* (10 a.m. to 3 p.m.), *afternoon drive time* (3 to 7 p.m.), *evening* (7 p.m. to midnight), and *late night* (midnight to 6 a.m.). Drive times draw the most listeners and command the highest ad rates.

TV time is priced highest during *prime time,* which runs from 8 to 11 p.m. The next most-expensive ad buys are in the hours adjacent to prime time, called *early fringe* (5 to 8 p.m.) and *late fringe* (after 11 p.m.).

>> **Flight:** A schedule of broadcast ads concentrated within a short time period. Ad flights create a level of awareness that generates a *carryover effect,* causing prospects to think that they just heard an ad even if it's been off-air for weeks.

>> **Increments:** Stations sell ads in lengths — *increments* — of 10 seconds (written as *:10s* and called *tens*), 15 seconds (:15s), 30 seconds (:30s), and 60 seconds (:60s). The majority of all TV ads are :30s.

REMEMBER

When buying radio time, :60s are usually only slightly more expensive — and sometimes no different in price — than :30s. If you opt for the longer ad, though, be sure you can create an interesting, entertaining ad capable of holding listener attention for a full minute. The rule in radio is to use only as much time as you need to say what needs to be said. If your offer is easy to explain, a :30s may be all you need. Shorter ads (:10s and :15s) are used as reinforcements, rotating into a schedule to build frequency through short reminder messages.

>> **Network affiliate:** A station that's affiliated with a national broadcast network (such as ABC, NBC, CBS, and FOX), usually resulting in larger audiences. A station not affiliated with a network is called an *independent station.*

>> **Sponsorship:** Underwriting a program in return for on-air announcements (called *billboards*) that tell the sponsor's name and tag line or brief message.

On commercial stations, advertisers can sponsor reports, such as the traffic update or the weather forecast, or they can sponsor public service announcements: "This safe driving reminder is brought to you by the doctors and nurses of St. Vincent's Hospital."

On public broadcast stations, sponsorships are the major vehicle available to marketers. Financial planners, medical and legal professionals, and others use program sponsorships to gain awareness without looking promotional. When you hear, "This program is brought to you with the generous support of . . .," you're listening to a sponsorship billboard.

>> **Spot:** The term *spot* has several meanings:

- The time slot in which an ad runs: "We're going to run 30 spots a week in prime time."

- The ad itself: "We're going to produce three spots to rotate over a month-long schedule."

- TV time purchased on specific stations rather than on an entire network: "We can't afford a four million-dollar Super Bowl network buy, so we're going to spend $500 to make a spot buy on our local channel."

>> **TAP or Total Audience Plan:** A radio package with a specified number of ads spread throughout each of the day parts. The station decides on the schedule, playing the agreed-upon number of your ads in each time period. Ads that run as part of TAPs are called *rotators*.

TAP programs are usually the most affordable packages that stations offer. Still, negotiate the deal. Ask about weighting the schedule toward the day parts when your prospects are most apt to be listening, or see whether the station will throw in additional spots to enhance the schedule. It's okay to beg — just don't get greedy!

Achieving broadcast reach, frequency, and rating points

Reach is the number of people who hear your ad or, in the case of TV, the number of households that are tuned in when your ad airs. *Frequency* is the number of times that an average prospect is exposed to your ad.

The accepted rule is that a broadcast ad needs to reach a prospect three to five times before it triggers action, which usually requires a schedule of 27 to 30 ad broadcasts. Book 5, Chapter 1 has more information about how reach and frequency work together in advertising schedules to put your message in front of enough prospects enough times to make a marketing difference.

If you have to choose, opt for frequency over reach. Instead of airing ads on ten stations (wide reach), choose two of the stations and talk to the same people repeatedly (high frequency).

Consider the following sections as you contemplate reach, frequency, and rating points for your ad.

Knowing how much is enough

The age-old question among broadcast advertisers is how much and how often ads need to air. This is where rating points come to the rescue. A *rating point* measures the percentage of the potential audience that a broadcast ad reaches. If an ad airs during a time that's calculated to reach 10 percent of the potential audience, then it earns 10 rating points.

Rating points are based on actual market performance, measured through surveys conducted by firms such as Arbitron and A. C. Nielsen. The findings have a margin of error, but they remain the best way to compare broadcast audiences within a market area. Stations subscribe to the findings and share the numbers with advertisers as part of their sales efforts.

Comparing gross versus target rating points

Gross rating points (GRPs) are the total number of rating points delivered by an ad schedule, usually over a one-week period. If you air 30 ads in a week, each reaching an average of 5 percent of the total potential audience, your schedule achieves 150 GRPs.

Target rating points (TRPs) are measured exactly like GRPs, except they count only your target audience. If your target market consists only of men age 35-plus, then your TRPs are measured as a percent of the men 35-plus who hear or see your ad.

GRPs measure your *total* reach; TRPs measure your *effective* reach.

Most media planners agree on the following scheduling advice:

>> **The rock-bottom minimum for GRPs is 150 per month.** If your budget can't cover a schedule with 150 GRPs over a month-long period, the effort likely won't be worth the investment.

>> **To build awareness, schedule at least 150 GRPs for three months in a row.** You can divide your schedule into 50 GRPs every week or 75 GRPs every other week, but commit to a multimonth schedule if you expect broadcast advertising to result in awareness for your business.

>> **Buy up to 500 GRPs per month to blitz the market.** For grand openings and major promotions, you need the kind of impact that only high-frequency broadcast buys can deliver.

You can make a broadcast buy without ever mentioning rating points, but you shouldn't. When a station rep offers to schedule for example, "Thirty spots at an average of $25 each," what are you really getting for your money? Follow up with a request: "Would you calculate how many gross rating points that schedule delivers? Also, what percentage of the audience fits our target profile of (for example) men age 35–plus?"

Bartering for airtime

Barter is the exchange of merchandise or services instead of monetary payment for advertising time. For example, a restaurant may trade for ad time by catering a station's holiday party, or a hotel may swap lodging packages that the station can use in on-air drawings. Here are a couple of ways to barter for airtime:

>> Trade a product or service that the station wants or needs — either for its own use or for use in on-air promotions.

>> Trade your product to a third-party business that then trades a like value of time or product to the station. For example, you trade $1,000 of plumbing services to a contractor, who then trades $1,000 of contracting services to a station's remodeling project. The station gives the contractor $1,000 of airtime, which you get as your end of the deal.

Unless you're making a direct trade with a station, bartering takes time and expertise. For assistance, search for barter services online or in the Yellow Pages or inquire with your media planner about making barter contacts.

When bartering, proceed with exactly the same care you'd exercise if you were making cash purchases of media time:

>> See that the schedule delivers adequate reach and frequency.

>> Verify that the station reaches your target audience.

>> Be sure that the timing matches your marketing plan.

>> Include an expiration date on product certificates you provide as part of your agreement. You don't want to end up paying for this year's advertising out of ad budgets in years to come.

>> Try to leverage your budget. You may be able to trade for airtime at up to two times your product value, but even a dollar-for-dollar trade saves money over a cash buy because your product price includes profit.

>> Be careful that on-air promotions involving your products are consistent with your business image and contribute to your brand's strength.

Looking At Broadcast Ad Guidelines

Whether you're producing a TV or radio ad, some general broadcast advertising guidelines apply. Later on, this chapter outlines best practices and advice for producing radio and TV ads specifically.

Establishing your own broadcast identity

Over time, you want listeners or viewers to recognize your business before they even hear your name. Consider the following identity-building techniques:

>> **Voice-over:** Have one announcer voice all your ads.

>> **Style:** Establish a broadcast ad style — for example, an ongoing dialogue between two people or ads that always advance a certain kind of message. (Want an example? Think of the two guys in the Sonic drive-in commercials.)

>> **Music/jingles:** If you use music or sound effects, use the same notable background in all your ads. As for jingles, some people love them, some hate them, and sooner or later, almost everyone tires of them. Before investing in a jingle, first be sure that you'll air enough ads to achieve an association between the jingle and your name. Second, the jingle must be appropriate to your brand image. Any station or studio can direct you to jingle producers.

Writing your ad

Don't write your own ad. Instead, put into words what you want your ad to accomplish, and then bring in professional help to develop your concept and write your script. Follow these tips:

>> **Write a *creative brief* (see Book 5, Chapter 1).** It should summarize whom you want the ad to talk to, what you want it to accomplish, and what consumer action you want it to inspire.

>> **Develop an ad concept capable of grabbing and holding audience attention without distracting from your ad message.** This is where professional writers really earn their fees.

>> **Grab audience attention.** Do so in the first three seconds, before your audience heads to the refrigerator or another station.

>> **Tell a story.** In a 30-second ad, you have about 20 seconds to inform, entice, and entertain — and even less if you cede time to a jingle or other sound or visual effects. The other seconds get divided between an attention-getting opening, your ad identification, and a call to action. Be sure to do the following in your ad:

- Feature your name (or product name) at least three times.

- Feature your call to action, preferably twice.

- If you include an address, provide an easy locator (for example, "Just across from the train station").

- If you want calls or website visits, present an easy-to-recall number or site address.

Turning your script over to the producers

When it's time to begin production, radio and TV stations usually offer their services. Whether you take them up on the offer (and if you want a unique ad, you may not want to) or use an independent producer, follow these steps:

1. Review the producer's work samples.

As you watch and listen to samples, ask yourself whether an ad enhances or diminishes your impression of the advertiser and the advertiser's commitment to quality. If you like what you see and hear, inquire about pricing, which, at station-based studios, is likely to be free or close to it.

2. Obtain a budget.

Request detailed allocations for studio time, tape and materials, music fees, talent, editing time, ad duplication, and other costs. Particularly, review the costs and usage restrictions for music, sound effects, and talent, following these tips:

- **Music and sound effects:** Studios have access to libraries of royalty-free or nominally priced music and sound effects, but always confirm costs and usage rights. Some rights are *outright* (you can air the ad wherever and whenever you want at no additional fee), whereas others cover only designated exposure and are *renewable* (meaning you pay again) for further use.

Never make the mistake of pulling favorite music from your personal collection for commercial use because whoever owns the rights can sue you for copyright infringement.

- **Talent:** Your ad may involve an announcer and possibly actors as well. For locally aired ads, you'll probably use talent that the studio provides. If you use members of a union, such as the Screen Actors Guild, be prepared for higher rates, paperwork, *and* more experienced talent.

  When using nonstation talent or recording outside the studio, obtain talent releases. Check with your production company and your attorney to be sure that you're requesting appropriate releases for your project.

3. Meet with the talent.

Before rolling tape or cameras, ask the talent to perform a dry run of the ad. Take time to correct the pronunciations of your name and products if necessary. Also, alter sentences that contain tongue twisters, and trim time-gobbling extra words. Then request another read to be sure the ad sounds right and fits within the allocated time frame.

TIP

If you don't like what you see or hear, speak up. Announcers can adjust their voices to sound younger, older, happier, sadder — or as if they're talking to children rather than adults or to an individual rather than a group. A good director can handle the talent direction for you, representing your thoughts while adding professional expertise.

4. Attend the editing session.

Editing is where dollars burn quickly. Make and approve decisions on the spot to avoid the need for a repeat session.

5. Produce your ad and provide all stations with duplicate copies, called *dubs*.

Unless you intentionally create a series of ads targeting various audiences, don't allow each station to air its own version of your ad. Frequency works only when people hear the same ad repeatedly.

TIP

Review your ad outside of the studio with its perfect sound system and lack of interruptions. Sit in your car, preferably in traffic, or in your living room with all its distractions. Turn on your ad while others are around to see whether they stop to tune in. Turn it on halfway through to see whether it still presents a coherent message. Then review it a dozen more times to see whether it holds your interest without driving you to distraction.

Producing Radio Ads

In 30 or 60 seconds, a good radio ad grabs attention, involves the listener, sounds believable, creates a mental picture, spins a story, calls for action, and manages to keep the product on center stage and the customer in the spotlight — all without sounding pushy, obnoxious, or boring.

Done perfectly, a radio ad is a one-on-one conversation with a single target prospect, written and produced so well that the prospect hears the introduction and says, in essence, "Shh, be quiet, you guys, I need to hear this. It's talking to me."

Great writers *write out loud* when creating radio ads. Here's how:

>> **Use language that's written exactly the way people talk.**

>> **Write to the pace that people talk, not to the pace at which they read.**

>> **Include pauses that give people time to think and announcers time to breathe.**

>> **Cut extra verbiage.** You wouldn't say "indeed," "thus," "moreover," or "therefore" if you were explaining something exciting to a friend. Don't do it in your radio ad, either.

>> **Rewrite elaborately constructed sentences full of phrases linked together with *who, which,* and *whereas.*** For example, instead of, "The new fashions, which just came off the Paris runways, where they made international news, are due to arrive in Chicago tomorrow at noon," go with, "The newest Paris runway fashions arrive in Chicago tomorrow at noon. You're invited to a premiere of the world's leading looks."

>> **Tell listeners what to do next.** Prepare them to take down your phone number ("Have a pen handy?") or repeat your number for them. Most important, help them remember your name so they can look you up later.

WARNING

Don't waste radio time telling people to "Look us up in the Yellow Pages." Chances are good they don't use the Yellow Pages, and if they do, they'll probably find your competitors there, too.

Producing TV Ads

"I saw it on TV" has become a mark of having made it into the advertising major leagues. To get there, though, be prepared to make a financial commitment. Successful TV advertisers have two things in common: They earmark adequate ad production budgets and they fund media schedules that span at least a multi-month period. If you can do both those things — produce a quality ad and fund an adequate schedule — TV advertising can deliver awareness and credibility for your business.

You can reduce costs by airing ads on cable channels at a fraction of the price of major station ad rates, but look long and hard to be sure the stations you choose reach adequate numbers of the audience you're targeting. Also, remember that even though the media cost of cable TV is relatively low, your ad's production value still needs to be high enough to meet viewer expectations and to show well in this competitive advertising arena.

Don't create your own TV ad or marketing video. Bring in the pros, share your objectives, leave room for creativity, and then evaluate their ad concepts and recommendations against the aims you seek to accomplish.

Why the insistence? Consider this: Your ad will play to an audience that has been trained to expect feature-film quality. To compete on a small business budget, you need a strong, simple ad concept and clean, well-edited visuals. The first step toward making a good impression is to get help from those who deal in video productions daily.

The following sections point out what you need to know about creating a TV ad.

Hiring professionals

As you select a creative partner for your ad production, consider the following resources:

>> **Advertising agencies:** If you want to receive major attention for a fairly small-budget project, interview small rather than large ad agencies.

>> **Video production services:** Search online for "video production services" and look for a studio that offers the full range of creative services, including scriptwriting, production, and editing.

>> **TV station production facilities:** Local stations can create your ad for almost nothing, but get a bid anyway. In the world of TV production, "nothing" can be enough to break your budget.

>> **Online options:** Check out websites like www.elance.com and www.upwork.com who have freelance professionals who perform these types of services as well.

Airing preproduced manufacturer ads

High-quality, ready-to-air ads may be available to you through your manufacturers or dealers. The ads feature the manufacturer's products, but they include time to add a tag line directing viewers to your local business. If you go this route, consider the following:

>> Run manufacturer ads only if your business is the exclusive regional representative.

>> Look into the possibility of obtaining the manufacturer's cooperative support in the form of shared media costs.

>> Ask your station to add your logo and tag line. In return for your ad buy, they'll probably perform the service for free or close to it.

Considering Infomercials

Infomercials are program-style ads that you come across when you're channel-surfing because you can't sleep. They promote housewares, financial and business opportunities, exercise and beauty items, self-help offerings, sports and workout equipment, and such aptitude development products as memory enhancement and reading programs. Oh, and psychic services.

Infomercials solicit viewer action in two ways:

>> **Sales-generating infomercials** invite viewers to call toll-free to place COD (cash on delivery) or credit card orders.

>> **Lead-generating infomercials** ask viewers to call for free catalogs, brochures, or other offers.

WARNING

With a success rate as low as one out of four, infomercials are high risk.

Still, the topic of infomercials comes up among small business marketers in part because of the direct and measurable results that infomercials generate and in part because the ads look fairly straightforward and easy to produce. Looks can deceive, though. As with all other broadcast ads, viewers have been trained to expect a certain caliber of production value.

Products featured in infomercials have markups high enough to absorb the significant cost of creating and airing the infomercial. For example, if an infomercial product sells for $19.95, it probably cost only $4 to $6 to manufacture. The average national infomercial production budget is more than $150,000, though you can find video production houses that will create your infomercial for a tenth of that amount — or less.

Big budget or small budget, all infomercials promote products with broad appeal that aren't available through retail channels and that most viewers can afford to buy without great deliberation.

If infomercials are in your marketing plan, keep these success factors in mind:

>> Make your product the star of the show. Describe its unique benefits, show how it solves a viewer problem, and tell why people should believe in it. Never fake product demonstrations. It's illegal. Enough said.

>> Use short sentences, short words, and short segments, broken at least three times during the program by your call to action.

>> Use unscripted testimonials that allow past buyers to ad lib as they share their praise.

>> Focus on selling, not on entertaining. Before airing the infomercial, be sure you're ready with a call center, a credit card merchant account, a shipping solution, and a website that can handle the anticipated traffic.

Most viewers respond, if they're going to, after watching the infomercial only once, so evaluate the ad's effectiveness immediately after the first showing. If it draws a good response, re-air it to reach yet more buyers. If it doesn't, head straight back to the editing booth. Start with the first three-minute segment, which is the portion that either grabs or loses most viewers.

Logging In to Webinars

Sometimes called *web seminars* or *webcasts*, a *webinar* is an event that a business or an individual hosts to address an audience that can be located anywhere that has access to online connections and phone lines.

In the context of advertising, webinars provide your customers or prospective customers valuable information through online presentations that help you achieve visibility in your field and a stronger reputation as a thought leader. They also help forge and deepen customer relationships.

To attend a webinar, participants log in via a web browser or web conferencing tool to view presentation visuals and to hear the webinar's audio portion, which can also be reached via a phone connection.

Some webinars simply share expertise. More often, though, they generate leads from those who listen in, like what they hear, and follow up by joining mailing lists, requesting meetings or proposals, registering to download e-books or other content, or taking other steps toward client relationships.

If you're thinking about hosting a webinar, consider these points:

>> **Upside:** When you host a webinar, you can speak from anywhere, using a web conferencing tool or Internet browser to share audio and visuals, usually in the form of PowerPoint slides, with people who can log on from anywhere.

>> **Downside:** The fact that almost no one likes the sound of the name *webinar* hasn't slowed webinars from becoming the content-delivery means of choice for those who want to establish themselves as experts and thought leaders. As a result, among invitees, webinars have acquired a dime-a-dozen reputation. As proof, just go to a site like www.webinarlistings.com to see the number of free and fee-based webinars in dozens of categories.

>> **Takeaway:** Expect your webinar to face strong competition for attendee attention. To succeed, you must

- Know the audience you want to reach, including what problems they face and want addressed.

- Decide on a topic that addresses a real problem that hasn't been addressed a million or a dozen times already.

- Select a presenter who is great in terms of reputation, expertise, and engaging style.

- Be prepared to announce and promote your event because no one is sitting around waiting for a webinar invitation.

TIP

- Host a terrific event by getting familiar with webinar-hosting tools like GoToMeeting, GoToWebinar, and AnyMeeting.

- Tape your presentation for post-presentation sharing and download, making up for what may be meager attendance with what can be terrific leveraging of webinar content after the fact.

IN THIS CHAPTER

Defining one-to-one marketing terms

Setting up for direct sales

Using direct mailers to market your product or service

Creating and sending your mailers by surface mail

Marketing through email

Chapter 4

Snail-Mailing and Emailing Your Customers Directly

Although television ads win awards and build awareness and social media wins buzz and launches relationships, direct mail wins customers and return-on-investment contests.

Direct mail is called *one-to-one communication* because it delivers your marketing message to carefully selected prospects and customers one at a time. One-to-one communication is the exact opposite of mass media advertising, which uses the shotgun approach — that is, you create an ad and use newspapers, magazines, and broadcast media to spread the message far and wide. One-to-one communication aims your message only at specific and well-defined individuals.

Most marketers believe that the two approaches work best in a tag-team arrangement: You use mass media advertising to build awareness, desire, and perceived value for your products, and then you use one-to-one marketing to call for the order.

If you can only afford to do one or the other, however, consider placing your bets on the one-to-one marketing approach, which this chapter discusses, aiming each dollar you spend straight at qualified prospects rather than scattering your budget through mass media to reach prospects and non-prospects alike.

Using One-to-One Marketing

When you employ one-to-one marketing, you bypass mass media vehicles and take your ad straight to the mailboxes, telephones, and computer screens of individuals who are prime prospects for your product or service. You may hear the terms *direct marketing, direct mail, direct-response advertising,* and *database marketing* used interchangeably in discussions about one-to-one marketing, but they each represent different aspects of the direct marketing arena. For the record, here are definitions of those terms and others:

>> **Direct marketing** involves a direct exchange between a seller and a buyer, without the involvement of retailers, agents, or other intermediaries.

>> **Direct mail** is the primary means of direct marketing communication. It involves sending promotional announcements in the form of letters, postcards, packages, or emails directly to targeted prospects.

>> **Direct-response advertising** announces a promotional offer and invites consumers to respond directly to your business — by phone, in person, or by clicking a QR code to reach a landing page on your website — to make a purchase or obtain additional information.

>> **Database marketing** entails compiling detailed information about customers and prospects and then using the data to match and send specialized offerings to consumers in different *customer segments,* based on the demography, interests, and values of customers in each group.

>> **Direct sales** are purchase transactions that occur directly between a buyer and seller. Mail order and e-commerce are the primary vehicles for direct sales.

>> **Telemarketing** involves communicating with prospects and customers over the telephone — either by *inbound calls* made by consumers to toll-free numbers that they see in ads, sales materials, or online, or by *outbound calls* made by a business to the homes or offices of target prospects.

WARNING

Be aware that most people hate outbound telemarketing calls so much that a majority of Americans have entered their phone numbers in the National Do Not Call Registry, which telemarketers are legally required to honor and to search at least once every 31 days. For more information, go to www.donotcall.gov.

Direct Sales: Do-It-Yourself Distribution

The name says it all: Marketers who employ *direct sales* strategies sell to consumers directly, without involving middlemen, retailers, agents, or other representatives. Instead, they use direct response ads, direct mailers, catalogs, and e-commerce to communicate one on one with prospective buyers.

EXAMPLE

Following are a couple of examples of how direct marketing tools can generate direct sales for small businesses:

>> **Direct response advertising:** A jewelry maker advertises his wares by placing small, black-and-white magazine ads. But instead of aiming to build general awareness, the ads invite readers to call toll-free to purchase the featured item or to visit the jeweler's website to view and order from his complete line. Either way, the instructions in the ad lead straight back to the jewelry maker and not to any retailer or other intermediary.

>> **Direct mail:** The self-publisher of a book featuring lists and ratings for summer youth camps promotes the book by sending direct mailers to a subscriber list rented from a major parenting magazine. She also works with bloggers and uses social media and online ads to build a network of inbound links to the page of her website featuring the book for sale.

>> **Catalog distribution:** A kitchen accessories company generates direct sales by mailing its catalog to the households of current and past customers, ad respondents, and subscribers of gourmet magazines.

The Direct Marketing Association warns against two big direct sales land mines: nondelivery of merchandise and misrepresentation of offers. Every year a few direct marketers hurt the reputation of all by implementing programs that fail to communicate honestly or to deliver the products as promised. If you sell directly, protect your own reputation and the reputation of all who participate in direct marketing by following this advice:

>> **Be clear, honest, and complete in your communications.** Your ad *is* the shopping experience for direct buyers, so make it thorough and consistent with what the customer will see when the order arrives. Make sure your ad accurately describes your product and represents your price, payment terms, and extra charges. Don't make outlandish claims and don't make promises that defy belief or that you can't live up to.

>> **Describe the commitment involved in placing an order.** Decide how to handle returns and communicate your policy in your marketing materials.

WARNING

Be aware that there are laws that enforce honesty in direct mail marketing. If you promise "satisfaction guaranteed" (or if you make a money-back guarantee), Federal Trade Commission regulations mandate that you give a full refund without question and for any reason. If you offer a risk-free trial, you can't charge the customer until the customer receives and is satisfied with the product. If you don't plan to refund a customer's money under any circumstances, your marketing materials must state, "All sales are final."

>> **State the estimated lag time between order receipt and product delivery.** If the average order takes four weeks for delivery, avoid complaints and concerns by informing customers of the delivery time frame in your marketing materials and when they place their orders.

>> **Get good customer data.** Your success relies on clear customer input. Whether online or in printed direct sales materials, provide detailed instructions on how to submit customer and payment information.

TIP

>> **Describe payment options.** Don't allow cash transactions. Credit card privileges increase response rates, so plan your policies accordingly.

>> **Keep track of consumer questions and complaints.** If, despite your best efforts, your ads result in misunderstandings, pull and revise them.

Marketing with Direct Mailers

All direct mailers, regardless of look, message, or purpose, are alike in one way: They go straight to your prospects' mailboxes or inboxes rather than reaching them through mass-media broadcast and print ads. Keep reading the following sections for more information about direct mailers.

Setting up for success with direct mail

Direct mailers are among the easiest of all marketing communications to monitor for success. With each mailing, you know exactly how many pieces you're sending and therefore how many prospects you're reaching. And because direct mailers almost always request an easy-to-track direct response (in the form of a sale, an inquiry, a visit to your business, a click, or some other prospect action), within days (for email) or weeks (for surface mail), you can count the responses to determine the effectiveness of your direct mail effort.

REMEMBER

Most successful direct mailers incorporate these factors:

>> **A targeted list:** To be great, a direct mail list must reach genuine prospects for your product or service. (See Book 1, Chapter 2 for help in creating a prospect profile.)

>> **A compelling offer:** The *offer* is the deal — the catalyst to which the consumer reacts.

>> **An attention-getting format:** Some mailers involve nothing more than a regular or oversized *(jumbo)* postcard. Others involve only a good sales message in a white envelope or an email message. Some are elaborate packages that contain samples and other enclosures (including brochures, CDs, or product samples). Just be sure that your approach is consistent with your company's brand image and capable of conveying your message and meeting your marketing objectives (see Book 5, Chapter 1).

Deciding between email and snail mail

Email tends to dominate conversations about direct mail, largely because it's so immediate and inexpensive. But don't write off the benefits of direct mailers sent by surface mail, primarily because you can send what's now called *snail mail* to new prospective customers, whereas email to strangers falls into the dreaded (and illegal) category of spam.

For a look at the differences between using surface mail or email to send direct mail, see Table 4-1.

TABLE 4-1 **Differences between Sending Direct Mail by Surface Mail and Email**

Surface Mail	Email
Is often considered junk mail	Is often considered and blocked as spam
Arrives in a mailbox with less mail than in previous years	Arrives in an increasingly crowded inbox
Can be sent to all prospective target prospects	Can be sent only to those who have opted in or had previous contact with your business
Typical response rates are 3 to 4 percent when mailings go to those on your house list of customers and prospects, and lower when sent to rented lists of people who match the profile of your target audience	House lists, which can include only established customers or those who have opted in to your mailings, result in open rates of around 20 percent and conversion rates just under 2 percent

(continued)

TABLE 4-1 *(continued)*

Surface Mail	Email
Can be used for reaching new prospects	Can be used for making offers to established contacts who have opted in to your list
Great for presenting photos, visuals, or samples	Great for conveying messages that prompt recipients to click for more information
Great for sending material with a "keeper" quality	Great for immediate response offers such as "register now" or "download now"
Costs time and money to produce and send	Can be produced and sent immediately and with little expense, and can be used to test and quickly alter headlines or offers

Making your offer

Good mailers make great offers that relate to — and build credibility in — your product or service. They're also unique, valuable, and attractive.

WARNING

Don't use your existing promotional materials or items emblazoned with your company name or logo as your offer. People get promotional material for free daily, and they certainly don't want to take the time to respond and ask for it unless it's extremely unique or exclusive.

TIP

A good offer contains the following elements:

>> **A great deal:** This may be a free sample or gift, a trial offer, a special price, an event invitation, or special payment terms, depending on the objective of your mailer and the nature of your product. In crafting your offer, be aware that the word *free* pulls more responses than discounts or other price offers.

>> **A guarantee:** To improve results, offer an assurance that working with your business is risk-free and reliable. For example, extend a money-back guarantee, a delivery guarantee, or a service guarantee. And keep your promise — for good business purposes and for legal reasons.

>> **A time limit:** This increases interest and response, even if the deadline is only implied (such as "Please reply by December 15").

Table 4-2 shows how a public relations agency that's seeking to build relationships with CEOs might weigh offers as bad, better, and improved.

WARNING

Don't go overboard with your offer. Remember that your goal is to receive *quality* responses. If your offer is *too* great, it will generate responses from people who simply want the deal.

TABLE 4-2   **Examples of Direct Mail Offers**

Bad Example	Better Example	Improved Example
Invite the CEO to request a free brochure featuring case histories of agency success stories.	Invite the CEO to request a free guide featuring advice on "How to Write News Releases and Manage Media Interviews."	Invite the CEO to specify how many free copies of "How to Write News Releases and Manage Media Interviews" she would like you to deliver.
Why?	*Why?*	*Why?*
A brochure is a promotional piece, and this "offer" asks the CEO to take time to request the kind of thing that other companies send out on a routine basis.	This free resource delivers a benefit to the recipient. It contains advice that public relations professionals usually sell by the hour. It also addresses the CEO's needs.	The CEO has a good reason to respond to this offer. It promises a valuable and unique item. Because only the CEO knows how many copies her company can use, the response request has meaning.

Personalizing your mailer

The best mailers are, above all, personal. (The opposite of a personalized mailing is one addressed to *Occupant* or *Resident*.) You can personalize your mailer in a number of ways:

» On envelopes you can use what looks like handwritten addresses. (Computers and mail-house technology automate this seemingly arduous task.)

» On printed letters you can personalize the salutation line, and on email messages you can personalize the subject line, so long as you're absolutely certain that you know you're using the recipient's name correctly. If you're not sure, don't guess and don't worry; the jury is still out on whether personalized subject lines lead to higher open rates.

» In letters and email messages, you can boost response rates by customizing your message to indicate awareness of the recipient's location, past purchases, or past interactions with your business. For example, a vet can send patients reminders about a pet's history, or a real estate agent can include information on homes in the recipient's immediate neighborhood.

WARNING

No matter what, don't make your mailer look like bulk mail by using an awful catch-all greeting such as *Dear Friend* or, worse, *Dear Valued Customer*. If your mailing is too extensive to allow for personalized greetings, replace the salutation with a headline.

Putting Surface Direct Mail to Work

With all other forms of advertising, you send messages through media channels matched to your market profile in general, but with direct mail, you aim your marketing investment precisely at those prospects who possess the exact characteristics that make them likely to buy from your business. These sections examine what you need to know about going the direct-mail route.

Developing a great list

Most surface direct mail programs involve one of the following types of lists:

>> **Demographic lists:** These include addresses for people who match the age, profession, household income, and other lifestyle aspects of those most apt to purchase your products.

>> **Geographic lists:** These include addresses for people who live in the cities or zip code areas that match your market area.

>> **Geodemographic lists:** These include addresses of individuals in your targeted geographic market area who also match the demographic attributes of your prospect profile. For example, a geodemographic list might target prospects in a specific zip code area who live in homes assessed at $300,000 or more.

You can create your own list, called a *house list,* by using your customer contacts as well as the names and addresses of prospects that you collect from other sources. Or you can choose to invest in *outside lists* from mailing service businesses and organizations, professional associations, magazines, or other list owners.

Creating your own house list

If you market in a local or clearly defined market area, you'll probably want to create your own list. As you go about assembling the names for your list, follow these steps:

1. **Include your established customer and prospect base.**

   Begin with the names of current customers, obtained from sales records, requests at the time of purchase or loyalty program enrollment, or through contest entries and other forms. Then add the names of those who have expressed interest by responding to your ads or in other ways sharing their names with your business.

2. **Turn to local business and community directories.**

For example, a golf club that's seeking to build its membership roster might create a mailing list that includes golfers in the target market area who have golfed as guests or in tournaments at the club, along with the names of all target market business CEOs. It may also form strategic partnerships with a local resort to acquire names through a joint promotion.

3. **Enter the names into a database.**

For this task, you can use database software, use the mail or data merge program in your word processor, or employ the resources of a professional database manager to keep your mailing list organized. (See the sidebar "Using mail specialists" later in this chapter.)

4. **Segment names according to geographic location, demographic profile, past purchasing patterns, or lifestyle interests.**

By segmenting your list, you can send tailored messages that match the interests of people in portions of your overall list.

Finding and renting good outside lists

Mailing services, printers, and list brokerage businesses can assist with list development or list rental. Define your target audience by stating where your most likely customers reside and who they are in terms of age, income, family size, education, and other lifestyle factors (see Book 1, Chapter 2). Then turn to the following resources for lists that suit your needs.

For publication subscriber lists, contact ad representatives at publications that serve your industry or market area to find out about list availability, prices, and terms. Ask each publication if it breaks down its subscriber list into interest or geographic segments. If so, you can rent a portion of the list to reach only those subscribers who are most likely to respond to your offer.

EXAMPLE

Suppose you're marketing a new travel bag. You can start by contacting a travel magazine to inquire about buying access to its subscriber list. But if your bag won't appeal to *all* subscribers, you can ask about ways the list can be *segmented*. You may be able to target your mailer geographically by obtaining names only for subscribers in, say, the Midwest. Or maybe you can send your mailer only to subscribers who list home addresses. (This eliminates the names of travel agents and others who receive the magazine in their offices.) Furthermore, you may be able to purchase a list segmented by subscriber income level or even by the type of travel the person prefers. You're on your way to a list tailored to your prospect profile!

If you decide to obtain lists through mailing services and list brokers, search the Internet for "mailing list brokers" to reach the sites of businesses that provide preassembled or customized lists for use in direct mail programs.

When renting a list, note the following:

>> You'll pay from $50 to several hundred dollars for one-time use of 1,000 names — and more for targeted industry and business lists.

>> You'll need to rent a minimum number of names (list owners usually require minimum orders well into the thousands).

>> You'll be required to conduct your mailing following the list owner's specifications. Most owners insist on handling the mailing from within their own operations or through a recognized, bonded mailing service to protect their list's value and to ensure against multiple use or resale of names.

>> Let list owners review and approve your mailer before you send it to the names on their list.

USING MAIL SPECIALISTS

Mailing services go by many names: *direct response specialists, bulk mailers, database managers, mail processors,* and *list managers.* They provide professional assistance in the following areas:

- Merging, updating, and maintaining databases, including deleting duplicate addresses, standardizing addresses, and inserting zip codes, carrier routes, and delivery-point bar code information
- Presorting your list by computer to qualify for the lowest possible postal rate
- Addressing envelopes with inkjet technology; label printing and affixing
- Folding, inserting, and sealing direct mail packages
- Packaging, sacking, and delivering mailings to the post office
- Generating postal reports and certification reports

For the names of direct mail specialists, look in the yellow pages under *Mailing Lists* and *Mailing Services,* or visit the Mailing & Fulfillment Service Association website at www.mfsanet.org.

TIP

To improve the quality of your list, consider renting two lists that reflect your prospect profile and then combine them (called a *merge/purge* operation). Names that appear on both lists are your best prospects. A destination resort may obtain the names of golfers age 35 and over living in a targeted metropolitan area *and* the names of homeowners of target market properties assessed at $500,000 or more. After merging and purging the lists, the resort has a better chance of reaching people with the interests *and* the financial abilities to match the resort's customer profile.

WARNING

When you purchase labels from a list owner, you're *renting*, not buying, the names. Don't try to use the list beyond the scope of your agreement or to duplicate the labels for additional mailings. The list usually includes names that tip off the list owner to misuse. After you conduct your mailing, however, individuals from the rented list may respond to your company for more information. From that point on, you may market to these respondents.

Creating your mailer

The best mailers feature the following materials and information:

>> **A clear offer:** Feature the offer on the envelope, the letter, the letter's post-script, and any additional enclosures.

>> **A free response mechanism:** Allow the customer to respond at no expense, whether through your website, a toll-free number, or a postage-paid card. Be sure to collect complete customer data, including an email address, allowing you to later invite the person to opt in for future digital communications.

TIP

>> **A reply card:** Some people prefer to mail in their responses, even if you also invite a response through a toll-free number or web address. On your reply card, give people a chance to say yes or no. It's counterintuitive, but giving them the chance to decline your offer increases the chance of them accepting it. To save money, contact your post office or a mailing service for help obtaining a business reply mail permit. That way you pay only for the responses you receive rather than paying to place a stamp on every reply card you enclose.

>> **A letter:** People may tell you that no one reads the letter or that the letter just gets in the way of other enclosures, but they're wrong. Unless your mailer takes the form of a postcard or self-mailer, the letter is an essential ingredient of direct mail.

Sending your mailers

The U.S. Postal Service website at www.usps.com offers instructions, advice, resources, postal rate information, and a service called Every Door Direct Mail that distributes mailers to all homes on a postal route without using individual addresses.

The post office gives this advice for sending mailers:

>> For a small mailing, it's probably easier to skip presorting and simply stamp and send your mailers.

>> For larger mailings, a mail service provider can help you select postal services and handle many of the details and much of the legwork.

>> To handle your own large mailing and to qualify for commercial pricing, be prepared to do your own presorting, meet postal regulations, apply for postal permits, complete all required documentation, and follow all the instructions for labeling, packing, and preparing your mailing.

Meeting postal regulations

Mailers must match precise dimensions in order for post office equipment to process them. Before printing your mailer, visit your post office or a mailing professional to make sure that your mailer conforms with regulations.

Take particular care when it comes to your mailer's address panel. Postal equipment reads addresses using high-tech, postal character–recognition equipment. If your recipient address doesn't appear in the correct place on the envelope or if other design elements intrude on the space, your mailer may take longer or cost more to process.

Taking advantage of postage discounts

If you prepare your mailers to meet processing and delivery regulations, the post office rewards you with reduced rates, called *standard mail (A)* or *bulk* rates. To take advantage of these discounts, you must obtain a mail permit, pay an annual bulk mail fee, send at least 200 identical pieces in each mailing (containing no checks or bills), include zip codes on each piece, and presort and bundle the mail following postal specifications.

TIP

To simplify presorting, use a list that's CASS (Coding Accuracy Support System) certified. When you purchase outside lists, ask to see the CASS certificate that the U.S. Postal Service provides.

You can receive further discounts by using zip+4 codes and adding bar codes that support the post office's automated systems. Various kinds of bar codes earn different discounts. Inquire at the post office or ask a mail consultant about the requirements to receive reduced rates.

Specifying postal instructions

When you send bulk mail, you can include instructions, or *endorsements,* that tell the post office what to do with mail that's undeliverable as addressed. Without an endorsement, returned items are thrown away.

TECHNICAL STUFF

An endorsement reading *Return Service Requested* instructs the post office to return the piece with the corrected address or the reason the mail was undeliverable. The item isn't forwarded, but you'll have the information you need to update your list. You can also instruct the post office to discard the piece but notify you of the new address (*Change Service Requested*) or to forward the piece (*Forwarding Service Requested*).

Each endorsement results in an additional charge, so base your instructions on the price you're willing to pay for the service, your confidence in the accuracy of your list, and your mailer's value. If you're sending a valuable gift in each mailer, you'll probably want to request return service.

Following up

REMEMBER

Half of all responses arrive within two weeks of the date that people receive a direct mailing in their mailbox, but keep your expectations in check. A 1 to 3 percent response rate is considered a home run with a purchased or outside list. If you use internal lists that are full of highly qualified names, you can hope for a higher return.

Responding quickly

Don't wait even one week to get back to your direct mail respondents. If you don't think you can handle the volume of responses in a timely manner, send your mailers out in *flights* — groups of several hundred every three or four days. This ensures that the responses are staggered as well. Do the following in your response:

>> **Thank the respondent for the inquiry.** Many people forget that they sent in a card, so refresh their memories.

>> **Provide the item that you promised in your initial mailing, along with a description that highlights its value.**

» **Introduce your business in terms of benefits that matter to the consumer.** See Book 5, Chapter 1 for advice on how features and customer benefits are different.

» **Offer the next step in the buying process.** Include an introductory offer, invitation, coupon for service, or some other means to heighten interest in an effort to convert the prospect into a customer.

Creating a database of respondents

After fulfilling the request, enter the respondent's name into a database for timely future contacts. Within eight weeks, contact prospects a second time by mail, phone, or — if they've invited you to do so — an email newsletter or update. (See the later section "Examining Email Marketing" for reasons *not* to send unauthorized email messages.)

As you enter names into your database, include

» The source of the lead

» The date of the first and each subsequent contact

» The respondent's name, mailing address, and email address

» Information that can help you customize future contacts (such as the answers to questions that you asked on your reply card)

» Additional space in which you can log follow-up activity

If your business has a limited number of prospects, you can maintain this database manually. But if you're managing a larger number of leads, consider using a customer relationship management software or a database management company.

Sending a second mailing to non-respondents

Within 30 days of your first mailing, contact recipients who haven't yet responded. (If you're using an outside list, rent the list for two-time usage and obtain a duplicate set of labels for this purpose.)

TIP

Research proves that following up with nonrespondents increases your overall response rate dramatically. Doing so also gives you much more value for the cost of the list rental because the second-time usage is usually a fraction of the cost of the initial usage. You can also make the second-round contact via email or phone. With any approach, your objective is to build on the first contact and move the prospect closer to buying action.

Keeping your list current

Surface mail address lists become outdated at a rate of almost 2 percent a month. To keep your list current, follow these steps:

>> Request address correction information from the post office. Make the request by including an endorsement on your mailer (see "Specifying postal instructions" earlier in the chapter).

>> Visit www.nationalchangeofaddress.com for information on the NCOA compilation of change-of-address records. When renting mailing lists or using mailing services, ask whether the lists have been updated against this file, which is licensed by the U.S. Postal Service.

>> Confirm the interest levels of those on your list. Every 12 or 18 months, give prospects in your database a chance to opt out of their relationship with you. It may sound crass, but disinterested prospects aren't prospects at all — they're simply a marketing expense.

When adding an opt-out option on your reply cards, consider these examples:

- "Yes, send me whatever great offer you're making in this mailing."

- "I'm not interested at the moment, but please keep my name on your list for future invitations."

- "No, I'm not in the market right now. Please remove my name from your list with the promise that you'll welcome me back in the future if my needs change."

EXAMPLE

Knowing the difference between direct mail and junk mail

Direct mail becomes junk mail when consumers feel that the offer isn't personal. For example, a high-rise apartment resident who gets a mailing for landscaping services automatically determines that it's junk mail. Timely and targeted messages that communicate information and offer good value, however, aren't considered junk mail. As a direct mail marketer, it's your job to toe the line.

Examining Email Marketing

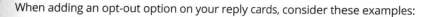

It's only partly coincidental that the preceding section on junk mail is followed by this section on email marketing. The sequence isn't meant to imply that email mass mailings *are* junk mail, but a good many of them belong in the junk mail category, and for legal and marketing reasons, you want to be sure yours don't.

WARNING

SPAM: IS IT OR ISN'T IT?

For the one in millions who may not know, *spam* is the term for electronic junk mail that's sent to a large number of email addresses. None of the addressees requested the information, and most of them feel invaded when they find the messages in their inboxes. Spam is the opposite of opt-in mailings and something to avoid at all costs.

What's more, it's illegal. In 2003, the U.S. government passed the CAN SPAM Act, requiring, among other things, that unsolicited commercial email be clearly identified as a solicitation or advertisement, that it contain a legitimate return email address as well as the sender's physical postal address, that it present a means to opt out or unsubscribe, and that unsubscribe requests be honored within a specific time frame. For a good explanation of the CAN-SPAM ruling and ways to comply, visit the Federal Communications Commission website at www.fcc.gov/guides/spam-unwanted-text-messages-and-email.

You also want to be sure that your email messages get opened trigger clicks, not just to your website but to a landing page where you're ready to capture contact information and fulfill interest with no additional navigation required. This section outlines best practices to follow.

Keeping your email legal and welcome

The unanimous advice from reputable online marketers regarding unsolicited email is this: *When in doubt, don't.* Instead, commit to an opt-in policy and limit your email marketing messages to the following recipients:

>> Those who have opted in by providing their email addresses and asking for more information. In fact, many email marketers now use a double opt-in system that allows a person who opts in to confirm (or deny) the decision by responding to a first email.

>> Friends, colleagues, suppliers, customers, or prospects who have requested similar information in the past.

>> Those who were referred to you by a colleague or by a group related to your business with the assurance that they'd appreciate receiving your information.

WARNING

Don't publish lists of your carefully collected email addresses on your site. You've probably seen company sites that include customer lists, event sites that post participant lists, or athletic event sites that post finish results, including names and email addresses. Opportunistic mailers cruise the Internet looking to cherry-pick from lists like these.

TIP

Also protect your customers by hiding their addresses when you send the same email to a list of recipients. To maintain the privacy of each recipient, enter your own address in the "To" line of your email and enter all recipient addresses as *blind carbon copies* by using the *BCC* address option.

Many Internet service providers won't allow you to email more than 50 people at a time, and breaking a large list into groups can be far too time-consuming. Instead, search online or in your market area for email marketing services. Providers such as Constant Contact and MailChimp are among many that offer safe, simple solutions, mailing advice, and analysis of mailing results.

Rating your email marketing

Email marketing efforts are evaluated based on the following terms, each involving the word *rate:*

>> **Bounce rate:** The percentage of undeliverable addresses that bounce back to the sender because the address doesn't exist (a hard bounce) or the person's inbox is too full or otherwise unavailable (a soft bounce).

>> **Delivery rate:** The percentage of mailers that actually make it through to recipients' inboxes.

>> **Click-through rate (CTR):** The percentage of recipients who click at least one link in the mailer, indicating their interest in the message.

>> **Sharing or forward rate:** The percentage of recipients who click to forward or share the email with others — the next to highest indicator of a successful mailer.

>> **Conversion rate:** The percentage of recipients who take the recommended action by filling out a form, subscribing to a newsletter, downloading a publication, or purchasing your product — the ultimate direct mail success indicator.

>> **Unsubscribe rate:** The percentage of recipients who ask to unsubscribe to your mailer. Honor unsubscribe requests quickly, and watch which mailings trigger the most unsubscribe requests, indicating a lack of interest in your message. At the same time, however, also watch which mailers have the lowest open rates, because many disinterested recipients don't even bother to unsubscribe — they just hit delete, pushing your open rates downward.

Sending email that gets read and gets results

Few marketing environments are less tolerant of intrusion than the email inbox. When you're confident that your email will be welcome in recipient inboxes, use these tips to make each mailing effective:

EXAMPLE

» **Extend a meaningful offer** that you announce in your subject line, explain in your message, and extend through your call to action.

» **Send your email from a real person or from your business**, but never from an anonymous sender like `info@ourcompany`.

» **Use a short subject line** (five to seven words) that headlines your mailer, draws attention, and builds recipient interest. Remember:

  • Use your subject line to alert recipients that the message is aimed specifically at them. For example, "Calling All Sausalito Mac Users" is far more targeted than "Closeout Computer Prices."

  • Keep the presentation of your subject line simple, with upper-lower case type, widely understood words, and absolutely no asterisks, symbols, exclamation marks, or the use of $, all of which trigger recipient suspicion — if your message makes it past spam filters.

» **Personalize your mailings** by using the recipient's name or indicating knowledge of the recipient's location, past purchases, or other distinctions that flag the mailing as a directed message and the opposite of spam.

» **Keep your message simple and easy to read at a glance.** Use up to ten lines of plain text broken into multiple paragraphs or bulleted lists, with few or no images, because most decision makers view email on mobile devices, which don't load images well. If images are important, consider including a link to an HTML web version of the message.

» **Include a clear, easy-to-follow call to action.** Tell people what to do to take advantage of the offer and why to do it now. Foster a sense of urgency and offer a one-click means of taking immediate action. Don't send people to your website and make them click again to reach the offer. Direct recipients to a landing page on your website to fulfill mailer interest.

» **Include an email signature** at the end of every message to present your business information, physical address and phone number, website address, email confidentiality statement, and promotional information such as a newsletter subscription invitation.

» **Include a "share this" along with a "forward to a friend" button.** Doing so allows recipients to post your offer on social networks and let friends invite friends to take advantage of your offer.

Chapter 5

Looking At Brochures, Promotions, Trade Shows, and More

Mass media advertising and direct mailings are the most obvious ways to promote your business, but the communications toolbox includes a long list of other effective communication vehicles. Brochures and fliers, free giveaway items known as *advertising specialties*, product promotions, and trade show appearances are all means of bypassing traditional advertising as you carry your message into the marketplace.

Most of these alternatives come with low price tags, so many small businesses use them with a nothing-ventured-nothing-gained-or-lost attitude. But even though large sums of money are rarely at risk when you print a stack of fliers or order pens imprinted with your name, your reputation is still on the line. This chapter offers advice so that every marketing investment you make — however large or small — works to your advantage while contributing to a favorable image of your business.

Publishing Brochures

People who aren't professional marketers hear the word *collateral* and think of the assets you have to pledge when you're trying to get a bank loan. To marketers, though, collateral means brochures, fliers, fact sheets, sales folders, posters, and all the other forms of printed material that carry your logo, message, and reputation into the marketplace.

Of all forms of collateral, you'll hear the most talk about brochures. It used to be that every business had a brochure. Even today, when most people turn to websites for business information, most marketers feel naked without a printed piece they can hand out. Few, though, can say *why* they need a brochure — and many don't.

You need a brochure if

>> Your business would benefit from a printed piece that you can send ahead of sales presentations to pave the way for your visit or that you can leave afterward to help the person you met with share key points about your business with others who may influence the purchase decision.

>> You're trying to communicate with individuals who aren't easily or affordably reached by mass media but who are likely to pick up literature at information kiosks or other distribution points.

>> Your service or product is complicated and involves details that your prospects need to study in order to make informed decisions.

>> The price of your product and the emotional involvement demanded by its purchase are high enough that prospects will consult with advisors, associates, or spouses before making the decision, in which case they'll benefit from a brochure that conveys your message in your absence.

Before you decide to produce a brochure or any other form of sales literature, see that you can answer yes to these questions:

>> **Do you have an adequate budget?** Can you allocate enough money to create a publication that makes a favorable impression of your business?

>> **Will the publication strengthen your image?** Can you commit to designing, writing, and printing a quality, image-enhancing piece?

>> **Do you have a distribution plan?** Do you know how you'll use the publication? Sales material does no good sitting in a back closet or the trunk of your car.

Differentiating types of brochures

Sales literature runs the gamut from elaborate folders filled with sets of matching fact sheets to laser–printed cards that sit on countertops or in racks. This section helps you sort through the opportunities.

TIP

>> **Capabilities brochure:** This "about our business" piece tells your story, conveys your business personality, and differentiates your offerings from those of your competitors. If you're marketing a professional service business (such as a law firm, accounting firm, financial services firm, or some other consulting business) or a business that offers high-emotion products (such as a home builder or a car company), this type of brochure is a marketing necessity. It gives prospects and customers a tangible piece to review as they deliberate their decision or, post-purchase, reinforce their positive thoughts about your company.

Capability brochures are among the most expensive kinds of brochures to produce, so give yours a keeper quality. A financial planner might include a net worth asset worksheet; a homebuilder may include a checklist for how to get the most value out of a home-building or remodeling budget. The goal is to give prospects a reason to hold onto and refer back to the piece.

>> **Product brochure:** This piece describes a specific offering of your business. This kind of brochure is important when marketing products that require more than spur-of-the-moment consideration, such as those with high prices, those purchased with input from more than one person, and those that involve cost and technical comparisons before a buying decision takes place.

>> **Modular literature:** This involves a number of sheets or brochures that all use a complementary design. This format allows you to assemble a package of easily updated individual pieces that you can mix and match inside a presentation folder or hand out individually, depending on the interests of your prospect and the impression you want to make.

REMEMBER

A modular format is a great approach if your business offers a range of products that you can represent on separate marketing pages, if your price lists or other information change frequently, or if your prospects have widely differing interests or needs. Just be sure that all pieces look like a matched set when they're viewed together but that each one is capable of serving as a stand-alone piece when presented separately.

>> **Rack cards:** These get their name from the fact that they fit into standard brochure racks that hold 4-x-9-inch literature. Some rack cards involve nothing more than a 4-x-9-inch card printed on one or both sides. Others take the form of a single, folded sheet that opens up to a multipanel brochure. Still others include a number of pages folded and stapled down the middle (called *saddle-stitched*). Many businesses create inexpensive rack cards by printing the same image three times on an 8½-x-11-inch sheet of paper (*3-up* is the printing term), which they then cut into three cards of 3⅔ x 8½ inches.

TIP

The most important thing to remember about rack cards is that only the top few inches are immediately visible to the consumer. The rest is hidden under the brochure that sits right in front of yours in the rack. So be sure that your name and a message announcing your customer benefit appear in that small, visible top space.

>> **Fliers:** The least expensive promotional piece you can print is a flier, which usually takes the form of an 8½-x-11-inch sheet of paper printed on one side or both to announce a sale, open house, or limited-time event. In producing a flier, write copy that people can understand at a glance (remember, a flier is a throw-away piece, so don't expect people to hang on every word). Design it following the advice for creating a print ad in Book 5, Chapter 2.

On a good printer or at a quick-print shop you can run off a thousand copies for very little money. For the investment, fliers usually look like what they are — low-cost handouts. The caliber of design and copy, the quality of paper and printing, and the way you get your fliers into circulation, however, can enhance the image they make.

Copywriting

The best brochures talk directly to your target audience, anticipating questions and providing answers before the reader even thinks to ask. Good brochures win your prospects' attention and interest and move those people a step closer to a buying decision.

Put differently, your brochure isn't about what you want to say; it's about what your prospective readers want and need to know in order to take the action you want them to take.

Your brochure text, called *copy*, needs to include the following:

>> **Appropriate headline and subheadlines:** They should convey at a glance what your business is, what it does, and how it provides unique benefits that address the interests of your target readers.

>> **Copy that talks directly to customers:** Use widely understood language that's similar to the way you would talk with them directly if you could — by answering their questions and addressing their solutions as if you were meeting face to face. For example, "Tired of the rising cost to heat your home? We can help. Here's how."

>> **Statements that convey the competitive advantages of your business:** Don't present these advantages as boastful statements but rather as facts that customers can count on and benefit from, including important licenses, registrations, patents, processes, awards, and achievements.

>> **Client lists and testimonials that allow satisfied customers to speak on your behalf:** Feature only statements that are believable (nothing is worse than testimonials that seem scripted) and for which you've obtained permission in writing to use the quotes with attribution.

>> **A clear call to action:** A brochure is a marketing tool. It needs to compel prospects to take the next step in the purchase process, whether you're aiming to prompt reservations, appointments, phone calls, business visits, website visits, or requests for additional information. Use your brochure copy to lead the consumer to the desired decision and then support your request with all the necessary information.

For example, if you're asking for phone calls, include your toll-free number on every page. If you're encouraging website visits, give a reason to visit and prominently display your site address, possibly with a QR code that readers can scan to reach your site quickly (see Book 5, Chapter 2 for the skinny on QR codes). If you want business visits, including your hours of operation, a street address, a map, and directions is a no-brainer.

Arrange your copy to address customer interests in this order: First, identify the customer's problem; second, tell specifically how you can help; and third (and never first), tell about you.

TIP

After you write your copy, don't initial your approval until it's been proofed multiple times. Proof it yourself and have the best writer on your staff proof it. Have a great friend or best customer read it. Proof it for typos, of course, but also for credibility and persuasiveness.

REMEMBER

Even if your brochure is intended for new customers, be sure it will ring true to those who know your business well. Brochures are read most carefully by people who are ready to finalize or who have just completed a purchase. By writing your brochure with committed consumers in mind, you minimize the tendency to oversell and instead focus on the benefits and promises that customers believe they can count on from your business.

Designing and printing brochures

Only a few years ago, design decisions revolved completely around budgets. Either you could afford professional printing or you couldn't. The same either-or option held true for printing brochures in full color over black and white and for using photos rather than easier-to-reproduce illustrations.

Today, between your own color printer and an ever-growing list of online brochure-production resources, design decisions center less on what you can afford and more on what image you want your brochure to convey. Effective brochures contribute to a positive image of your company by presenting a design and message consistent with the reputation and brand of your business.

For top-quality printing of highly customized brochures, brick-and-mortar printers are still the top choice. But for producing standard-sized brochures on tight budgets, online resources are increasingly the way to go.

Open a search engine and type in "brochure printing online" to find sites that allow you to use brochure templates or to upload your own customized brochure design file. You choose the quantity, pay the surprisingly affordable price, and receive your order within days. For a comparison of top online printing sites, see http://online-printing-services-review.toptenreviews.com.

For a quick comparison of using local printers versus online services, see Table 5-1.

TABLE 5-1   Local Printers versus Online Printing Sites

Local Printers	Online Printing Sites
Customized printing of your original design	Printing from your uploaded brochure design file or from your choice of a range of templates, not only for brochures but for all forms of printed sales material
Convenient location proximate to your business	Online service with lower pricing due to the lack of bricks and mortar overhead
Personal service from people familiar with you and your business	Convenient access online whenever and from wherever you wish, sometimes but not always backed by personal assistance
Your choice of paper and design features, including unusual sizes, folds, cuts, and special effects	A range of templates, sizes, and papers from which to choose
The option of extremely quick turnaround, for a price	Quick turnaround plus shipping time
Assurance of a completely original piece	Templates can result in brochures that lack originality or reflection of your business and brand image

Here are a couple steps to take and issues to consider in the design and printing phases of creating your brochures:

>> Match the quality of paper, printing, and design to your brand image, your marketing message, and your brochure purpose.

>> Be sure your business name and contact information are prominent on the brochure back. For rack brochures, be sure your name is visible along the upper portion of the front cover. For multipage brochures, include contact information on every single page or two-page spread.

REMEMBER

If you don't have design skills within your company, don't risk trying to create your own brochure. Even customizing a template involves an eye for design and a level of production skill. Invest in the talents of a graphic artist or choose a print shop that provides design assistance so you end up with a unique piece that reflects your business and message.

Getting brochures into the marketplace

Great brochures can't address customer questions or strengthen your company's image if they're sitting in a storage room, so don't hoard them.

Printing the first brochure is the most expensive. After that, you're paying only for ink and paper, so print enough brochures to ensure that you won't feel a need to protect your supply. Then follow these steps to get them into circulation:

>> Send copies to customer, media, and industry contacts.

>> Convert the brochure to a PDF and then add the PDF to your website as well as social media sites.

>> Send a copy in advance of face-to-face meetings so that your prospect gets a sense of you before meeting you.

TIP

>> Contract with a brochure distribution service to maintain supplies of your brochure in brochure racks such as those in visitor welcome centers. For the names of services in your area, contact the International Association of Professional Brochure Distributors at www.iapbd.org.

>> Use your brochure as a step in your sales process, sending a copy, along with a customized letter, as a follow-up to in-person meetings and as a way of staying in touch with pending prospects.

Making the Most of Newsletters

Unlike brochures, which deliver marketing messages to target audiences, newsletters are informal, friend-to-friend communications. They reach customers and those who've indicated an interest in your business with newsworthy information, useful updates, reminders of what your business does, and interesting, helpful ideas.

Newsletters can accomplish the following for your business:

>> Build credibility and reputation

>> Provide a means of frequent communication

>> Deliver news from your company and your industry

>> Answer questions, usually through a question-and-answer column

>> Offer tips that enhance your company's credibility while also building customer confidence and loyalty

>> Share profiles of employees, customers, and success stories

>> Convey industry information (with permission, of course)

These sections point out what you need to know if you plan on using newsletters to market your business.

Planning your newsletters

Newsletters work only when they're distributed on a consistent basis, which means you have to commit to the long haul before you produce the first issue. As you make your decision, consider the following:

>> **Define the purpose of your newsletter.** Who is it for? What does your target audience need and want to know? What kind of information will you share? Know what you expect from your newsletter before you design or write the first issue.

>> **Establish how often you'll produce and send your newsletter.** How often are you and your staff able to get a newsletter assembled and distributed? How often is your customer interested in hearing from you?

>> **Determine your initial mailing list.** You may start with a list that includes customers, prospects, suppliers, and other business friends. Then grow your

list by featuring a free newsletter subscription invitation on your website and in direct mailers and other marketing pieces.

>> **Decide how you'll deliver your newsletter.** How many will you send and how often? Will you handle the task in-house or hire assistance from writing, design, and mail service pros? Will you print and send the newsletters by surface mail or produce digital newsletters to send by email? Tally the costs and be sure you can afford to commit to the project for at least a full year.

Packing newsletters with useful content

Here's great news for small budget marketers: The most effective newsletters look inexpensive, newsy, and current, which translates to the fact that newsletters are among the most economical of marketing materials.

Whether you're creating printed or digital newsletters, consider the following points:

>> **Stick with a simple format issue after issue.** The more your newsletter looks like a highly designed marketing piece, the less it looks newsy.

>> **Feature many short items rather than a few long ones.**

>> **Include invitations that require reader response to deepen customer relationships and to help you gauge the effectiveness of your newsletter.** For instance, if you announce a new product, offer to provide trial samples on request.

WARNING

>> **Include valid dates when presenting time-specific offers.** Prospects may read printed newsletters in particular well into the future, long after your offer has expired.

>> **Use your newsletter to promote reasons to visit your business or website.** For example, a resort may include this item:

EXAMPLE

Our new online reservation service is off to a great start. More than half of our visitors click to view room photos and floor plans, and 38 percent of those who view our property online make a reservation request. If you haven't visited our site lately, go to www.ourhotel.com. Be sure to click to enter our web-only sweepstakes for a free weekend stay. Also, if you'd rather receive our newsletter electronically than by mail, just click the e-newsletter request icon and we'll transfer your mailing information to our confidential electronic file. Either way, we look forward to sending you quarterly updates, special packages, and resort news.

EXAMPLE

>> **Combine sales messages with news updates so that readers view your newsletter as more than a promotional mailing.** For example:

Rocky Mountain vacations are more popular than they've been in years, based on the number of toll-free reservation calls and website visits. Calls in April 2015 were up 22 percent over April 2014, with Thanksgiving and Christmas reservations already ahead of pace. As soon as you know your vacation dates, call us at 1-800-555-5555 or click to make an online reservation so we can reserve your stay.

>> **Prominently feature your business identification and contact information.** On printed newsletters, include your logo, phone number, mailing address, email address, and website address on every page of every issue to encourage communications. On digital newsletters, include your street address and phone number so people can follow up in person.

TIP

MailChimp features a library of free, downloadable templates you can use when producing printed newsletters. Go to www.mailchimp.com.

For help producing digital newsletters, see the advice from widely recognized e-newsletter expert Michael Katz in the nearby sidebar, "Tips from a gargantuan, elephantine fan of e-newsletters."

Producing and circulating e-newsletters

People subscribe to online newsletters because they want

>> Work-related news from their employer or business organization, or news pertaining to their personal interests and hobbies.

>> News about prices, sales, and special offers.

>> Advance notice of upcoming events.

The key word is *news*. Keep your newsletter current, informative, relevant, and to the point. Also keep the language casual — as if you're talking one on one — and easy to skim through in a matter of seconds.

Formatting your e-newsletter

The first rule of newsletter production is to know the purpose and frequency of your newsletter and stick to what you promise to provide. The second rule is to create a newsletter that's easy to open and read on the greatest number of screens, including mobile devices, where most executives and others now get their email.

Using plain text in your newsletter makes it easy to assemble and easy to open on all devices. Using HTML is more complicated, but it allows you to present colors, fonts, and graphic images and to track the rate at which recipients open your mail or click through to links. HTML comes with some cautions, however. For one thing, spam filters sometimes block all-HTML email messages or HTML messages with a heavy images-to-text ratio.

TIP

If you opt for an HTML format, consider these tips:

>> Make life easy by typing your newsletter into a preformatted template, available through email services or findable through an online search for "free email templates."

>> Consult a web designer to set up at least your first issue.

>> Contract with an email marketing service such as Constant Contact, which offers information and a trial offer at www.constantcontact.com. Another email marketing service is MailChimp. Check out www.mainchimp.com for more information.

>> Send your newsletter in both HTML and plain-text formats so people can read it one way or the other. As an alternative, set up your newsletter opt-in form so that people can choose the format they want to receive at the time they subscribe.

TIP

Companies such as Constant Contact, Emma, Delivra, AddressTwo, and ExactTarget have attractive, customizable templates on their websites that you can format without a working knowledge of HTML.

Following opt-in rules when sending e-newsletters

Don't send unsolicited newsletters, ever. Instead, take the time to inform people about your newsletter and invite them to become free subscribers. Follow these guidelines as you build your electronic mailing list:

>> Make it easy to sign up by simply clicking to open a subscription form on your website's home or landing page.

>> Reply to each subscription request by welcoming the subscriber, describing the newsletter's purpose and frequency, and providing an easy way for the recipient to confirm interest or unsubscribe.

>> Don't reveal the names on your distribution list. Your software should allow you to send bulk emails so that recipients can't see who else is on the same list.

>> Test your newsletter by emailing it to a few email accounts before sending the full distribution. Use the test to check the formatting and to be sure the links all work.

>> Send the newsletter in batches if your distribution list is large. By sending a portion of the list each day instead of, say, a weeklong period, you can better manage the responding emails and phone calls.

>> Include an opt-out function and promptly honor unsubscribe requests. Otherwise, you're in violation of CAN SPAM regulations, which you can read about in Book 5, Chapter 4.

Finding Marketing Opportunities throughout Your Business

For all the money that small businesses spend on marketing, they often look right past free opportunities to add marketing messages to their own products, vehicles, and more. With the right moves, which the following sections discuss, you can amplify your marketing message with practically no investment at all.

Turning your packages into ad vehicles

Every time you package a product for a customer, you're creating a vehicle that can give your marketing message a free ride. You incur practically no cost when you add an in-pack advertising message that's certain to reach a valid prospect because the recipient has already made a purchase.

Manufacturers can affix or print ads right onto product cartons or enclose materials in the box to invite the purchase of accessories, warranties, service programs, or other offers. Repair businesses can affix service labels that remind owners who to call for future needs.

EXAMPLE

Retailers can drop into each shopping bag an invitation to join a frequent customer club, to request automatic delivery of future orders, or to redeem a special offer on a future purchase (called a *bounce-back offer* because it aims to bounce a customer back into your business). For example, a pool or hot tub chemical supply company can enclose a flier offering a monthly service program, automatic twice-a-year chemical delivery, or an annual maintenance visit.

Building business with gift certificates

It's astonishing how many small businesses make a gift certificate request seem like an inconvenience, when actually it's the sincerest form of customer compliment. If someone wants to give your business offerings as a gift, roll out the red carpet. Here's how:

>> **Create a gift certificate form.** This form can convey the gift's details while also enhancing the gift's perceived value simply by its creative presentation. Use quality paper, a professional design that matches your company image, and a look that's appropriate to the nature of your business offering.

>> **Package the certificate in an envelope or a gift box.** The gift certificate buyer is a current customer making an effort to bring a new person into your business. Reward the effort with a package that flatters both the gift giver and your business.

>> **When the gift is redeemed, get in touch with both parties.** Reinforce your relationship with the gift buyer by sharing that the certificate was redeemed and that you and your staff were flattered by the gift choice. Send a separate mailing to the gift recipient, welcoming the person to your business and enclosing an offer such as a free subscription to your newsletter, a special new-customer invitation, a frequent-shopper club membership, or some other reason for the person to become a loyal customer of your business.

>> **If the deadline is nearing on an unredeemed certificate, contact the gift recipient.** Offer a short extension or invite a phone or online order to build goodwill rather than let the certificate lapse.

Getting good use out of business cards

Even as talk of business-card obsolescence rages, people are ordering more cards today than ever before. That's because business cards are still the tools that break the ice, make good impressions, and ease follow-up contact for you and your business.

Even the highest-quality business cards cost only a few cents each, and the price keeps going down with each new card-printing service that opens online. You'll be hard-pressed to find a more economical way to get your name and brand image into your marketplace.

To create a business card that makes a strong statement, use a professional design, a typestyle and ink selection that match the graphic image of your brand, quality paper, good printing, and a straight cut (nothing looks cheaper than a card with a crooked cut). Follow this advice:

TIP

>> **Invest a few hours with a graphic designer to achieve a distinctive, professional design that enhances your company image.** Unless you're certain of their design talents, don't ask staff members or quick-print shop designers to create your card.

For online production, compare options at www.toptenreviews.com. Click Small Business and then Business Card Printing.

>> **Be sure your card features your business name and logo, your phone number, and your contact information in a type size that people can easily read.** Also include either a slogan or tagline or a short description of your business offerings.

>> **Keep your card design simple.** Use a standard size that's convenient for recipients to file, and present contact information in a typeface that scanning software can read.

>> **Print cards for each employee.** Business cards are great for staff morale, and when employees use their cards to introduce your business to their friends and business contacts, you recoup the cost of the cards many times over.

TIP

If you print the back of your card with simple directions or other information, keep your logo, name, title, and contact information on the front. Many people scan business cards or keep them in files in which only the front side is visible.

Making the most of advertising specialties

Advertising specialties are ubiquitous and inexpensive mind-joggers for your business. They include giveaways such as pens, pencils, refrigerator magnets, mouse pads, matchbooks, notepads, paperweights, pocketknives, calendars, calculators, T-shirts, golf towels, and a long list of other items that can be printed, engraved, embossed, or emblazoned with a business logo.

Most specialty advertising items are cheap — and they often look it. When investing in an advertising specialty, follow this advice:

>> Select items that relate to your business and that advance a reminder of the benefits you offer.

>> Choose items that your customers want or need and things that they'll notice, pick up, and keep for at least a short time.

>> Opt only for items that add to your business image, not detract from it.

>> Decide how to feature your name on the item. If the item is targeted for prospects or clients who value quality and exclusivity, make your name subtle and scaled to the item rather than in a gaudy design that monopolizes the item and assures its quick trip to the trash can.

>> Know how you'll distribute the items before you place an order for advertising specialties.

For information on the unbelievably wide range of specialties available, search online for "ad specialties and promotional items."

Choosing and Using Trade Shows

Trade shows bring together businesses, suppliers, customers, and media representatives for a daylong or multiday extravaganza of selling, socializing, entertaining, product previewing, and competitive sleuthing.

Attending trade shows is a great way to maintain customer contacts, introduce suppliers and customers to your business, develop and maintain media relations, and stay on top of industry and competitive developments. The drawback — and it's a big one — is that regardless of your industry, you have a long list of trade shows from which to choose.

Because attendance at even one show costs a significant amount of time, money, and energy, choose cautiously, using these guidelines:

>> Study shows carefully. Track the number of presenters and attendees over recent years (if the number is going up, it probably indicates a well-regarded show). Also see whether leading media outlets are among the sponsors, another indication of the show's reputation.

>> Decide whether you need to invest in a booth or whether you can achieve visibility by buying an ad in the show guide, making a presentation, hosting a reception, or simply working the floor.

>> If you host a booth, know whom you want to attract to your booth, what you want to communicate, and what action you want to inspire.

>> Know how you'll capture trade show visitor information and how you'll follow up with your trade show contacts.

Table 5-2 presents advice to follow and actions to avoid.

TABLE 5-2   ## Do's and Don'ts for Trade Show Attendance

Do's	Don'ts
Do prospect before the show, using letters, direct mailers, phone calls, and email to encourage prospects to visit your booth.	Don't count on prospects to seek you out or find you on their own. Most shows simply have too many distractions.
Do arrive at the show with preset appointments for meetings with your top-choice media reps, journalists, customer prospects, and vendors.	Don't count on spontaneous encounters with key contacts at the show. Take the time in advance to introduce yourself and schedule appointments.
Do use your staff well. Be sure they wear business identification or, better yet, logo shirts or uniforms. Present with your best presenters and turn other team members loose to meet with suppliers and do competitive research.	Don't let your whole team hang out in your show booth, which gives the impression of a dull spot. Instead, have ongoing client or media meetings underway, a greeter visiting with passers-by in the entry area, and other staff members out working the show.
Do have moderately priced handouts and logo items for distribution, along with a means for collecting prospect names for follow-up. After the show, send a thoughtful letter and gift to prospects who were serious enough to complete a short form to qualify their interest.	Don't set up for trick-or-treaters. You don't have to give something to every visitor, and you shouldn't waste money (or weigh down your prospects) by giving out expensive or heavy literature or catalogs. Prospects will appreciate follow-up packages delivered upon their return from the show.
Do invest in a professionally designed booth that reflects your business image and current marketing message.	Don't try to do it on a tight budget by using a self-designed booth and do-it-yourself graphics.
Do use lights, banners, moving displays, bright colors, floor carpeting, and counters to break your booth into parts, along with other devices that draw attention and make your booth look like a hub of activity.	Don't be bland and don't expect a banner with your logo to double as a booth design. You need ad enlargements, graphics, and huge, colorful photos to draw attention to your booth.
Do gather competitive intelligence. Visit other booths to get brochures and listen in on presentations. Beyond that, position your staff at buffets, in areas where people are making calls, and other locations where show attendees are talking about their businesses.	Don't be vulnerable to eavesdroppers. Reserve private rooms, hospitality suites, or other places to make presentations to clients or to gather your staff to share trade show intelligence. When you're done, take all your notes with you so they aren't available for others to see.

Building Sales through Promotions

The purpose of a promotion is to create a desired consumer action over a short period. Businesses stage promotions to attract new customers, to win back lapsed customers, to alter customer buying patterns (for example, by prompting larger or more frequent purchases), to develop business during slow seasons or hours, or — increasingly — to attract customers into social media networks for easy and ongoing interaction.

Regardless of the promotion purpose, the objective is accomplished by offering one of the following types of action incentives:

>> **Price savings:** Incentives include percentage discounts, two-for-one deals, and other appealing reductions. The bigger the incentive, the more attractive it is to the consumer, of course. But be careful to come up with an offer that can inspire customers without giving away your store or attracting interest only from those who want the deal, with no interest in a long-term relationship.

>> **Samples:** Businesses introducing new products or trying to win over competitors' customers offer samples or free trials to prove their advantage and get their products into circulation. First, be sure that your product shows well in comparative tests. Second, accompany the sample with a bounce-back offer that prompts the customer to make an after-sample purchase or to take a follow-up action (for example, subscribing to your newsletter) to cement the new relationship.

>> **Events and experiences:** Events draw crowds, spurring increased sales and sometimes even attracting media coverage. Use product launches, VIP visits, new inventory arrivals, business milestones, holidays, and other occasions as reasons to invite customers and prospects into your business.

>> **Coupons and rebates:** A *coupon* provides an offer that a customer can redeem at the time of purchase. A *rebate* provides an offer that a customer can redeem following the purchase, usually by completing and sending in a form. Less than 2 percent of coupons in circulation are redeemed, yet coupons remain a popular promotion staple. They catch reader attention when placed in ads, and they provide a measurable way to reward customers with price reductions. When using coupons, protect your profitability through small-print advisories that state expiration dates and that the coupon *is not valid with other special offers.*

Before staging a promotion, be clear about each of the following points:

>> The objective you're working to achieve.

>> How you'll measure success.

>> The target audience that you intend to influence with the promotion.

>> The incentive you'll offer and why you're confident that it's capable of motivating your target audience.

» How you'll inform and train your staff to handle promotion response. Nothing is worse for a consumer than to respond to a promotion or to arrive at what's billed as a promotional event only to discover that no one at the host business seems to know anything about it.

TIP

Keep the promotion description simple. If you can't explain the promotion and incentive in a single sentence, it's too complicated for the quick response you want to generate, and as a result, the idea almost certainly won't fly.

6 Measuring Results

Contents at a Glance

Chapter 1

Delving into Data

W *eb analytics* is the practice of analyzing performance and business statistics for a website, social media marketing, and other online marketing efforts to better understand user behavior and improve results. Some may call web analytics more art than science; to others, it's black magic.

The amount of data that can be acquired from online marketing efforts vastly exceeds the amount available using traditional offline methods. That statement alone makes online marketing, including social media, an attractive form of public relations and advertising.

In the best of all possible worlds, the results of your marketing efforts should appear as increased profits — in other words, as an improved bottom line with a nice return on investment (ROI). You're more likely to achieve this goal if you make analytics part of a process of continuous quality improvement.

TIP

Before getting mired in the swamp of online marketing data, assess the performance of your hub website. If you aren't making a profit from that core investment, it doesn't matter whether you fill the conversion funnel (see Book 2, Chapter 2) with fantastic traffic from social media, exhibit a soaring click-through rate, or tally revenues through the roof. If you aren't sure how your hub site is performing, use the tools in this chapter and ask your web developer and bookkeeper for help.

Planning a Measurement Strategy

The basic principle "You can't manage what you don't measure" applies doubly to the online universe. Do you know whether Facebook or LinkedIn drives more traffic to your site? Whether more people buy after reading a blog post about pets than after reading a blog post about plants? If not, you're simply guessing at how to expend your precious marketing dollars and time.

To make the most of your effort, return to the goals and objectives you established on your Social Media Marketing Goals statement (see Book 2, Chapter 2). Ask yourself what you need to measure to determine your accomplishments. Would interim measurements help you decide whether a particular aspect of a social media campaign is working?

For instance, if one of your goals is to substitute social media marketing for paid advertising, compare performance between the two. If you initiated social media activities to improve a ranking on Search Engine Results Pages (SERP), you must measure your standing by keywords at different times. In either case, of course, you might want to track visitors to the site who arrive from either a social media referral or from natural search to see whether they continue to a purchase.

Fortunately, computers do one thing extremely well: count. Chances are good that if you have a question, you can find an answer.

WARNING

Because computers count just about everything, you can quickly drown in so much data that you find it impossible to gather meaningful information, let alone make a decision. The last thing you need is a dozen reports that you don't have time to read.

Unless you have a large site, monitoring statistics monthly or quarterly is usually sufficient. You may check more often when you first initiate a specific social media campaign or another online marketing activity, if you invest significant amounts of money or effort into a new campaign, or if you support your site by way of advertising.

REMEMBER

On your Social Media Marketing Plan (see Book 2, Chapter 3), add your choice of measurement parameters and analytical tools, as well as the names of the people who will be responsible for creating reports. Schedule the frequency of analytical review on your Social Media Activity Calendar (see Book 2, Chapter 3 for more on that as well).

These sections take a closer look at how you can strategize and include measurement to your Social Media Marketing Plan.

Monitoring versus measuring

This chapter only discusses quantitative data as part of the measurement process. Use monitoring tools to review such qualitative data from social media as

>> The degree of customer engagement

>> The nature of customer dialog, sometimes called *sentiment*

>> Your brand reputation on a social network

>> The quality of relationships with your target market

>> The extent of participation in online conversations

>> Positioning in your industry versus your competitors

If you have no monitoring tools in place yet, turn to Book 2, Chapter 1.

REMEMBER

"Real people" usually review subjective monitoring data to assess such ineffable qualities as the positive or negative characteristics of consumer posts, conversational tone, and brand acknowledgment. Notwithstanding Hal in the movie *2001: A Space Odyssey*, analytical software with the supple linguistic sophistication of the human brain isn't available . . . yet.

Setting aside the squishy qualitative data, you still have two types of quantitative data to measure:

>> **Internal performance measurements:** Measure the effectiveness of your social media, other marketing efforts, and website in achieving your objectives. Performance measurements include such parameters as traffic to your social pages or website, the number of people who click-through to your hub presence, which products sell best, and *conversion rate,* or the percentage of visitors who buy or become qualified leads.

>> **Business measurements:** Primarily dollar-based parameters — costs, revenues, profits — that go directly to your business operations. Such financial items as the cost of customer or lead acquisition, average dollar value per sale, the value assigned to leads, the break-even point, and ROI fall into this category.

Deciding what to measure

Most of the key performance indicators (KPI) and business criteria you measure fall into one of the following categories:

>> **Traffic:** You must know the number and nature of visitors to any of the sites that are part of your web presence.

>> **Leads:** Business-to-business (B2B) companies, service professionals, and companies that sell expensive, complex products often close their sales offline. Online efforts yield prospects, many of whom — you hope — will become qualified leads as they move down the conversion funnel.

>> **Financials:** Costs, sales, revenue, and profits are the essential components of business success. Analytics let you track which sales arrive from which sources and how much revenue they generate.

>> **Search marketing:** As discussed in Book 2, Chapter 4, optimizing social media can improve visibility in search engine results. Not only do many social media sites appear in search results, but your hub site also gains valuable inbound links from direct and indirect referrals.

>> **Other business objectives:** You may need customized analytics to track goals and objectives that don't fall into the other categories.

Book XI, Chapter 2 discusses KPIs in depth.

Don't plan on flying to the moon based on the accuracy of any statistical web data. For one thing, definitions of parameters differ by tool. Does a new visitor session start after someone has logged off for 24 minutes or 24 hours? For another, results in real-time tools sometimes oscillate unpredictably.

TIP

If a value differs from what you expected, try running your analytics again later or run them over a longer period to smooth out irregularities.

Relative numbers are more meaningful than absolute ones. Is your traffic growing or shrinking? Is your conversion rate increasing or decreasing? Focus on ratios or percentages to make the data more meaningful. Suppose that 10 percent of a small number of viewers to your site converted to buyers before you started a blog, compared to only 5 percent of a larger number of viewers afterward. What does that tell you?

Figure 1-1 shows what most businesses are measuring online. You can find a lot of research about typical performance on different statistical parameters. Though it's nice to know industry averages for benchmarking purposes, the only statistics that matter are your own.

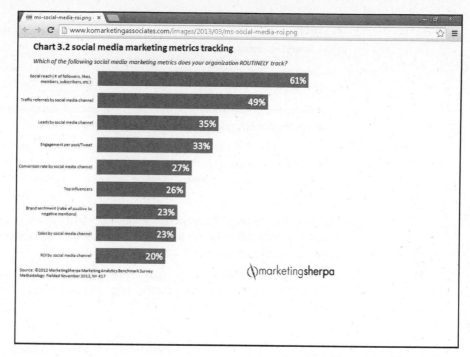

FIGURE 1-1:
Social media
marketing
metrics routinely
tracked by
businesses.

TIP

Regardless of how you go about the measurement process, you must define success before you begin. Without some sort of target value, you can't know whether you've succeeded. Keep your handy, dandy Social Media Marketing Goals (see Book 2, Chapter 2) accessible while you review this chapter.

A good measurement strategy determines how much data to leave out, as well as how much to measure. Unless you have a huge site or quite a complex marketing campaign, you can focus on just a few parameters.

Establishing responsibility for analytics

Chances are good that your business isn't large enough to field an entire team whose sole responsibility is statistical analysis. Even if you aren't running an employment agency for statisticians, you can still take a few concrete steps to ensure that the right data is collected, analyzed, and acted on:

1. **Ask your marketing person (Is that you?) to take responsibility for defining what needs to be measured based on business objectives.**

   Consult with your financial advisor, if necessary.

Delving into Data

2. **Have your programmer, web developer, or go-to IT person select and install the analytics tools that will provide the data you need.**

   Make ease of use, flexibility, and customizability important factors in the decision.

3. **If it isn't part of the analytical package, ask your IT person to set up a one-page** *dashboard* **(a graphical** *executive summary* **of key data).**

   Try the Google Analytics dashboard, shown in Figure 1-2, or the HubSpot dashboard for multiple media, shown in Figure 1-3. Dashboards display essential results quickly, preferably over easy-to-change time frames of your choice.

4. **Let your marketing, IT, and content management folks work together to finalize the highest priority pages (usually landing pages and pages within your conversion funnels).**

   When possible, set up tracking codes for links coming from social marketing pages. IT should test to ensure that the data collection system works and adjust it as needed.

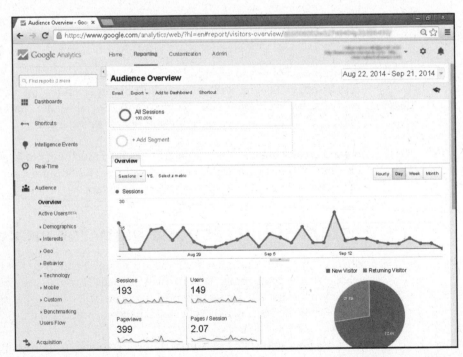

FIGURE 1-2:
A typical Google Analytics dashboard displays key web statistics.

Source: www.google.com

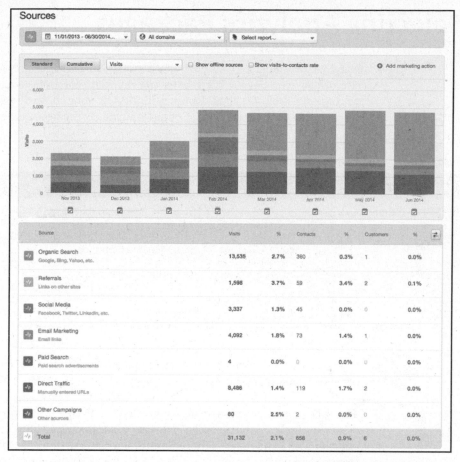

Reproduced with permission of HubSpot, Inc.

FIGURE 1-3:
A HubSpot page showing the distribution of visits by source.

5. **Your marketing person can be responsible for regularly monitoring the results, adjusting marketing campaigns, and reporting to you and other stakeholders.**

    Have your IT person validate the data and audit tracking tags at least twice a year — they can easily get out of sync.

6. **Always integrate the results of your social media and online marketing efforts with offline marketing and financial results for a complete picture of what's happening with your business.**

    Compare against your business goals and objectives and modify as needed.

TECHNICAL STUFF

Aggregate all analytics into one place. You're unlikely to find a premade dashboard that includes everything you need to measure for your specific campaigns. Your programmer may have to export data into Excel, PDF, or email format; save it all in one place; and then build a custom spreadsheet to generate combined reports for your review.

Delving into Data

Selecting Analytics Packages

Ask your developer or web host which statistical packages are available for your site. Unless you have a fairly large site or need real-time data, one of the free packages in Table 1-1 should work well. Review your choices to select the best fit for your needs. In many cases, Google Analytics is the best answer.

TABLE 1-1   **Free Analytics Packages**

Name	URL	Notes
AFS Analytics	`www.afsanalytics.com/`	Graphical display; real-time, adjustable time frame
Clicky	`http://clicky.com`	All the basics for a single website; 3,000 daily page view max; offers paid options
Google Analytics	`www.google.com/ analytics`	Can include social media
Piwik	`http://piwik.org`	Open source analytics

WARNING

If your developer or web host tells you that you don't need statistics, find another provider. Measuring success without easy access to statistics is nearly impossible.

The specific suite of statistical results that a package offers may influence your choice of tools. Unfortunately, you can't count on getting comparable results when you mix and match different tools. Each one defines parameters differently (for example, what constitutes a repeat visitor). Consequently, you need to watch trends, not absolute numbers.

Of this list, you should start with Google Analytics. If you have a large site with heavy traffic or extensive reporting requirements, free packages — even Google Analytics — may not be enough. If so, consider using `www.inc.com/ guides/12/2010/11-best-web-analytics-tools.html`.

REMEMBER

Not all marketing channels use the same yardstick — nor should they. Your business objectives drive your choice of channels and therefore your choice of yardsticks.

Some paid statistical packages are hosted on a third-party server. Others are designed for installation on your own server. Generally, higher-end paid statistical solutions offer several benefits:

- >> Real-time analytics (no waiting for results)

- >> Sophisticated reporting tools by domain or across multiple domains, departments, or enterprises

- >> Customizable data-mining filters

- >> Path-through-site analysis, tracking an individual user from entry to exit

- >> Integrated traffic and store statistics

- >> Integrated qualitative and quantitative analytics for multiple social media services

- >> Analysis of downloaded PDF, video, audio, or another file type

- >> Mapping host addresses to company names and details

- >> Clickstream analysis to show which sites visitors arrive from and go to

REMEMBER

Don't collect information for information's sake. Stop when you have enough data to make essential business decisions.

Reviewing analytical options for social media

Depending on what you're trying to measure, you may need data from some of the analytical tools available internally from a particular social media channel or statistics from social bookmarking sites such as AddToAny (`http://www.addtoany.com`) or from URL shorteners, discussed in the following section.

Table 1-2 summarizes which social media services integrate with Google Analytics for traffic monitoring purposes and which also offer their own internal performance statistics.

TABLE 1-2   **Analytics for Specific Social Networks**

Website	URL	Integrates with Google Analytics?	Own Analytics Package?
Facebook Page Insights	`www.facebook.com/help/336893449723054`	Yes	Yes
Google+ Platform Insights	`https://developers.google.com/+/features/analytics`	Yes	Yes

(continued)

Delving into Data

TABLE 1-2 *(continued)*

Website	URL	Integrates with Google Analytics?	Own Analytics Package?
LinkedIn Analytics Tab	`http://help.linkedin.com/app/answers/detail/a_id/26032/~/analytics-tab-for-company-pages`	Yes	Yes
Meetup Group Stats	`http://help.meetup.com/customer/portal/articles/868781-meetup-group-stats`	Yes	Yes
Twitter Analytics	`https://analytics.twitter.com/about`	Yes	Yes
YouTube Analytics	`www.youtube.com/analytics`	Yes	Yes (must have an account with a channel)

REMEMBER

Register for free optional statistics whenever you can.

Selecting a URL-shortening tool for statistics

One type of free optional statistics is particularly handy: traffic generated by shortened URLs, as described in Book 2, Chapter 1. Be sure to select a free shortener that offers analytics, such as

>> **Bitly** (`http://bitly.com`): A free account (registration required) to track statistics from shortened links

>> **Google URL Shortener** (`http://goo.gl`): Google's free URL shortener

>> **Ow.ly** (`http://ow.ly`): Hootsuite's free URL shortener

TIP

To access a shortcut to results for links shortened with Bitly, paste the short URL into a browser, followed by the plus sign (+) (for example, `https://bitly.com/Xv1TDI+`). A page appears showing how many clicks the short URL received. After you sign into your Bitly account, you can see additional metrics, such as those shown in Figure 1-4.

TIP

You can use a dashboard tool like Netvibes to see all your stats in one convenient place. See Book 1, Chapter 4 for more details about dashboards.

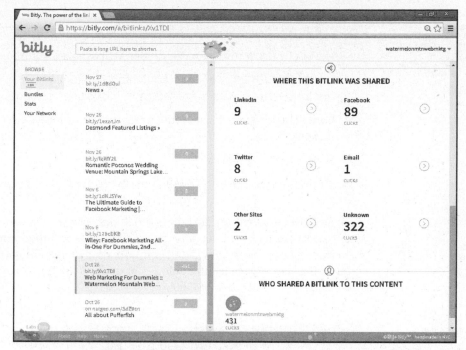

FIGURE 1-4:
After you log into your account, Bitly offers several displays for traffic statistics for a shortened URL.

Getting Started with Google Analytics

Google Analytics is so popular that it justifies its own discussion. This free, high-quality analytics tool works well for most website owners. It now incorporates many social media services as part of its analysis and scales well from tiny sites to extremely large ones.

TIP

Start with the free Google Analytics and switch to an enterprise-level solution when and if your web effort demands it.

Among its many advantages, Google Analytics offers

>> More in-depth analysis than most other free statistical packages

>> Plenty of support, as Table 1-3 shows

>> Easy-to-set specific time frames to compare results to other years

>> Many of the more sophisticated features of expensive software, such as path-through-site information

>> Customization of the dashboard display

» Conversion funnel visualization, as Figure 1-5 shows

» Analysis by *referrer* (where traffic to your site has linked from) or search term

» Tracking of such key performance indicators as returning visitors and *bounce rate* (percentage of visitors who leave without visiting a second page)

» Customizable reports to meet your needs that you can have emailed automatically to you

» Social analytics capabilities

» Seamless integration with AdWords, the Google pay-per-click program

Google provides steps for installing Analytics at `www.google.com/analytics`. This task definitely isn't for anyone who is faint-of-programming-heart. Get help from your developer. For detailed information on installing Google Analytics, refer to the help sites listed in Table 1-3 or go to `https://support.google.com/analytics/?hl=en#topic=3544906`.

TABLE 1-3   **Helpful Google Analytics Resource URLs**

Name	URL	Description
"15 Google Analytics Tricks to Maximize Your Marketing Campaign"	`www.forbes.com/sites/ jaysondemers/2014/08/20/ 15-google-analytics- tricks-to-maximize- your-marketing-campaign/`	Useful Google Analytics tips and tricks
Analytics Academy	`https://analyticsacademy. withgoogle.com/explorer`	Google Analytics Academy courses
About Social Analytics	`https://support.google.com/ analytics/answer/1683971?hl`	Guide to the features of Google's social media tools
Analytics Help Center	`https://support.google.com/ analytics/?hl=en - topic=3544906`	Google Analytics support
Google Analytics Blog	`http://analytics.blogspot.com`	Google blog for all things analytics
"How to Prepare for Google Analytics IQ"	`https://support.google.com/ analytics/answer/3424288?hl=en`	Online Google Analytics training
KISSmetrics 50+ Google Analytics Resources	`https://blog.kissmetrics.com/ google-analytics-resources-2014/`	Collection of Google Analytics guides

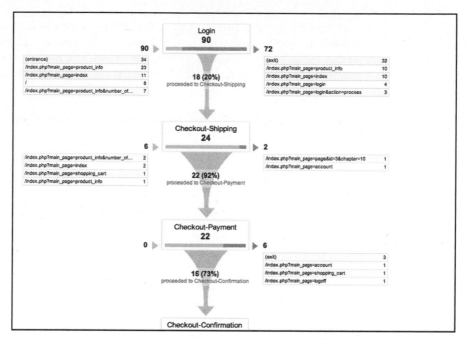

Reproduced with permission of WebReach Ireland Ltd.; www.webreach.ie

TECHNICAL STUFF

You must tag each page of your website with a short piece of JavaScript. The tagging task isn't difficult. If your site uses a template or a common server-side include (for example, for a footer), you place the Analytics code once, and it appears on all pages. You should start seeing results within 24 hours.

Integrating Google Analytics with Your Social Media

To be sure, you can still identify traffic arriving at your site from social media services simply by looking at All Referrers under Acquisition in your Google Analytics account.

However, Google's Social Media Analytics makes it much easier to integrate statistical results from social media services into your reports and to assess the business value of social media. Take advantage of the Social option to pre-filter for social-site referrers only.

Start by clicking Acquisition in the left navigation, as usual. Then click again to expand the Social option and select Network Referrals. As shown in Figure 1-6, Google Social Analytics compares sessions from social media to all sessions in the graphs and lists traffic from individual social media sources below the graphs.

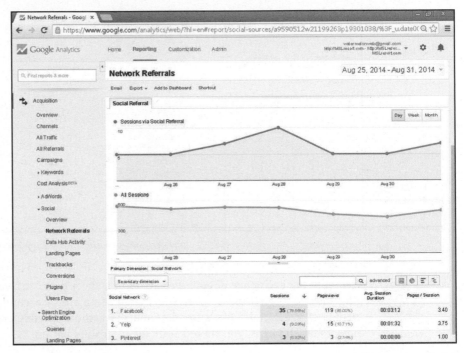

Source: www.google.com

FIGURE 1-6:
The Social section of Google Analytics makes it easy to collect and compare referrals from social networks.

Alternatively, below the Social options in the left navigation, click Users Flow. In the Select Segment drop-down list (at the top of the Social Users Flow page), select Referral Traffic. The resulting display, shown in Figure 1-7, appears.

Some social media services, such as Ning, Facebook, and Meetup, make it easy to integrate their data with Google Analytics by enabling you to place Google Analytics tracking code on your social media pages. Of course, the Google-owned Blogger, Google+, and YouTube, as well as the RSS service FeedBurner, are already compatible with Analytics.

REMEMBER

Web analytics, from Google or anywhere else, are valuable only if you use them to improve users' experience on your site and your bottom line.

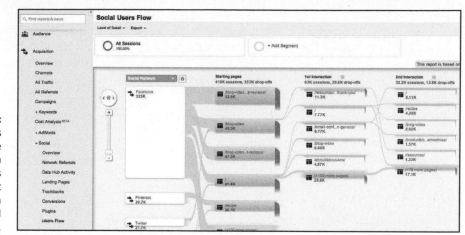

FIGURE 1-7:
The Social Users
Flow page
displays the path
taken by visitors
who arrive at
your site from
various social
media.

Source: *https://megalytic.com/blog/social-insights-from-google-analytics*

TIP

The URLs for funnel and goal pages don't need to have identical domain names, as long as the correct tracking code appears on the pages. The thank-you page for a purchase is sometimes on a third-party storefront, for instance. Or perhaps you want to track how many people go from a particular page on your main website to post a comment on one of your social network sites or blog.

Chapter 2

Comparing Metrics from Different Marketing Techniques

By now, you may be asking yourself whether web *metrics* (the science of measurement) are worth the trouble. They certainly matter if you have a business with a finite amount of time, money, or staff — which covers just about every business.

Metrics aren't about determining whether your company is the best in any particular marketing or advertising channel. They're about deciding which channels offer your company the best value for achieving your business objectives. Not to denigrate your instinct, but metrics are simply the most objective way to optimize your marketing effort. This chapter explains what you need to know about using metrics in marketing your small business.

REMEMBER

Marketing isn't rocket science. If your metrics show that a particular tactic is working, keep doing it. If they show it isn't working, try something else.

Establishing Key Performance Indicators

The most important items to measure — the ones that reflect your business goals and objectives — are *key performance indicators* (KPIs). They may vary by type of business, but after they're established, they should remain consistent over time.

An e-retailer, for instance, may be more interested in sales by product category or at different price points, though a business-to-business (B2B) service company might want to look at which sources produce the most qualified prospects. The trick is to select five to ten relevant metrics for your business.

REMEMBER

If something isn't measured, it can't be evaluated. If it can't be evaluated, it isn't considered important.

While you read this chapter, you can establish your own KPIs. Then you can combine them with other information about how your various marketing efforts contribute to sales and leads, to your bottom line, and to your return on investment (ROI). Armed with this information, you'll be in a position to make strategic business decisions about your marketing mix, no matter what size your company.

TIP

Enter at least one KPI for each business goal on your Social Media Marketing Plan (see Book 2, Chapter 2). Some business goals share the same KPI. Schedule a review of the comparative metrics on your Social Media Activity Calendar (discussed in Book 2, Chapter 4) at least once per month — or more often if you're starting a new endeavor; you're running a brief, time-constrained effort; or you handle a large volume of traffic.

Overcoming measurement challenges

Measuring success among forms of social media, let alone between social media and any other forms of marketing, is a challenge. You're likely to find yourself comparing apples not only to oranges but to mangoes, pineapples, kiwis, pears, and bananas too. In the end, you have to settle for a fruit salad or smoothie.

TIP

Install the same statistical software, whether it's Google Analytics or another package, on all your sites. Your sites may not have identical goals (for instance, users may not be able to purchase from your LinkedIn profile or request a quote from your wiki), but using the same software will ensure that metrics are consistently defined. In fact, the availability of compatible analytics packages may influence your selection of a host, development platform, or even web developer.

Using A/B testing

You may want to apply *A/B testing* (comparing a control sample against other samples in which only one element has changed) to your forays into social media. Just as you might use A/B testing to evaluate landing pages or emails, you can also compare results between two versions of a blog post or compare performance of two different headlines for an update on a social media service, while keeping all other content identical.

If you're comparing performance (click-throughs to your site) of content placed in different locations — for example, on several different social bookmarking sites or social news services — use identical content for greater accuracy.

REMEMBER

Don't rely on absolute measurements from any online source. Take marketing metrics with a shaker full of salt; look more at the trends than at the exact numbers. Be forewarned, though, that the temptation to treat numbers as sacrosanct is hard to resist.

To no one's surprise, an entire business has grown up around web metrics. If you have a statistical bent, join or follow the discussions on the resource sites listed in Table 2-1.

TABLE 2-1 **Online Metrics Resources**

Site Name	URL	What It Offers
eMetrics	www.emetrics.org	Events and conferences on marketing optimization
HubSpot	http://blog.hubspot.com/marketing/how-to-run-an-ab-test-ht	A/B testing how-to FAQs article
Digital Analytics Association	www.digitalanalyticsassociation.org	Professional association for analytics practitioners

(continued)

TABLE 2-1 *(continued)*

Site Name	URL	What It Offers
Web Analytics Demystified Blog	`http://blog.` `webanalyticsdemystified.com`	Digital measurement techniques
WebProNews	`www.webpronews.com`	Breaking news blog for web professionals, including analytics topics
Webtrends	`http://webtrends.com/resources/` `overview`	Resources for analytics and other marketing topics

Comparing Metrics across Social Media

Each genre of social media services has its own arcane measurements, from hashtags to comments, from posts to ratings, from membership numbers to sentiment.

TIP

Use medium-specific metrics to gauge the efficacy of different campaigns within that medium or to compare results from one site within a genre to another.

However, to assess the overall effectiveness of social media efforts and your total marketing mix, common metrics cross boundaries. Surprise! These common metrics look a lot like the statistics discussed in Book 6, Chapter 1. By using the right tools, or by downloading analytics to a spreadsheet and creating your own graphs, you can compare data for various social media.

Online traffic patterns may vary for all sorts of reasons and for different businesses. Watch for cyclical patterns across a week or compare the same time frames a year apart. Merchants often do this for same-store sales to compare how a store is performing compared to past years.

Carefully aggregate measurements over exactly the same time frame and dates. You obviously don't compare weekly data from a blog to monthly data for a website. But neither should you compare Tuesday traffic on one source to Saturday traffic on another, or compare November and December clicks for an e-commerce site that sells gift items (which is probably quite high) to January and February clicks (which are probably low). Compare, instead, to the same time frames from the preceding year.

These sections take a closer look at social media and what you need to know when studying metrics across your different social media sites.

Recognizing the important metrics

In most cases, these metrics become some of the KPIs on your list:

>> **Traffic (visits):** The overall measure of the number of visits (not visitors) made to your site or to a particular social media presence over a set period. Facebook (see Figure 2-1) offers page administrators traffic data in its free analytics at www.facebook.com/insights (you must be logged in). Google Social Analytics enables you to compare traffic from different social media sources, as discussed in Book 6, Chapter 1.

>> **Unique users:** The number of different users (or, more specifically, IP addresses) who visited. Depending on your business model, you may want to know whether you have ten visits apiece from 100 ardent fans (multiple repeat users) or 1,000 users, each of whom drops in once. This type of detail is available for some, but not all, social media services.

>> **Keywords:** The list of search terms or tags used to find a particular web posting. Phrases are often more useful than individual words.

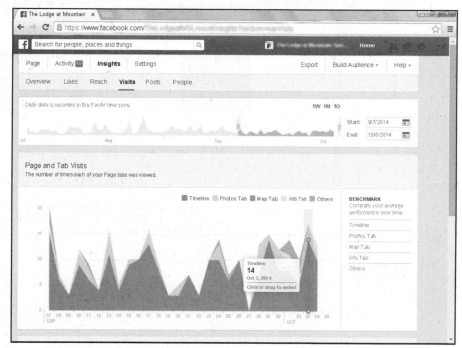

FIGURE 2-1:
Facebook's Insights analytics tool displays Facebook traffic over a customized report time frame.

Source: www.facebook.com

» **Referrers:** A list of traffic sources that tells you how many visitors arrive at your web entities from such sources as search engines, other websites, paid searches, and many, but not all, other social media services. Some even identify referrers from web-enabled cellphones.

You can find a section like this in most analytics programs. Those traffic sources may be aggregated and displayed graphically for easy review, as shown in Shoutlet's Social Analytics feature (see Figure 2-2). This feature compares the performance of social posts across networks for a holistic view of campaign metrics.

Keeping track of users' paths among many components of a complicated web presence isn't easy, but it's worth it. You may find that your marketing strategy takes B2B prospects from LinkedIn to your blog and then to a microsite. Or you may watch business-to-consumer (B2C) clients follow your offers from a social news service to a store widget on Facebook before they conclude with a purchase on your site. Refer to the next section for more about tracking your links.

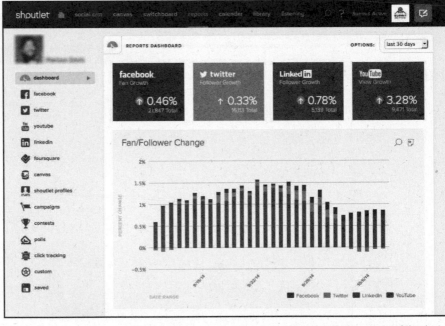

FIGURE 2-2:
The Shoutlet analytics report provides the total number of referrals by source in the top boxes and a graph depicting the relative growth of traffic by source at the bottom.

Reproduced with permission of Shoutlet, Inc.

» **Click-through rate (CTR):** The number of click-throughs to your site from a particular source divided by the number of visitors (traffic) that arrived at that source. If 40 people view your Facebook stream in one day, for instance, and 4 of them click-through to your primary site, the CTR is 10 percent (4 ÷ 40). You may need to derive this data by combining traffic measurements from particular social media services with information from the Referrers or Entry Pages sections of your analytics program. In some cases, the CTR becomes the conversion measure for a particular social media service.

Table 2-2 suggests some useful KPIs that can track by genre and social media platform.

TABLE 2-2   **Social Media by Genre and KPI**

Social Genre	Site Examples	Useful KPIs to Check
Bookmarking	Delicious, StumbleUpon	traffic, keywords, CTR
Community	Forums, Ning, Google Groups, Yahoo! Groups	traffic, users, time, keywords, CTR
Information	Blogs, webinars, wikis	traffic, users, time, keywords, referrers, CTR
Media sharing	Podcasts, YouTube, Pinterest, Instagram	traffic, users, time, keywords, CTR, number of views, Likes, Followers
Network	Facebook, LinkedIn, Google+, Twitter	traffic, users, time, keywords, CTR
News	Digg, Reddit	traffic, keywords, CTR
Review	Angie's List, Epinions, TripAdvisor, Yelp	traffic, CTR, user ratings, leads

Tagging links

Tagging your links with identifying code is especially helpful for tracking clicks that arrive from e-newsletters, email, widgets, banner ads, and links from a mobile phone because they otherwise aren't distinguishable in the referrer list.

TECHNICAL STUFF

Tagging links offers one other advantage: the ability to track the impact of dark social media traffic. *Dark traffic* arrives at your site via an intermediate stop on some site other than the social media page on which you posted your original link. (For instance, someone shares the link you placed on Facebook with one of their friends via email or text message.) Unless you tag your links, Google can't identify traffic from these sources, so it gets reported as direct traffic.

An unidentified referrer is usually displayed on a row with only a / (slash) in its name. This unspecified / category includes people who type your URL on the address bar of their browsers because they remembered it, were told about it, or have bookmarked your site.

Tagging links manually

If you have only a few such unspecified sources, simply tag the inbound link with additional, identifying information. Add ?src= and the landing page URL. Follow that, in any order, with the source (where the link appeared, such as MerchantCircle), the medium (pay-per-click, banner, email, and so forth), and campaign name (date, slogan, promo code, product name, and so on). Separate each variable with an ampersand (&). The tagged link will look something like www.yoursite.com/landingpage?src=yahoo&banner&july14.

REMEMBER

Google AdWords does this tracking for you automatically. Be sure that you have linked your Analytics and AdWords accounts together and enable auto-tagging. You can still use either the manual method described in this section or the Google tag builder described in the following section for all non–AdWords campaigns.

Using Google's URL builder to tag links

Google's automated tool for creating tagged links can be used for any advertising campaign or medium, not just Google AdWords. Follow these steps:

1. **Go to** https://support.google.com/analytics/answer/1033867.

2. **Enter your website's address in the Website URL text box.**

3. **In the Campaign Source text box, enter the referrer, such as Facebook, newsletter, Google Ads, and so on.**

4. **Enter the type of ad in the Campaign Medium text box.**

    For example, the ad type may be promoted post, banner, retargeting, or print.

5. **(Optional) Enter keywords or target audience demographics in the Campaign Term text box.**

6. **(Optional) Include text from the body or headline of each ad in the Campaign Content text box to differentiate ads.**

    This step is often helpful for A/B testing when you're trying to decide which headline or offer works better in an ad.

7. **In the Campaign Name text box, enter an easily identifiable product name, slogan, promo code, holiday, or theme.**

8. Click the Submit button.

Your custom URL, which appears below the button, looks something like www.watermelonweb.com/?utm_campaign=holidayparties2014&utm_medium=banner&utm_source=chambernewsletter.

As far as the user is concerned, the link automatically redirects to the correct landing page. However, you can count each distinctive URL in a list of referrers or, in the case of Google Analytics, by choosing Acquisition > Campaigns, as shown in Figure 2-3.

TIP

You can use tagged links to identify traffic coming from offline sources. Create an obvious, easy-to-remember URL for print, radio, or TV ads that looks something like www.yoursite.com/tv. Then ask your programmer to create a redirect from the obvious URL to your tagged link. Because the tagged link will show up as the referrer in Google Analytics, you can determine how successfully your offline advertising drives traffic to your site. Redirects are a great way to distinguish how often your video ads are seen on YouTube versus television, for example.

Click Campaigns under Acquisition

Campaign names

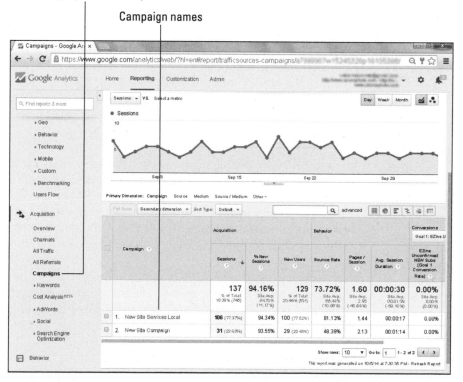

FIGURE 2-3: You can easily track results for non-AdWords campaigns in Google Analytics.

Reproduced with permission of Brad Cavanaugh, Air One, Inc.

The process of tagging links may be time consuming, but being able to monitor a particular campaign more accurately is worth your trouble.

REMEMBER

Generate a separate, unique, shortened link for tweets, LinkedIn updates, and mobile sites, if needed. *Always* test to ensure that the modified link works correctly.

Analyzing the clickstream

Clickstream analysis is a fancy name for tracking users' successive mouse clicks (the *clickstream*) to see how they surf the web. Clickstream analytics are usually monitored on an aggregate basis.

Server-based clickstream analysis provides valuable insight into visitor behavior. For instance, by figuring out which paths users most frequently take on a site and which routes lead to sales, you can make changes in content and calls to action, as well as identify ways to simplify navigation and paths to check out.

On a broader level, clickstream analysis gives you a good idea where your visitors were before they arrived at your website or social media service, and where they went afterward.

REMEMBER

Aggregated data about user behavior or industry usage is useful while you design your social media marketing strategy. This analysis may also help explain why a campaign is or isn't working.

In the end, however, the only data that truly matters is the data that shows what's happening with your business, your web presence, your customers, and your bottom line.

REMEMBER

You can easily see your *upstream analysis* (where visitors came from). That's the same as your referrers. What's harder to see is where visitors go when they leave your site. Figure 2-4 displays a clickstream analysis of where visitors were before arriving at Twitter in 2014. The URLs of the top five upstream sites are available free on the Competitive Intelligence tab for a site on Alexa. To view downstream clicks, you must upgrade to Alexa's paid version.

Or you can try the Interest Affinity or Site Affinity Index on Quantcast for quantified sites. It doesn't provide specific clickstream data, but it compares the interest in other sites or areas by those who use a specific property to that of average Internet users.

Clickstream data varies over time while users run hot and cold about a particular service, while the user population changes, or while a social media technique evolves.

Top five upstream sites

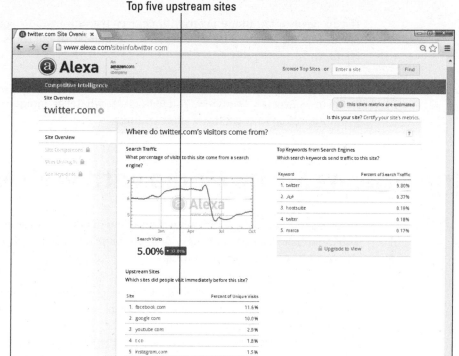

FIGURE 2-4:
Alexa displays the top five upstream sources for visitors before they arrive at a specific site; in this case, Twitter.

Source: www.alexa.com

You can also set up a clickstream analysis for sites in Google Analytics by choosing Audience > Users Flow. For more information, visit `https://support.google.com/analytics/answer/2519989`.

Tracking your own outbound links

Google Analytics lets you track outbound, downstream clicks from your own pages. Your programmer must tag all outbound links you want to track, which involves some JavaScript customization. Send your programmer to `https://support.google.com/analytics/answer/1136920`.

For additional help, have your programmer visit Google's Universal Analytics Upgrade Center at `https://developers.google.com/analytics/devguides/collection/upgrade`. If you haven't already upgraded to Google's Universal Analytics, you'll find that upgrading makes the entire tracking process easier.

If you need to tag many external links, try the automated tagging solution we discuss in the section "Using Google's URL builder to tag links," earlier in this chapter.

To see the number of clicks to each external link in Google Analytics, choose Behavior > Events > Overview, and look under whatever category name your programmer set up to track these external links.

Integrating Social Media with Web Metrics

In addition to creating your hub website, you may have developed sites either as subdomains within your primary domain name or with auxiliary domain names. These sites may take several forms:

>> **Microsites:** These small, dedicated sites that have their own domain names are usually developed for a specific event, product or product line, service, or another promotion, or as specialized landing pages for an advertising campaign. Whether the microsite is permanent or temporary, you must make a strategic choice to create one, judging cost, branding needs, search engine optimization (SEO), and other marketing efforts against potential benefits.

>> **Blogs:** All blogs and other information-sharing sites, such as webinars and wikis, can be fully tracked with analytical software. Some sites, such as Ning (www.ning.com/ning3help/set-up-google-analytics/) and Blogger (http://www.bloggertipstricks.com/?s=set+up+google+analytics), offer Google Analytics integration, but not all hosted solutions do so. Although you can obtain statistics from certain hosted communities or third parties, you may not be able to customize them or integrate them with your other statistics.

>> **Communities:** All Ning communities, as well as forums, chat rooms, and message boards, fall into this category. Although they may have their own internal statistics, also investigate whether you can customize those statistics to meet your needs before you select software or a hosted platform. For instance, Yahoo! Groups (https://groups.yahoo.com/neo) and Google Groups (https://groups.google.com/forum/#!overview) are inexpensive community alternatives, but they provide only limited statistics.

The use of KPIs at these additional sites makes it easier to integrate user activity on your social media channels with what happens after users arrive at your primary website. To complete the analysis, add a few more comparative indicators, each of which you can analyze independently:

>> **Conversion rate:** You're already computing the percentage of visitors who complete tangible goals on your primary website, whether they purchase a product or complete a request form. Now compare the conversion rate (for the same available goal) by traffic source to the average conversion rate across all sources for that goal. Figure 2-5 displays the Social Value option in Google Analytics, which analyzes conversion rate to assess the relative value of links from various social media. (Go to Acquisition > Social > Overview and scroll down.)

>> **Sales and lead generation:** These numbers may come from your storefront package or be based on measurements tracked offline.

>> **Downloads:** Track the number of times users download video or audio files, slide-show PDF files, white papers, or application forms from your sites.

TECHNICAL STUFF

To track downloads, email links, and phone calls derived from clicks, you can use the same approach that you do for tracking outbound links, as discussed in the section "Tagging links," earlier in this chapter. Visit the event-tracking guide for more information (https://developers.google.com/analytics/devguides/collection/analyticsjs/events).

>> **Pages per view, pages viewed:** Microsites, communities, and blogs usually offer enough content to make these parameters reasonable to measure. Tracking this information by social source, however, as shown in Figure 2-5, can be valuable. Page views are available for most blogs but not necessarily for all other services.

>> **Time per visit:** The average length of time spent viewing material is a good, but not exact, proxy for the number of pages per view. Naturally, users spend less time reading a single tweet than they might spend on your blog or website, but fractions of a second are indications of trouble everywhere.

>> **Bounce rate:** For another indication of interest in your content, determine the percentage of visitors who leave without visiting a second page (related to time per visit). Like with pages per view or time per visit, the bounce rate may be a bit misleading. If many people have bookmarked a page so that they can immediately find the information they want, your bounce rate may be higher than expected, although pages per view or time per visit may be low. You may want to sort bounces by upstream source.

Click this option see the relative value of links from social media.

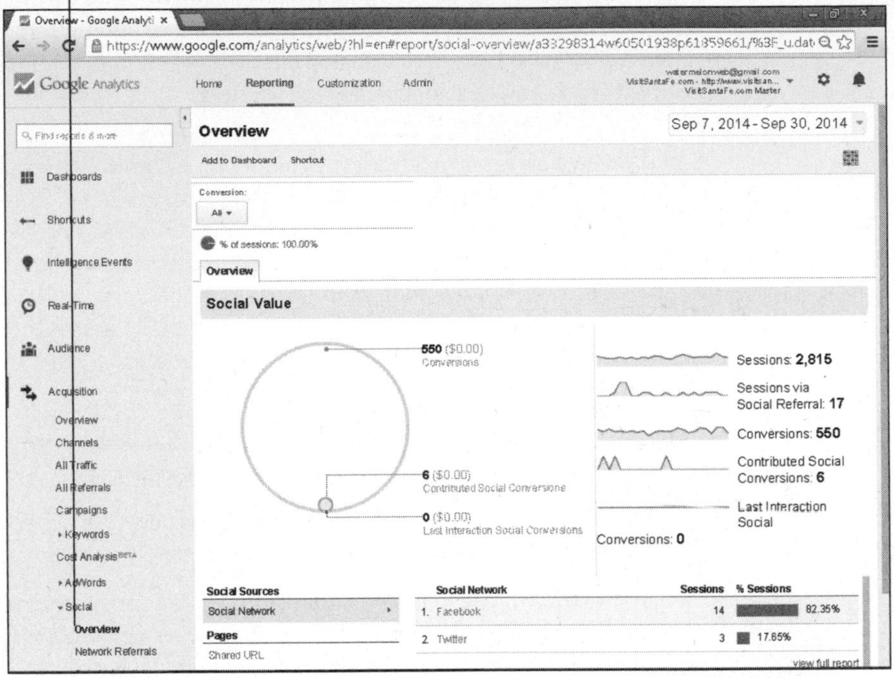

FIGURE 2-5: Google Analytics displays Social Value in chart and linear forms as part of the Social Overview page.

Reproduced with permission of Hutton Broadcasting, LLC

Using Advertising Metrics to Compare Social Media with Other Marketing Types

Because you generally don't pay social media services, social media marketing is incredibly appealing as a cost-effective substitute for paid ads. You can convert the advertising metrics in the following sections to compare the cost effectiveness of your various social media efforts or to analyze social media outlets versus other forms of promotion, online and off.

Obtaining metrics for paid advertising

With the exception of pay-per-click advertising, which exists only online, the metrics used for paid advertising are the same whether you advertise online or offline. Most publishers offer advertisers a *media kit* that includes demographics, ad requirements, and ad rates based on one or more pricing models.

Advertising costs vary over time based on demand and availability, as well as the overall economy. Ad prices are generally based on *what the market will bear* — that is, the most that an advertiser is willing to bid. New, real-time bidding schemes for online advertising may make prices even more volatile. Life is negotiable in many advertising marketplaces, except for those that operate as self-service networks. It never hurts to ask for what you want. For more information, see the most recent edition of *Google AdWords For Dummies* by Howie Jacobson, Joel McDonald, and Kristie McDonald (John Wiley & Sons, Inc.).

REMEMBER

Many social media sites don't charge for posting content because their true goal is to sell either premium services or advertising. Your content generates what they sell: an audience. The more user eyeballs a social media service can deliver to its advertisers, the greater its own advertising revenue. In essence, you manufacture their product in exchange for getting some of that traffic for yourself.

CPM

Cost per thousand (CPM — confusingly short for *cost per mille*) impressions, one of the most consistently used metrics in advertising, work across all forms of media. CPM is based on the number of times an ad is viewed, whether it's calculated for ads on TV, billboards, or in print magazines; received as dedicated emails; or viewed on web pages.

CPM is simple to calculate: Divide the cost by (.001) of the number of impressions (views). The more narrowly defined the audience, the higher the CPM. You can find a handy CPM calculator at www.clickz.com/static/cpm-calculator.

For instance, the CPM for a 30-second broadcast Super Bowl ad in 2014 averaged almost $36, but the actual dollar cost — $4 million — was high because the audience was 111.5 million TV viewers. By contrast, CPM for a small, highly targeted audience of CEOs in high-tech companies may run $100 or more.

Because you may have difficulty tracking from impression to action in some channels, CPM models are often used to measure branding campaigns. Figure 2-6 compares the range of CPM rates for a variety of media. CPM rates vary widely within each category based on a variety of factors.

CPA and CPC

Compare CPM with a *cost-per-action* (CPA) advertising model and its subset, *cost-per-click* (CPC) ads. CPA advertising triggers payment only when a user takes a specific action, such as downloading a white paper; signing up for a newsletter; registering for a conference; or becoming a fan, friend, or follower. At the far end of the CPA spectrum, when CPA is based on a user purchase, it approaches a sales commission model.

Range of CPMs for Different Advertising Methods		
Media Type	**Lower Range**	**Upper Range**
Social Media	$1.00	$4.00
Display Advertising	$2.80	$4.86
Billboard	$3.00	$5.00
PPC Keywords	$4.00	$20.00
Magazine	$8.00	$20.00
Direct Mail	$26.00	$27.00

FIGURE 2-6: The relative range of CPM rates for various forms of advertising in 2014.

Sources: http://smallbusiness.chron.com/typical-cpm-74763.html and www.ehow.com/info_12200588_average-banner-cpm.html

TIP

In the classic definitions of CPA, CPC, and CPM, rates don't include the cost of producing an ad, the commission paid to an agency, or your own labor to research and review ad options. From a budget point of view, you need to include all these factors in your cost estimates.

A web-only metric, CPC (or sometimes *PPC*, for pay-per-click) falls within the CPA model because advertisers are charged only when a viewer clicks a link to a specified landing page. The CPC model is often used for ads in the rightmost columns of search engines and also for clicks obtained from banner, video, and online classified ads, and from shopping comparison sites and paid directory listings. For additional resources for paid online advertising, consult Table 2-3.

REMEMBER

Always ask which statistics a publisher provides to verify the results of your ads. Some confirm impressions, as well as clicks or other actions (check against your own analytics program); some provide only impressions; and some publishers can't — or won't — provide either one.

Even if you pay a flat fee, such as for an annual directory listing, you can compute CPC and CPM after the fact, as long as the publisher provides you with the number of impressions and you can identify click-throughs.

Reach

Reach is the estimated number of potential customers (qualified prospects) you can target in a specific advertising medium or campaign. You can apply the concept of reach, by extension, to specific social media channels, anticipated traffic on your website, or other populations, such as the addresses on your email list. Reach is sometimes expressed as a fraction of the total audience for an advertising campaign (for example, potential customers divided by total audience).

The number of potential customers may be the total number of viewers in a highly targeted campaign, or only a segment of them. In the case of the Super Bowl example in the earlier section "CPM," for instance, a beer ad may be targeted at males ages 25 to 64; only that demographic percentage of the audience should be calculated in reach.

TABLE 2-3 **Online Advertising Resources**

Name	URL	What You Can Find
ADOTAS	http://research.adotas.com	Online advertising research and news
Adwords by Google	www.adwords.google.com	Ad management and solutions
Interactive Advertising Bureau	www.iab.net/wiki/index.php/category:glossary www.iab.net/guidelines/508676/508767/displayguidelines	Glossary of interactive advertising terms List of standard online ad sizes
Internet Advertising Competition	www.iacaward.org/iac	Annual Internet ad competition produced by the Web Marketing Association
Small Business Association	www.sba.gov/content/online-advertising	Resources for online advertising
The Webby Awards	www.webbyawards.com	Interactive advertising competition
Word of Mouth Marketing Association	http://womma.org	Membership group, resources, events

TIP

For the best results, identify advertising venues where the number of potential customers (reach) represents a large share of potential viewers (impressions). Return to your early market research for viewer demographics from Quantcast or review media kits to estimate the reach of each publication or social media site you're considering.

Applying advertising metrics to social media

Because publishers receive no payments for most social media appearances, comparing free social media marketing to paid advertising requires a little adjustment. How can you compare the CPM or CPC for something that's free versus something you pay for? Though you can acquire information about page views (*impressions*), clicks, and other actions (conversion goals) from your analytics program, cost requires a little thought.

One possibility is to modify the cost of advertising to include labor and hard costs for production, management, and commission, and any fees for services, such as press release distribution. Then estimate the hard costs and the amount of work in labor dollars required to create and maintain various elements of your social media presence. If you outsource the creation of ads or social media content to contractors such as copywriters, videographers, photographers, or graphic designers, include those expenses.

TIP

Don't go crazy trying to calculate exact dollar amounts. You simply estimate the relative costs of each medium or campaign to compare the cost-effectiveness of one form of promotion to another. Social media marketing may be relatively inexpensive, but if you see only one action or impression after 20 hours of labor, you need to decide whether it's worth it.

Contrasting Social Media Metrics with Other Online Marketing

Regardless of any other online techniques you use, you can combine links with source tags, analytics program results, and advertising metrics to compare social media results to results from other online techniques.

Refine your list of KPIs for these elements:

>> **Email newsletters:** Whether you use your own mailing list or rent one, you measure

- *Bounces:* Bad email addresses

- *Open rate:* The percentage of good addressees that open your newsletter, roughly equivalent to reach as a percentage of impressions

- *Click-through rate (CTR):* The percentage of people who click through to a web page after opening a newsletter

- *Landing pages:* Where newsletter recipients go when they click a link in a newsletter

Well-segmented, targeted lists result in better reach. If you rent lists, be sure to include the acquisition CPM names, as well as the transmission cost, in your total cost for CPM comparison. Most newsletter services and list-rental houses provide all these metrics.

>> **Coupons, promotion codes:** Online coupons can be tracked similarly to regular banner ads. However, for both promotion codes and coupons, track the offers that produce the best results, which are almost always sales or registrations.

>> **Press releases:** Sometimes press releases are hard to track online because many free press distribution services don't provide information on page views or click-throughs. By contrast, most paid distribution services tell you the click-through rate and the number of impressions (or number of times someone viewed your release) on their servers. Although these services can tell you where the release was distributed, they don't know what happened afterward. A press release is a good place to include an identifier in the links, as described earlier in the "Tagging links" section. The tag enables you to track entry pages. You may also see a spike in daily or hourly traffic to your site shortly after the distribution time.

>> **Product placement in games and other programs:** Advertisers can now place the equivalent of banner ads or product images within online video games. If the ads are linkable, you can find the CTR and impressions to calculate CPM and CPC (cost per click). Offline games with product placement must be treated as offline marketing elements.

>> **Online events:** Track live concerts, chats, speeches, and webinars with KPIs for registration — request an email address, at minimum — even if the event is free. Though not everyone who registers attends, this approach also provides a helpful set of leads and a built-in audience to notify of future events. Of course, you can also check referrers and entry pages.

>> **Disaggregated components, such as third-party blogs, chat rooms, RSS feeds, regular email, or text messaging:** Tagged links that pass through from these forms of communication are probably your best bet.

You can incorporate a special tag for links forwarded by others, although you may not be able to tell how they completed the forwarding (for example, from a Share This feature versus email) unless you have implemented social media plug-ins. It all depends on what you're trying to measure.

TIP

Be sure to register for optional analytics when you install a Share function from sites such as AddThis or ShareThis, which integrate with Google Analytics. Then you can see where and how often users forward your link through these services.

Assessing Word-of-Web and Word-of-Mouth

Word-of-mouth is, without a doubt, the most cost-effective form of advertising. Ultimately, that force powers all social media, with its peer-to-peer recommendations and referrals.

Try to keep your expectations in check. According to Microsoft research in 2012, less than 1 percent of social media content goes viral. In this case, *viral* is defined as reaching a much larger audience via peer-to-peer sharing compared to the audience reached by the original post.

Recent research on the impact of social media as a form of word-of-mouth is both intriguing and contradictory:

>> Mention (www.mention.com) found that 76 percent of more than 1 billion brand mentions on the web and social media were basically "meh" — neither positive nor negative. The remaining mentions are more likely to stand out.

>> According to eMarketer, about 68 percent of social media users 18 to 34 years old, and 53 percent ages 33 to 35 are at least somewhat likely to be influenced to make a purchase based on a friend's social media posting.

>> Lithium Technologies found that 70 percent of consumers read online reviews when considering a brand.

Keep these points in mind while you consider the positive and negative impacts of participation in social media. Review sites can have a significant impact on your marketing, but the impact of individual recommendations may be overrated except in special cases.

Your analytical task here is to compare the efficacy of "word-of-web" by way of social media to its more traditional forms. Tracking visitors who arrive from offline is the trickiest part. These visitors type your URL in the address bar of their browsers either because they've heard of your company from someone else (word-of-mouth) or as a result of offline marketing.

Offline marketing may involve print, billboards, radio, television, loyalty-program key-chain tags, promotional items, packaging, events, or any other great ideas you dream up.

By borrowing the following techniques from direct marketing, you can find ways, albeit imperfect, to identify referrals from offline sources or other individuals:

>> **Use a slightly different URL to identify the offline source.** Make the URL simple and easy to remember, such as http://yourdomain.com/tv; http://yourdomain.com/wrapper; http://yourdomain.com/nyt; or http://yourdomain.com/radio4. These short URLs can show viewers a special landing page — perhaps one that details an offer or a contest encouraged by an offline teaser — or redirect them to an existing page on your site. Long, tagged URLs that are terrific for online sourcing and hard-to-remember shortened URLs aren't helpful offline.

>> **Identify referrals from various offline sources.** Use different response email addresses, telephone numbers, extensions, or people's names.

>> **Provide an incentive to the referring party.** "Tell a friend about us. Both of you will receive $10 off your next visit." This technique can be as simple as a business card for someone to bring in with the referring friend's name on the back. Of course, the card carries its own unique referral URL for tracking purposes.

>> **Stick to the tried-and-true method.** Always ask, "May I ask how you heard about us?" Then tally the results.

You can then plug these numbers into a spreadsheet with your online referral statistics to compare offline methods with online social media.

HubSpot (www.hubspot.com) compared the subjective importance of various sources of B2B lead sources by marketing channel, including some offline activities, in its *2013 State of Inbound Marketing* survey. The results, shown in Figure 2-7, indicate that marketing professionals view online activities as more important sources of leads than traditional offline marketing venues, with social media, natural search (SEO), and email seen as the most important. Think about where you're spending your marketing dollars.

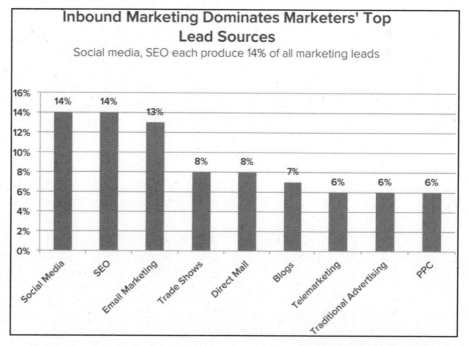

FIGURE 2-7: In a HubSpot survey, businesses rated social media, SEO, and email as more valuable sources of leads than traditional marketing activities.

Reproduced with permission of HubSpot, Inc.

Chapter 3

Making Decisions by the Numbers

The 2014 *Social Media Marketing Industry Report* from Social Media Examiner showed that only 37 percent of professionals whose companies use social media said that they're able to measure their return on investment (ROI). By using the tools for assessing qualitative and quantitative results, including ROI, you can certainly count yourself among those happy few who do.

However, there's no point in collecting metrics just to save them in a virtual curio cabinet. The challenge is to figure out how to use the numbers to adjust your online marketing campaigns, whether they need fine-tuning or a major overhaul. This chapter shows you how to analyze problems, see what your data reveals, and then use the results to modify your marketing approach.

Using Metrics to Make Decisions

Despite of the hype, social media is, at its core, a form of strategic marketing communications. As a business owner, you must balance the subjective aspects of branding, sentiment, goodwill, and quality of leads with the objective performance metrics of traffic and click-through rate (CTR) and the business metrics of customer acquisition costs, conversion rate, sales value, and ROI. The balance point is unique to each business at a specific time. Alas, no fixed rules exist.

As part of your balancing act, you'll undoubtedly also tap your instincts, incorporating casual feedback from customers, the ever-changing evolution of your market, your budget, and your assessment of your own and your staff's available time and skills.

Even after you feel confident about your marketing program, keep watching your metrics as a reality check. Data has a funny way of surprising you.

TIP

Don't become complacent. Continue to check your performance and business metrics at least monthly. How do they compare to what your instinct is telling you?

Knowing When to Hold and When to Fold

Watch for a few things in your metrics. As always, you evaluate comparative results, not absolute numbers. Keep an eye on these characteristics:

>> Negative and positive trends that last for several months

>> Abrupt or unexpected changes

>> No change in key performance indicators (KPIs), in spite of social media marketing activities

>> Correlations between a peak in traffic or sales with a specific social marketing activity

Layering activity timelines with metrics, as shown in Figure 3-1, is a simple, graphical way to spot this type of correlation. Establishing baseline metrics for your hub presence first truly helps in this process. It also helps if you add social media techniques one at a time — preferably with tracking codes.

TIP

Don't make *irreversible* decisions based on one event or from an analytical time frame that's too short for the marketing channel you're trying to implement. There are no rules for a time frame that is too short or too long. Your overall campaign may be designed to take off like a rocket in less than a week, or it may be set up to take 6 to 12 months to bear fruit. Be patient. Monitor your social media campaigns and rely on your business instincts.

You may find a time delay between the initiation of an effort and its impact on metrics, for these reasons:

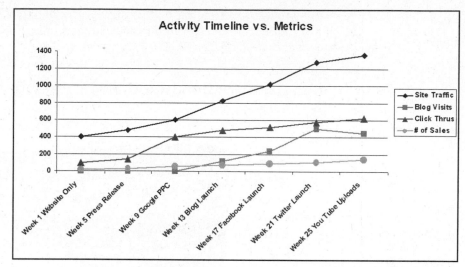

FIGURE 3-1:
Correlating an activity timeline with key performance indicators provides useful information.

>> Viewers may wait to see a history of posts before engaging, let alone clicking through to your main hub.

>> By definition, establishing a relationship with viewers or prospects takes time, just as it does in real life.

>> Our brains haven't changed despite the Internet: As every brand marketer knows, most people still need to see something seven times to remember it.

>> Many types of social media display a greater cumulative effect over time as viral marketing takes hold.

>> Your mastery of a new medium usually improves as you climb the learning curve.

With positive results, the answer is simple: Keep doing what you're doing, and even more so. After you identify the elements responsible for your success, repeat them, amplify them, multiply them, and repurpose them.

Neutral or negative results force you to evaluate whether you should drop the activity or invest the effort needed to identify the problem and try to fix it. Ultimately, only you can decide whether you want to continue sinking time and effort into a social marketing method that doesn't produce the results you want.

Make a chart for yourself like the one from Social Media Examiner shown in Figure 3-2. It shows how 2,800 marketers rank their accomplishments from using social media. How do your efforts stack up?

FIGURE 3-2: Compare the benefits you receive from social media with the benefits identified by marketers in other businesses.

Reproduced with permission of Social Media Examiner

TREKKING THROUGH SOCIAL MEDIA

Inspired by a love of the outdoors, KEEN, Inc., manufactures hybrid outdoor and casual footwear with an innovative design that supports the lifestyles and outdoor adventures of active people around the world. Founded in 2003, KEEN is one of the fastest-growing brands in the outdoor industry and has quickly become a well-respected brand, with a loyal following. Through its Hybrid Care giving program, KEEN has partnered with nonprofit organizations around the world that are working towards building stronger communities and a healthier planet, and stands behind those partners that are actively working to inspire responsible outdoor participation and land and water conservation.

According to Eric King, KEEN's Social Strategist, the company's social media presence has evolved to "meet our fans wherever they are." KEEN started with Facebook in 2008 as part of a sustainability campaign targeting college students, and has added other channels incrementally since then. "Since social marketing is constantly evolving, it can be tricky to know exactly what to plan for, but we try to do everything possible to stay on top of the latest tools and trends and be nimble enough to take advantage of the right opportunities that come along," King says.

King's approach is driven by content. "We decide which content we need first, create that content, and then determine the most appropriate posting dates and times by looking at our analytics. We do schedule most of our content in advance, but also leave some slots open for opportunities that come up in real-time."

KEEN aims for a broad range of content, including product photography, brand story-telling, Ambassador and Hybrid Care partner updates, sneak peeks, and fan photos. One dedicated person in-house plus employee contributors and some outside content creators manage this effort.

King tries to tailor content for each social media channel separately, considering everything from age demographics to topic affinities. He then researches which themes or content mediums will work best for each channel. "For example," he finds, "Instagram and Tumblr are ideal for posting lookbook-style inspirational images, while Facebook and Twitter are better suited for asking our community questions and then responding to their suggestions."

(continued)

(continued)

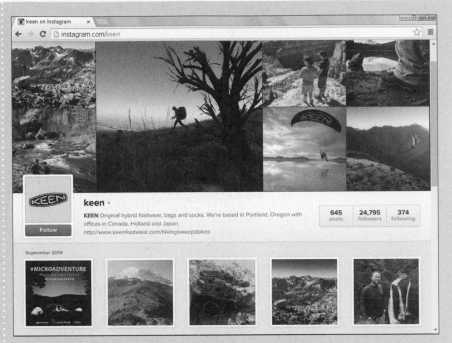

To keep track of all this social media traffic, KEEN uses a sophisticated analytics program called Crimson Hexagon for "social listening." KEEN manages the analysis in-house, going beyond just the numbers to understand the why. As King explains, "We study what's being said about KEEN online, how much of the conversation is positive or negative, how it compares to what's being said about our competitors, and then how we can use all this information to inform future strategy."

King's advice to other marketers is straightforward: "Know exactly what your goals are and how you plan on tracking them at the start of every year and every campaign. Be consistent with your tracking and set clear KPIs [key performance indicators] that can be tied back to definitive numbers. Finally, make sure that everyone who is involved is on the same page and working toward one common goal."

He follows his own advice. KEEN's goals, which are to increase brand awareness and engagement, have evolved over time as KEEN has "placed more priority in listening to what our fans have to say . . . so we can be more intentional with how we're communicating with them. . . . We want to make it clear that we're listening and that we care about what the community has to say."

KEEN's web presence:

- www.keenfootwear.com

- www.facebook.com/KEEN

- http://twitter.com/keen

- http://pinterest.com/keenfootwear

- http://instagram.com/keen

- www.youtube.com/user/keenoutdoor

- www.keenfootwear.com/blog

Diagnosing Problems with Social Media Campaigns

Put on your business hat when you detect a problem. Some techniques may be worth modifying and trying again, but others should be dropped. Ultimately, it's a business decision, not a technological one.

Be patient when assessing cost of customer acquisition and ROI, although a few trend lines in your metrics might give you pause:

>> Traffic to a social media service never picks up or falls and remains low after an initial burst.

>> Traffic to the social media site holds steady, but the CTR to your master hub or other sites is low.

>> Follow-through on intermediate calls to action is low in performance metrics.

>> Traffic and click-throughs increase, but the leads aren't well qualified.

>> Traffic and engagement, which had been increasing for quite a while, fall and continue to fall; small dips and rises are natural.

>> A conversion rate tracked back to a social media service is unintentionally lower than from other sources, and average sales value is lower. (Good strategic reasons for these results might exist, of course. You might deliberately target the younger student audience on Yelp with less-expensive options than those offered to an older, more affluent audience on Facebook.)

>> The cost of customer or lead acquisition is much higher than for other channels, making the ROI unattractive. For example, a high-maintenance blog may generate a few leads but be relatively expensive compared to prescheduled tweets that drive more traffic successfully.

Fixing Problems

Underlying problems with low traffic on social media usually can be slotted into a few categories:

>> Problems locating your social media presence

>> Mismatch between channel and audience

>> Poor content

>> No audience engagement

>> Problems with the four Ps of marketing: product, price, placement or position (distribution), and promotion

After these problems are diagnosed, they can be handled in roughly the same way, regardless of the social media venue used. The following sections help you solve some common issues that your small business may have.

Before you panic, make sure you've set reasonable expectations for performance and business metrics. Research the range of responses for similar companies or view your competitors' social media sites to see how many responses, comments, and followers they have. Although you can't foretell their ROI, you can assess their traffic and inbound links. Your results from social media may be just fine!

Be careful with interpretation. If your competitors began working on their social media campaigns long before you did, they're likely to have very different results.

Remember that the social media audience is quite fickle. A constant demand exists for changes in content, approach, tools, and tone to keep up.

Your social presence can't be found

Driving traffic to your social media presence is as challenging as driving people to your site. If traffic is still low after about four weeks, ensure that all your social media sites are optimized for external search engines such as Google and internal (on-site) search tools used by different social media services. Turn to Book 2, Chapter 5 for optimization techniques.

The source of the problem may be poorly selected search terms or tags, a headline or description that contains no keywords, or content that hasn't been optimized. Unless your hub presence, whether it's a blog or website, is well optimized itself, your social media presence may suffer, too.

TIP

Be sure that posts occur often enough for your social media page to appear in real-time search results.

Inappropriate match between channel and audience

The symptoms for a mismatch usually show up quickly: People take little or no interest in your social media postings, you suffer from low CTR, and your bounce rate is high whenever visitors do click through.

To start with, you may have chosen an inappropriate social media service or the wrong group within a network. For example, young tech males like Reddit, but if you want a social site about weddings and interior decor, try Pinterest instead.

The solution: Return to your Social Media Marketing Plan (see Book 2, Chapter 3). Review the demographics and behavioral characteristics for the social media service you're using. They may have changed over time; for example, Facebook is still enormously popular with 18- to 29-year-olds, despite recent growth in older users, but that may not last. The youngest of social media users are already migrating toward Instagram and Snapchat! Find a social venue that's a better fit, revise your plan, and try again.

REMEMBER

Use Quantcast or Alexa to check demographics on social media sites if you aren't sure.

Your site has poor content

Content problems are a little harder to diagnose than visibility problems, especially if the problem appears with your first posts. In that case, the problem may also look like a channel mismatch, with content that simply doesn't appeal to your target market or is inappropriate for the channel.

However, if you experience a persistent dip in traffic, comments, or CTR from your blog, Facebook stream, Pinterest, podcast, YouTube, or any other social media account, you have other difficulties. Perhaps the content isn't timely, or isn't updated frequently enough.

Or perhaps content quality itself has degraded. Content creators are commonly enthusiastic at the beginning of a project but may lose interest after a period of time. Or they may have a backlog of media and ideas that can be repurposed and posted initially; after that's depleted, they may run out of ideas. As a result, later content may not be as valuable to your market, lack appropriate production values, or simply become boring.

REMEMBER

Watch for burnout. After the backlog of media is used up, the insistent demands for new content can easily become a burden. Creators often lose interest, or they focus on quantity rather than on quality.

Compare the individual posts that produced an increase in traffic, responses, or CTR to ones that are failing. Tally posts by the names of their creators and what the posts were about. Start by asking previously successful creators to develop new material along the lines of older, successful content. If that doesn't work, watch the most popular tags to see what interests visitors and try to tie new content into those topics, if appropriate.

Finally, try assigning fresh staff members, recruiting guest writers and producers, or hiring professionals for a while. If this change produces better results, you have indicators for a long-term solution.

Lack of audience engagement

If you see traffic to the social media service holding steady but lack follow-throughs from calls to action, or you have an unusually low CTR to your hub site, you may not be engaging your audience. Watch especially for engagement parameters that never take off or that dip persistently.

TIP

Review user comments, retweets, and other interactions on each service. You can use the internal performance metrics for Twitter, Facebook, and your blog to assess numerical results of engagement. Then review the chain for interaction between social media visitors and your staff. Are visitor responses being acknowledged? Is there follow-up? One of the biggest challenges in social media is establishing a relationship with your visitors and maintaining a back-and-forth conversation. A lack of engagement may presage a lack of brand recognition, loss of customer loyalty, and reduced referrals from visitors to their friends or colleagues.

You've forgotten the four Ps of marketing

Perhaps you're getting traffic and click-throughs to your hub site and generating plenty of leads but still not closing or converting to sales. It may be time to go back to the basics.

Review a web analytics report generated before you started your social media marketing efforts. Make sure your website is well optimized for search, your online store (if you have one) is working well, and your conversion rate is solid. Fix any problems with your website before you try to adjust your social media campaign.

Product, price, placement or position (distribution), and promotion — the four Ps — are considered the basic elements of traditional marketing. These terms apply to social media and other forms of online marketing, as well.

Product

Your *product* is whatever good or service you sell, regardless of whether the transaction takes place online or off. Product also includes such elements as performance, warranties, support, variety, and size. Review your competition to see which features, benefits, or services they offer, and which products they're featuring in social media. If you have an online store, look at your entire product mix and merchandising, not just at individual products. Ask yourself these questions:

>> Are you selling products that the people you're targeting with social media want to buy?

>> Do you have enough products or services to compete successfully in this environment?

>> Are you updating your offerings regularly and promoting new items often?

Price

Price-comparison sites such as Shopping.com and discount stores online already put price pressure on small businesses. Now mobile social media shopping sites, with the rapid viral spread of news about special offers and price breaks, have put cost-conscious shoppers firmly in the driver's seat.

No longer can you check only competitors' websites and comparison-shopping sites for prices. Now you must check to see what they offer visitors to their Facebook, Twitter, or LinkedIn pages; their blog readers; those who receive their e-newsletter; and social shopping page customers to gain new customers and hold onto them as loyal, repeat buyers. Any single product or service may now have multiple prices, depending on who's buying.

Use social shopping and other sites to assess your prices against your online competition. Are yours significantly higher or lower, or are they price competitive?

Your small business can have difficulty competing in the market for standard manufactured goods such as baby clothes or DVDs unless you have excellent wholesale deals from manufacturers or distributors. But you can compete on price on customized goods or services or by offering unique benefits for buying from your company.

If you must charge higher prices than your social media competitors, review your value proposition so that people perceive an extra benefit. It may be a $5 promotional code for a discount on another purchase, a no-questions-asked return policy, exclusivity, or very accessible tech support.

Be careful not to trap yourself into matching prices against large companies with deep pockets. Make tactical financial decisions about loss leaders and discounts for users of particular social media. Consider a less-than-fullfeatured product or service package for social media users if needed (sometimes called the *freemium* business model).

Placement or position

Placement or position refers to how products and services are delivered to consumers (distribution channels). Where and how are your products and services available? Your website needs to serve as a 24/7 hub for customer research, support, and sales online, but social media offers brand-new opportunities to serve your clients. Best Buy, for example, has already become famous for its *twelpforce*, in which employees use Twitter to field customer support questions and make product recommendations.

With multiple social marketing outlets, you must be alert for the effects of *channel cannibalization* (the use of multiple distribution channels that pull sales from each other). Products or services sold directly from social media outlets may depress the sales numbers on your website.

Promotion

Your online and social media marketing plans fall into the *promotion* category, which includes all the different ways you communicate with customers and prospects, both online and offline. This also includes making people aware of your multiple points of visibility online, almost as though you're marketing another product. Careful cross-promotion among all your online venues is now as critical as integrating online and offline advertising. Are people aware of all your social media pages? Are you using the right calls to action on those pages to get people to buy?

TIP

Don't continue investing in a social media technique just because everyone else is doing it.

Adjusting to Reality

Many times, expectations determine whether a marketing technique is seen as a success, a waste of time, or something in between. It isn't possible for a particular social media service to produce extraordinary changes in traffic or conversions. In most cases, though, your victories will be hard-won, whereas you cobble together traffic from multiple social media sources to build enough of a critical mass to gain measurable sales.

Achieving that goal usually involves many people, each of whom may become a committed champion of the method she has been using. When you decide to pull the plug on one of your social media techniques — or just decide to leave it in a static state — try to still keep your employees engaged.

Unless social media participants have proved themselves to be nonperformers, try to shift them into another channel so that they can retain a direct relationship with customers.

Avoid the temptation to recentralize your social media marketing in one place, whether it's PR, marketing communications, management, or customer support. Instead, try to maintain the involvement of someone from each of those functional areas, as well as subject area experts from such diverse departments as manufacturing, sales, and research and development (R&D).

REMEMBER

Marketing is only part of a company, but all of a company is marketing.

As wild a ride as social media may seem, it's more of a marathon than a sprint. Given that it may take months to see the return on your marketing efforts, you may need to nourish your social media sites for quite a while.

Feeding the hungry maw of the content monster week in and week out isn't easy. You need to not only keep your staff engaged and positive, but also keep your content fresh. Take advantage of brainstorming techniques that involve your entire team to generate some new ideas each month. Here are a few suggestions to get you started:

>> Create unique, themed campaigns that last one to three months. Find an interesting hook to recruit guest posts or writers, perhaps letting a few people try your product or service and write about it.

- » Distribute short-term deals using social media channels, such as providing location-based coupons on cellphones or distributing offers to Meetup attendees.

- » Write a Wikipedia entry about your product or business from a consumer's point of view.

- » Make friends on Facebook by incorporating an interactive application, such as a poll or sweepstakes entry.

- » If you aren't gaining traction with groups on LinkedIn or Facebook, post on someone else's old-fashioned forum, message board, or chat room on a relevant topic.

- » Tell a story about your product or service in pictures or video and upload it to Instagram, Vine, Pinterest, YouTube, or another image service.

REMEMBER

Every marketing problem has an infinite number of solutions. You have to find only one of them!

Index

G

GanttProject (website), 159
geodemographics, 19
geographics
  definition of, 18
  locating target areas, 23–24
  social media marketing and, 134–137
geographic targeting, 55
Getbarometer.com (website), 96
gift certificates, 499
Gifts feed (Pinterest), 368
goals
  budget and, 68–71
  in content marketing, 270–271
  definition of, 64
  in marketing communication, 418–419
  purpose statement, 63–64
  putting into action, 66
  setting, 65
  in social media marketing, 121–124, 391
  vision, mission, and, 62
GoDaddy.com (website), 281
goMobi (website), 403
Good Keywords (website), 385
Goodreads (website), 140
Google
  Advanced Search, 247, 261
  Adword Keyword Planner, 186–187, 219
  Adwords, 539
  Alerts, 98, 247, 261
  Analytics, 20, 512, 514, 517–521, 534, 536
  Business Pages, 225–226
  Calendar, 160, 161
  Chrome, 34–35
  Display Planner, 392
  Google+, 231–233, 407
  Google + Platform Insights, 515
  Groups, 534
  Index Status page, 203
  Insights, 186
  Maps, 34
  News, 103
  PageRank, 206–208
  Plus, 230
  purpose statement, 63

  search engine market share, 183–184
  Spreadsheet Marketing Budget Template for Start-ups, 71
  Toolbar, 392
  Trends, 23, 98, 141
  unique visitors, 180
  Universal Analystics Upgrade Center, 533
  URL builder to tag links, 530–532
  URL Shortener, 516
  users, 113
  Webmaster Central, 206
Google AdWords For Dummies (Jacobson et al), 537
GooglePing (ping service), 84
Googling yourself, 34
Graphiq.com (website), 452
gray-market link sites, 211
gross rating points, 459
growing business, 12
growth phase, product life cycle, 43–44
guest blogging, 287–289
Gunelius, Susan, *Blogging All-in-One For Dummies*, 283

H

handouts, 333
Hashtagify.me (website), 103
hashtags
  Instagram, 357–358
  Pinterest, 362
  Twitter, 307–308
headline
  adding power to, 438
  attributes of good, 437
  crafting, 437–438
  definition of, 436
  font, 442
  power of, 436–437
Heap, Imogen (artist), 320
HideMyAss (website), 35
Highwire (website), 95
home contractors, 363
Hootsuite (website), 79, 162, 164
HostGator.com (web site), 281
HowSociable (website), 99
HubSpot (website), 77, 143, 392, 513, 525, 543

I

J

K

L

Yelp, 112, 173
Yext.com (website), 204, 210
YouTube
  Analytics, 516
  services, 108

Z
zip codes, 24
Zoominfo (website), 34

About the Authors

Scott Ayres is a professional blogger and social media consultant who currently blogs and heads up training for the Facebook scheduling app Post Planner (www.postplanner.com) as well as podcasts on the popular "Facebook Answerman" show (www.FacebookAnswerman.com). He became addicted to social media even before MySpace (the first time around). He's a horrible Internet marketer because he's more concerned about teaching than turning a quick buck. On any given day, he spends 20+ hours on Facebook!

Kelby Carr is the founder and CEO of Type-A Parent (www.typeaparent.com), a social network and online magazine-style blog founded in 2007 for parent bloggers, and Type-A Parent Conference (www.typeaconference.com), an annual blogging and social media conference founded in 2009 that attracts major corporations and hundreds of parents who blog. She is a social media and blogger outreach consultant. She is a frequent speaker on new media topics.

She's been coding since 1982, social networking online since 1984, web publishing since 1992, blogging since 2002, and tweeting since 2007. She was an early adopter of Pinterest, and is active there daily with thousands of followers and hundreds of pins.

Jamie Crager is the founder and CEO of crowdshifter.com, blazefly.com, and Crowdshifter Media, a digital marketing company that helps businesses use digital and social media to expand their companies. He also teaches social networking and digital marketing classes in the continuing education department of Iowa Western Community College and sits on the advisory board of several companies. Some of his most recent achievements are voted Best Social Media Consultant 2011 by Omaha Businesses via B2B Magazine, Google AdWords Qualified Individual, 2011 Stevie Awards Finalist for National Accounts Manager of the Year, and Miller Heiman Certified.

Joel Elad, MBA, is the head of Real Method Consulting, a company dedicated to educating people through training seminars, DVDs, books, and other media. He holds a master's degree in business from UC Irvine, and has a bachelor's degree in computer science and engineering from UCLA.

Joel has written seven books about various online topics, including *Facebook Advertising For Dummies, Starting an Online Business All-In-One Desk Reference For Dummies, Starting an iPhone Application Business For Dummies,* and *Wiley Pathways: E-business.* He has contributed to *Entrepreneur* magazine and Smartbiz.com, and has taught at institutions such as the University of California, Irvine, and the University of San Diego. He is an educational specialist trained by eBay and a former Internet instructor for the Learning Annex in New York City, Los Angeles, San Diego, and San Francisco.

Barbara Findlay Schenck helps business leaders start, grow, market, brand, and, when they're ready, sell their companies. She has worked with hundreds of businesses and shares what she's learned in a shelf-full of business books that include the book you're holding (including its first and second editions), *Branding For Dummies, Selling Your Business For Dummies,* and *Business Plans Kit For Dummies* (now in its 5th edition).

Barbara is a marketing strategist and small business advocate who contributes to a number of news sites and is called upon for presentations and advice by a long list of businesses and business groups.

Laura "@Pistachio" Fitton has had a long, crazy, wild ride with Twitter, which she hopes continues for many years to come. Laura is credited with convincing Guy Kawasaki and thousands of tech execs that Twitter would have real business value. She founded the first Twitter for business consultancy, Pistachio Consulting, in 2008 and has been speaking professionally about the business use of Twitter since 2007. In addition to co-writing all three editions of *Twitter For Dummies,* she was the sole founder/CEO of the venture-capital funded tech startup oneforty.com, acquired in 2011 by HubSpot. Today Laura serves as HubSpot's inbound marketing evangelist.

Susan Gunelius is president & CEO of KeySplash Creative, Inc. (www.keysplashcreative.com), a marketing communications company. Her clients include large and small companies around the world, such as Citibank, Cox Communications, and many more.

She has more than 20 years of experience working in the marketing field with the first decade of her career spent directing marketing programs for some of the largest companies in the world, including divisions of AT&T and HSBC. Today, Susan often speaks about marketing, branding, copywriting, and social media at events around the world. Susan is the author of numerous books about marketing, branding, and social media, including *Blogging All-in-One For Dummies, Google Blogger For Dummies, 30-Minute Social Media Marketing, Kiss-ass Copywriting in 10 Easy Steps,* and more.

Alexander Hiam has led creative retreats for top consumer and industrial firms to facilitate innovative thinking about strategic plans, branding, naming, and product ideas. He is the author of *Marketing Kit For Dummies* and *Business Innovation For Dummies.*

Rising from the media and journalism world, **Anum Hussain** quickly realized her content and communication skills had a home in the world of marketing. While at HubSpot, she has written countless blog posts, e-books, and reports on Twitter effectiveness and strategy that have been viewed by more than 1.2 million readers.

After being forced to use Twitter by a college professor, **Brittany Leaning** soon found herself "Leaning" into the social media site for good. Since then, she's directly managed social media strategy and execution for brands such as HubSpot, Vermont Teddy Bear, PajamaGram, and Hoodie-Footie, developing an obsession for driving real business results through Twitter along the way. She believes that Twitter is a tool beyond personal enjoyment — it connects students with teachers, organizations with donors, job seekers with employers, and so much more.

Deborah Ng is a former freelance writer who used her gift of gab to grow a successful blog into the number one online community for freelance writers before selling in 2010. Deb is the former community manager for several online brands. When she's not oversharing on the social networks, Deb blogs at Kommein.com and enjoys her time with her extremely handsome husband and brilliant son.

Jan Zimmerman has found marketing to be the most creative challenge of owning a business for the more than 35 years she has spent as an entrepreneur. Since 1994, she has owned Sandia Consulting Group and Watermelon Mountain Web Marketing (www.watermelonweb.com) in Albuquerque, New Mexico. (Sandia is Spanish for watermelon.) Jan's web marketing clients at Watermelon Mountain are a living laboratory for experimenting with the best social media, search engine optimization, and other online marketing techniques for bottom-line success.

She has written three editions of *Web Marketing For Dummies,* four editions of another book about marketing on the Internet, as well as the books *Doing Business with Government Using EDI* and *Mainstreaming Sustainable Architecture.* She has also co-authored two previous editions of *Social Media Marketing All-in-One For Dummies* and co-authored the third edition of *Facebook Marketing All-in-One For Dummies.* Her concern about the impact of technological development on women's needs led to her book *Once Upon the Future* and the anthology *The Technological Woman.*

Publisher's Acknowledgments

Acquisitions Editor: Stacy Kennedy, Katie Mohr
Compilation Editor: Corbin Collins
Project Manger/Copy Editor: Chad R. Sievers
Technical Editor: William B. Donato
Art Coordinator: Alicia B. South

Production Editor: Antony Sami
Cover Photos: Hero Images/Getty Images, Inc

JOIN THE
U.S. CHAMBER

Running a small business is complicated. You have a unique outlook and face new challenges every day.

That's why the U.S. Chamber of Commerce created **Small Business Nation.** Join today for free to get access to a nationwide network of entrepreneurs who understand what small business is all about, as well as a lot of other great resources, including a subscription to our weekly email newsletter, *The Startup Rundown.*

OVER 96%
of U.S. Chamber of Commerce members have fewer than 100 employees

The U.S. Chamber of Commerce is the world's largest business organization representing the interests of more than 3 million businesses of all sizes, sectors, and regions. Our members range from mom-and-pop shops and local chambers to leading industry associations and large corporations. They all share one thing—they count on the Chamber to fight for their interest in Washington, D.C.

Join Small Business Nation today
uschamber.com/JoinSBN